BIBLICAL RHETORIC AND RHETORICAL CRITICISM

Hebrew Bible Monographs, 45

Series Editors
David J.A. Clines, J. Cheryl Exum

Editorial Board
A. Graeme Auld, Marc Brettler, David M. Carr, Paul M. Joyce,
Francis Landy, Lena-Sofia Tiemeyer, Stuart D.E. Weeks

BIBLICAL RHETORIC AND RHETORICAL CRITICISM

Jack R. Lundbom

SHEFFIELD PHOENIX PRESS
2015

Copyright © 2013, 2015 Sheffield Phoenix Press

First published in hardback, 2013
First published in paperback, 2015

Published by Sheffield Phoenix Press
Biblical Studies, University of Sheffield
45 Victoria Street
Sheffield S3 7QB

www.sheffieldphoenix.com

All rights reserved.
No part of this publication may be reproduced or transmitted in any form or by any means, electronic or mechanical, including photocopying, recording or any information storage or retrieval system, without the publisher's permission in writing.

A CIP catalogue record for this book
is available from the British Library

Typeset by CA Typesetting Ltd
Printed by Lightning Source Inc.

ISBN 978-1-910928-06-6 (paperback)
ISBN 978-1-907534-56-0 (hardback)

ISSN 1747-9614

To

Cao Jing

Contents

Preface	xi
Abbreviations	xiv

Hebrew Rhetoric and the Method of Rhetorical Criticism

Chapter 1
HEBREW RHETORIC — 3

Chapter 2
CHRISTIAN SCHOETTGEN'S *EXERGASIA SACRA* — 9

Chapter 3
RHETORICAL CRITICISM:
HISTORY, METHOD, AND USE IN THE BOOK OF JEREMIAH — 16

Chapter 4
DELIMITATION OF UNITS IN THE BOOK OF JEREMIAH — 37

Chapter 5
SECTION MARKINGS IN BIBLE SCROLLS — 60

The Primary History

Chapter 6
ABRAHAM AND DAVID IN THE THEOLOGY OF THE YAHWIST — 65

Chapter 7
PARATAXIS, RHETORICAL STRUCTURE, AND THE DIALOGUE
OVER SODOM IN GENESIS 18 — 73

Chapter 8
SCRIBAL CONTRIBUTIONS TO OLD TESTAMENT THEOLOGY — 81

Chapter 9
GOD'S USE OF THE *IDEM PER IDEM* TO TERMINATE DEBATE — 89

Chapter 10
THE DECALOGUE IN THE PRIMARY HISTORY 99

Chapter 11
THE INCLUSIO AND OTHER FRAMING DEVICES IN DEUTERONOMY 1–28 102

Chapter 12
THE LAWBOOK OF THE JOSIANIC REFORM 121

Chapter 13
STRUCTURE IN THE SONG OF MOSES (DEUTERONOMY 32.1-43) 131

Chapter 14
ELIJAH'S CHARIOT RIDE 150

THE PROPHETS

Chapter 15
RHETORICAL DISCOURSE IN THE PROPHETS 165

Chapter 16
THE LION HAS ROARED: RHETORICAL STRUCTURE IN AMOS 1.2–3.8 202

Chapter 17
DOUBLE-DUTY SUBJECT IN HOSEA 8.5 213

Chapter 18
CONTENTIOUS PRIESTS AND CONTENTIOUS PEOPLE IN HOSEA 4.1-10 216

Chapter 19
POETIC STRUCTURE AND PROPHETIC RHETORIC IN HOSEA 232

Chapter 20
JEREMIAH AND THE BREAK-AWAY FROM AUTHORITY PREACHING 240

Chapter 21
RHETORICAL STRUCTURES IN JEREMIAH 1 259

Chapter 22
RUDIMENTARY LOGIC IN JEREMIAH 277

Chapter 23
THE DOUBLE CURSE IN JEREMIAH 20.14-18 290

Chapter 24
NEW COVENANT IN JEREMIAH AND LATER JUDAISM   303

THE GOSPELS

Chapter 25
NEW COVENANT IN THE EARLY CHURCH AND IN MATTHEW   313

Chapter 26
CLOSURE IN MARK'S GOSPEL   323

Index of Biblical References   332
Index of Authors   349

Preface

This collection of essays brings together work I have been doing over a period of years in rhetorical criticism of the Bible. The first essay, 'Elijah's Chariot Ride', was published in 1973. This essay was a paper read at the Annual Meeting of the Society of Biblical Literature in Toronto in 1969, a year after James Muilenburg gave his memorable lecture to the SBL Meeting in Berkeley in 1968, 'Form Criticism and Beyond'. When I read my paper in Toronto there was no section in SBL given over to rhetorical criticism, so I was put into the section on form criticism. This turned out, however, to be an unexpected boon for a young graduate student, as form criticism was what everyone was doing at the time, so the room was filled. Discussion afterwards showed a definite interest in this new twist on form criticism, and in subsequent years rhetorical criticism has taken its rightful place alongside other methods of biblical criticism.

Rhetorical criticism owes a singular debt to Muilenburg, who in 1968 finally named a method he had been practicing for years. Rhetorical criticism for him was an adjunct to form criticism, combining as it did his earlier interest in a literary study of the Bible with the form criticism he learned from Hermann Gunkel. Muilenburg met Gunkel in Germany in 1929–30, and is the one credited with introducing the form critical method to America.

As I point out in my essay, 'Rhetorical Criticism: History, Method, and Use in the Book of Jeremiah', rhetorical criticism is largely an American method, having first been developed in American universities as a result of pioneering work done at Cornell in the 1920s. Other literary studies of non-biblical texts, many carried out in Classical Departments of American universities beginning in the early 1900s, were rhetorical in nature even though they were not named as exercises in 'rhetorical criticism'. Outside America, a literary criticism not unlike Muilenburg's own was done in the mid 20th-century by Roman Catholic scholars at the Pontifical Biblical Institute in Rome, where again, those practicing it did not call it 'rhetorical criticism'. But that is what it was. It went beyond biblical stylistics to deal with matters of rhetorical structure, structure being another component of ancient rhetoric as understood by rhetors in the classical world.

My own scholarly work is eclectic in nature. I do rhetorical criticism, but I also do other things. Muilenburg did rhetorical criticism as an adjunct (and corrective) to form criticism. I combine it broadly with all types of biblical criticism, using whatever I find useful in explicating a biblical text or some larger issue within a biblical text. I seek whenever possible to use rhetorical criticism to confirm conclusions—many of them well-established—that have been reached by those employing other methods of biblical criticism, and very often rhetorical work corroborates these conclusions. The present essays, then, are not simply in rhetorical criticism, but all in some way make use of rhetorical criticism.

The second point I wish to make is that rhetorical criticism, at least as I practice it, is not simply a *synchronic* method, as it is commonly characterized by those wanting to distinguish it from other biblical criticism *diachronic* in nature. My rhetorical criticism can be either synchronic or diachronic. It is true, I joined forces long ago with those who chose to begin with the biblical text in its present form, to see if any structure and coherence might exist there, rather than positing some *Urform* and arguing for a development to the text we now possess. If I can find structure and coherence in the text as it now stands, which happens often enough when one does rhetorical criticism, I question and often reject the atomistic divisions proposed by critics working along diachronic lines. To this extent, my rhetorical criticism is synchronic in nature.

But I also use rhetorical criticism diachronically, showing how in some cases beneath the present text lie rhetorical structures hidden or partially hidden as a result of later redactional activity. My first essay, 'Elijah's Chariot Ride', applied rhetorical criticism to 2 Kings 1–2, and showed that a rhetorical structure lay hidden beneath the present text containing a Deuteronomic obituary notice. Rhetorical criticism was here used diachronically. One will also see a diachronic use of the method in my article, 'The Lion Has Roared: Rhetorical Structure in Amos 1.2–3.8', as well as in passages discussed in my *Jeremiah* commentary, e.g., the 'Jehoiakim and Zedekiah Clusters' lying beneath the disarrayed prose in chaps. 24–36 (see 'Excursus III: The Composition of Jeremiah 24–36' in my *Jeremiah 21–36* [AB, 21B; New York: Doubleday, 2004], pp. 253-54). Rhetorical criticism is concerned about redaction, but it is a different take on redaction than one meets up with in the German school of 'redaction criticism'.

To David Clines, my sincere gratitude for his ready willingness to publish 26 essays on biblical rhetoric and rhetorical criticism, most of which appeared earlier over a span of nearly 40 years in various journals, Festschriften, and other publications. Two of the essays, 'The Decalogue in the Primary History' and 'Structure in the Song of Moses (Deuteronomy 32.1-43)', and part of a third, 'New Covenant in the Early Church and in Matthew', are here published for the first time.

I wish to thank my teaching assistant at Garrett-Evangelical Seminary, Amanda R. Morrow, for much appreciated help in retyping some of the essays for publication. Retyping was done also by Krista McNeil and Julia Humenik of the Academic Affairs Office at Garrett, and to them also I say a word of thanks. In the documentation I have added recent English translations of German works, and in some cases omitted citations of the German originals. I have also included subsequent reprints of articles about which I am aware.

I dedicate this book to my esteemed colleague and friend, Dr Cao Jing, currently teaching at Xiangfan University in Hubei Province, China. Jing, in possession of an earned doctorate and a scholar and teacher in her own right, was my student at the Lutheran Theological Seminary in Hong Kong. She is one of the bright lights of China, combining in her own way a love for country, an interest in the Bible, and a vibrant Christian faith.

Jack R. Lundbom
Garrett-Evangelical Theological Seminary, February 2012

ABBREVIATIONS

AB	Anchor Bible
ABD	*The Anchor Bible Dictionary* (ed. David Noel Freedman; New York: Doubleday, 1992)
ADAJ	*Annual of the Department of Antiquities of Jordan*
AJP	*American Journal of Philology*
AJSL	*American Journal of Semitic Languages and Literatures*
AnBib	Analecta biblica
ANE	Ancient Near East(ern)
$ANET^3$	James B. Pritchard (ed.), *Ancient Near Eastern Texts Relating to the Old Testament* (3rd edn, with supplement; Princeton: Princeton University Press, 1969)
AOAT	Alter Orient und Altes Testament
APOT	R.H. Charles (ed.), *Apocrypha and Pseudepigrapha of the Old Testament in English* (2 vols.; Oxford: Clarendon Press, 1913)
ATANT	Abhandlungen zur Theologie des Alten und Neuen Testaments
ATD	Das Alte Testament Deutsch
AV	Authorized Version
BA	*Biblical Archaeologist*
BASOR	*Bulletin of the American Schools of Oriental Research*
BDB	Francis Brown, S.R. Driver and Charles A. Briggs (eds), *A Hebrew and English Lexicon of the Old Testament* (Oxford: Clarendon Press, 1907)
BET	Beiträge zur biblischen Exegese und Theologie
BH	*Biblia hebraica*
BHK	*Biblia hebraica* (1st edn; ed. R. Kittel, 1906)
BHK^3	*Biblia hebraica* (3rd edn; ed. R. Kittel, 1937)
BHS	*Biblia hebraica stuttgartensia* (ed. K. Elliger and W. Rudolph; 'Liber Jeremiae' prepared by W. Rudolph; Stuttgart, 1970)
BHT	Beiträge zur historischen Theologie
BiRev	*Bible Review*
BJRL	*Bulletin of the John Rylands Library*
BK	Biblischer Kommentar
BN	*Biblische Notizen*
BWANT	Beiträge zur Wissenschaft vom Alten und Neuen Testament
BWAT	Beiträge zur Wissenschaft vom Alten Testament
BZ	*Biblische Zeitschrift*
BZAW	Beihefte zur Zeitschrift für die alttestmentliche Wissenschaft
CB	The Century Bible (ed. W.F. Adeney)
CBQ	*Catholic Biblical Quarterly*
CBSC	The Cambridge Bible for Schools and Colleges (OT ed. A.F. Kirkpatrick)
CCC	*College Composition and Communication*
CD	The Damascus Document (= The 'Zadokite' Document)
CJ	*Classical Journal*

CJT	*Canadian Journal of Theology*
CP	*Classical Philology*
CQ	*Classical Quarterly*
CTA	A. Herdner (ed.), *Corpus des tablettes en cunéiformes alphabétiques découvertes à Ras Shamra–Ugarit de 1929 à 1939* (Paris: Imprimerie nationale Geuthner, 1963)
D	The 'Deuteronomic' source of the Pentateuch
DH	The 'Deuteronomic Historian'
DJD	Discoveries in the Judaean Desert
DLZ	*Deutsche Literaturzeitung*
E	The 'Elohist' source of the Pentateuch
EncJud	*Encyclopaedia judaica* (ed. C. Roth and G. Wigoder; Jerusalem, 1971–1973)
EncPhil	*Encyclopedia of Philosophy* (ed. Paul Edwards; New York, 1967).
EncRhet	*Encyclopedia of Rhetoric* (ed. Thomas O. Sloane; Oxford and New York, 2001)
ET	*Expository Times*
GKC	*Gesenius' Hebrew Grammar* (2nd edn; ed. E. Kautzsch; trans. A.E. Cowley; Oxford, 1963)
GNB	Good News Bible (New York, 1976)
GRBS	*Greek, Roman and Byzantine Studies*
HAT	Handbuch zum Alten Testament (ed. Otto Eissfeldt)
HDB	*A Dictionary of the Bible* (ed. James Hastings; New York, 1902)
Heb	Hebrew
HKAT	Handkommentar zum Alten Testament (ed. D.W. Nowack)
HSM	Harvard Semitic Monographs
HTR	*Harvard Theological Review*
HUCA	*Hebrew Union College Annual*
IB	*The Interpreter's Bible* (ed. George Buttrick)
ICC	The International Critical Commentary (ed. S.R. Driver, A. Plummer, and C.A. Briggs)
IDB	*The Interpreter's Dictionary of the Bible* (ed. George Buttrick; New York, 1962)
IDBSup	*IDB*, Supplementary Volume (ed. Keith Crim; Nashville, 1976)
IEJ	*Israel Exploration Journal*
Int	*Interpretation*
JAOS	*Journal of the American Oriental Society*
JB	The Jerusalem Bible (Garden City, NY, 1966)
JBL	*Journal of Biblical Literature*
JCS	*Journal of Cuneiform Studies*
JE	Combined 'Yahwist' and 'Elohist' sources of the Pentateuch
JHS	*Journal of Hellenic Studies*
JJS	*Journal of Jewish Studies*
JNES	*Journal of Near Eastern Studies*
JNSL	*Journal of Northwest Semitic Languages*
JQR	*Jewish Quarterly Review*
JR	*Journal of Religion*
JSOT	*Journal for the Study of the Old Testament*
JSOTSup	*Journal for the Study of the Old Testament*, Supplement Series
JTS	*Journal of Theological Studies*
KAT	Kommentar zum Alten Testament (ed. E. Sellin)

KB³	Ludwig Köhler and Walter Baumgartner, *Hebräisches und aramäisches Lexikon zum Alten Testament* (3rd edn; Leiden, 1967–1990)
KHC	Kurzer Hand-Commentar zum Alten Testament
LA	*Liber annuus*
LCL	Loeb Classical Library
LXX	Septuagint, according to *Septuaginta II* (8th edn; ed. Alfred Rahlfs; Stuttgart, 1965)
M^A	Masoretic Text according to the Aleppo Codex (Codex A)
M^L	Masoretic Text according to the Leningrad Codex B19^A (Codex L)
M^P	Masoretic Text according to the St Petersburg Codex of the Prophets B3 (Codex P)
MNTC	Moffatt New Testament Commentary
MT	Masoretic Text, according to *BHK*³ or *BHS*
NAB	The New American Bible (New York, 1970)
NEB	New English Bible (Oxford and Cambridge, 1970)
NIV	New International Version (Grand Rapids, 1973)
NJB	The New Jerusalem Bible (New York, 1985)
NJV	The New Jewish Publication Society of America Translation of the Holy Scriptures: The Prophets (Philadelphia, 1978)
NKZ	*Neue kirchliche Zeitschrift*
NRSV	The New Revised Standard Version (New York, 1989)
NT	New Testament
OLZ	*Orientalistische Literaturzeitung*
OS	Oudtestamentische studiën
OT	Old Testament
OTL	Old Testament Library
OTP	James Charlesworth (ed.), *The Old Testament Pseudepigrapha* (2 vols.; Garden City, NY, 1983–1985)
P	The 'Priestly' source of the Pentateuch
PBA	*Proceedings of the British Academy*
PhRh	*Philosophy and Rhetoric*
QJS	*Quarterly Journal of Speech*
REB	The Revised English Bible (Oxford and Cambridge, 1989)
RJ	*Rechtshistoriches Journal*
RSV	Revised Standard Version (New York, 1953)
Sam	The Samaritan Pentateuch
SBLDS	SBL Dissertation Series
SBT	Studies in Biblical Theology
SEÅ	*Svensk exegetisk årsbok*
SJOT	*Scandinavian Journal of the Old Testament*
St.-B.	H.L. Strack and P. Billerbeck, *Kommentar zum Neuen Testament aus Talmud und Midrasch* (Munich, 1922–1961)
TAPA	*Transactions and Proceedings of the American Philological Association*
TDNT	Gerhard Kittel and Gerhard Friedrich (eds.), *Theological Dictionary of the New Testament* (trans. Geoffrey W. Bromiley; 10 vols.; Grand Rapids: Eerdmans, 1964–1976)
TDOT	G.J. Botterweck, Helmer Ringgren, and H.-J. Fabry (eds.), *Theological Dictionary of the Old Testament* (trans. David Green *et al.*; 16 vols; Grand Rapids, Eerdmans, 1974–2006)
tiq soph	*tiqqune sopherim* (corrections of the ancient scribes)
TLZ	*Theologisches Literaturzeitung*

TSK	*Theologische Studien und Kritiken*
TU	Texte und Untersuchungen zur Geschichte der altchristlichen Literatur
UF	*Ugarit-Forschungen*
Vulg	Vulgate
VT	*Vetus Testamentum*
VTSup	*Vetus Testamentum*, Supplements
WADB	*Weimar Ausgabe Deutsche Bibel*
WMANT	Wissenschaftliche Monographien zum Alten und Neuen Testament
ZAW	*Zeitschrift für die alttestamentliche Wissenschaft*
ZDA	*Zeitschrift für deutsches Altertum*

Hebrew Rhetoric and the Method of Rhetorical Criticism

Chapter 1

Hebrew Rhetoric*

Hebrew rhetoric developed from an already ancient pre-classical rhetorical tradition that dates to the beginning of recorded history. Sumerian scribal schools, called 'tablet houses', produced a literate class now known to have preserved a rich legacy of rhetorical discourse in this early society (c. 3000 BCE). The Sumerians wrote poetry having repetition, parallelism, epithet, and similes, the latter occurring with some frequency, as one might expect from a people given to analogical thinking. Cuneiform texts of the third and second millennia show that this tradition survived in Old Babylonia, Assyria, and Ugarit. A rhetorical tradition doubtless developed in Egypt during the same period, where scribal schools are known to have existed from the early third millenium, and where poetry was also written, but about this tradition little is known.

Israel's oldest literature, to judge from its earliest lyric poems (Exodus 15; Judges 5), are finished works of fine art. A simplified 22 to 30 letter alphabet, introduced at Ugarit two to three centuries before Israel's 13th-century entry into Canaan, created still more possibilities for oral and written discourse, as words began replacing older cuneiform signs. Ancient Hebrew rhetoric survives largely in the Hebrew Bible/Old Testament, from which it may be concluded that during the 8th- to 6th-centuries, it had already experienced its 'golden age', a full three centuries and more before the art achieved classical expression by Aristotle in Greece, and by Cicero, Quintilian, and others at Rome.

Hebrew poetry existed from the earliest times, this fact having been recognized in the major medieval codices of the Hebrew Bible (10th–11th centuries CE), and in the older Dead Sea Scrolls (c. 2nd-century BCE to 1st-century CE), where portions of text are written in block form (Exodus 15; Judges 5; Deuteronomy 32; Psalms; Proverbs; and Job). The recognition in modern times that Hebrew poetry is characterized largely by parallelism derives from Bishop Robert Lowth, who demonstrated this in Lecture 19 of his now-famous *De sacra poesi Hebraeorum praelectiones* (Oxford,

---

* *Encyclopedia of Rhetoric* (ed. Thomas Sloan; Oxford: Oxford University Press, 2001), pp. 325-28.

1753), given at Oxford beginning in 1741. Lowth also showed that large portions of prophetic discourse were in fact poetry, not prose, as previously thought (Lecture 18). Lowth based his parallelism doctrine on a 16th-century essay by Rabbi Azariah de Rossi of Ferrara, who discussed Hebrew rhythm in his larger work, *Me'or 'enayim*. The recognition of parallelism in Hebrew poetry, but more along rhetorical lines, appeared also in the early 18th-century work of Christian Schoettgen, *Horae hebraicae et talmudicae I* (Leipzig, 1733), where the phenomenon was called *exergasia* (Lat. *expolitio*). Hebrew poetry, in addition, has stanza formation, as can be seen from the existence of acrostics and refrains.

Hebrew rhetorical tradition produced neither theoretical work the likes of Aristotle's *Rhetoric* (322–320 BCE), nor handbooks such as the *Rhetorica ad Herennium* (c. 86–82 BCE) or Quintilian's *Institutes* (c. 90 CE). Nevertheless, in the Bible are figures performing the same functions as in classical rhetoric, also modes of argumentation known and classified by the later Greek and Roman authors. On occasion, one will meet up with figures and argumentative strategies that appear to be uniquely Hebraic, or possibly Semitic, in that they are not cited in Aristotle or any of the classical rhetorical handbooks. Yet some turn up in modern discourse.

The importance of repetition in Hebrew rhetoric can hardly be overstated. Repetitions express the superlative ('holy, holy, holy' in Isa. 6.3), provide emphasis (*epanalēpsis*), give structure to psalms, prophetic oracles, and other compositions, and terminate debate. In the Bible's *locus classicus* on divine revelation (Exod. 3.12-15), repetition assumes a debate-closure function. There, God promises a hesitant Moses regarding the trek out of Egypt, 'I will be with you' (v. 12). But Moses demurs, wanting to know God's name. God then responds, 'I will be what I will be' (v. 14), which terminates the debate, but does furnish Moses and Israel with a name for future generations: 'I will be', modified to 'He will be' = Yahweh (v. 15). This *idem per idem* tautology, as it is called, occurs in Arabic and in modern discourse, but is not mentioned in the classical rhetorical handbooks.

The Bible's rhetorical prose *par excellence* is in Deuteronomy, also less prominently in Kings and portions of Jeremiah, where an array of figures embellish, provide structure, and effect closure in legal, historical, biographical, and sermonic discourse. Deuteronomy is characterized by stereotyped phrases and an abundance of accumulation (*accumulatio*), where nouns and verbs heap up in twos, threes, and fours, and longer phrases balance rhythmically in parallelism (4.28: 'and there you will serve gods of wood and stone, the work of men's hands, that neither see, nor hear, nor eat, nor smell'). The core Deuteronomy (chapters 1–28) makes extensive use of the *inclusio*, which gives emphasis to parenetic admonitions, restores focus, and brings about closure:

> These are the *statues and ordinances* which *you shall be careful to do* in the land... (Deut. 12.1)
> *Every word* that I command you, *you shall be careful to do*; you shall not add to it or take from it (Deut. 12.32)
>
> *For you are a people holy to Yahweh your God* (Deut. 14.2)
> *For you are a people holy to Yahweh your God* (Deut. 14.21)

The preachers of Deuteronomy were probably Levitical priests, some of whom were trained scribes and went by the name *scribe* (2 Chron. 34.13). But the real rhetors in ancient Israel were the prophets, who reflect the same rhetorical tradition as other literates in society, suggesting that they must have received training in letters and the arts before venturing forth as heralds of the divine word. Isaiah, Jeremiah, and Ezekiel may well have attended a Jerusalem school where writing and rhetorical skills were taught. In Jeremiah's time (622 BCE), this school would have been headed by Shaphan, the scribe, and attached to the temple as in neighboring societies (2 Kgs 22.8-10).

Prophets embellish their oracles and other public discourse with an array of rhetorical figures, such as metaphor, simile, comparison, euphemism, epithet, *chiasmus*, *asyndeton*, alliteration, rhetorical question, *hyperbolē*, *paronomasia*, and irony. Amos is the prophet of the rhetorical question; Hosea, the framer of oracles with broken bicolons, also the prophet of extraordinary *pathos*; Isaiah, the master of verbal irony; and Ezekiel, the prophet of the extended metaphor. But the prophet with greatest rhetorical skill is unquestionably Jeremiah, who can hold rank with the best of the Greek and Roman rhetors, anticipating them as he does in style, structure, and modes of argumentation.

Hebrew rhetoric does not employ reason (*logos*) to the extent that Greek rhetoric does. For Aristotle, logic was everything, the true aim of rhetoric being to prove your point, or seem to prove it. However, if the prophet's message is set over against the controlling message of Deuteronomy, where the latter is assumed by the prophet, but left unexpressed, a great enthymeme emerges:

> [Deuteronomy: An Israel in violation of the covenant will be punished]
> The prophets: Israel has violated the covenant
> Israel will therefore be punished.

Hebrew rhetoric appeals only occasionally to the emotions (*pathos*), as, for example, in the preaching of Hosea (11.1-4, 8-9) and Jeremiah (3.19-20; 31.15-20). *Ēthos* appeals are similarly rare, seen occasionally in Jeremiah's confessions to Yahweh (Jer. 8.6; 12.3; 18.20), but not usual in public discourse. The place of *ēthos* is taken largely by authority, which is the dominant element in Hebrew rhetoric, and the driving force in almost all prophetic preaching. Yet in Jeremiah, there is an observable break away from authority preaching; that is, oracles become open-ended, and the audience is thereby made a partner with the prophet in discerning the import of the divine word (3.1-5; 5.1-8).

Jeremiah makes extensive use of repetition, not simply as a stylistic device, but to structure his oracles. Examples abound of *anaphora* and *epiphora*, the former enriched often by onomatopoeia. A fivefold repetition of 'sword' (50.35-38) simulates the repeated stabbing of victims, where, at the end, is a climactic paronomasia with the similar-sounding 'drought'. On a happier note, a threefold 'again' (31.4-5) simulates the resumption of city life in a resettled Zion. A change in rhythm is another way of creating onomatopoeia, for example, in Jeremiah's chaos vision (4.23-26), where decreasing colon length simulates a cessation of life in the entire created order. Jeremiah also repeats verbal roots in succession: In 11.18: 'Yahweh made me know, and I knew'.

Repeated words and phrases—otherwise synonyms or fixed word pairs—structure stanzas as well as entire poems. Jeremiah constructs elaborate word schemes, often with inversion (*chiasmus*). Keyword *chiasms* (2.5-9; 5.1-8; 51.34-45), are similar to those in Lamentations 1–2. Reflecting the homiletical prose of Deuteronomy, Jeremiah makes liberal use of the *inclusio* in both prose (7.3-7, 8-11, 12-14) and poetic (3.1-5; 20.7-10) oracles, also in his defense before the court (26.12-15):

> *Yahweh sent me* to prophesy against this house and against this city—*all the things* that you have heard... (26.12)
>
> ...for in truth *Yahweh sent me* to you to speak in your ears *all these things* (26.15).

The *inclusio* frames oracles by the prophet Huldah (2 Kgs 22.16-20) and by Jeremiah's adversary, Hananiah (Jer. 28.2-4). This figure is present in Akkadian poetry, in classical poetry, where it is called 'ring composition', and in modern poetry (e.g., the poems of Carl Sandburg).

Jeremiah's discouse, like that in Deuteronomy, is replete with *accumulatio* (in poetry: 1.10; 12.7; in prose: 7.5-6, 33-34). It also contains *asyndeton* (in poetry: 4.5; 5.1; in prose: 7.9), which classical authors used to heap up praise or blame. The string of six infinitive absolutes in one of the Temple oracles (7.9) assigns blame. Jeremiah uses this figure to enliven a judgment on the nations (25.27) and underscore the joy in announcing Israel's salvation (31.7).

The expansion of Hellenism in the 4th-century BCE, followed by Rome's entry into the eastern Mediterranean in the 1st-century BCE, brought an infusion of Greco-Roman rhetoric into postexilic Jewish intellectual life. We see now a use of the 'sortie' (Gk. *climax*; Lat. *gradatio*) in Jewish writings (*Pirqe Aboth* 1.1; Wis. 6.17-19), which is a catalogue of statements, each picking up a keyword from the statement preceding, leading finally to a climax. The sortie is used often by Paul in the New Testament (Rom. 5.3-5: 'More than that we rejoice in our *sufferings*, knowing that *suffering* produces *endurance*, and *endurance* produces *character*, and *character* produces *hope*, and *hope* does not disappoint us'; see also Rom. 8.29-30; 10.14-15. The locust parade of Joel (1.4), 'what the *cutting locust* left, the *swarming locust* has eaten; what the *swarming locust* left, the *hopping locust* has eaten; and what the *hopping locust* left, the *destroying locust* has eaten', is not really a sortie, but a chain created in the interest of expressing totality, which is another defining characteristic of the older Hebrew rhetoric.

Jewish apocryphal and pseudepigraphal works, supplemented by the sectarian documents found at Khirbet Qumran (Dead Sea Scrolls), all provide valuable insights into Hebrew rhetorical tradition as it developed during the so-called Intertestamental period. Rhetorical discourse from the proto-tannaitic and tannaitic periods (c. 100 BCE to 200 CE) survives in the Mishnah and Talmud, the latter completed c. 500 CE in Babylon. Here Hellenistic philosophy and rhetoric are seen to have influenced rabbinic methods of interpretation, particularly the hermeneutical rules developed by the great Pharisee Hillel (c. 30 BCE). We should also not overlook the New Testament as an important 1st-century CE document of Hebrew rhetoric, even though it survives (and was probably written from the beginning) in Greek, not Hebrew or Aramaic. It teems with figures, structures, and modes of argumentation derived from ancient Hebrew rhetoric. In the early Middle Ages, and again in modern times, Jewish rhetoric has been influenced by contemporary philosophical thought, and has combined it in each case with its own rich tradition of rhetoric rooted in preclassical antiquity.

Bibliography

Daube, David, 'Rabbinic Methods of Interpretation and Hellenistic Rhetoric', *HUCA* 22 (1949), pp. 239-64. Reprinted in *Understanding the Talmud* (ed. Alan D. Corré; New York: Ktav, 1975), pp. 275-89.
Fischel, Henry A., 'The Uses of Sorties (*Climax, Gradatio*) in the Tannaitic Period', *HUCA* 44 (1973), pp. 119-51.
Herder, Johann Gottfried von, *The Spirit of Hebrew Poetry* (2 vols.; trans. James Marsh; Burlington, VT: Edward Smith, 1833). English translation of *Vom Geist der ebräischen Poesie*, 2 vols. first published in 1782–83. A classic work on the inner spirit of ancient Hebrew poetry.
Kramer, Samuel Noah, 'The Sumerian School: A Pre-Greek System of Education', in George E. Mylonas (ed.), *Studies Presented to David Moore Robinson* (St Louis: Washington University Press, 1951), pp. 238-45.
—'Sumerian Similes: A Panoramic View of Some of Man's Oldest Literary Images', *JAOS* 89 (1969), pp. 1-10.
—*The Sacred Marriage Rite* (Bloomington, IN: Indiana University Press, 1969). See especially Chapter 2: 'The Poetry of Sumer: Repetition, Parallelism, Epithet, Simile'.
Lowth, Robert, *Lectures on the Sacred Poetry of the Hebrews* (trans. G. Gregory; Boston: Joseph P. Buckingham, 1815). English translation of *De sacra poesi Hebraeorum*

praelectiones, first published in 1753. The standard work on parallelism in ancient Hebrew poetry.

Lund, Nils W., 'The Presence of Chiasmus in the Old Testament', *AJSL* 46 (1930), pp. 104-26.

—*Chiasmus in the New Testament* (Chapel Hill, NC: University of North Carolina, 1942; Reprinted: Peabody, MA: Hendrickson, 1992). The primary text for chiasmus in large panels in both the Old and New Testaments.

Lundbom, Jack R. 'God's Use of the *idem per idem* to Terminate Debate', *HTR* 71 (1978), pp. 193-201. Discusses the two important Old Testament passages on divine revelation in Exodus (3.12-15; 33.18-23).

—'Poetic Structure and Prophetic Rhetoric in Hosea', *VT* 29 (1979), pp. 300-308. The broken bicolon is shown here to be a structural and closure device in Hosea's preaching.

—'Jeremiah and the Break-away from Authority Preaching', *SEÅ* 56 (1991), pp. 7-28. Qualifies the widely held view that Hebrew (also early Christian) discourse is based solely on authority.

—'Jeremiah (Prophet)', in *ABD* 3, edited by David Noel Freedman, pp. 684-98. Includes section on 'Rhetoric and Preaching'.

—'The Inclusio and Other Framing Devices in Deuteronomy i–xxviii', *VT* 46 (1996), pp. 296-315. The *inclusio* is shown here to be the controlling structure in the homiletical discourse of Deuteronomy 1–28.

—*Jeremiah: A Study in Ancient Hebrew Rhetoric* (2nd enlarged edn; Winona Lake, IN: Eisenbrauns, 1997, first published in 1975). Contains an introductory essay, 'Rhetorical Criticism: History, Method and Use in the Book of Jeremiah' (pp. xix-xliii); also an English translation of Christian Schoettgens's *Exergasia sacra* in an Appendix (pp. 155-63).

—*Jeremiah 1–20* (AB, 21A; New York: Doubleday, 1999; New Haven: Yale University Press, 2009). Introduction contains sections on the modern method of rhetorical criticism (pp. 68-85), rhetoric and composition in the book of Jeremiah (pp. 85-92), and rhetoric and preaching of the prophet (pp. 121-39).

Muilenburg, James, 'A Study in Hebrew Rhetoric: Repetition and Style', in *Congress Volume Copenhagen* (VTSup, 1; Leiden: E.J. Brill, 1953), pp. 97-111. Reprinted in Thomas Best, *Hearing and Speaking the Word* (Chico, CA: Scholars Press, 1984), pp. 193-207.

—'Form Criticism and Beyond', *JBL* 88 (1969), pp. 1-18. Reprinted in Thomas Best, *Hearing and Speaking the Word* (Chico, CA: Scholars Press, 1984), pp. 27-44. The first essay to define Old Testament rhetorical criticism as a method.

Schoettgen, Christian, *Horae hebraicae et talmudicae I* (Leipzig and Dresden: F. Hekel, 1733). See Dissertatio VI: *De exergasia sacra*, pp. 1249-264. Contains ten canons on *exergasia* in Hebrew poetry.

Chapter 2

CHRISTIAN SCHOETTGEN'S *EXERGASIA SACRA**

It has been customary to credit Robert Lowth with the discovery of Hebrew parallelism even though we realize that he did not actually discover it.[1] Lowth's primary source was an essay on Hebrew rhythm by Azariah de Rossi, a rabbi from Ferrara, who included this in his larger work *Me'or enayim*, published in 1574.[2]

More recent research has shown that biblical parallelism was widely known by the end of the 17th-century. Roman Jakobson has called attention to studies done in Scandinavia 50 years before Lowth which compared Hebrew parallelism with parallelism in Finnish poetry.[3] Among Lowth's other predecessors there were two who defined the phenomenon in rhetorical categories. One was the Italian Alessio Simmaco Mazzocchi, the other a German named Christian Schoettgen. Mazzocchi saw parallelism as 'epesegesi', whereas for Schoettgen it was 'exergasia'. The contributions of both scholars have been relatively unknown, although some years ago Mazzocchi was given his redress.[4] It is now proper, then, to give to Schoettgen what is due him.

Very little is known about Schoettgen's *Exergasia sacra*, and even less is known about Schoettgen himself. To make matters worse, what has been passed on about Schoettgen in the English tradition is not entirely correct. The one scholar in the English tradition who seems to have seen Schoettgen's dissertation in *Horae hebraicae et talmudicae* was John Jebb, who, like Schoettgen himself, is another scholar not well known.[5] Jebb makes numerous references to the work in his *Sacred Literature*, but he evidently

---

* *Jeremiah: A Study in Ancient Hebrew Rhetoric* (SBLDS 18; Missoula, MT: Society of Biblical Literature and Scholars Press, 1975), pp. 121-27 [repr. Winona Lake, IN: Eisenbrauns, 1997, pp. 155-63].

1. For the most recent article on Lowth, see Aelred Baker, 'Parallelism: England's Contribution to Biblical Studies', *CBQ* 35 (1973), pp. 429-40.

2. מאור עינים [The Light of the Eyes] (Volna; R.M. Romma, 1866); see chap. 60, 'Essays in Criticism' (אמרי בינה), pp. 477-85.

3. 'Grammatical Parallelism and Its Russian Facet', *Language* 42 (1966), p. 403.

4. See Ugo Bonamartini, 'L'epesegesi nella S. Scrittura', *Biblica* 6 (1925), pp. 424-44; cf. Baker, 'Parallelism: England's Contribution to Biblical Studies', p. 433.

5. See Frederick Bussby, 'Bishop Jebb, A Neglected Biblical Scholar', *ET* 60 (1948–49), p. 193.

does not know the author. He discusses the *Exergasia sacra* with other works by Abarbanel and Azariah in a paragraph entitled, 'Two *or three* rabbinical dissertations' (italics mine).[6] This is cautious, but nevertheless incorrect. Schoettgen was not a rabbi but a Christian scholar living in the 18th-century in Germany.

Another erroneous belief has crept into English scholarship, although this is not the responsibility of Jebb. Both Charles Briggs and Theophile Meek have made statements to the effect that Lowth used the earlier work of Schoettgen's.[7] Yet nowhere in either Lowth's *Lectures on the Sacred Poetry of the Hebrews* or *Isaiah* does he even mention Schoettgen. Jebb notes this too.[8] This appears then to be decisive, because Jebb knows of no writer (presumably in the English tradition) who has cited Schoettgen when discussing Hebrew poetry,[9] in addition to the fact that both Briggs and Meek appear to be ultimately dependent upon Jebb for their information.[10] Briggs seems to be the one who first made the connection, and unless evidence is forthcoming which shows that he had independent information, we are more correct to assume that Lowth worked independent of Schoettgen and did not use the *Exergasia sacra* as one of his sources.

It is time now to set the record straight, which we can do with the help of an article on Schoettgen in *Biographie universelle*.[11] Christian Schoettgen was a philologist born in 1687 at Wurzen in Saxony, not far from Leipzig. His father was a shoemaker, but having had himself a literary education, was in a position to give his son the same. After early training at the gymnasiums, the young Schoettgen matriculated at the University of Leipzig for a course in theology, at which time he also began a study of the oriental languages. Nine years were spent at Leipzig giving lessons and doing literary work of one kind or another. At the request of the local library Schoettgen undertook the revision of a 1667 manuscript by Thomas Reinesius entitled *Eponymologicum*. This was a glossary explaining ancient inscriptions. Schoettgen's teaching career began in 1716 when he was named rector at the gymnasium of Frankfurt on the Oder. In 1719 he became professor of literature. Then in 1728 he became rector at one of the gymnasiums at Dresden, where he remained until his death on October 15, 1751. Schoettgen

---

6. Jebb, *Sacred Literature* (London: T. Cadell & W. Davies, 1820), pp. 14-15.
7. Briggs, *Psalms* I (ICC; Edinburgh: T. & T. Clark, 1952), p. xxxv; Meek, 'The Structure of Hebrew Poetry', *JR* 9 (1929), p. 528.
8. Jebb, *Sacred Literature*, p. 14.
9. Jebb, *Sacred Literature*, p. 14.
10. Briggs's remarks about Schoettgen are immediately followed by a reference to Jebb's *Sacred Literature*. Meek in his discussion then repeats what Briggs says almost verbatim.
11. Ed. J.F. Michaud, Vol. 38 (Graz, Austria: Akademische Druck- u. Verlagsanstalt, 1969), p. 409.

was married and had eight children. He was a much respected teacher and was remembered also for his interest in fellow-citizens and strangers.

Besides being an expert in philology and historical scholarship, Schoettgen mastered to a rare degree the oriental and rabbinic literature. He was often consulted by Jewish scholars who venerated him until they found out about his desire to prove from the Old Testament that Jesus was the Messiah. The second volume of *Horae hebraicae et talmudicae* (1742)[12] is taken up almost entirely by a discussion of the Messiah. This work was then followed in 1748 by *Jesus le vrai Messie*.

Schoettgen published many other works. Some were updated editions of works done by earlier scholars, while others were his own. Included among the former were the works of Lambert Bos on the Greek ellipsis and Walter on the Hebrew ellipsis. Schoettgen also published a new edition of Pasor's *Lexique* on the New Testament. In 1746 he published a better lexicon himself, and a third edition of this with later additions by Krebs and Spohn was considered by Thomas Horne in the 19th-century to be the best Greek–Latin lexicon of the New Testament currently available.[13]

The first volume of *Horae hebraicae et talmudicae* was published in 1733, predating the Lowth Lectures by eight years. It is mostly commentary on the books of the New Testament, with eight dissertations on various subjects at the back. The sixth of these is *Exergasia sacra*. In this dissertation Schoettgen first gives a general explanation of *exergasia*, equating it with the Latin figure *expolitio*. The *exergasia* had already been thoroughly discussed by Julius Scaliger, so the reader is referred to him for further information. Then follows 10 canons of 'exergasia sacra', which are now presented here for the first time in English translation. Each canon is illustrated by three biblical texts, and in two instances—in Canons III and VII—Schoettgen makes some additional comments. The 10 canons are then given further demonstration following their enumeration. Here I will present only the canons and the illustrative texts. After these have been looked at I will conclude with some comparisons to Lowth's doctrine of parallelism as well as to subsequent restatements that have come more recently.

Canon I. *Exergasia is complete when each member of the two cola so corresponds to the other that one is neither greater nor less than the other.*

Psalm 33.7
Gathering together/as in a bottle/the waters of the sea
and putting/in a storehouse/the abyss

---

12. In the biographical article in *Biographie universelle* (see note above), Schoettgen's second volume is given a publication date of 1740. The second volume in my possession is dated 1742.

13. Thomas H. Horne, *An Introduction to the Critical Study and Knowledge of the Holy Scripture*, II (4th edn; Philadelphia: E. Littell, 1831), pp. 705-706.

Numbers 24.17

>It comes/a star/out of Jacob
>>and it is raised/a scepter/out of Israel

Luke 1.47

>It magnifies/my soul/the Lord
>>and it exults/my spirit/in God my savior

Canon II. *Sometimes, however, in the second part of the total thought, the subject is not repeated, but by ellipsis is omitted, and by common usage is understood.*

Isaiah 1.18

>If your sins/be as scarlet/they shall be white as snow
>>and if —/red as a berry/they shall be as wool

Proverbs 7.19

>Whereas the husband/is not in his house
>>—/is gone on a distant journey

Psalm 129.3

>Upon my back plowed/the plowers
>>cut their furrows long/—

Canon III. *Sometimes, also, only part of the subject is missing.*

Psalm 37.30

>The mouth of the just/meditates/upon wisdom
>>his tongue/speaks/justice

Here only part of the subject is repeated, viz., the suffix 'his', not indeed the whole subject.

Psalm 102.29

>Sons of your servants/will dwell
>>and their seed/before your face will be

Isaiah 53.3

>And he/was wounded/for our transgressions
>>—/was bruised/for our sins

Canon IV. *Examples appear, where in the repeated line of the exergasia, the predicate is omitted.*

Numbers 24.5

>How beautiful they are/your tents/O Jacob
>>—/your habitations/O Israel

2. *Christian Schoettgen's* Exergasia sacra

Psalm 33.12:
> Happy/that nation/whose Lord is God
> —/that people/whom he willed in his inheritance

Psalm 123.4:[14]
> It is sated/our soul/with the mockery of the arrogant
> —/—/with the contempt of the proud

Canon V. *Sometimes only part of the predicate is missing.*

Psalm 57.10:[15]
> I will acknowledge you/among the peoples/O Lord
> I will sing songs/among the nations/—

Psalm 103.1:
> Bless/O my soul/the Lord
> and —/all my innards/the name of his holiness

Psalm 129.7:
> So that he does not fill up/his hands/the reaper
> or —/his fists[16]/the binder of sheaves

Canon VI. *Some elements may be added in one member when not present in the other.*

Numbers 23.18
> Arise/Balak/and hear
> —/son of Zippor/give ear to me

Psalm 102.29
> The children of your servants/—/shall dwell
> and their seed/before your face/shall be established

Daniel 12.3
> And those who make people wise[17]/—/shall shine/as the brightness of the firmament
> and those who make just/many/—/as the stars/forever

Canon VII. *Sometimes two propositions treating different things occur, but which, arranged by means of a distribution, can and should be interpreted as one general proposition.*

---

14. Correction; Schoettgen text has 123.6.
15. Correction; Schoettgen text has 57.11.
16. Compare 'bosom', in both the Hebrew and the Vulgate. Is he striving after a more exact parallelism with 'hands'?
17. Schoettgen supplies *reddunt* to render the Hebrew hiphil (compare modern English versions).

Psalm 94.9[18]
> The one who plants/the ear/does he not hear?
> the one who forms/the eye/does he not see?

Psalm 128.3
> Your wife/as a fruitful vine/in the company of your house
> your sons/as olive plantings/around your table

Sirach 3.16
> As a blasphemer is he/who forsakes/his father
> and cursed by the Lord/who incites to wrath/his mother

No one supposes here that we believe the 'eye' to be the 'ear', or the 'father' to be the 'mother', etc., for these two propositions refine one generalization. Thus, in the first saying, the general proposition is this: 'God knows everything'; in the second: 'Fruitful will you be in marriage'; in the third: 'Unhappy is he who strikes his parents'.

> Canon VIII. *Exergasia also occurs when the second proposition expresses the opposite of the first.*

Proverbs 15.8
> The sacrifice/of the wicked/is an abomination to the Lord
> and the prayers/of the upright/are his good pleasure

Proverbs 14.1
> The wisdom of women/builds a house
> and foolishness within her hands/destroys it

Proverbs 14.11
> The house/of the wicked/will be devastated
> and the tent/of the righteous/will flourish

> Canon IX. *We also have examples of this kind of exergasia where whole propositions correspond, although the subject and predicate are for the most part not the same.*

Psalm 51.7
> Behold, in iniquity I was brought forth
> and in sin my mother conceived me

Psalm 119.168
> I have kept your injunctions and your testimonies
> because all my ways are before you

---

18. Correction; Schoettgen text has 94.8.

Jeremiah 8.22
> Is there no balm in Gilead, nor a doctor there?
> for why has the daughter of my people not come to health?

Canon X.   *There occur even three-member exergasias.*

Psalm 1.1
> Blessed is the man/who has not gone/in the counsel/of the wicked
>   and —/— has not stood/in the way/of sinners
>   and —/- has not sat/in the seat/of scoffers

Psalm 130.5
> I have waited for the Lord
> my soul has waited
> and in his word have I hoped

Psalm 52.9[7]
> Behold the man, who would not make God his help
>   and — has confided in the multitude of his riches
>   and — was hardy in his emptiness

Schoettgen's canons cover all Lowth's categories: I–VII and X are what Lowth calls 'synonymous parallelism'; VIII is 'antithetical parallelism'; and IX is 'synthetic parallelism'. And like Lowth's third category, Canon IX is the weakest: Ps. 51.7 may perhaps fit, but neither Ps. 119.168 nor Jer. 8.22 is exergasia. Schoettgen lists more types of synomymous parallelism and in so doing anticipates the later refinements of Lowth by G.B. Gray. In Gray's terminology, Canons II–V would be 'incomplete parallelism without compensation', and Canon VI 'incomplete parallelism with compensation'.[19]

But the real importance of Schoettgen's dissertation is that it emphasizes the rhetorical nature of parallelism. We are shown how parallelism strives after *totality* (Canon VII), which is what Muilenburg continually stressed.[20] And we see too the *elliptical* quality of Hebrew poetry (Canon II). This latter observation has been made repeatedly by Dahood in his *Psalms I–III*, where he shows how all parts of speech and even suffixes can do 'double-duty' for more than one colon of poetry.[21]

Schoettgen thus deserves his rightful place alongside Lowth. Not only does his work predate Lowth, but more important, it shows how parallelism *functions* for the Hebrew poet.

19. G.B. Gray, *The Forms of Hebrew Poetry* (New York; Ktav, 1972), p. 74. Lowth has also recognized this, however; cf. Lowth, *Lectures on the Sacred Poetry of the Hebrews* (trans. G. Gregory; Boston: Joseph T. Buckingham, 1815), pp. 262-63.

20. J. Muilenburg, 'A Study in Hebrew Rhetoric: Repetition and Style', in *Congress Volume Copenhagen* (VTSup, 1; Leiden: E.J. Brill, 1953), p. 99.

21. See especially, M. Dahood, *Psalms III* (AB, 17A; Garden City, NY: Doubleday, 1970), pp. 429-44.

Chapter 3

RHETORICAL CRITICISM:
HISTORY, METHOD, AND USE IN THE BOOK OF JEREMIAH*

Rhetorical criticism as a non-prescriptive, analytical method for the study of discourse, ancient and modern, oral and written, in prose and in poetry, was born roughly 75 years ago on American soil, where it also developed in subsequent years (1) among non-biblical scholars working in the university and (2) among biblical scholars working largely outside the university. For most of its history neither group has had much direct contact with the other.

Rhetorical Criticism in the American Universities

The beginnings of rhetorical criticism belong to a revival of classical rhetoric that took place in American colleges and universities between 1900 and 1925, a time, ironically enough, when an older rhetoric movement in many of the same institutions had only recently died out. Key figures in this revival included Fred Newton Scott of the University of Michigan, Charles Sears Baldwin of Yale, and after 1914, of Columbia University and Barnard College, James M. O'Neill of Dartmouth and later the University of Wisconsin, and James Albert Winans of Cornell and later Dartmouth.[1] It was with faculty in the Department of Speech at Cornell—notably Everett Lee Hunt, Hoyt Hudson, and Herbert Wichelns—that graduate work in rhetoric

---

* *A Study in Ancient Hebrew Rhetoric* (Winona Lake, IN: Eisenbrauns, 2nd edn, 1997), pp. xix-xliii.
1. Carroll C. Arnold, 'Rhetoric in America since 1900', in *Re-establishing the Speech Profession: The First Fifty Years* (ed. Robert T. Oliver and Marvin G. Bauer; [Mineola, NY]: Speech Association of the Eastern States, 1959), pp. 3-7; Wayne C. Booth, 'The Revival of Rhetoric', in *New Rhetorics* (ed. Martin Steinmann, Jr.; New York: Charles Scribner's, 1967), pp. 1-15; Robert J. Connors *et al.*, 'The Revival of Rhetoric in America', in *Essays on Classical Rhetoric and Modern Discourse* (ed. Robert J. Connors *et al.*; Carbondale, IL: Southern Illinois University Press, 1984), pp. 1-15; Donald C. Stewart, 'The Status of Composition and Rhetoric in American Colleges, 1880–1902: An MLA Perspective', *College English* 47 (1985), pp. 734-46.

was first undertaken in America, and rhetorical criticism as we know it today in the American universities was born.[2]

Classical rhetoric had experienced an earlier revival in the mid-18th-century, when, for the first time, the works of Cicero and Quintilian became widely available and new textbooks on rhetorical theory and practice were written. When John Quincy Adams became the first Boylston Professor of Rhetoric at Harvard in 1806, rhetoric as an academic discipline was broadly conceived, although still essentially *prescriptive* in nature. The subject was taught to produce skilled public speakers.[3]

A century later things had changed dramatically. A shift from oral to written discourse had occurred in the universities, with the result that departments of rhetoric were now largely departments of English. Gone were the oral examinations, student debate societies, recitations, and public disputations associated with college commencement. In 1874, Harvard added written exams for its applicants, and two years later, in 1876, a new Chair of English Literature was created for James Francis Child, occupant of the Boylston Chair of Rhetoric.

The 19th-century also witnessed a specialization of disciplines that truncated rhetoric to the point that it became associated primarily with *belles lettres*. Its emphasis was now largely on correctness, style and the aesthetic appreciation of literature. Style and delivery (*elocutio* and *pronunciatio*) formed the core of rhetorical instruction at Harvard, as it was even before the classical revival of the 18th-century. Style, that darling of the Renaissance, dominated rhetorical instruction in other American colleges and universities through the end of the 19th-century,[4] with the result that by 1900 rhetoric found itself in sharp decline.

Yet in 1903 Fred Scott created a Department of Rhetoric at the University of Michigan. A renewal of classical scholarship had begun, more critical in nature than what preceded, and it was helped along by individuals such as Charles Sears Baldwin, who, in 1914 contributed an important essay on rhetoric to Monroe's *Encyclopaedia of Education*. This essay was a fresh inquiry into the nature of classical rhetorical theory.[5] A decade later Baldwin published his *Ancient Rhetoric and Poetic*.[6]

---

2. Everett Lee Hunt, 'Herbert A. Wichelns and the Cornell Tradition of Rhetoric as a Humane Study', in *The Rhetorical Idiom* (ed. Donald C. Bryant; Ithaca, NY: Cornell University Press, 1958), pp. 1-4; Edward P. Corbett, 'The Cornell School of Rhetoric', in *Selected Essays of Edward P.J. Corbett* (ed. Robert J. Connors; Dallas: Southern Methodist University Press, 1989), pp. 290-304.
3. Connors *et al.*, 'The Revival of Rhetoric in America', pp. 1-2.
4. Connors *et al.*, pp. 2-4.
5. Arnold, 'Rhetoric in America since 1900', p. 5.
6. Charles S. Baldwin, *Ancient Rhetoric and Poetic* (Gloucester, MA: Peter Smith, 1959).

The year 1914 was pivotal. In this year a group of speech professors decided to break away from the National Council of Teachers of English and form the National Association of Academic Teachers of Public Speaking (later the Speech Communication Association). This new association, led by James Winans and James O'Neill, began campaigning immediately for separate departments of rhetoric and public speaking in the universities. Many such departments were thus formed between 1915 and 1920.

The Department of Speech and Drama at Cornell never became a Department of Rhetoric in name; nevertheless, Cornell in the 1920s was the center of this new interest in classical rhetoric and became the place where rhetorical criticism was born. The history of the so-called 'Cornell School of Rhetoric' is well known, beginning with the celebrated graduate seminar on classical rhetoric offered by Alexander Drummond and Everett Hunt in 1920, said to have been 'the first significant graduate seminar in classical rhetoric offered at a major American university in the twentieth century'.[7] Hoyt Hudson defined graduate course work for the study of rhetoric,[8] and Hunt, in addition to his graduate seminar, offered an undergraduate course in argumentation where rhetorical discourse from both classical and modern periods was studied. Finally, it was Herbert Wichelns's highly influential essay, 'The Literary Criticism of Oratory',[9] which defined 'rhetorical criticism' and mapped out its agenda.[10] These three individuals on the Cornell faculty, Hunt, Hudson and Wichelns, all understood rhetoric in its broad classical sense, and for each of them rhetoric was a humane discipline, not a science.

Wichelns's essay transcended its own title by making a distinction between literary and rhetorical criticism that is now classic. Literary criticism, he said, is out to find the permanent value in a literary work; it looks at the

---

7. Corbett, 'The Cornell School of Rhetoric', pp. 295-96.

8. Hoyt H. Hudson, 'The Field of Rhetoric', *QJS* 9 (1923), pp. 167-80 [= Raymond F. Howes (ed.), *Historical Studies of Rhetoric and Rhetoricians* (Ithaca, NY: Cornell University Press, 1961), pp. 3-15]; cf. Cornell Faculty in the Department of Public Speaking, 'Some Subjects for Graduate Study Suggested by Members of the Department of Public Speaking of Cornell University', *QJS* 9 (1923), pp. 147-53.

9. *Studies in Rhetoric and Public Speaking in Honor of James Albert Winans* (ed. A.M. Drummond; New York: The Century Co., 1925), pp. 181-216 [= Bryant, *The Rhetorical Idiom*, pp. 5-42]. For a briefer version, see Wichelns, 'Some Differences between Literary Criticism and Rhetorical Criticism', in *Historical Studies of Rhetoric and Rhetoricians* (ed. Raymond F. Howes; Ithaca, NY: Cornell University Press, 1961), pp. 217-24.

10. Corbett, 'The Cornell School of Rhetoric'; Mark S. Klyn, 'Toward a Pluralistic Rhetorical Criticism', in *Essays on Rhetorical Criticism* (ed. Thomas R. Nilsen; New York: Random House, 1968), p. 154; Charles J. Stewart, 'Historical Survey: Rhetorical Criticism in Twentieth Century America', in *Explorations in Rhetorical Criticism* (ed. G.P. Mohrmann *et al.*; University Park, PA and London: Pennsylvania State University Press, 1973), pp. 2-6.

work's thought and eloquence to see what gives it enduring quality over the ages—its 'perennial freshness'. Rhetorical criticism, on the other hand,

> is not concerned with permanence, nor yet with beauty. It is concerned with effect. It regards a speech as a communication to a specific audience, and holds its business to be the analysis and appreciation of the orator's method of imparting his ideas to his hearers.[11]

Wichelns was after a speech's persuasive quality, for which reason he said rhetorical criticism 'is concerned with effect'. This revived a central idea from Aristotle (*Rhetoric* I ii 1). But the key term is really 'audience', and by audience Wichelns meant the original audience, not the subsequent reader.[12] It was left to later rhetorical critics to expand the term to include subsequent readers.[13] What was important in Wichelns's program, however, was the renewed emphasis on the classical triumvirate of speaker, text, and audience, a delineation again going back to Aristotle (*Rhetoric* I iii 1). Today these combine into or else are supplemented by what is called the 'rhetorical situation'. Lloyd Bitzer says the rhetorical situation is 'the context in which speakers or writers create rhetorical discourse'.[14]

We may now sum up the main characteristics of rhetorical criticism as it emerged in the early 20th-century revival of rhetoric within American colleges and universities—a revival some call the 'new rhetoric(s)',[15] although New Rhetoric derives from the French (*la nouvelle rhétorique*) and is associated largely with the argumentative rhetoric of Chaim Perelman:[16]

1. Rhetorical criticism is first of all a modern, analytical discipline. In classical times, in the Renaissance, and up through the end of the 19th-century, rhetoric was studied for its prescriptive value; its aim was to train people for effective public speaking. Rhetorical criticism analyzes discourse—ancient and modern, written and oral, in poetry and in prose—asking questions

---

11. Wichelns, 'The Literary Criticism of Oratory', p. 209.
12. Wichelns, 'The Literary Criticism of Oratory', p. 201.
13. Edwin Black, *Rhetorical Criticism* (New York: Macmillan, 1965), p. 11; Chaim Perelman and L. Olbrechts-Tyteca, *The New Rhetoric* (trans. John Wilkinson and Purcell Weaver; Notre Dame, IN: University of Notre Dame Press, 1969), p. 7.
14. Lloyd F. Bitzer, 'The Rhetorical Situation', *PhRh* 1 (1968), p. 1 [= Walter R. Fisher (ed.), *A Tradition in Transition* (East Lansing, MI: Michigan State University Press, 1974), pp. 247-48]; cf. Perelman and Olbrechts-Tyteca, *The New Rhetoric*, pp. 412, 460-65, 491.
15. Corbett, 'Rhetoric and Teachers of Rhetoric', *QJS* 51 (1965), pp. 376-80; Bryant, 'Rhetoric: Its Function and its Scope *Rediviva*', in Donald C. Bryant, *Rhetorical Dimensions in Criticism* (Baton Rouge: Louisiana State University Press, 1973), pp. 9-10 [= W.R. Fisher, *A Tradition in Transition*, pp. 235-36].
16. Perelman, 'The New Rhetoric: A Theory of Practical Reasoning', in *The Great Ideas Today 1970* (trans. E. Griffin-Collart and O. Bird; ed. Robert M. Hutchins and Mortimer J. Adler; Chicago: Encyclopaedia Britannica, 1970), pp. 273-312; 'The New Rhetoric and the Rhetoricians: Remembrances and Comments', *QJS* 70 (1984), pp. 188-96; and with L. Olbrechts-Tyteca, *The New Rhetoric*.

about structure, style, intention, impact upon the audience, and how these together create a rhetorical situation.

2. Rhetorical criticism builds upon the broad classical tradition, which is to say its concern is not simply with style (*elocutio*), but with structure (*dispositio*) and all the other classical components of suasive discourse.

3. Rhetorical criticism goes beyond the simple identifying and cataloguing of figures; it wants to know how figures *function* in discourse.

4. Finally, rhetorical criticism focuses on the 'audience', which sets it off most clearly from earlier forms of literary criticism, and is doubtless responsible for the shift to 'reader-response' and other more recent forms of literary criticism. Rhetorical criticism studies a text with an eye to discerning its impact on single and multiple audiences, beginning with the original audience and extending up to current audiences made up of hearers or readers, individuals or members of a group.

Since the 1920s the study of rhetoric has continued among so-called 'neo-Aristotelians' at the University of Chicago during the 1940s and 1950s; at Michigan State University and the University of Iowa where the Communication Skills Movement originated during the 1940s and 1950s, then at other midwestern state universities; and at the University of California, Berkeley through the turbulent 1960s and 1970s, to name some of the more prominent centers in America.

Rhetoric today is a respected academic discipline, although few schools have, as the University of California, Berkeley does, a department of rhetoric with a graduate program. In some universities, however, graduate programs in rhetoric can be found in departments of English. Harvard and Princeton, despite well-known rhetoric faculty and many years of undergraduate teaching in rhetoric, have never had graduate programs in rhetoric.[17]

The division that existed earlier between English and Speech/Rhetoric faculties has all but disappeared, and since the mid-1960s, rhetoric has been well represented in a number of interdisciplinary programs.[18] In the universities we are even beginning to see signs of an emerging synthesis between classical rhetorical theory and the study of the Bible, for example among such people as George Kennedy of the University of North Carolina at Chapel Hill,[19] and Hans Dieter Betz at the University of Chicago. Betz, who does not come out of the American rhetorical movement, has been studying Paul against the Socratic tradition.[20] These beginnings could be helped

---

17. Corbett, 'The Cornell School of Rhetoric', p. 302.
18. Connors, *et al.*, 'The Revival of Rhetoric in America', pp. 11-13.
19. See e.g., George Kennedy, *Classical Rhetoric and its Christian and Secular Tradition from Ancient to Modern Times* (Chapel Hill, NC: University of North Carolina Press, 1980); and *New Testament Interpretation through Rhetorical Criticism* (Chapel Hill, NC and London: University of North Carolina Press, 1984).
20. See, e.g., H.D. Betz, *Der Apostel Paulus und die sokratische Tradition* (BHT, 45;

along by more interdisciplinary programs, and by joint seminary–university programs, such as the one that developed and flourished for a time between the University of California and Graduate Theological Union in Berkeley.

Mention should also be made of other studies in the American universities, many of them in departments of Classics, which have been rhetorical despite their not being so named. A turn-of-the-century work on chiasmus in classical writers was done by R.B. Steele,[21] and structural works of a more expansive sort appeared later on the Homeric epics and Herodotus by J.L. Myres, George E. Duckworth, Cedric Whitman, and others,[22] and on Pindar,[23] Euripides,[24] Propertius,[25] Horace,[26] Vergil,[27] and Plutarch[28] by various scholars. Mark Rose has shown in an important study[29] that the Shakespearean plays, before acts came into being, were structured by design, not plot, and as a result were symmetrical. Literature has thus been compared to balancing movements in Beethoven and Mozart,[30] and to artwork on ancient pottery (Myres; Whitman).

Tübingen: J.C.B. Mohr [Paul Siebeck], 1972); *Galatians* (Hermeneia; Philadelphia: Fortress Press, 1979); *2 Corinthians 8 and 9* (Hermeneia; Philadelphia: Fortress Press, 1985).

21. R.B. Steele, 'Anaphora and Chiasmus in Livy', *TAPA* 32 (1901), pp. 154-85; 'Chiasmus in the Epistles of Cicero, Seneca, Pliny and Fronto', in *Studies in Honor of Basil L. Gildersleeve* (Baltimore: The Johns Hopkins University Press, 1902), pp. 339-52.

22. J.L. Myres, 'The Last Book of the "Iliad"', *JHS* 52 (1932), pp. 264-96; 'The Structure of Stichomythia in Attic Tragedy', *PBA* 34 (1948), pp. 199-231; 'The Pattern of the Odyssey', *JHS* 72 (1952), pp. 1-19; *Herodotus: Father of History* (Oxford: Clarendon Press, 1953); George E. Duckworth, *Foreshadowing and Suspense in the Epics of Homer, Apollonius and Vergil* (Princeton, NJ: Princeton University Press, 1933); Cedric Whitman, *Homer and the Heroic Tradition* (Cambridge, MA: Harvard University Press, 1958); Henry Immerwahr, *Form and Thought in Herodotus* (Cleveland: Western Reserve University Press, 1966); Stephen Bertman, 'Structural Symmetry at the End of the *Odyssey*', *GRBS* 9 (1968), pp. 115-23.

23. Gilbert Norwood, *Pindar* (Berkeley: University of California Press, 1945).

24. T.V. Buttrey, 'Accident and Design in Euripides' "Medea"', *AJP* 79 (1958), pp. 1-17.

25. O. Skutsch, 'The Structure of the Propertian "Monobiblos"', *CP* 58 (1963), pp. 238-39; William R. Nethercut, 'Notes on the Structure of Propertius Book IV', *AJP* 89 (1968), pp. 449-64.

26. R.W. Carrubba, 'The Technique of the Double Structure in Horace', *Mnemosyne* Series 4, 20 (1967), pp. 68-75.

27. Gilbert Norwood, 'Vergil, *GEORGICS* iv, 453–527', *CJ* 36 (1940–41), pp. 354-55; George E. Duckworth, *Structural Patterns and Proportions in Vergil's Aeneid* (Ann Arbor: University of Michigan Press, 1962).

28. T.F. Carney, 'Plutarch's Style in the *Marius*', *JHS* 80 (1960), p. 27.

29. Mark Rose, *Shakespearean Design* (Cambridge, MA: Belknap/Harvard University Press, 1972).

30. George Thomson, 'Notes on *Prometheus Vinctus*', *CQ* 23 (1929), p. 158.

James Muilenburg and Rhetorical Criticism

Rhetorical criticism had its beginning in Old Testament (OT) with James Muilenburg, whose celebrated Presidential Address to the 1968 Meeting of the Society of Biblical Literature in Berkeley, 'Form Criticism and Beyond', laid out the method.[31] Muilenburg defined *rhetorical criticism* in this address as understanding and exhibiting in Hebrew poetry and prose 'the structural patterns that are employed for the fashioning of a literary unit...and...the many and various devices by which the predications are formulated and ordered into a unified whole'.[32]

The rhetorical critic, said Muilenburg, should seek to discover 'the texture and fabric of the writer's thought' by undertaking 'a responsible and proper articulation of the words in their linguistic patterns and in their precise formulations'.[33] Muilenburg wanted to go beyond form criticism because the emphasis there was too much on the typical features of a genre and not enough on those features that made the biblical passage unique. He said, 'The passage must be read and heard precisely as it is spoken'.[34]

In this lecture Muilenburg named a method he had been using for 45 years or more, and in this sense 'rhetorical criticism' was not new. The name was new. Yet, only for the first time was Muilenburg able to distance himself sufficiently from his work to explain precisely what he had been doing. Rhetorical study in the literary tradition of Robert Lowth and R.G. Moulton, and the stylistics of E. König and more recently Luis Alonso Schökel, was for him a supplement to form criticism.[35] Muilenburg's combined use of these two critical methodologies, form criticism and the yet-to-be-named rhetorical criticism, reached a brilliant climax in his II Isaiah commentary in the *Interpreter's Bible*.[36]

Others besides Alonso Schökel at Rome's Pontifical Biblical Institute were doing structural work on the biblical text without calling it rhetorical

---

31. James Muilenburg, 'Form Criticism and Beyond', *JBL* 88 (1969), pp. 1-18.
32. Muilenburg, 'Form Criticism and Beyond', p. 8.
33. Muilenburg, 'Form Criticism and Beyond', p. 7.
34. Muilenburg, 'Form Criticism and Beyond', p. 5.
35. Robert Lowth, *Lectures on the Sacred Poetry of the Hebrews* (trans. G. Gregory; Boston: Joseph T. Buckingham, 1815); *Isaiah, Preliminary Dissertation and Notes* (10th edn; London: T.T. & J. Tegg, 1833); Richard G. Moulton, *The Literary Study of the Bible* (New York: D.C. Heath & Co., 1895); Ed. König, *Stilistik, Rhetorik, Poetik in Bezug auf die biblische Literatur* (Leipzig: Dieterich'sche Verlagsbuchhandlung, 1900); 'Style of Scripture', in *HDB Extra Volume* (1904), pp. 156-69; and Luis Alonso Schökel, *Estudios de poética hebrea* (Barcelona: Juan Flors, 1963); *A Manual of Hebrew Poetics* (Rome: Pontifical Biblical Institute, 1988).
36. James Muilenburg, 'Isaiah', in *IB*, V (ed. George A. Buttrick; New York: Abingdon Press, 1956), pp. 381-773.

per se; for example, William Moran and Norbert Lohfink[37] in their studies on Deuteronomy were carrying on the tradition of earlier Scripture scholars A. Condamin, Cardinal A. Bea, and H. Galbiati.[38] There was also the important research of Nils W. Lund done during the 1930s and early 1940s at the University of Chicago.[39] These scholars isolated in the biblical text keyword, motif, and speaker distributions that formed inclusios and large chiasmi (Moran and Lohfink called the latter 'concentric inclusions'). Lund in his study of chiasmus built as Muilenburg did on the English tradition, in his case on the works of John Jebb and Thomas Boys.[40]

The rhetorical criticism of Muilenburg was at once broader and narrower than the rhetorical criticism of Wichelns and those working in the universities. It was broader by virtue of its being an adjunct to form criticism, from which it gained much of its vitality. Form criticism took for granted the oral provenance of OT literature, also seeking out 'life situations' (*Sitze im Leben*) in which the biblical passages were originally 'at home'. Hermann Gunkel, the founder of form criticism (*Gattungskritik*), was an eclectic scholar of the first order, making form criticism broad in scope from the very beginning. Muilenburg met Gunkel while he was in Germany in 1929–1930 and became the person chiefly responsible for introducing Gunkel's method to America.[41]

Compared with the rhetorical criticism practiced in the universities, however, the Muilenburg program appears somewhat narrow.[42] It does not, for

37. Moran's class notes at the Pontifical Biblical Institute, *Adnotationes in libri Deuteronomii capita selecta* (Rome: Pontifical Biblical Institute, 1963), and Lohfink's class notes, *Lectures in Deuteronomy* (trans. S. McEvenue; Pontifical Biblical Institute, 1968), had limited circulation among their students. See also Moran, 'Deuteronomy', in *A New Catholic Commentary on Holy Scripture* (ed. Reginald C. Fuller; Camden, NJ and London: Thomas Nelson & Sons, 1969), pp. 256-76; and Lohfink, 'Darstellungskunst und Theologie in Dtn 1,6–3,29', *Biblica* 41 (1960), p. 123 n. 2 [= Lohfink, *Studien zum Deuteronomium und zur deuteronomistischen Literatur*, I (Stuttgart: Verlag Katholisches Bibelwerk, 1990), pp. 32-33 n. 70]; *Das Hauptgebot* (Rome: Pontifical Biblical Institute, 1963).

38. The two important works by Condamin were *Le Livre de Jérémie* (Paris: Librairie Victor Lecoffre, 1920); and *Poèmes de la Bible* (2nd edn; Paris: Gabriel Beauchesne et ses Fils, 1933).

39. Lund's major work was *Chiasmus in the New Testament* (Chapel Hill, NC: University of North Carolina Press, 1942; reprint: Peabody, MA: Hendrickson Publishers, 1992).

40. John Jebb, *Sacred Literature* (London: T. Cadell & W. Davies, 1820); Thomas Boys, *A Key to the Book of Psalms* (London: L.B. Seeley & Son, 1825).

41. Muilenburg, 'The Gains of Form Criticism in Old Testament Studies', *ET* 71 (1959–60), pp. 229-33.

42. See e.g., Michael V. Fox, 'The Rhetoric of Ezekiel's Vision of the Valley of the Bones', *HUCA* 51 (1980), pp. 1-4, and C. Clifton Black, 'Rhetorical Criticism and Biblical Interpretation', *ET* 100 (1989), pp. 254, 256.

example, evaluate discourse over against its 'audience', unless one takes *Sitz im Leben* to include audience. Nor does it deal much with classical concerns associated with a speaker's ability to persuade, that is, intent, stance, strategies, ethos moves, etc. Most of the effort is expended doing close work on the biblical text—engaging in 'a responsible and proper articulation of the words in their linguistic patterns and in their precise formulations'. Rhetorical criticism in the Muilenburg tradition is therefore perceived by many as being little more than an exercise in textual description—perceptive and sensitive description, to be sure, especially when the master was at work—but textual description all the same.

There are reasons for this limited agenda, besides the obvious one that rhetorical criticism gained its dynamism from form criticism and was largely adjunct to it. To cite the prophetic material, in which one finds precisely the sort of discourse a rhetorical critic would be most eager to study, conditions for doing rhetorical criticism of the broad type could hardly be worse. Little or no background information is available. We lack biographical material on the speaker, and relevant historical data on the speech, such as date, what the occasion was, or who the audience happened to be, are scanty at best, usually unavailable. There is only the speech, and to make matters worse, speeches are placed end to end in the biblical text, making delimitation difficult, if not impossible. Interpolations are common. In some instances, part of a speech appears to be missing. Ancient methods of composition were quite different from modern methods, and we are still learning about the ancient methods and what sort of logic lay behind them.

In the book of Jeremiah, where conditions are good, perhaps the best, speeches embedded in the prose of chaps. 18–45 do contain bits of historical information, less often speaker and audience data. Only in rare cases (for example, 26.1-19; 29) does one find all three. The bulk of the speeches—which are poetry and appear grouped together in chaps. 1–20, 22–23, 30–31, and 46–51—typically lack a historical context and contain few clues about audience, occasion, and intent. We are therefore left inferring a rhetorical situation from the text itself. Muilenburg was aware of this problem.[43]

So while it is true that the book of Jeremiah contains a relatively large amount of background material—substantially more than any other prophetic book—solid correlations to the book's oracles, confessions, and other prophetic utterances remain few. It is no wonder, then, that biblical scholars say nothing or else talk sparingly about the prophet's intent, stance, strategy, or argumentation in a given speech, not to mention what the audience response might have been.

We can sum up the Muilenburg agenda for rhetorical criticism as follows:

---

43. Muilenburg, 'Form Criticism and Beyond', p. 6.

1. One must first define the limits of the literary unit. Where does the unit begin and where does it end? This is priority one. Delimiting the unit is essential for grasping the author's 'intent and meaning'. Muilenburg finds that once the literary unit has been delimited, major motifs stated at the beginning are seen to find resolution at the end. Keywords make inclusios. He says, 'No rhetorical feature is more conspicuous and frequent among the poets and narrators of ancient Israel than the proclivity to bring successive predications to their culmination'.[44]

2. Second, one must perceive the structure of the literary unit or, in Muilenburg's words, 'discern the configuration of its component parts'. This means close analysis of poetic bicola and tricola where particular attention is paid to keywords, figures of speech, and particles appearing in 'strategic collocations' or in 'crucial or climactic contexts'. Repetitions are all-important, and one must be alerted also to the use of chiasmus. Muilenburg says 'rhetorical devices...are employed for marking, on the one hand, the sequence and movement of the pericope, and on the other, the shifts or breaks in the development of the writer's thought'.[45] In poetry one must also look for 'refrains', as well as for other clusters of bicola and tricola termed 'stanzas' or 'strophes'. Refrains are deemed rhetorically important by critics working outside the Bible.[46] Muilenburg was also of the opinion that Hebrew poetry contained 'climactic or ballast lines'.[47]

Muilenburg then did move beyond textual description by showing an interest in discerning the author's intent, development of thought, and meaning. But his agenda is still too limited for rhetorical critics with classical and modern interests. This is due more to the unique circumstances under which OT rhetorical criticism is forced to operate than to narrow scholarly interests on the part of Muilenburg. Rhetorical critics working on Lincoln's Second Inaugural, the Lincoln–Douglas Debates, Kennedy's speech at the Berlin Wall, or Martin Luther King's 'Moses on the Mountain' speech have at their disposal vast amounts of information on speaker and audience and seldom, if ever, do they need wonder where their text begins and ends. Even those working with classical texts have an easier time delimiting speeches and coming up with speaker and audience data.

Whereas the beginning of OT 'rhetorical criticism' is dated from Muilenburg's 1968 lecture to the Society of Biblical Literature, for Muilenburg's graduate students at the San Francisco Theological Seminary and the GTU the beginning came a year earlier. In a graduate seminar on Deuteronomy, offered in the fall of 1967, members of the seminar told Muilenburg that

---

44. Muilenburg, 'Form Criticism and Beyond', p. 9.
45. Muilenburg, 'Form Criticism and Beyond', pp. 10, 14-16.
46. Gene Montague, 'Rhetoric in Literary Criticism', *CCC* 14 (1963), p. 173.
47. Muilenburg, 'Form Criticism and Beyond', p. 9.

what they wanted from him was less 'form criticism' and more 'rhetoric and composition'. Though the master teacher continued to serve up a healthy amount of both—and a healthy amount of much else, I might add—this seminar marked a turning point. Muilenburg did in fact accent rhetoric and composition in his teaching, and this emphasis continued in subsequent seminars taught up until his retirement in 1971. Largely as a result of these seminars and his SBL address of December, 1968, the GTU saw a flurry of dissertations on rhetorical criticism in the decade following—in both Old and New Testament. GTU faculty also came under Muilenburg's influence. Since then, rhetorical criticism following Muilenburg's lead, if not done precisely along Muilenburg lines, has become widely practiced in America and abroad.[48]

The Question of Method

It has been argued since Aristotle that rhetoric is an art, not a science.[49] What then is rhetorical criticism? Is it also an art? Hunt, as we mentioned earlier, believed speech to be a humane discipline, but his senior colleague at Cornell, James Winans, was of the opinion that the study of speech must be carried on along scientific lines. The program developed by Charles H. Woolbert of the University of Illinois and adopted in the midwestern universities built on the same premise.[50] It seems that with 'method' being more at home in the sciences, the question becomes, 'Can criticism of and within a basically humane discipline be reduced to a method?'

Muilenburg called rhetorical criticism a method, yet for him it was a practiced art, not a science. He said, 'in matters of this sort there is no substitute for literary sensitivity'.[51] Although he might cite Near Eastern materials to compare with the biblical text when it was possible, when it came to identifying a climactic line, an inclusio, an important shift signaled by a particle, and so on, it was the sensitivity of the critic that controlled interpretation. If you asked him how he knew it was a climactic line, an inclusio, or an important shift by a particle, he would likely say, 'Well, it just is!' The charge then sometimes made about there being too much subjectivity in

---

48. Black, 'Rhetorical Criticism and Biblical Interpretation'; Phyllis Trible, *Rhetorical Criticism: Context, Method, and the Book of Jonah* (Minneapolis: Fortress Press, 1994); see more recently the studies of Pieter van der Lugt, *Rhetorical Criticism and the Poetry of the Book of Job* (OS, 32; Leiden: E.J. Brill, 1995); P.A. Smith, *Rhetoric and Redaction in Trito-Isaiah* (VTSup, 62; Leiden: E.J. Brill, 1995); and Robert H. O'Connell, *The Rhetoric of the Book of Judges* (VTSup, 63; Leiden: E.J. Brill, 1996).

49. See W.R. Fisher, *A Tradition in Transition*, p. x; D.C. Stewart, 'The Status of Composition and Rhetoric in American Colleges, 1880–1902', pp. 738-39.

50. Corbett, 'The Cornell School of Rhetoric', pp. 292-94.

51. Muilenburg, 'Form Criticism and Beyond', p. 9.

Muilenburg's method is not entirely groundless. Muilenburg believed that subjectivity was required to do the job.

Clifton Black says the Muilenburg program is not a *bona fide* method, as is the rhetorical criticism of George Kennedy, which 'is truly a method, not merely an interpretative perspective'.[52] Some rhetorical critics, however, fear that once rhetorical criticism becomes a method, the freedom of the critic is taken away and the whole enterprise returns to being prescriptive.[53]

A mediating position is that rhetoric is a 'mixture of science and art',[54] which would seem to allow for the possibility that rhetorical criticism too might be both science and art. This seems to be a happy compromise, particularly if an art admittedly ancient is subjected to an analysis admittedly modern. Whatever the final verdict on art versus science, the method question is one that must be addressed. When dealing with an ancient text—particularly a biblical text where interpretation rides on so many variables—one had better employ some method, with some controls; otherwise what is passed off as art may not be art at all but simply random and subjective reflections producing little or no yield. Sad to say, much current rhetorical criticism of the Bible is precisely this.

University scholars doing rhetorical criticism of the broad variety have understood their work as being methodological in nature,[55] although some insist that method ought to be pluralistic.[56] It would seem that method is as appropriate to the study of rhetoric as to the study of any other humanistic discipline. The term is not wholly owned by the sciences. If Muilenburg's rhetorical criticism assumes for 'method' an interpretation too loose to be meaningful, then some controls must be put into place that will either objectify insights credited to a critic's acute sensitivity or else show the same to be invalid, and if not invalid, at least unlikely.

Rhetorical Criticism and the Book of Jeremiah

We turn now to discuss an agenda for rhetorical criticism in the biblical book of Jeremiah. Some overlap here with matters of composition will be unavoidable, since at virtually every point the prophet's discourse has been preserved in combination with other discourse to serve the ongoing needs of a worshiping community.

52. So Black, 'Rhetorical Criticism and Biblical Interpretation', pp. 256-57.
53. Klyn, 'Toward a Pluralistic Rhetorical Criticism'.
54. Arnold, 'Rhetoric in America since 1900', p. 7.
55. Montague, 'Rhetoric in Literary Criticism', p. 168.
56. Stewart, 'Historical Survey: Rhetorical Criticism in Twentieth Century America', pp. 22-23. Klyn ('Toward a Pluralistic Rhetorical Criticism', p. 146) earlier lobbied for pluralism, but not when it came to methodology. For him 'rhetorical criticism... should only mean intelligent writing about rhetoric'.

The Text. Rhetorical criticism of the book of Jeremiah must begin with the text, that is, the biblical text. There really is no other place to begin. Extrabiblical sources telling us about the prophet and audiences he addressed in the late 7th and early 6th-centuries BCE are nonexistent. Also largely nonexistent are outside sources corroborating the book's narrative and other prose. All the speaker and audience information we possess is within the book of Jeremiah, and only there.

This brings us to clarify at the outset our use of the word *text*. In reference to the Bible *text* has both a broad and a narrow meaning. *Text* in the broad sense means *the present biblical text in all its complexities*. Any portion of the Jeremiah book is text—4, 8, or 12 lines of poetry, with or without supplements; oracles, confessions and liturgies, with or without interpolations, singly or in collections; small and large blocks of narrative prose; and books within the present book, for example, chaps. 1–20; 21–23; 30–33; 37–44; 46–51. All this is text and may be subjected to rhetorical criticism.

Embedded in the biblical text are also 'texts' that were at one time self-standing, namely oracles, confessions, prayers, liturgies, letters, proverbs, memoirs, narratives, colophons, and so on. On these rhetorical criticism may also be done, and with potentially greater yield. Once individual texts are delimited, one may begin asking questions about speaker—or speakers, if the discourse happens to be a dialogue of which there are many in Jeremiah; how the discourse begins and ends; the flow of the argument; who the audience might be; and so on. The context in some cases will be of help. But more often the rhetorical situation has to be recreated—with help from the imagination—on the basis of the text alone.

Delimitation of the Literary Unit. For Muilenburg the first order of business was delimiting the literary unit. This had priority also on the form-critical agenda, although criteria there were different, and in the case of certain literary genres—not the prophetic speeches, however—content alone would make clear where the unit began and ended. Delimitation of prophetic speeches is difficult, though not as difficult as one might imagine. The attempt, in any event, has to be made. Synchronic analysis that pays little or no attention to literary units will not pass for rhetorical criticism and ends up being a throw-back to precritical study of the Bible. University scholars, also, who have the broad agenda for doing rhetorical criticism betray a similar narrowness when they use as their text a King James or rabbinic Bible, neither of which distinguishes prose from poetry or has any of the other interpretive formatting derived from modern biblical research.

In Jeremiah the delimitation of literary and discourse units can in fact be done reasonably well with the use of both rhetorical and nonrhetorical criteria. There is a relative abundance of *setumah* (ס) and *petuḥah* (פ) section markers, which we now know from the Dead Sea Scrolls to be very old.[57] In chaps. 1–20, where poetic texts are compiled end to end, these are particularly useful and more often than not corroborate rhetorical data in marking the end of one unit and beginning of another. Yet these are not always present. Also, ancient and medieval manuscripts are not entirely consistent in their use. Occasionally they have to be disregarded. But section markings should always be taken into account. In the main, they are reliable indicators of where the breaks should be.

Chapter divisions go back only to about the 8th- or 9th-centuries CE, and verse numbers come later—with the advent of printed Bibles in the 15th and 16th-centuries. Both have only limited value. Superscriptions are much older and generally prove to be reliable markers for delimitation. Messenger formulas—usually 'thus said Yahweh' (כֹּה אָמַר יהוה) or 'oracle of Yahweh' (נְאֻם־יהוה)—are likewise helpful when present. In Jeremiah these formulas appear at the beginning or end of oracles, occasionally at both beginning and end, and only rarely in the middle. Once other textual assessments have been made, it is usually clear where the formula fits in a given oracle.

In Jeremiah interspersed prose and poetry give an added bonus in delimitation. Sometimes one can delimit on the basis of content or genre, but both are tricky, especially in the poetry, and corroborating criteria are a must. The form-critical search for genres, such as the 'lawsuit' (רִיב), 'prophetic call', 'judgment oracle on the individual', 'judgment oracle on the nation', 'summons to repentance', and so on, has been largely unsuccessful, the reason being that Jeremianic discourse is structured not according to form-critical models but according to canons of ancient Hebrew rhetoric.

The inclusio, once established, has proved to be of great value in delimitation, since by definition it ties in beginning and end.[58] Some scholars use *inclusio* to refer to almost any repetition, but the term should be reserved for repeated or balanced vocabulary or else a clear return of thought that brings about closure. In ancient as in modern discourse the inclusio returns the audience to the point of beginning. Chiastic structures—both keyword and speaker—also aid in delimitation. Occasionally a chiasmus will exist

---

57. The Dead Sea Scrolls do not contain the sigla; they simply have spacing in the text.

58. Muilenburg, 'Form Criticism and Beyond', pp. 9-10; Jack R. Lundbom, *Jeremiah: A Study in Ancient Hebrew Rhetoric* (SBLDS, 18; Missoula, MT: Society of Biblical Literature and Scholars Press, 1975), pp. 23-60 [2nd edn; Winona Lake, IN: Eisenbrauns, 1997, pp. 36-81]. Moulton, *The Literary Study of the Bible*, pp. 56-58, spoke of an 'envelope figure'. Barbara Herrnstein Smith, *Poetic Closure: A Study of How Poems End* (Chicago: University of Chicago Press, 1968), pp. 53-54, does not use the term 'inclusio', but recognizes the phenomenon all the same. Classical scholars use the term 'ring composition'; see J.A. Notopoulos, 'Continuity and Interconnection in Homeric Oral Composition', *TAPA* 82 (1951), pp. 81-101; and Whitman, *Homer and the Heroic Tradition*, pp. 252-54.

within a larger unit, in which case other data must help determine the beginning and end.

Structure. Once the literary or discourse unit is delimited, the rhetorical critic moves on to discern the arrangement of parts, that is, the unit's structure. Some refer to this as 'formal analysis'.[59] A structural feature of discourse, defined most simply, is any portion of the discourse that, if missing, substantially diminishes the whole. The controlling structures of the Jeremianic oracles, confessions, and other utterances are all rhetorical. Larger compositional structures in the book are both rhetorical and non-rhetorical.

In Jeremiah entire poems are structured by the inclusio and the chiasmus. These are usually formed by repeated or balancing words or, if the discourse has dialogue, by alternate speaking voices (6.8-12; 8.18-21; 17.13-16a). Sometimes poems have both (5.1-8; 8.13-17). It is difficult to overestimate the importance of repetition, which Muilenburg considered the very basis of ancient Hebrew rhetoric.[60] Jeremianic poetry is seen in other ways to be particularly well balanced, for example, the wordplay on 'see' (יִרְאֶה) and 'fear' (יִרָא Kt) in the parallel stanzas of 17.5-8.

One finds in Jeremiah much argument, some of it stimulated by rhetorical questions. The threefold question in the form הֲ...אִם...מַדּוּעַ ('If... if...why then...?') is a signature of the prophet (2.14, 31; 8.4-5, 19, 22; etc.), as also the question used to set up the 'but my people' contrast (2.11, 32; 5.22a, 23; 18.14-15). Arguments make use of the classical *distributio* (28.8-9). In 26.14, the prophet defends himself by using what ancient rhetoricians called 'surrender' (classical *permissio*). Jeremiah is familiar also with the argument *a minori ad maius* (Heb. *qal vechomer*; 3.1; 12.5; 25.29; 49.12), with protasis–apodosis (4.1-2; 7.5-7; 16.11-13; 31.36, 37), and with the technique of arguing by way of circumlocution (inclusio: 3.1-5; chiasmus: 5.1-8).

Particles signal discourse shifts, as Muilenburg rightly pointed out, for example, וְעַתָּה ('and now') in 2.18, which not only divides a poem in two but separates a foil from the prophet's preferred subject. Shifts in speaker perform a structural function in the Jeremianic oracles (2.5-9; 5.1-8; 8.18-21), with dialogue occurring everywhere—between Yahweh and Jeremiah, between Yahweh and the people, between Jeremiah and the people, and between Jeremiah and himself. Even the enemy is heard from (6.4-5).

---

59. Bernard Weinberg, 'Formal Analysis in Poetry and Rhetoric', in *Papers in Rhetoric and Poetic* (ed. Donald C. Bryant; Iowa City: University of Iowa Press, 1965), p. 36.

60. James Muilenburg, 'A Study in Hebrew Rhetoric: Repetition and Style', in *Congress Volume Copenhagen* (VTSup, 1; Leiden: E.J. Brill, 1953), pp. 97-111.

Refrains, which were important for Muilenburg as they are also for rhetorical critics working in modern poetry,[61] in Jeremiah conclude stanzas of oracles (2.14-19); take the form of doxologies in liturgical compositions (10.6-7, 10); and appear as stereotyped rhetorical questions later added at the end of oracles (5.9; 9.8 [Eng. 9.9]) or else interpolated into them (5.29).

Juxtaposition is another structural device in composition, a way for theological statements to be made without so much as a word being said. In Jeremiah the juxtaposition of chaps. 34 and 35, which are out of chronological sequence, sets up a contrast between disobedience and obedience.[62]

In discerning the structure of discourse, rhetorical criticism can isolate added material in the text and material that appears to have fallen out.[63] It can point up major breaks, minor breaks, and breaks that are not breaks at all.[64] Now and then it will illuminate differences between the MT and the LXX, helping to decide which text is better, if not the one that is more original (e.g., 10.1-10).

Style. Rhetorical criticism pays attention to matters of style in order to discern the texture of a text, as well as to measure such things as the level of abstraction, degree of ambiguity, and whether there is hidden meaning. Style has much to do with effect. Jeremiah's discourse is filled with wordplays, metaphors, similes, accumulation (*accumulatio*) and various other types of repetition. Here the interest goes beyond mere identification and cataloguing. The rhetorical critic seeks to find out how figures *function* in discourse,[65] with the great resources here being the classical rhetorical handbooks, such as Aristotle's *Rhetoric*, the *ad Herennium*, and Quintilian's *Institutes*.

Repetition may be for emphasis (*geminatio*) or embellishment (*exergasia*), but it has other functions. Anaphora simulates the sense (*onomatopoeia*) by driving home judgment (the fourfold 'they shall eat up' simulating a consuming enemy in 5.17; the fivefold 'sword' simulating the repeated stabbing of the victim in 50.35-38; the ninefold 'I will break in pieces' simulating a

---

61. Muilenburg, 'Form Criticism and Beyond', p. 11; Montague, 'Rhetoric in Literary Criticism', p. 173.
62. Lundbom, 'Scribal Contributions to Old Testament Theology', in *To Hear and Obey: Essays in Honor of Frederick C. Holmgren* (ed. Bradley Bergfalk and Paul Koptak; Chicago: Covenant Publications, 1997), pp. 42-49.
63. On possible loss in Jer 9.2-5 [3-6], see Lundbom, *Jeremiah: A Study in Ancient Hebrew Rhetoric*, pp. 86-88 [1997, pp. 114-16]; in Jer 20.14-18, see Lundbom, *Jeremiah: A Study in Ancient Hebrew Rhetoric*, pp. 46-48 [1997, pp. 65-67]; 'The Double Curse in Jeremiah 20.14-18', *JBL* 104 (1985), pp. 589-600.
64. Lundbom, 'Rhetorical Structures in Jeremiah 1', *ZAW* 103 (1991), pp. 193-210.
65. Donald C. Bryant, 'Uses of Rhetoric in Criticism', in *Papers in Rhetoric and Poetic* (ed. Donald C. Bryant; Iowa City: University of Iowa Press, 1965), p. 9.

pounding hammer in 51.20-23, or building up hope (the threefold 'again' simulating renewed activity in Zion in 31.4-5). Asyndeton functions to create a sense of urgency (verbs in 4.5 and 5.1). *Accumulatio* functions as it does for the later classical orators to heap up praise or blame. The accumulation of six infinitive absolutes in 7.9 heaps up blame.

Metaphors, similes and other tropes add strength to discourse, functioning also to kindle the hearer's imagination. Jeremiah's metaphors describe Yahweh, false gods, the nation, Judah's kings, the enemy, and even Jeremiah himself. They also heighten the enormity of evil and the destruction this evil will bring upon the nation. One of the harsher tropes is the *abusio*, which is an implied metaphor. It behaves somewhat extravagantly, in that a word is taken from a common usage and put to a usage that is uncommon, perhaps unique. So, for example, in 4.4: 'remove the foreskins of your *hearts*'; 5.8: 'each man *neighing* for his neighbor's wife'; in 18.18: 'come, let us smite him with the *tongue*'; in 51.44: 'the nations shall no longer *flow* to him'.

Jeremiah's style includes an abundance of paronomasia, hyperbole and verbal irony, showing also an unmistakable flair for the dramatic. On paronomasia see 1.10; 18.7; 31.28; on hyperbole see 1.5 (where Yahweh is speaker); 2.20, 28; 6.10; 8.16; and on verbal irony see 2.33; 4.22; 5.31. Fertility worship is mocked when Jeremiah deliberately reverses sexual preferences in 2.27, making the tree masculine and the stone feminine. Drama is seen in the use of apostrophe (2.12; 4.14; 22.29, 30; 47.6) and in the alternation of speakers.

Keywords. Rhetorical critics make much of 'keywords', which are normally repeated words or word cognates in a given discourse.[66] But they can also be synonyms, antonyms or fixed-pairs that balance one another. According to Martin Buber, 'the recurrence of keywords is a basic law of composition in the Psalms'.[67] It is a basic law of composition in Jeremiah as well.

How does one identify keywords? Repeated words, for example, may have little significance or none at all. Muilenburg says keywords are words appearing in 'strategic collocations' or in 'crucial or climactic contexts'. Repetitions at the beginning or end of successive cola, lines, or stanzas (anaphora; epiphora) qualify as keywords (see both in 8.22–9.1 [Eng. 9.2]). So also do verb clusters, regardless of position (שוב in 8.4-5), as well as

---

66. Thomson, 'Notes on Prometheus Vinctus', p. 157; Muilenburg, 'Form Criticism and Beyond', pp. 11, 13, 16-17; Montague, 'Rhetoric in Literary Criticism', pp. 173-74; Richard L. Graves, 'Symmetrical Form and the Rhetoric of the Sentence', in *Essays on Classical Rhetoric and Modern Discourse* (ed. Robert J. Connors *et al*.; Carbondale, IL: Southern Illinois University Press, 1984), p. 174.

67. Buber, *Good and Evil* (New York: Charles Scribner's Sons, 1953), p. 52.

3. History, Method, and Use in the Book of Jeremiah

repetitions at the beginning and end of a discourse unit (inclusio), or repetitions forming an abb'a' pattern (chiasmus) in the same. In the commission passage (1.13-19), keywords structure the parts and connect parts to one another.[68]

What controls exist for identifying keyword inclusios or chiasmi, which returns us to the method question raised earlier in connection with the Muilenburg program of rhetorical criticism? The most obvious answer would be other data delimiting the same unit. But what if there are no corroborating data, or the corroborating data remain ambiguous? The proposed inclusio may simply rest upon the repetition of one or two words in 8 lines of poetry or poetry where 10 or 20 chapters lie in between. In such cases one internal control can be applied that seems to have validity. If a word or word combination repeats at what appears to be the beginning and end of a rhetorical unit, *but occurs nowhere else in reasonable proximity to that beginning or end*, one may reasonably propose that the said repetition is an inclusio. Holladay, for example, has argued that the repetition of 'sow' in 2.2 and 4.3 makes an inclusio between two oracles, 2.2b-3 and 4.3-4, noting that the verb does not appear again in the book until 12.13.[69]

As it turns out, Holladay has other data to support his argument. Rubrics introducing the two oracles contain other keywords, namely, 'Jerusalem' in both 2.2 and 4.3. This is significant, because in 2.1–4.4 the audience is otherwise (Northern) Israel (2.4; 3.12). Also 2.1–4.4, which is the unit delimited by Holladay's inclusio, is agreed on other grounds as being a 'harlotry cycle' of oracles. This example, then, has an internal control of 'isolated keywords in context' and an external control of coroborating non-rhetorical data. Rhetorical criticism that works in this fashion is a method; keywords are not randomly identified, nor are judgments based solely on literary sensitivity.

One other example. Questions have been raised about my inclusio delimiting chaps. 1–20,[70] which is based upon the repetition, 'you came forth from the womb' in 1.5 and 'from the womb came I forth' in 20.18.[71] This verb–noun combination appears in these two places and nowhere else in chaps. 1–20, in fact, nowhere else in the entire book of Jeremiah. The

---

68. Lundbom, 'Rhetorical Structures in Jeremiah 1', p. 205; *The Early Career of the Prophet Jeremiah* (Lewiston, NY: Mellen Biblical Press, 1993), p. 65.

69. William L. Holladay, *Jeremiah 1* (Hermeneia: Philadelphia: Fortress Press, 1986), p. 68.

70. Black, 'Rhetorical Criticism and Biblical Interpretation', p. 254, and earlier James Crenshaw, 'A Living Tradition: The Book of Jeremiah in Current Research', *Int* 37 (1983), p. 119. Crenshaw expresses a preference for the linking of chaps. 1 and 24; see also Alexander Rofé, 'The Arrangement of the Book of Jeremiah', *ZAW* 101 (1989), pp. 390-98.

71. Lundbom, *Jeremiah: A Study in Ancient Hebrew Rhetoric*, p. 28 [1997, p. 42].

keywords are also inverted, which is a stylistic nicety often seen in this type of inclusio.

Corroborating non-rhetorical data were also cited in support of this inclusio. That 1.5 begins a literary unit needs no defense; it is the first poetry after the book's superscription. As for 20.18, a number of things point to it being a conclusion, besides the universal judgment that the verse ends the confession in 20.14-18:

a. after 20.18 is a change from poetry to prose;
b. a *petuḥah* (פ) section marker appears after 20.18; and
c. there is a chapter designation at 21.

That 20.18 marks an even greater termination point is indicated by the onset of dated prose in 21.1, the verse following. I pointed out that no dated prose from the reigns of either Jehoiakim or Zedekiah exists prior to 21.1; in fact, Jehoiakim and Zedekiah are not even mentioned in chaps. 1–20, except in the superscription of 1.1-3.[72] Finally, a major break after 20.18 is indicated by the separate delimitation of chaps. 21–23, which is a collection of utterances against kings and prophets. All this corroborates the keyword inclusio said to occur in 1.5 and 20.18. We are not talking here about proof; we are talking about method and controls that make for sound biblical interpretation.

Other keyword repetitions combine to form chiastic structures.[73] These occur in bicola and double bicola and in stanzas of oracles where they become the controlling structure (2.5-9; 5.1-8; 8.13-17; 51.34-45). Again, questions of method and controls are rightly asked about such structures. In Lamentations 1–2, where the phenomenon was first discovered by Condamin,[74] stanzas of an acrostic provided a control over the keyword distribution. In Jeremiah, stanzas delimited by speaker provide in some cases, though not all, a control for the keyword distribution. There is interpretation here, to be sure, but there is also the working out of a method and results that merit consideration. And it should also be pointed out that these chiastic structures, like the inclusio structures, are frequently supported at various points by non-rhetorical data as well.

Catchwords. Catchwords (hook words; *Stichwörter; mots crochets*) are keywords, basically, that connect originally independent discourse or literary units in the present biblical text. These could be mnemonic devices

---

72. Lundbom, *A Study in Ancient Hebrew Rhetoric*, pp. 28-30 [1997, pp. 42-44].

73. Nils W. Lund, 'The Presence of Chiasmus in the Old Testament', *AJSL* 46 (1930), pp. 104-126; *Chiasmus in the New Testament;* Lundbom, *Jeremiah: A Study in Ancient Hebrew Rhetoric*, pp. 61-112 [1997, pp. 82-146]; and John W. Welch (ed.), *Chiasmus in Antiquity* (Hildesheim: Gerstenberg Verlag, 1981).

74. Albert Condamin, 'Symmetrical Repetitions in *Lamentations* I and II', *JTS* 7 (1905), pp. 137-40.

used by the oral poet that have been carried over into the written text or else scribal devices used in early editing of the scrolls.⁷⁵ In chaps. 1–20 almost all the individual poems, and some of the prose units, show a linking by catchwords.

It stands to reason that catchwords cannot be identified until after the discourse or literary units have been delimited. In Amos 1–2 stereotyped oracles provide a ready-made control for catchword identification.⁷⁶ In Jeremiah, catchwords can be identified in prose juxtaposed to poetry (e.g., 'terror on every side' in 20.3 and 10), or when passages are delimited on other grounds. One notes in Jeremiah that some of the same words, for example, הִנֵּה ('look!') and אָסַף ('gather'), turn up as catchwords in different parts of the book.

Audience. Once discourse and literary units have been delimited and rhetorical criticism has done its full complement of work on the text, insights will be forthcoming on the speaker's interaction with his audience. In 3.1-5, for example, the audience is brought back at the oracle's end to the 'Would you return to me?' question posed at the beginning. In 5.1-8, Jeremiah abandons authority preaching by leaving it to the audience to decide at the end whether Yahweh can indeed pardon Jerusalem.⁷⁷ It is said that speakers commonly 'work against a pattern of expectation, and that expectation is not in the work but in the audience'.⁷⁸ Jeremiah plays with audience expectation in 50.35-38, where, after a fivefold repetition of חֶרֶב ('sword') he ends with the similar-sounding חֹרֶב ('drought'). Amos, as has already been noted, did precisely the same sort of thing.⁷⁹

I called attention earlier to Jeremiah's 'rhetoric of descent'.⁸⁰ Once discourse units are delimited, arguments are seen to go quite consistently from

---

75. Theophile J. Meek, 'The Poetry of Jeremiah', *JQR* ns 14 (1923–24), p. 283; Sigmund Mowinckel, 'Die Komposition des deuterojesajanischen Buches', *ZAW* 49 (1931), pp. 242-60; Edwin M. Good, 'The Composition of Hosea', *SEÅ* 31 (1966), p. 24; and Menahem Haran, 'Book-Size and the Device of Catch-Lines in the Biblical Canon', *JJS*, 36 (1985), pp. 8-11. In the commentaries, see W. Rudolph, *Jeremia* (HAT; 3rd edn; Tübingen: J.C.B. Mohr [Paul Siebeck], 1968), p. 75; J. Bright, *Jeremiah* (AB, 21; Garden City, NY: Doubleday, 1965), pp. lxxv, 73, 134; and Claus Rietzschel, *Das Problem der Urrolle* (Gütersloh: Gütersloher Gerd Mohn, 1966), pp. 24, 128.

76. Shalom M. Paul, 'Amos 1.3–2.3: A Concatenous Literary Pattern', *JBL* 90 (1971), pp. 397-403.

77. Lundbom, 'Jeremiah and the Break-away from Authority Preaching', *SEÅ* 56 (1991), pp. 7-28.

78. Montague, 'Rhetoric in Literary Criticism', p. 169.

79. David Noel Freedman, 'Deliberate Deviation from an Established Pattern of Repetition in Hebrew Poetry as a Rhetorical Device', in *Proceedings of the Ninth World Congress of Jewish Studies (Jerusalem August 4–12, 1985). Division A: The Period of the Bible* (Jerusalem: World Union of Jewish Studies, 1986), pp. 45-52.

80. Lundbom, *Jeremiah: A Study in Ancient Hebrew Rhetoric*, pp. 116-17 [1997, pp. 150-51].

the ironic to the straightforward, the figurative to the literal, the general to the specific, and the abstract to the concrete. In the oracles and other utterances, Jeremiah moves in the direction of lowering the level of abstraction, which means the encounter with his audience is most immediate at the end. This observation and others are but a modest beginning in the kind of broad rhetorical criticism that doubtless holds more promise yet in future study of the book of Jeremiah.

Chapter 4

DELIMITATION OF UNITS IN THE BOOK OF JEREMIAH*

James Muilenburg and Rhetorical Criticism

Interest in delimiting units within the biblical text began in earnest during the last century with James Muilenburg, whose 1968 Presidential Address to the Society of Biblical Literature, 'Form Criticism and Beyond',[1] argued for supplementing form criticism with a rhetorical criticism that would, among other things, better identify both macro- and micro-units of biblical speech and composition. In this lecture, Muilenburg said:

> The first concern of the rhetorical critic, it goes without saying, is to define the limits or scope of the literary unit, to recognize precisely where and how it begins and where and how it ends... An examination of the commentaries will reveal that there is great disagreement on this matter, and what is more, more often than not, no defence is offered for the isolation of the pericope. It has even been averred that it does not really matter. On the contrary, it seems to me to be of considerable consequence, not only for an understanding of how the *Gattung* is being fashioned and designed, but also and more especially for a grasp of the writer's intent and meaning. The literary unit is in any event an indissoluble whole, an artistic and creative unity, a unique formulation.[2]

Muilenburg found in biblical compositions many marks indicating that a finale had been reached. One important rhetorical figure delimiting units of poetry and prose is the inclusio, which Moulton earlier called an 'envelope figure',[3] and classical scholars refer to as 'ring composition'.[4] Although the inclusio is doubtless a thought pattern, it is most convincingly argued in the biblical text when words or phrases at the beginning of a pericope are seen

---

* *The Impact of Unit Delimitation on Exegesis* (ed. Raymond de Hoop *et al.*; Leiden: E.J. Brill, 2009), pp. 146-74.
  1. James Muilenburg, 'Form Criticism and Beyond', *JBL* 88 (1969), pp. 1-18.
  2. Muilenburg, 'Form Criticism and Beyond', pp. 8-9.
  3. Richard G. Moulton, *The Literary Study of the Bible* (New York: D.C. Heath & Co.), pp. 56-58.
  4. James A. Notopoulos, 'Continuity and Interconnexion in Homeric Oral Composition', *TAPA* 82 (1951), pp. 81-101; Cedric H. Whitman, *Homer and the Heroic Tradition* (Cambridge, MA: Harvard University Press, 1958), pp. 252-54.

to repeat at the end. Sometimes it is word cognates, associated words, or fixed word pairs repeating. But the inclusio—like also the chiasmus, to be discussed shortly—is typically, one is tempted to say always, anchored in specific vocabulary of the biblical text, not consisting of some vague 'idea', which all to often ends up being a subjective and incorrect projection of the modern reader in search of a now well-documented rhetorical device in Hebrew literary composition.

The repetition, in my view at least, should also be at beginning and end, not anywhere in the composition. Some scholars, e.g., Dahood on the Psalms, use 'inclusio' with this broader meaning, which has no value in delimiting units. The biblical speaker or writer uses the inclusio to tie-in the end of a discourse or discourse compilation with its beginning, making this an intentional closure device for ancient people who hear words spoken or listen to them being read aloud. The repetition sends out a signal that the discourse has ended. Repeated words and phrases also drive home points the speaker wishes to emphasize, compare, or contrast. On occasion, the same establish subtle continuities or contain weighty theological truths. Modern readers must then be alerted to this important structure in biblical discourse, for in structures lie keys to meaning and interpretation.

Muilenburg agreed with those who found lines of Hebrew poetry existing in well-defined clusters, saying that each possessed its own identity, integrity, and structure. These he called 'strophes' or 'stanzas',[5] which in his view also possessed clear beginnings and ends. Stanzas—now the preferred term—have traditionally been argued in biblical poetry on the basis of acrostics and refrains, the latter being found in such texts as Exod. 15.3, 6, 11, 16b; Pss. 42.6, 12 [42.5, 11]; and 43.5. Muilenburg noted that stanzas frequently conclude with 'climactic' or 'ballast' lines. Ballast lines he learned from George Adam Smith, who in his *Schweich Lectures* of 1910 called attention to 'a longer, heavier line, generally at the end of a strophe... similar to what the Germans call the "Schwellvers" in old German ballads'.[6] Smith found instances of this heavy line in the Song of Deborah (Judg. 5.3, 8, 10, 12, 19, 23, 27), the Song of Moses (Deut. 32.14b, 42b, 43b), and elsewhere in biblical poetry.

In his commentary on Second Isaiah,[7] Muilenburg delimited stanzas of poetry by Israel's consummate prophet of the Exile on the basis of climactic lines that lift up the name of Yahweh (Isa. 44.23c; 47.4; 48.2; 51.15-16; 54.5, 15). Climactic lines naming Yahweh occur also in other OT poetry (Exod. 15.3; Deut. 32.3, 9, 27b; Amos 4.13; 5.8; 9.6; Hos. 12.6 [12.5]), and

5. Muilenburg, 'Form Criticism and Beyond', pp. 9-12.
6. George Adam Smith, *The Early Poetry of Israel in its Physical and Social Origins* (London: Henry Frowde, Oxford University Press, 1912), pp. 20-21, 77.
7. Muilenburg, 'Isaiah', in *IB*, V (ed. George A. Buttrick; New York: Abingdon Press, 1956), pp. 392, 510, 544-635.

4. Delimitation of Units in the Book of Jeremiah

in Jeremiah the name of Yahweh is lifted up climactically at the conclusion of the hymn in Jer. 10.16 [= 51.19].

Muilenburg delimited stanzas at beginning and end in the Psalms, Second Isaiah, and elsewhere using other criteria, e.g., keyword repetitions, succession of interrogatives, vocatives addressed to God, shifts of speaker, audience, or motif, and the collocation of rhetorical questions and particles, especially the particle כִּי.[8] Muilenburg believed that even little words took on importance in Hebrew poetry. He said:

> Particles play a major role in all Hebrew poetry and reveal the rhetorical cast of Semitic literary mentality in a striking way. Chief among them is the deictic and emphatic particle כִּי, which performs a vast variety of functions and is susceptible of many different renderings, above all, perhaps, the function of motivation where it is understood causally. It is not surprising, therefore, that it should appear in strategic collocations, such as the beginnings and endings of strophes.[9]

Other particles found to delimit stanzas were לָמָה, לָכֵן, הִנְנִי, הֵן, הִנֵּה, and וְעַתָּה.[10] All of these particles delimit units in Jeremiah: The Jeremianic oracle most commonly begins with הִנֵּה or הִנְנִי together with a participle;[11] in 3.1-5 הֵן and הִנֵּה make an inclusio for an oracle; other oracles or stanzas of oracles begin and end with לָמָה (2.29; 6.20; 14.8-9, 18; 15.18; 20.18; etc.), or with לָכֵן (2.9; 5.2, 6; 6.15; 8.10 and 12 [inclusio]; 23.12; 49.26; etc.); oracles and stanzas of oracles frequently close with כִּי (4.6b, 8b; 5.6c; etc.) and in 2.18 the poem is nicely divided by וְעַתָּה, which shifts focus to the present at the beginning of the second stanza. Jeremiah also begins many of his poems and stanzas of poems with קוֹל, כִּי קוֹל, or מִקּוֹל (3.21; 4.15, 19c, 29, 31a; 9.18 [9.19]; 10.22; 30.5; 31.15; 47.3; 48.3; 50.22; 51.54).

History of Textual Delimitation in Jeremiah

Critical scholars began the work of delimitation in Jeremiah and other books of the OT long before Muilenburg. In the modern era, we must begin not surprisingly with Robert Lowth's all-important *Lectures on the Sacred Poetry of the Hebrews*,[12] best known for its pioneering work on poetic parallelism (Lecture XIX). But as important as this pivotal lecture became, and it was important, in another lecture (Lecture XVIII) Lowth argued that

---

8. Muilenburg, 'The Linguistic and Rhetorical Usages of the Particle כִּי in the Old Testament', *HUCA* 32 (1961), pp. 135-60.
9. Muilenburg, 'Form Criticism and Beyond', pp. 13-14.
10. Muilenburg, 'Form Criticism and Beyond', pp. 13-17.
11. Lundbom, *Jeremiah 1–20* (AB, 21A; New York: Doubleday, 1999; New Haven: Yale University Press, 2009), pp. 235, 242.
12. Lowth, *Lectures on the Sacred Poetry of the Hebrews* (trans. G. Gregory; Boston: Joseph T. Buckingham, 1815, originally 1753).

much of the prophetic writings were in fact poetry, not prose, as previously thought. Medieval codices of the Hebrew Bible (M^P, M^A, M^L)[13] did not format this discourse as poetry, and the *Hebrew University Bible* (in the fascicule on *The Book of Jeremiah*) carries on this tradition by continuing not to print prophetic poetry as poetry.[14]

Lowth said that poetry and prose seemed to be about evenly divided in Jeremiah,[15] but it was Benjamin Blayney, in his *Jeremiah* commentary of 1784, who was the first, so far as I know, to distinguish poetry from prose throughout the book.[16] His judgments, as one might expect, differ at points from judgments made today, but he made a good start, and came up with a credible work strikingly similar to both *Biblica hebraica* and modern versions of the Bible. The main differences in Blayney's commentary, when compared, say, to the RSV, are the following:

a. Blayney takes all of chapter 1 as prose; the RSV takes some of vv. 4-10 as poetry;
b. Blayney puts more bona fide Jeremiah utterances in poetry than the RSV, e.g., 4.9-12; 7.2b–8.3 (the RSV isolates 7.29 as a poetic fragment); 9.22-25 [9.23-26]; 11.9-17, 21-23; 12.14-17; 13.9-14; 14.11-16; 15.1-2a, 3-4, 10-14 (I take vv. 10-14 as poetry); 16.1-18, 21; 17.1-4 (I take most of vv. 1-4 as poetry); 18.6-12; 22.1-6, 24-27; 23.1-8 (I take vv. 5-6 as poetry), 23-40; 31.23-34, 38-40.
c. Blayney makes into poetry passages now recognized to be scribal additions, which the RSV takes as prose, e.g., 3.15-18, 24-25, 5.18-19; 9.11-15 [9.12-16]; 22.8-9, 11-12; 23.16-17; 25.33; 30.8-9; 46.25-26.
d. Blayney also did not distinguish superscriptions and subscriptions, usually taking them with the oracles to which they are joined. The RSV takes these as prose, distinguishing them from the poetry of the oracles.

Blayney recognizes most of chaps. 30–31, and virtually all the Foreign Nation Oracles in chaps. 46–51, as poetry. What makes this early work of Blayney so important is that poetry and prose are interspersed throughout much of the Jeremiah book, and in the shifts from prose to poetry and poetry to prose we have an important aid in the delimitation of literary units.

13. The sigla refer to the following manuscripts: M^P = St Petersburg Codex of the Prophets, M^A = Aleppo Codex, M^L = Leningrad Codex.
14. *The Hebrew University Bible: The Book of Jeremiah* (ed. C. Rabin *et al.*; Jerusalem: Magnes Press, The Hebrew University, 1997).
15. Lowth, *Lectures on the Sacred Poetry of the Hebrews*, p. 291.
16. Benjamin Blayney, *Jeremiah and Lamentations: A New Translation with Notes Critical, Philological, and Explanatory* (Oxford: Clarendon Press, 1784).

It was Bernhard Duhm who sharpened the identification of poetry in Jeremiah, although in his commentary[17] he went too far in appropriating the metrical theories of Julius Ley,[18] applying them with astounding rigidity. Duhm argued, for example, that Jeremiah's *ipsissima verba* could be found only in pentameter or *qina* (3:2) verse. Yet, Duhm became an important predecessor to Rudolph Kittel, who identified and formatted the Jeremiah poetry in his First Edition of *Biblia hebraica* (1906). Kittel's work has stood up remarkably well, exerting even today a major influence on how the Jeremiah poetry is scanned and interpreted.

Scholars of the Wellhausen school of literary (source) criticism were interested in doublets in the biblical text. In Jeremiah some passages appear twice (5.9, 29; 9.8 [9.9]; 6.13-15 = 8.10b-12; 10.12-16 = 51.15-19; 15.13-14 = 17.3-4; 23.19-20 = 30.23-24; 30.10-11 = 46.27-28), and the repetition thus becomes another aid in delimiting literary units. In a couple of cases, passages have been slightly rewritten for later use (6.22-24 = 50.41-43; 23.5-6 = 33.14-16), but here too delimitation of the early and later version is not difficult. Also, some duplications in MT are not present in the LXX,[19] providing yet another aid in identifying the MT passages as self-standing units.

The contribution of form-criticism to the work of delimitation in Jeremiah has been mixed. On the positive side, it was Gunkel who argued that genres had stereotyped beginnings,[20] leading Muilenburg to discover specific examples of this in Second Isaiah and elsewhere. But Jeremiah commentators have paid scant attention to this phenomenon, even though, as we pointed out above, certain particles and keywords repeatedly begin and end the Jeremiah poems. One could cite other stereotyped beginnings in Jeremiah, e.g., in 2.20-28 a succession of poems begins 'Now you say...not' (v. 20b); 'How can you say...not' (v. 23a); 'Now you say...No' (v. 25b); and '...they say...' (v. 27c).[21]

Gunkel on his work in Genesis and the Psalms had little difficulty in delimitation. Of a Genesis legend he could simply say, 'Everyone can see that the story ends here'.[22] Delimiting psalms was also not much of a prob-

---

17. Duhm, *Das Buch Jeremia* (Tübingen and Leipzig: J.C.B. Mohr [Paul Siebeck], 1901).

18. Ley, *Grundzüge des Rhythmus des Vers- und Strophenbaues in der hebräischen Poesie* (Halle: Verlag der Buchhandlung des Waisenhauses, 1875); *Leitfaden der Metrik der hebräischen Poesie* (Halle: Verlag der Buchhandlung des Waisenhauses, 1887).

19. Lundbom, *Jeremiah 1–20*, p. 59.

20. Gunkel, 'Israelite Literary History', in *Water for a Thirsty Land* (Minneapolis: Fortress Press, 2001), p. 33.

21. Lundbom, *Jeremiah 1–20*, p. 275.

22. Herman Gunkel, *The Legends of Genesis* (trans. W.H. Carruth; New York: Schocken Books, 1966), p. 43.

lem. But everyone cannot see where the prophetic speech ends, and many later form-critics have realized this, going first to the prose to find their speech outlines and then working back to the poetry, instead of allowing the poetry to articulate itself. Gunkel correctly identified two psalm-like compositions in Jeremiah: Jer. 2.14-19, with its repeated refrain,[23] and the wisdom psalm in 17.5-8.[24] The latter he thought was imitated by the author of Psalm 1.

Gunkel's greatest contribution to Jeremiah research was in pointing out that the prophet's so-called 'confessions' were in fact individual laments, the same as what one finds in the Psalter.[25] Gunkel identified Jer. 3.22b-25 and 14.7-9, 19-22 as communal laments containing confessions of sin. He believed that in both the individual and communal lament Jeremiah was imitating genres from the cult, using them to give expression to his own feelings and also to make an impression on people who were receptive to the forms.[26] This pioneering work of Gunkel was carried forward in an important monograph on the laments in Jeremiah by Walter Baumgartner.[27] Other scholars found in Jer. 14.1–15.4 a Temple liturgy, said to have been recited at a fast called in response to a drought.[28]

Form-critics depend heavily upon content for unit delimitation, which is especially true with individual and communal laments.[29] This has resulted in improper delimitation of units, and words of lament not being identified in larger structures of which they form a part. Gunkel said simply that the lament in prophetic material typically contains two parts: (1) a passionate appeal; and (2) a divine response. But things are more complex than this. It is true that many Jeremianic laments are joined with a divine response (11.18-23; 12.1-6; 15.15-21; 20.14-18 with 1.5), but some are not (10.19-21; 10.23-25; 17.16b-18; and 18.19-23). Also, other combinations exist, e.g., some laments appear in dialogues containing multiple speakers (8.18-21; 17.13-16a), and the lament in 20.7-10 is joined with a hymn of

---

23. 'Schriftstellerei und Formensprache der Propheten', in Gunkel, *Die Propheten* (Göttingen: Vandenhoeck und Ruprecht, 1917), pp. 116-17.

24. Gunkel, *The Psalms: A Form-Critical Introduction* (trans. Thomas M. Horner; Philadelphia: Fortress Press, 1967), p. 27.

25. Gunkel, *Introduction to the Psalms: The Genres of the Religious Lyric of Israel* (completed by Joachim Begrich; trans. James D. Nogalski; Macon, GA: Mercer University Press, 1998, originally 1933).

26. Gunkel, *The Psalms: A Form-Critical Introduction*, pp. 1-2.

27. Walter Baumgartner, *Jeremiah's Poems of Lament* (trans. David E. Orton; Sheffield: Almond Press, 1988).

28. Lundbom, *Jeremiah 1–20*, p. 692.

29. Lundbom, *Jeremiah: A Study in Ancient Hebrew Rhetoric* (SBLDS, 18; Missoula, MT: Society of Biblical Literature and Scholars Press, 1975), p. 7 [2nd edn; Winona Lake, IN: Eisenbrauns, 1997, p. 12].

confidence, concluding climactically with a lyrical word celebrating Yahweh's deliverance (20.11-13).

Westermann's work on prophetic speech forms offers no help whatever in delimitation; in fact, it frustrates the enterprise.[30] In his work on the 'judgment speech', Westermann is either unable or does not bother to delimit the literary unit, and what is more, he does not avail himself of help from others who have delimited. What he does is to rearrange the Jeremiah text in order to suit his imagined genre, with the result that the text is carved up into pieces that cannot possibly be put together. It becomes clear in this work that Jeremiah texts have been put into a mold that they just do not fit.[31] Muilenburg spoke to this weakness in the form-critical method when he said:

> To state our criticism in another way, form criticism by its very nature is bound to generalize because it is concerned with what is common to all the representatives of a genre, and therefore applies an external measure to the individual pericopes. It does not focus sufficient attention to what is unique and unrepeatable, upon the particularity of the formulation. Moreover, form and content are inextricably related. They form an integral whole. The two are one. Exclusive attention to the *Gattung* may actually obscure the thought and attention of the writer or speaker. The passage must be read and heard precisely as it is spoken.[32]

Attempts to find a 'lawsuit' (ריב) genre in Jeremiah 2 have also fared poorly.[33] Here, again, we have no model to work from, since the 'lawsuit'—much less the 'prophetic lawsuit'—genre has yet to be uncovered in documents of the ancient Near East. What Gunkel did was to create his *Gerichtsrede* from an array of biblical passages, relying heavily on Psalm 82.[34] The idea of a 'prophetic lawsuit' came later from Herbert Huffmon.[35] The attempts by Huffmon and also Julian Harvey[36] to find a 'lawsuit' genre in Jeremiah 2 must be judged a failure. Elements in the Jeremah text are again 'out of order', leaving the composition that exists in hopeless disarray. Attempts to find other genres in Jeremiah have foundered in a similar way.[37] The reason

---

30. Claus Westermann, *Basic Forms of Prophetic Speech* (trans. Hugh Clayton White; Philadelphia: Westminster Press, 1967).
31. Lundbom, *Jeremiah: A Study in Ancient Hebrew Rhetoric*, p. 10 [1997, pp. 16-17].
32. Muilenburg, 'Form Criticism and Beyond', p. 5.
33. Lundbom, *Jeremiah: A Study in Ancient Hebrew Rhetoric*, pp. 10-12 [1997, pp. 18-21].
34. Gunkel, *Introduction to the Psalms*, pp. 279-80.
35. Herbert Huffmon, 'The Covenant Lawsuit in the Prophets', *JBL* 78 (1959), pp. 285-95.
36. Julien Harvey, 'Le "Rîb-Pattern", réquisitoire prophétique sur la rupture de l'alliance', *Biblica* 43 (1962), pp. 172-96.
37. Lundbom, *Jeremiah: A Study in Ancient Hebrew Rhetoric*, p. 12 [1997, pp. 21-22].

is simple: Jeremianic discourse is structured not according to form-critical models, but according to canons of ancient Hebrew rhetoric.³⁸

The most form-critical help in delimiting oracles of Jeremiah comes from messenger formulas if they happen to be present, and quite often they are. It was Ludwig Köhler who argued that prophetic speech was essentially 'messenger speech', with the prophet now seen to be not an ecstatic but a royal messenger in the employ of Yahweh the king.³⁹ The typical Jeremiah oracle begins with 'Thus said Yahweh' (כֹּה אָמַר יְהוָה), or ends with 'oracle of Yahweh' (נְאֻם־יְהוָה), although some oracles, particularly those in prose, contain 'oracle of Yahweh' formulas near the beginning and, on rare occasion, elsewhere in the oracle (7.12-15 in prose; 51.34-45 in poetry). A few oracles have messenger formulas at beginning and end (2.2-3; 2.5-9), but usually an oracle contains only one formula. In my *Jeremiah* commentary I found these formulas very useful in delimiting units. In only one case, 6.9, I judged a messenger formula to be misplaced because on rhetorical grounds I concluded that 6.1-7 and 6.8-12 were companion poems.

The traditio-historical school of OT study has had little impact on the delimitation process, and much of it is in need of correction. It begins with what is believed to be large blocks of tradition still observable in the final composition, working methodologically just the reverse of the form-critics. Four 'tradition complexes' are identified in Jeremiah: (1) 1–24; (2) 25, 46–51; (3) 26–35/36; and (4) 36/37–45.⁴⁰ Agreement has not been reached on whether chap. 36 ends one complex or begins another. Too much importance is placed here on the divergence between the MT and LXX at 25.13a,⁴¹ which is important, but does not affect the delimitation of prose in chaps. 24–36. Rhetorical criticism—working diachronically—shows that chap. 25 belongs with chaps. 26, 35 and 36 in a compositional cluster, not with chaps. 46–51.⁴² It also shows that chap. 24 belongs with chaps. 27–29 in another compositional cluster. Therefore, chaps. 1–24 do not make up a unit, and chap. 36 is the end, not the beginning, of an editorial compilation.⁴³

---

38. Lundbom, *Jeremiah: A Study in Ancient Hebrew Rhetoric*, pp. 20-21 [1997, p. 35].

39. Ludwig Köhler, 'Formen und Stoffe', in *Deuterojesaja (Jesaja 40–55) stilkritisch untersucht* (BZAW, 37; Giessen: Alfred Töpelmann, 1923), pp. 102-42.

40. Lundbom, *Jeremiah: A Study in Ancient Hebrew Rhetoric*, pp. 14-15 [1997, pp. 25-27].

41. Lundbom, *Jeremiah: A Study in Ancient Hebrew Rhetoric*, p. 15 [1997, p. 26].

42. Lundbom, *Jeremiah 21–36* (AB, 21B; New York: Doubleday, 2004), pp. 253-54.

43. Lundbom, *Jeremiah 21–36*, pp. 222-23, 582-83.

4. Delimitation of Units in the Book of Jeremiah

Unit Delimitation in the Book of Jeremiah

My early work followed Muilenburg and others in applying rhetorical criticism to the delimitation of units in the book of Jeremiah.[44] I made more use of chiasmus than Muilenburg did, following Nils W. Lund in finding larger chiastic patterns in both Jeremiah poetry and prose.[45] I also found convincing Condamin's argument that keyword chiasms were present in Lamentations 1–2,[46] which took on added importance in that these structures turned up in acrostics, giving him a control for his rhetorical argument. In my *Jeremiah* commentary I returned to make more use of form-critical criteria, particularly the messenger formula introducing the Jeremianic oracle, appearing as it does most often at beginning or end. I also began to take account of section markings, the *setumah* (ס) and the *petuḥah* (פ), since they had turned up in the Dead Sea Scrolls and were therefore not medieval in origin. In addition, I made an attempt at delimiting Jeremiah oracles in prose, which earlier commentators had not done. These oracles, as it turned out, had some of the same rhetorical structures as the oracles in poetry.

Although my study of Jeremiah gives prominence to the method of rhetorical criticism, when all is said and done it is really eclectic, bringing together a variety of methods with the broad aim of explicating the meaning of the biblical text by whatever means possible. The work of delimitation must also make use of all criteria available, rhetorical and non-rhetorical. I have paid a modest debt to form-criticism by identifying three expanded colophons in Jer. 36.1-8, 45.1-5, and 51.59-64.[47] This builds on the work of Mowinckel, who noted in a later work how Baruch made a self-presentation in chap. 45.[48] Here real form-critical work is possible because we have at our disposal a large number of colophons in documents of the ANE for purposes of comparison.[49]

In identifying rhetorical structures I always look for corroborative data to support arguments for an inclusio, chiasmus, or other balancing word pattern. Rhetorical arguments need as much objectification as possible,

---

44. Lundbom, *Jeremiah: A Study in Ancient Hebrew Rhetoric* (1975, 1997).

45. Nils W. Lund, 'The Presence of Chiasmus in the Old Testament', *AJSL* 46 (1930), pp. 104-26; *Chiasmus in the New Testament* (Chapel Hill, NC: University of North Carolina Press, 1942 [reprint: Peabody, MA: Hendrickson, 1992].

46. Albert Condamin, 'Symmetrical Repetitions in *Lamentations* Chapters I and II', *JTS* os 7 (1905), pp. 137-40; cf. Lundbom, *Jeremiah 1–20*, pp. 81-82.

47. Lundbom, 'Baruch, Seraiah, and Expanded Colophons in the Book of Jeremiah', *JSOT* 36 (1986), pp. 89-114.

48. Sigmund Mowinckel, *Prophecy and Tradition* (Oslo: Jacob Dybwad, 1946).

49. Hermann Hunger, *Babylonische und assyrische Kolophone* (AOAT, 2; Neukirchen–Vluyn: Neukirchener Verlag, 1968).

and corroborative data provide controls for arguments that may otherwise founder because they are too subjective. For example, if keywords are said to make an inclusio or chiasmus in a given passage, it is important that these words do not appear elsewhere in the system, or in reasonable proximity to the passage under consideration.[50] In my argument that 'you came forth from the womb' in 1.5 makes an inclusio with 'from the womb came I forth' in 20.18, it should be noted that this noun–verb combination occurs nowhere else in Jeremiah; indeed, it occurs nowhere else in the Hebrew Bible.

In my argument that 20.18 marks the conclusion of a major early composition in the present book of Jeremiah (I call chaps. 1–20 the First Edition), I cite the following as evidence:[51]

1. The poetry in 20.14-18 is a self-standing composition, having its own integrity and identifiable internal structure.
2. A keyword repetition (with inversion) exists in 20.18 and 1.5.
3. 1.5 is the first poetry in the book.
4. After the poetry in 20.18 is a return to prose.
5. A *petuḥah* section marking exists after 20.18, followed by a chapter designation at 21.1 added later (13th-century CE).
6. Chapter 21 is the first dated prose in the book of Jeremiah not counting the superscription in 1.1-3; from this point onward most—but not all—of the Jeremiah prose is dated.
7. Chapters 21–23 are delimited as separate collections of utterances against kings and prophets.

In delimiting macro- and micro-units in the book of Jeremiah I use the following criteria, some old, some new, some rhetorical, and some non-rhetorical:

1. Shifts from prose to poetry, and poetry to prose.
2. Duplication of verses or larger passages appearing in different contexts.
3. Genres and content of genres: oracles (judgment and salvation); individual laments (some with divine answers); communal laments (some with confessions of sin; some with calls to repentance); Temple liturgies; hymns; doxologies; prayers (some with answers); proverbs; letters; vision reports; narrative; colophons; parables; midrash.

---

50. Lundbom, 'Rhetorical Criticism: History, Method and Use in the Book of Jeremiah', in *Jeremiah: A Study in Ancient Hebrew Rhetoric* (2nd edn, 1997), pp. xxxix-xl.
51. Lundbom, *Jeremiah: A Study in Ancient Hebrew Rhetoric* (2nd edn, 1997), pp. xl-xli.

4. Superscriptions and subscriptions.
5. Messenger formulas.
6. Section markings (*setumah* and *petuḥah*).
7. Inclusio.
8. Editorial inclusios.
9. Balance and parallelism.
10. Stereotyped beginnings of oracles and other discourse.
11. Keyword and/or speaker chiasms.
12. Editorial chiasms.
13. Other patterned repetition.
14. Change from Hebrew to Aramaic (10.11).

Delimitation of Oracles in Jeremiah Poetry

I will now present seven selected texts of Jeremiah poetry (2.5-9, 33-37; 5.1-9; 8.18-21; 8.22–9.1 [9.2]; 20.7-13, 14-18), showing in each case how I have delimited macro- and micro-units. After these, two selected texts of Jeremiah prose will be presented, both containing oracle clusters (7.1-15; 31.23-40), and show how I have gone about delimiting the units they contain.

Jeremiah 2.5-9

These verses are delimited at the top end by a 'Thus said Yahweh' messenger formula, which introduces a divine oracle. Prior to that is a superscription (v. 4), preceded by a *petuḥah* section marking. The problem has been in determining the lower limit of the unit. Commentators generally extend the unit to v. 13. There are no subsequent section markings until the *setumah* after v. 28, which means delimitation of the oracle must be determined solely on the basis of formal and rhetorical criteria. I believe the oracle extends through v. 9 for two reasons: (1) there is a concluding 'oracle of Yahweh' formula in v. 9; and (2) a chiastic structure identifies vv. 5-9 as a rhetorical unit. Most Jeremiah oracles have only one messenger formula, but this one, like 2.2b-3, has two: one at the beginning, and one at the end. The chiastic structure consists of balancing keywords (bold), and also a speaker alternation, which we find in other Jeremiah oracles. Here the speaker throughout is Yahweh, but in segments B and B' Yahweh cites what others should have said, but did not (cf. 8.6b). The oracle then contains the following structure:[52]

---

52. Lundbom, *Jeremiah: A Study in Ancient Hebrew Rhetoric*, pp. 70-74 [1997, pp. 94-98]; *Jeremiah 1–20*, pp. 256-58.

        2 ⁵Thus said Yahweh:
        What did **your fathers** find wrong in me
A   that they wandered far from me?
        They went/after The Nothing
        and became nothing

              ⁶**They did not say, 'Where is Yahweh**
              who brought us up from the land of Egypt
              who led us in the wilderness
      B   in a land of desert and pit
              in a land of drought and death shadow
              in a land through which a person does not pass
              and a human being does not dwell there?'

              ⁷**Then I brought you into** the garden **land**
      C   to eat its fruit and its goodness
              But you came in and polluted **my land**
              and my heritage you made an abomination

        ⁸**The priests did not say, 'Where is Yahweh?'**
          those handling the law did not know me
      B'   The shepherds rebelled against me
          the prophets prophesied by Baal

        After No Profits /they went
         ⁹Therefore I still have a grievance with you
A'   —oracle of Yahweh—
        and with **your children's children** I will have a grievance!

This oracle is not structured according to any 'lawsuit' genre, but rather according to canons of ancient Hebrew rhetoric. Here we see a balancing verse at the center, which Lund noted in many large keyword chiasms,[53] and which occurs with frequency in Jeremiah (2.33-37; 5.1-8; 6.1-7; 6.8-12; 8.13-17; 23.18, 21-22; and 51.34-45). The present rhetorical structure also contains an argument, i.e., that the sins of the fathers will be meted out on the children's children, a well-established retribution theory in the OT (Exod. 34.7).

Jeremiah 2.33-37
These verses may also be a prophetic oracle, but if so, the text contains no introduction, no section markings, and no messenger formula, only a chapter division after v. 37, which means delimitation must be solely by rhetorical analysis. As it turns out, this is one of the most carefully crafted of the Jeremiah poems, which makes delimitation easy. A keyword structure,

---

53. Lund, *Chiasmus in the New Testament*, p. 40.

which includes inversion, shows this poem to divide into three stanzas of four lines, two lines, and four lines.[54] This structure, with a short center, has been identified on a smaller scale in Hebrew poetry by Dahood.[55] The structure here with its keywords (in bold) is outlined as follows:

2 ³³**How** well you make **your way**
    to seek love
So **even** you can teach
    your wicked ways
³⁴**even** on your skirts are found
    bloodstains of the innocent needy
Not in burglary you found them
    indeed despite all these things

³⁵**Now you say**, 'Indeed I am innocent
    surely his anger has turned away from me'
Look I am entering into judgment with you
    for **your saying** 'I have not sinned'

³⁶**How** very casually you act
    to change **your way**
even by Egypt you will be shamed
    as you were shamed by Assyria
³⁷**even** from this you will come away
    your hands upon your head
Indeed Yahweh rejects your 'trusted ones'!
    and you will **not** succeed by them.

A	*How………your way…..to…*	מַה………דַּרְכֵּךְ ל………	v. 33a
	…even………………………	…גַּם…………………………	v. 33b
	even……………………………	………………………גַּם…	v. 34a
	Not…………………indeed…	לֹא……………כִּי……………	v. 34b
B	*Now you say…………………*	……………………וַתֹּאמְרִי…	v. 35a
	……………………your saying…..	…………אָמְרֵךְ………………	v. 35b
A'	*How…………to……your way*	מַה………ל………דַּרְכֵּךְ	v. 36a
	even………………………………	……………………………גַּם	v. 36b
	even………………………………	……………………………גַּם	v. 37a
	Indeed……………and not…	כִּי……………וְלֹא…………	v. 37b

Here again, only this time in the center of the poem, Yahweh brings in other voices. He first cites what the people have said, then what they should have

---

54. Lundbom, *Jeremiah: A Study in Ancient Hebrew Rhetoric*, pp. 74-75 [1997, pp. 98-100]; *Jeremiah 1–20*, p. 294.
55. Mitchell Dahood, 'A New Metrical Pattern in Biblical Poetry', *CBQ* 29 (1967), pp. 574-79.

said, but did not. It is unclear who is speaking in the first stanza, but however that is decided, a dialogue is going on, because Jeremiah is clearly the speaker in the final stanza ('Indeed Yahweh rejects your "trusted ones"!').

Jeremiah 5.1-9
These verses are delimited at the top end in M^A, M^L, and M^P with a *petuhah* before 5.1, and at the bottom end with a *setumah* after 5.9. Rhetorical criticism refines delimitation by showing that vv. 1-8 constitute an extraordinary five-stanza poem in which a keyword chiasmus and a chiasmus of speaker work simultaneously to provide the structure.[56]

Yahweh begins and ends the discourse, with Jeremiah speaking in the center. The LXX clarifies the speaker at the outset by adding λέγει κύριος ('oracle of the Lord') at the end of v. 1. The center also has internal keyword balance like 2.7. Audiences also change: Yahweh addresses a search team at the beginning (A), and the city of Jerusalem at the end (A'). Jeremiah addresses Yahweh in Stanzas 2 and 4 (B and B'), and is heard talking to himself at the center (C):

Yahweh to Searchers	A	5 ¹Go back and forth in the streets of Jerusalem
		    look please, and take note
		And search in her squares
		    Surely you can find **a man**
		Surely there is one doing justice
		    one searching for integrity
		    that I may pardon her!
		²Just as surely they say, 'By Yahweh's life'
		    therefore **they swear** to The Lie

Jeremiah to Yahweh	B	³Yahweh, your eyes
		    are they not for integrity?
		You struck them down but they did not writhe
		    you finished them, they refused to take correction
		They made their faces harder than rock
		    they refused to repent

Jeremiah to Self	C	⁴Then I said to myself, 'But **poor folk!**
		    they, they have no sense
		For they know not Yahweh's way
		    the justice of their God
		⁵Let me go for myself to the **great ones**
		    and let me speak to them
		For they, they know Yahweh's way
		    the justice of their God'

---

56. Lundbom, *Jeremiah: A Study in Ancient Hebrew Rhetoric*, pp. 75-78 [1997, pp. 100-104]; *Jeremiah 1–20*, pp. 372-75.

Jeremiah to Yahweh:		But they together, they have broken the yoke they have snapped the straps ⁶Therefore a lion from the forest **has struck them down** and a wolf of the steppes will destroy them A leopard is prowling around their cities everyone going out from them will be torn apart For their rebellions are very many their regressions are numerous
	B'	
Yahweh to Jerusalem:		⁷Why then **will I pardon you?** your children have forsaken me and **have sworn** by 'no gods' When I fed them full they committed adultery and to a whorehouse they cut a path ⁸well-endowed early-rising horses they were Each **man** for his neighbor's wife, they neighed
	A'	

Verse 9 lies outside the chiastic structure, and because it is stereotyped and occurs two other times in the book (5.29; 9.8 [9.9]), we can take it here as an add-on. It contains an 'oracle of Yahweh' messenger formula, identifying the preceding as a prophetic oracle:

> ⁹Because of these things shall I not call to account?
> —oracle of Yahweh—
> And against a nation such as this
> shall I not vindicate myself?

This main poem does not conclude at v. 6, as some commentators assume, which builds on the notion that Yahweh is concluding a discourse with a word of judgment. In my view, Yahweh is not the speaker in v. 6; it is Jeremiah, who is expressing horror at past, present, and future judgment, and perhaps also attempting to intercede with Yahweh for the people.

Jeremiah 8.18-21

These verses contain a three-way dialogue among Jeremiah, the people, and Yahweh, who unexpectedly interrupts in the center. It is structured into a speaker chiasmus, with Jeremiah lamenting at beginning and end, and other voices speaking in between:[57]

a		Jeremiah		v. 18
	b	Jeremiah for the people		v. 19ab
		c	Yahweh	v. 19c
	b'	Jeremiah for the people		v. 20
a'		Jeremiah		v. 21

---

57. Lundbom, *Jeremiah: A Study in Ancient Hebrew Rhetoric*, pp. 84-86 [1997, pp. 111-14]; *Jeremiah 1–20*, pp. 528-29.

A similar speaker chiasmus occurs in Jer. 17.13-16a. The upper limit is secured by a *setumah* in M^P, M^A, and M^L before v. 18, where 4QJer^a also has a section. The lower limit has been in doubt, with M^P and M^A having a *setumah*, and 4QJer^c a *petuhah*, after v. 22. Older scholars, however, extended the unit even farther to include 8.23 [Eng. 9.1], after which another *setumah* occurs in M^A. Baumgartner concluded the unit at v. 23, but did discern the sequence of speakers correctly in vv. 18-21.[58] The unit, as a rhetorical analysis will show, is 8.18-21 (RSV, NRSV). The lament following, as we will see next, is delimited to 8.22-9.1 [9.2].

Jeremiah	8.18My joy is gone
	   grief is upon me
	      my heart is sick

People	19Listen! a voice (a cry of my dear people from a land far off):
	   '*Is* Yahweh not in Zion?
	      Is her King not in her?'

Yahweh	*So why* have they provoked me to anger with their images with their foreign nothings?

People	20The harvest is past
	   the summer is ended
	      and we are not saved!

Jeremiah	21For the brokenness of my dear people
	   I am broken, I mourn
	      desolation has gripped me.

In v. 19 is a threefold rhetorical question in the הַ...אִם...מַדּוּעַ ('Is... Is... So why...') form (italics), which is a signature of Jeremiah occurring eight times in the book (2.14, 31; 8.4-5, 19, 22; 14.19; 22.28; 49.1).[59] Its use here differs from elsewhere in the book in that Yahweh is interrupting two questions of the people with a third question of his own.

Jeremiah 8.22–9.1 [9.2]

Here is an individual lament spoken in its entirety by Jeremiah. We get no help in this case from formal criteria or section markings, which means another unit determined solely by rhetorical criteria. The latter proves to be possible because of an interlocking balancing pattern (*epiphora* and *anaphora* in bold), which sets the verses off from what precedes and what follows.[60]

---

58. Baumgartner, *Jeremiah's Poems of Lament*, p. 84.
59. Lundbom, *Jeremiah 1–20*, p. 271.
60. Lundbom, *Jeremiah 1–20*, pp. 535-36.

4. Delimitation of Units in the Book of Jeremiah

Delimitation is further aided by another rhetorical structure occurring in 9.2-5 [Eng. 9.3-6].[61]

> [8.22]*Is* there no balm in Gilead?
> *Is* there no healer there?
> Indeed *so why* has it not arisen
> healing for **my dear people**?
>
> [9.1]**Who can make** my head waters
> and my eyes a well of tears
> So I might weep day and night
> for the slain of **my dear people**?
>
> [2]**Who can make** for me in the desert
> a traveler's lodge
> So I might forsake my people
> and go away from them?
>
> For all of them are adulterers, a faithless bunch.

The final line of v. 2 is to be taken as a later add-on, the first part of which may derive from Hos 7.4. In this lament is another occurrence of the Jeremianic threefold rhetorical question (italics).

Jeremiah 20.7-13
In these verses I delimit two poems linked by catchwords: vv. 7-10, and vv. 11-13. They seem to be separate genres: vv. 7-10 an individual lament, and vv. 11-13 a hymn of confidence concluding with joyful praise. In the Psalms one often finds internal movement from complaint to confident assurance (Psalms 6; 13; 22; 28; 30; 31; 35), which means lament and thanksgiving can be present in a single composition. The lament here has some striking affinities to Psalm 31, for example, v. 10 and Ps 31.13. Gunkel therefore took vv. 11-13 of the present composition as the prophet's 'certainty of hearing', a formal feature in the lament psalms.[62] But here I think two separate compositions have been joined in a way similar to the joining of judgment and salvation oracles in chaps. 30–31.[63] Linkage is provided by catchwords (italics). The lament in vv. 7-10 contains keywords making an inclusio (bold).[64]

---

61. Lundbom, *Jeremiah: A Study in Ancient Hebrew Rhetoric*, pp. 86-88 [1997, pp. 114-16]; *Jeremiah 1–20*, pp. 540-41.
62. Gunkel, *Introduction to Psalms*, p. 181.
63. Lundbom, *Jeremiah 1–20*, pp. 97-98; *Jeremiah 21–36*, p. 379.
64. Lundbom, *Jeremiah: A Study in Ancient Hebrew Rhetoric*, pp. 45-46 [1997, pp. 63-65]; *Jeremiah 1–20*, pp. 852-53.

The upper limit of the lament is established by the shift from prose to poetry in v. 7, and section markings in M^P. M^A, and M^L prior to v. 7. The next sections in M^P, M^A, and M^L come after vv. 12 and 13, suggesting that v. 13 may be a later add-on. Verse 12 may also be an addition, since it is duplicated in 11.20.

Jeremiah's lament:

> [20.7]**You enticed me,** *Yahweh,* **and I was enticed**
> you laid hold of me, and *you overcame*
> I have become a joke all the day
> they all make fun of me
>
> [8]For too often I speak, I cry out
> violence and destruction, I proclaim
> For the word of Yahweh has become for me
> reproach and ridicule all the day
>
> [9]Then I say, I will not mention him
> I will not speak any longer in his name
> But it becomes in my heart like a burning fire
> shut up in my bones
> I am weary from holding it in
> and ***I cannot overcome***
>
> [10]For I hear whispering in the crowd:
> 'Terror-on-every-side!
> tell, let us tell on him!'
> All my trusted friends watch for my fall:
> **'Perhaps he can be enticed** *and we will overcome him*
> and we will take *our revenge* on him'.

Hymn of confidence:

> [11]But *Yahweh* is with me like a fearless warrior
> therefore my pursuers will stumble and *will not overcome*
> They are greatly shamed, for they did not succeed
> eternal disgrace will not be forgotten!
>
> [12]Yahweh of hosts, who tests the righteous
> who sees the inner being and the heart
> let me see *your vengeance* upon them
> when to you I have confided my case.
>
> [13]Sing to *Yahweh*
> praise *Yahweh*
> For he rescued the life of the needy
> from the hand of evildoers!

4. Delimitation of Units in the Book of Jeremiah

Jeremiah 20.14-18
Here at the end of the First Edition is the most deeply moving lament in the book. It can be delimited by content, rhetorical structure, and section markings in M^P, M^A, M^L, and 4QJer^a at both top and bottom. As we noted earlier, a major break in the present book exists between chaps. 20 and 21. With reconstruction, the lament is seen to have an original keyword chiasmus (bold).[65] In its immediate context, the lament is without a divine response. Von Rad says: 'The God whom the prophet addresses no longer answers him'.[66] But in the compilation making up the First Edition (chaps. 1–20), an answer comes in 1.5.[67] The tie-in is created by a keyword inclusio (italics).

Jeremiah's lament:

> 20.14**Cursed be the day**
>   on which I was born
>   the day my mother bore me
> Let it not be blessed
>
> 15**Cursed be the man**
>   who brought my father the news:
> 'A male child is born to you'
>   making him very glad
>
> 16**Let that man be like** the cities
>   which Yahweh overthrew and did not pity
> Let him hear a cry in the morning
>   and an alarm at noontime
>
> 17 **[Let that day be like…]**
>   because he did not kill me in the womb
> So my mother would have been my grave
>   and her womb eternally pregnant
>
> 18Why this: *from the womb came I forth*
>   to see hard times and sorrow
>   and **my days** end in shame?

Divine response:

> 1.5Before I formed you in the belly I knew you
>   and before *you came forth from the womb* I declared you holy
>   a prophet to the nations I made you.

---

65. Lundbom, *Jeremiah: A Study in Ancient Hebrew Rhetoric*, pp. 64-68 [1997, pp. 65-67]; 'The Double Curse in Jeremiah 20.14-18', *JBL* 104 (1985), pp. 589-600; *Jeremiah 1–20*, pp. 865-69.

66. Gerhard von Rad, *Old Testament Theology*, II (Edinburgh and London: Oliver & Boyd, 1965), p. 204.

67. Lundbom, *Jeremiah: A Study in Ancient Hebrew Rhetoric*, pp. 28-30 [1997, pp. 42-44]; *Jeremiah 1–20*, p. 869.

The prophet's wrenching question receives an answer, when the scribe compiling the First Edition makes a tie-in between v. 18 of the lament and the word of call in 1.5. The larger message is that Jeremiah came forth from the womb because Yahweh called him before he came forth.

Delimitation of Oracles in Jeremiah Prose

In my *Jeremiah* commentary I delimited for the first time oracles in the prose, finding that they have rhetorical structures, just as the poetic oracles do. This presents a more accurate picture of the Jeremiah prose in that it delimits units and thereby aids the interpretive process.

Jeremiah 7.1-15

The prose of 7.1-15 has been taken as the text of Jeremiah's so-called 'Temple sermon', a summary of which appears together with background information in chap. 26. But a closer reading of the text, in which attention is paid to rhetorical structures, messenger formulas, and section markings, shows that vv. 3-14 contain not a single 'Temple sermon', but rather three distinct 'Temple oracles' brought together into a cluster.[68]

I   7.3Thus said Yahweh of hosts, the God of Israel:
Make good your ways and your doings and **I will let you dwell in this place**. 4Do not trust for yourselves in the deceptive words, 'The temple of Yahweh, the temple of Yahweh, the temple of Yahweh are these'. 5For if you really make good your ways and your doings, if you really act justly each man toward his fellow, 6the sojourner, the orphan, and the widow you do not oppress, and the blood of the innocent you do not shed in this place, and after other gods you do not go, to your own hurt, 7then **I will let you dwell in this place**, in the land that I gave to your fathers for all time.

II   7.8**Look**, you trust for yourselves in the deceptive words to no avail. 9Do you think you can steal, murder, and commit adultery, and swear to The Lie, and burn incense to Baal, and go after other gods that you have not known, 10and then come and stand in my presence, in this house upon which my name is called, and say, 'We are safe!'—only to keep doing all these abominations? 11A robber's den is this house upon which my name is called in your eyes? As for me, **Look!** I have seen!—oracle of Yahweh.

III   7.12Go indeed, would you, to **my place** that was **in Shiloh**, where I first made my name dwell, and see what I did to it because of the evil of my people Israel. 13Now then, because you have done all these doings—oracle of Yahweh—when I spoke to you—constantly I spoke—but you did not hear, and I called you but you did not answer, 14I will do then to the house upon which my name is called, in which you trust, yes to **the place** that I gave to you and to your fathers, as I did **to Shiloh**.

---

68. Lundbom, *Jeremiah 1–20*, pp. 454-59.

¹⁵So I will cast you away from my presence, as I cast away all your brothers, all the offspring of Ephraim.

Verses 1-2 are 'Introduction', containing a superscription and section markings in M^P, M^A, and M^L before v. 1 and after v. 2. Oracle I (vv. 3-7) has a beginning 'Thus said Yahweh of hosts, the God of Israel' messenger formula in v. 3, but no section markings in the medieval codices after v. 7. Oracle II (vv. 8-11) has a concluding 'oracle of Yahweh' messenger formula in v. 11, and a *setumah* in M^L and M^P after v. 11. Oracle III (vv. 12-15) has an 'oracle of Yahweh' messenger formula midway in v. 13 (yet LXX omits), but no section markings in the medieval codices after v. 14. Section markings appear in M^P, M^A, M^L and 4QJer^a after v. 15, which concludes the larger unit. All three oracles contain keyword inclusios, indicating that v. 15 is probably an add-on to Oracle III, making a comparison between Judah and Ephraim (cf. 3.6-11):

I	...*I will let you dwell in this place*...	v. 3
	I will let you dwell in this place...	v. 7
II	*Look* (הִנֵּה)...	v. 8
	Look! (הִנֵּה)...	v. 11
III	...*my place... in Shiloh*	v. 12
	the place...to Shiloh.	v. 14

Here the identification of three self-standing oracles aids the interpretive process, which has been frustrated due to a lack of coherence in one and the same sermon: vv. 3-7 are conditional preaching, calling for a return to covenant obedience; vv. 12-14 are unmitigated judgment for covenant disobedience. With three self-standing oracles, we see that Oracle I is conditional reform-type preaching; Oracle II indictment for covenant violation; and Oracle III unmitigated judgment.

Jeremiah 31.23-40
In these verses we have a collection of prose oracles, including the important new covenant prophecy, which together with other material expands the core poetry (30.5–31.22) and creates what becomes Jeremiah's first Book of Restoration (chaps. 30–31). These oracles announce that Israel's future will have both continuity and discontinuity with the past.[69] A rhetorical structure points up the continuity or discontinuity, employing the keywords 'Look days are coming', and 'again' (עוֹד) or 'not again' (לֹא...עוֹד). The second

---

69. Lundbom, *Jeremiah: A Study in Ancient Hebrew Rhetoric*, pp. 34-36 [1997, pp. 50-52]; *Jeremiah 21–36*, pp. 453-55.

'not again' in v. 34 makes an inclusio with 'again' in v. 23. The expansion occurs in two stages: (1) the addition of vv. 23-34; (2) then the addition of vv. 35-40. Each oracle of the present compilation is further delimited by a messenger formula. M^P, M^L, and 4QJer^c have section markings prior to v. 23, and M^P, M^A, and M^L have section markings after v. 40.

First stage of expansion:

I $^{31.23}$Thus said Yahweh of hosts, God of Israel: **Again** they shall say this word in the land of Judah and in its cities, when I restore their fortunes:

> May Yahweh bless you
> > righteous pasture
> > > O holy mountain

^{24}And Judah and all its cities shall dwell in it, together the farmers and they who set out with the flock. ^{25}For I will saturate the thirsty soul, and every languishing soul I will fill.

> Intervening verse (31.26)

II ^{27}**Look, days are coming**—oracle of Yahweh—when I will sow the house of Israel and the house of Judah with the seed of human and the seed of beast.

^{28}And it will be as I have watched over them to uproot and to break down, and to overthrow and to destroy, also to bring evil, so I will watch over them to build and to plant—oracle of Yahweh.

^{29}In those days they shall **not again** say:

> Fathers have eaten sour grapes
> > and children's teeth become set on edge

^{30}But each person in his iniquity shall die. Every human who eats the sour grapes, his teeth shall become set on edge.

III ^{31}**Look, days are coming**—oracle of Yahweh—when I will cut with the house of Israel and with the house of Judah a new covenant, ^{32}not like the covenant that I cut with their fathers in the day I took them by the hand to bring them out from the land of Egypt, my covenant that they, they broke, though I, I was their master—oracle of Yahweh.

^{33}But this is the covenant that I will cut with the house of Israel after those days—oracle of Yahweh: I will put my law in their inward parts, and upon their hearts I will write it. And I will be God to them, and they, they will be a people to me. ^{34}And they shall **not again** instruct each person his fellow and each person his brother, saying, 'Know Yahweh', for they, all of them, shall know me, from the least of them to the greatest of them—oracle of Yahweh—for I will forgive their iniquity, and their sin I will **not** remember **again**.

Second stage of expansion:

> Intervening poetry (31.35-37)

IV ³⁸**Look, days are coming**—oracle of Yahweh—when the city shall be rebuilt for Yahweh from the Tower of Hananel to the Corner Gate. ³⁹And the measuring line shall go out again, straight over Gareb Hill and turn to Goah. ⁴⁰And all the valley land, the corpses and the ashes, and all the terraces up to the Brook Kidron, up to the corner of the Horse Gate toward the east, shall be holy for Yahweh. It shall not be uprooted, and it shall **not again** be overthrown—forever.

The 'not again' here in v. 40 makes an inclusio with 'For look days are coming' in 30.3, bringing the first Book of Restoration to completion.

Chapter 5

SECTION MARKINGS IN BIBLE SCROLLS*

What induced me to consult the Taylor–Schechter Genizah fragments in the Cambridge University Library was an interest in section markings in ancient biblical manuscripts. Modern critical editions of the Hebrew Bible, for example, *Biblia hebraica stuttgartensia*, designate these sections open or closed, the former by a symbol פ (*petuḥah*), the latter by a symbol ס (*setumah*).

Medieval manuscripts lack such sigla, simply having blank spaces like those found today in printed texts which set off paragraphs of prose, verses of poetry, or discourses in either genre which are independent literary units. There are indentations at the beginning of lines, spaces at the end of lines, spaces in the middle of lines, and entire lines left blank when sections cannot be indicated in one of these other ways.

Little attention had been paid to section markings until they turned up in the Dead Sea Scrolls, which predate the medieval manuscripts by 700 to 1,000 years. With the use of sections being much older than previously thought, these devices deserve a fresh look for whatever insights they might contain into the delimitation of units within the biblical text.

In the Prophets, particularly, proper delimitation is essential for getting at texts within the text, and reaching beyond these towards correct meanings and interpretations. In preparing a forthcoming *Jeremiah* in the Anchor Bible commentary series, I examined more than 350 Jeremiah fragments in the Cambridge Genizah Collection (9 in the Cambridge–Westminster Collection) for the purpose of comparing section markings with those in Leningrad Codex B19^A (M^L), the Aleppo Codex (M^A), and the Dead Sea Scroll fragments of Jeremiah (2QJer; 4QJer).

I was interested primarily in Genizah fragments of the Hebrew Bible, which are generally (but not in every case) distinguishable from Genizah liturgical texts. Sections in the latter may well represent a different development. But in the great majority of cases, these sections were found to correspond exactly to sections in the Hebrew Bible, which means at the very least that they should not be relegated to a status of insignificance.

* *Genizah Fragments* 32 (October 1996), p. 2.

There was a high degree of correspondence between the Genizah fragments and the Ben Asher texts of M^L and M^A, as well as the Qumran fragments of Jeremiah. But there were divergences, a few of which struck me as being significant. For example, Genizah fragment NS 58.42 has a section after Jer. 5.25 where rhetorical analysis and content both indicate closure. M^L and M^A both lack a section marking. No Qumran text exists for comparison.

Some Genizah fragments lack a section marking where other manuscripts have one that seems either misplaced or superfluous. This could indicate that the demarcation is unoriginal, or else not that important. A section marking or its absence in a Genizah manuscript—with or without corroboration from a DSS fragment—is at least as good as the judgment of a modern scholar, who, for reasons unexplained, makes or does not make a break in interpreting the larger Jeremianic text.

The Primary History

Chapter 6

ABRAHAM AND DAVID IN THE THEOLOGY OF THE YAHWIST*

Just over a century ago Julius Wellhausen published his *Geschichte Israels* I (1878), which had such enormous influence upon Old Testament studies. This influence has of course waxed and waned, and Wellhausen's particular type of literary criticism (now 'source criticism') has given way to other methods such as form criticism, tradition-historical criticism, and rhetorical criticism. Nevertheless, certain assumptions made by him about the composition of the Pentateuch and about how it relates to later material in the Old Testament, notably Samuel and Kings, are as valid today as they were a century ago, and remain the foundation for all future work.

We are still committed, for example, to the idea that certain materials in the primeval and patriarchal histories of Genesis were written and edited by someone preferring the divine name Yahweh, for which reason we call him the Yahwist. This Yahwist adapts traditions from outside Israel (Genesis 2–11), and makes use also of indigenous traditions originating in northern Israel (Jacob and Joseph stories in Gen. 25.19–50.26), but is himself oriented towards the south, where Abraham looms large in traditions surviving around Hebron (Gen. 12.1–25.18) and David is the recent figure of prominence from Jerusalem. The Yahwist does his writing in Jerusalem from the perspective of the United Monarchy. His audience is Israel in the 10th-century BCE, most probably the generation living during the early reign of Solomon,[1] which includes among its number some who retain a living memory of David. A date of 950 BCE is about right. This is a time of high literary culture and international vision—an 'enlightenment', to quote von Rad.[2] The current focus of the Yahwist, however, is not upon Solomon, but upon David.

---

* *The Word of the Lord Shall Go Forth: Essays in Honor of David Noel Freedman* (ed. Carol L. Meyers and M. O'Connor; Winona Lake, IN: American Schools of Oriental Research and Eisenbrauns, 1983), pp. 203-209.

1. Gerhard von Rad, 'The Form-Crtitical Problem of the Hexateuch', in his *The Problem of the Hexateuch and Other Essays* (trans. E.W. Trueman-Dicken; New York: McGraw–Hill, 1966), p. 69; H.W. Wolff, 'The Kerygma of the Yahwist' (trans. Wilbur A. Benware). *Int* 20 (1966), pp. 135-36.

2. G. von Rad, 'The Beginnings of Historical Writing in Ancient Israel', in *The Problem of the Hexateuch and Other Essays*, p. 203.

Wellhausen also argued that a literary work about antiquity is a primary source only for the historical situation out of which it arose. For the time about which it gives information, it is but a secondary source. Wellhausen said the following about the patriarchal narratives in Genesis 12–50:

> It is true, we attain to no historical knowledge of the patriarchs, but only of the time when the stories about them arose in the Israelite people; this later age is here unconsciously projected, in its inner and its outward features, into hoar antiquity, and is reflected there like a glorified mirage.[3]

Obviously, this is an exaggeration. The patriarchal epics—and indeed also the primeval history in Genesis 2–11—are not merely idealized retrojections from the United Monarchy. Their *origins* lie somewhere in 'hoar antiquity', though admittedly in much less focused and much less theological form. Having said this, however, we concede at the same time that Wellhausen expounds a valid principle. Yahwistic Genesis is a product of the 10th-century, and events of the 10th-century—including their interpretation—leave upon the work a decisive mark. The same can be said *mutatis mutandis* about certain modern writings. In George Mendenhall's *The Tenth Generation*[4] and Norman Gottwald's *The Tribes of Yahweh*[5] modern sociological and political theory—also social revolutions of the 20th-century—control to a large extent the authors' interpretation of the Hebrew Conquest. They likewise become a primary source only for the age of their composition (20th-century CE), and a secondary source for the period about which they give information (13th-century BCE).

From the early Solomonic era comes another important biblical document. I refer to the so-called Court History of David (2 Samuel 7, 9–20; 1 Kings 1–2), or, as some call it, the Succession Document.[6] This work has been discussed thoroughly by von Rad[7] who builds on an earlier study by L. Rost. The Court History seems to have been composed shortly after the events themselves took place,[8] making it the earliest specimen of historical writing in ancient Israel.[9] This document in all likelihood was accessible to the Yahwist, in which case it could have influenced him in his writings

---

3. J. Wellhausen, *Prolegomena to the History of Ancient Israel* (trans. J.S. Black and A. Menzies; New York: World, 1965), pp. 318-19.
4. G.E. Mendenhall, *The Tenth Generation* (Baltimore: The Johns Hopkins University Press, 1973).
5. N.K. Gottwald, *The Tribes of Yahweh* (Maryknoll, NY: Orbis Books, 1979).
6. O. Eissfeldt, *The Old Testament: An Introduction* (trans. P.R. Ackroyd; New York: Harper & Row, 1965), pp. 137-39; P.F. Ellis, *The Yahwist: The Bible's First Theologian* (Notre Dame, IN: Fides, 1968), pp. 77-85.
7. Von Rad, 'The Beginnings of Historical Writing in Ancient Israel'.
8. D.N. Freedman, 'Pentateuch', in *IDB*, III: p. 726.
9. Von Rad, 'The Beginnings of Historical Writing in Ancient Israel', p. 176; J.J. Jackson, 'David's Throne Patterns in the Succession Story', *CJT* 11 (1965), p. 183.

about antiquity. Working from his assumption, Walter Brueggemann[10] attempted a few years ago to show that the Yahwist's compilation of Genesis 2–11 was dependent upon a sequence of events in the Court History. But this effort, in my opinion, was only partly successful.[11] What appears to be much clearer is that events described in the Court History served rather as a catalyst for the Yahwist in the recall, the shaping, and the preservation of traditions about the patriarchs (Genesis 12–50). That is, traditions we possess about Abraham were determined to some extent by things happening later to David, and the theological importance of both finds its common source in the mind of the Yahwist. D.N. Freedman has shown very well how the unconditional covenant given to Abraham (Gen. 12.1-3; 15) parallels the unconditional covenant given to David (2 Samuel 7).[12]

In the present essay I wish to narrow the focus to the two passages linking together the primeval and patriarchal histories, namely, the Tower of Babel story (Gen. 11.1-9) and the Call of Abraham (Gen. 12.1-3); and the chapter I take as the beginning of the Court History, namely, 2 Samuel 7.[13] My thesis is that 2 Samuel 7—with its message about what kind of house Yahweh really wants—provides the Yahwist with just the inspiration he needs to complete the transition from primeval to patriarchal history. It leads him to juxtapose

10. W. Brueggemann, 'David and his Theologian', *CBQ* 30 (1968), pp. 156-81.
11. Of the four parallels that Brueggemann sets up, only the first two, viz., David and Bathsheba // Adam and Eve; and Ammon and Absalom // Cain and Abel are likely to have been consciously made by the Yahwist. The rebellion of Absalom makes for a weak comparison with Noah and the Flood. And the fourth parallel of Solomon // Tower of Babel turns out to be no parallel at all because Solomon's building activities, his subsequent prosperity, and the final disintegration of his rule—all of which contribute to the alleged parallel—come not in the Court History, but in 1 Kings 5ff. Brueggemann indicates early on (p. 159) that he is using only 1 Kings 1–2, but before he is through he has gone far beyond that point. According to von Rad (*Old Testament Theology*, I [trans. D.M.G. Stalker; London: Oliver & Boyd, 1962], p. 164) and G. Fohrer (*Introduction to the Old Testament* [trans. David E. Green; New York: Abingdon Press, 1968], p. 88), the Yahwist inherited a fixed cosmological scheme long in existence. At the same time, he may well have fashioned his superb account of the Fall (Genesis 3) with David and Bathsheba in mind. The Cain and Abel story has affinities with the story of Ammon and Absalom because both recount brotherly rivalries, yet the almost opposite characters of Ammon and Abel argue more for discontinuity than continuity in this parallel.
12. D.N. Freedman, 'Pentateuch', pp. 714-15; 'Divine Commitment and Human Obligation', *Int* 18 (1964), p. 13 [repr. in *Divine Commitment and Human Obligation: Selected Writings of David Noel Freedman*, I (ed. John R. Huddlestun; Grand Rapids: Eerdmans, 1997), p. 177].
13. The beginning of the Court History is, of course, much in dispute. For the various views, see Eissfeldt, *The Old Testament: An Introduction*, pp. 137-38. The inclusion of chap. 7 is essential, in my opinion, because without the promise about David's house of royal descendants, the whole struggle of succession—which is what the Court History is all about—loses all significance and 1 Kings 1–2 has no climactic value whatsoever.

the Tower of Babel story and the Call of Abraham, and in so doing a theological judgment is rendered about 'hoar antiquity' that comes very close to being the same as one already made in the Court History. The net result is to strengthen the link he intends between David and Abraham, and to undergird at the same time those covenants given by Yahweh to each of them.

The Babel story and the Call of Abraham are both from the Yahwist's hand.[14] The former was at his disposal, and the latter was perhaps composed by him *de novo*, and not a piece of fixed tradition.[15] The Yahwist is credited also with the basic editorial work, that is, he juxtaposed the passages prior to the time when the Priestly genealogies of 11.10-27 were inserted.[16]

It has long been recognized that the Yahwist's editorial work contributes greatly to his theological purpose. Von Rad has shown how the primeval history as a whole contains a sin/punishment/grace cycle, which then makes 12.1-3 its proper end. After sin and punishment at Babel, Yahweh shows his grace anew to Abraham.[17] And the universal elements in each passage combine to give theological importance to all history. Whereas the judgment at Babel results in the scattering of people over the whole earth (11.9), the blessing to Abraham is to be for 'all the families of the earth' (12.3). The Yahwist has yet another point to make. While the men of Babel seek for themselves a name, in Abraham's case, Yahweh gives the name.[18] In Gen. 11.4 the men say: 'And let us *make* for ourselves a *name*'. But in Gen. 12.2 Yahweh says to Abraham: 'And I will *make* of you a great nation, and I will bless you, and I will make great your *name*'.

The Yahwist in his editorial work creates a dialectic similar to one existing in the Babel story itself. Rashi[19] and Herder[20] both observed long ago that at Babel Yahweh deliberately imitates the men's resolves. Whereas they say: '*Come let us* make bricks... *Come let us* build ourselves a city and a tower...' (11.3-4), Yahweh says, '*Come let us* go down and there confuse

---

14. J.E. Carpenter and G. Harford-Battersby, *The Hexateuch*, II (London: Longmans, Green & Co., 1900), pp. 17-19.

15. Von Rad, 'The Form-Critical Problem of the Hexateuch', p. 67, following Gunkel; W. Zimmerli, 'Promise and Fulfillment' (trans. James Wharton), in *Essays on Old Testament Hermeneutics* (ed. Claus Westermann; Richmond, VA: John Knox Press, 1963), p. 91.

16. Von Rad, *Genesis* (OTL; trans. John H. Marks; Philadelphia: Westminster Press, 1961), p. 150.

17. Von Rad, *Old Testament Theology*, I, pp. 163-64; 'The Form-Critical Problem of the Hexateuch', p. 65.

18. Von Rad, *Genesis*, p. 155; H.W. Wolff, 'The Kerygma of the Yahwist' (trans. Wilbur A. Benware), *Int* 20 (1966), pp. 141-42.

19. *Rashi—Commentaries on the Pentateuch* (selected and trans. Chaim Pearl; New York: Viking, 1970), pp. 38-39.

20. J.G. Herder, *The Spirit of Hebrew Poetry*, I (trans. James Marsh; Burlington, VT: Edward Smith, 1833), pp. 203-204.

their language...' (11.7). The purposed ascent of man and the descent of God are 'placed silently side by side', says Herder. So we see how the Yahwist in his editorial work duplicates theology contained in the very material he makes use of. The same technique is used in editorial work done within the book of Jeremiah.[21]

But in the transition from primeval to patriarchal history the references to 'making a name' function to contrast in a subtle way the hubris at Babel with God's graciousness to Abraham and subsequent humanity. Yahweh is also seen to be a God who seizes the initiative. But the real key to the Yahwist's mind is found by observing a play here on words. 'Making a name' means one thing in 11.4, but quite another in 12.2. In the Babel story, men seek a name by erecting a city within which there is a religious temple.[22] Some have thought the latter structure to be a ziggurat of the type built by Nabopolassar and Nebuchadnezzar in the 7th- and 6th-centuries BCE, but Speiser[23] contends the reference is rather to a more ancient structure such as we have described in *Enuma elish* VI, 60-66 (cf. *ANET*³, pp. 68-69). In any case, the word 'tower' found in most English translations (AV, RSV, NEB, JB, NAB) is misleading. Reference is to a religious temple. Abraham, however, will achieve his name by having a myriad of descendants. These will become a great nation, which no doubt is what the men of Babel are also striving for as they set out to build their city.[24]

With this play on words the Yahwist makes his main point. He wants above all to contrast descendants on the one hand with imposing structures on the other. We can refine this a bit more. If we take 2 Samuel 7 as the passage providing primary inspiration for the Yahwist, we find out there that Yahweh is averse not to structures in general, but to temples in particular, especially temples of a pretentious sort.

2 Samuel 7 in its present form betrays (in v. 13 at least) work of a later editor who seeks to harmonize the original promise to David with 1 Kings 8. Solomon, after all, did finally build Yahweh a temple. Yet despite the editing there

---

21. J.R. Lundbom, *Jeremiah: A Study in Ancient Hebrew Rhetoric* (SBLDS, 18; Missoula, MT: Society of Biblical Literature and Scholars Press, 1975), p. 32 [2nd edn. Winona Lake, IN: Eisenbrauns, 1997, p. 47].

22. Gunkel's source analysis of the passage (*Genesis* [Göttingen: Vandenhoeck & Ruprecht, 1966], pp. 92ff.), in which he proposed two original accounts, a city recension (*Stadtrezension*) and a tower recension (*Turmbaurezension*), is no longer taken seriously. One of the most obvious problems with this view is that the phrase, 'Let us make for ourselves a name', is placed in the city recension. Even von Rad (*Genesis*, pp. 144-46), who is sympathetic to this view, recognizes that the tower (not the city) is what symbolizes the men's will to fame. U. Cassuto (*A Commentary on the Book of Genesis* II [Jerusalem: Magnes Press, 1964], pp. 235-38) is no doubt correct when he says that the city and the tower were meant to be together from the beginning.

23. E.A. Speiser, *Genesis* (AB, 1; Garden City, NY: Doubleday, 1964), pp. 75-76.

24. Professor Freedman is to be given credit for this observation.

is in v. 9 the promise of a 'great name' to David; also in David's prayer we find a request for Yahweh's 'blessing' (v. 29). Both reinforce the connection between David and Abraham. David is chosen for greatness just as Abraham was. Also, David fulfills the promise of Gen. 12.1-3, making him Abraham's spiritual son. More importantly, the editing does nothing to obscure the main point of the chapter: whereas David wants to build Yahweh a house, Yahweh says he will instead build a house for David.[25] Again Yahweh seizes the initiative. Here a wordplay on בית, 'house', brings home the basic theological affirmation. David has in mind a house of stone and cedar, that is, a lavish temple, but Yahweh is thinking of a house of royal descendants.

So the Yahwist's thrust in Genesis 11–12 is basically the same as 2 Samuel 7. Yahweh rejects temples planned by ambitious individuals. Instead he initiates work on a structure of his own choosing, which in each case is a line of perpetual descendants.

Writing then in the early part of Solomon's reign, the Yahwist intends, I believe, a quiet protest against the building of a temple. We know from the Yahwist's work elsewhere that he tends to be less than direct. Von Rad, writing about the patriarchal traditions says:

> In these stories we are not confronted with an account of the history which furnishes the reader with explicit theological judgments, or which constantly allows him to participate in extensive theological reflection upon the history, as the Deuteronmistic account does. In the stories of the patriarchs the reader will look in vain for any formulation of the narrator's own theological judgment. This being the case, there is more prospect of success in attempting to arrive at an indirect understanding of the narrator and his opinion.[26]

We must not, however, attribute the Yahwist's indirectness only to his style. There are political reasons for what he does. The temple is perhaps already under construction, and public sentiment is behind it. Thus he cannot be any more explicit in his criticism.

What we are saying, then, is that the Yahwist is anti-temple. This squares with von Rad's view that the Yahwist is not concerned about the cult, but interested rather in Yahweh's activity in history.[27] But it challenges von Rad's notion that the Yahwist has sympathies with the Settlement tradition. According to him, it was the Yahwist who integrated the patriarchal history with the idea of the Settlement.[28] Of course, von Rad also believed that the Settlement recorded in Joshua constituted the 'proper end' of what

---

25. S.R. Driver, *Notes on the Hebrew Text and the Topography of the Books of Samuel* (Oxford: Clarendon Press, 1966), pp. 275-76; H.W. Hertzberg, *I and II Samuel* (trans. J.S. Bowden; Philadelphia: Westminster Press, 1964), p. 283.
26. Von Rad, *Old Testament Theology*, I, p. 165.
27. Von Rad, 'The Form-Critical Problem of the Hexateuch', p. 71.
28. Von Rad, 'The Form-Critical Problem of the Hexateuch', p. 60.

he thought was a 'Hexateuch', but Noth[29] has convincingly shown that a Hexateuch as such never existed. Instead Deuteronomy begins a separate history that extends through the end of 2 Kings. It is the Deuteronomic School, as von Rad also knows well enough, that puts the emphasis on the Settlement.[30] Even so, the 'rest' that the Settlement makes possible is controlled always by the Mosaic (Sinai) Covenant, which is conditional in nature. Israel must obey the commandments if this covenant is to remain in force.[31] If it does not, the land will be lost (Deuteronomy 28).

Thus I am inclined to see in the Yahwist more of a 'pilgrim mentality'. This explains why he is so interested in recovering the traditions of the patriarchs. Also, when the Yahwist looks at the Court History he can find ample evidence for his thesis that Abraham and David both journey like pilgrims through history. The Court History makes no attempt to hide the fact that rest in the land is a prelude to trouble, while salvation comes to the one who trusts the Lord of History. It was after Yahweh had given David rest from all his enemies round about (2 Sam. 7.1), that David decided to build Yahweh a permanent resting place, and as we have seen, Yahweh turned that plan down. From the Court History we learn too that only after David is settled well enough in Jerusalem as to remain there while Joab and others go out to fight the spring battle with the Ammonites (2 Sam. 11.1), is he led straightaway into trouble with Bathsheba, wife of Uriah the Hittite. Finally, David is forced into being a pilgrim in the wilderness when his son Absalom moves to overthrow him (2 Samuel 15–18), which teaches him again that kingship—at least his—is tied not to settlement in the land, but to Yahweh's deliverance in history.

The Yahwist then is not pro-Settlement, nor is he even mildly concerned about Settlement traditions current in the 10th-century. As far as he is concerned, Yahweh would rather that revelation be kept in the sphere of historical events where people are the important thing and continuity through the generations counts for more than continuity with the land. It is in support of this theology that the Yahwist labors. He shows that both Abraham and David are brought into covenant after Yahweh rejects permanent places of worship. Temples signify divine settlement—indeed permanent divine settlement, as Jeremiah found out later to his utter dismay (Jer. 7.1-15).

Jeremiah in his famous 'Temple Sermon' (Jeremiah 7; 26) is not the only prophet to speak in opposition to the temple. According to P. Hanson,[32] that

29. M. Noth, *A History of Pentateuchal Traditions* (trans. Bernhard W. Anderson; Englewood Cliffs, NJ: Prentice–Hall, 1972), p. 6.
30. Von Rad, 'There Remains Still a Rest for the People of God', in *The Problem of the Hexateuch and Other Essays*, pp. 94-102.
31. Freedman, 'Divine Commitment and Human Obligation'.
32. Paul D. Hanson, *The Dawn of Apocalyptic* (Philadelphia: Fortress Press, 1975), pp. 161-86.

nameless prophet of the exile speaking for the disenfranchised in Second Isaiah is concerned not at all about the temple. The tradition lives on in Jesus, who, in speaking to his disciples (Mk 13.1-2) and also to the Samaritan woman (Jn 4.21-24), points beyond a temple to the true locus of worship. Elsewhere in the New Testament, 1 Pet. 2.4-10 describes Jesus as a 'living stone' and the church as more 'living stones...built into a spiritual house'. Finally, Rev. 21.22 teaches that the New Jerusalem will have no need of a temple, for its temple will be Yahweh God the Almighty and the Lamb.

Chapter 7

Parataxis, Rhetorical Structure, and the Dialogue over Sodom in Genesis 18*

I

Erich Auerbach in his classic work, *Mimesis* (1953),[1] contrasted the epic styles of Homer and the Bible and concluded that the Greeks and Hebrews had very different ways of comprehending and representing reality. From the 'recognition scene' of Odysseus in Book 19 of the *Odyssey*, Auerbach came to characterize Greek epic style as essentially 'hypotactic',[2] that is, in direct discourse as well as in narrative more generally, descriptions are commonplace and in them is much detail. Syntactic connections between narrative parts create a kind of framework, with the result that nothing remains in obscurity, everything is clear—even story-line interruptions end up bringing persons, things, and incidents together logically and in a flowing manner. Feelings and thoughts are also externalized, making an epic type of all foreground. Hypotactic style has no background, says Auerbach, nothing hidden or unexpressed, 'never...a form left fragmentary or half-illuminated, never a lacuna, never a gap, never a glimpse of unplumbed depths'.[3] Without background there is also no suspense. Even interruptions, instead of setting up tension, relax it because of where they are placed or how they integrate into the narrative as a whole.

The biblical passage used for contrast was the sacrifice of Isaac in Genesis 22. Auerbach concluded from this narrative that Hebrew epic style is essentially 'paratactic', that is, a style typified by economy of detail, and what detail there is functions indirectly to express such things as resolve, obedience, or one's moral position in relation to God. There are no characterizations of persons. Syntactic connections between narrative parts are

---

* *The World of Genesis: Persons, Places, Perspectives* (ed. Philip R. Davies and David J.A. Clines; Sheffield: Sheffield Academic Press, 1998), pp. 136-45.

1. Erich Auerbach, *Mimesis* (trans. W.R. Trask; Princeton, NJ: Princeton University Press, 1974), pp. 3-23.

2. The term 'hypotaxis', and Auerbach's contrasting term for Hebrew epic style, 'parataxis', are introduced later; see *Mimesis*, pp. 70-75, 99-122.

3. Auerbach, *Mimesis*, pp. 6-7.

few in number, or else non-existent, and those which do appear are of such a rudimentary sort that much is left in obscurity. Feelings and thoughts of persons are not externalized, that is, motives are lacking and purposes remain unexpressed. Speeches by persons are often fragmentary. In the Genesis 22 passage we meet with that 'heavy silence' between Abraham and his son as they walk to the mountain of sacrifice. Hebrew epic is all background, says Auerbach, which allows it to teem with suspense and convey mystery with exceptional facility. The latter capacity works to good advantage when it comes to speaking about God, for 'the [Hebrew] reader knows that God is a hidden God'.[4] Auerbach finds parataxis in other Old Testament narratives, for example, those about Saul and David.

In this essay I should like to discuss the well-known dialogue between Yahweh and Abraham over the fate of Sodom in Gen. 18.23-32, a passage embodied in narrative (Gen. 18–19) similar to Genesis 22. Here we might expect to find more paratactic style of the type described by Auerbach— economy of detail, loose syntactic connections, feelings and thoughts not externalized, purposes left unexpressed, rich background, suspense, etc.— and because of the argument, an opportunity is afforded to test for parataxis in direct discourse, largely unavailable in Genesis 22, where Auerbach found only that 'heavy silence' between Abraham and his son.

Auerbach's classic distinction between parataxis and hypotaxis has been picked up by Chaim Perelman in his discussion of argumentation.[5] Perelman says hypotaxis is the argumentative construction *par excellence* because it creates frameworks, controls the audience by forcing it to see particular relationships, and restricts what interpretations may be considered. Its inspiration comes primarily 'from well-constructed legal reasoning'. Parataxis, on the other hand, 'leaves greater freedom, and does not appear to wish to impose a particular viewpoint'. Perelman also believes that enumeration, in some of its uses, exemplifies the paratactic construction.

Parataxis is deserving of more consideration in evaluating biblical argumentation. If we moderns tend to think hypotactically, as we seem to, we are likely left with an uneasy feeling when encountering many a biblical argument—much the same as in reading biblical narrative—that something is missing. Something usually *is* missing, which is precisely the point. Parataxis doubtless accounts for our inability to recognize a genuine dialectic in the Old Testament, what with thoughts not sufficiently externalized, connections in the argument not there, and all the rich background admitting other interpretations.

---

4. Auerbach, *Mimesis*, p. 15.
5. C. Perelman and L. Olbrechts-Tyteca, *The New Rhetoric: A Treatise on Argumentation* (trans. J. Wilkinson and P. Weaver; Notre Dame, IN: University of Notre Dame Press, 1969), pp. 157-58.

II

Genesis 18–19 forms a unit that preserves stories about renewing the covenant promise to Abraham that Sarah will bear a son (18.1-15), and about the destruction of the Gentile cities of Sodom and Gomorrah (18.16–19.28). These stories are said to have been reworked by the Yahwist who includes them—along with Genesis 22—into his rendering of patriarchal history.[6]

We can only speculate about earlier forms the stories may have taken. In my view, one of the three visiting men (שְׁלֹשָׁה אֲנָשִׁים) in 18.2, two of whom are called '(divine) messengers' (מַלְאָכִים) in 19.1 and 15, originally carried on the discourse with Abraham and Sarah about Sarah bearing a child in old age. As it is now, he speaks only in 18.10, with Yahweh taking over the discourse in 18.13-15. Verse 14 looks to be a duplicate of v. 10 as both speak about a return visit in the spring. The spokesman for the three may have spoken the soliloquy in 18.17-19 as well, after which divine thoughts are revealed to Abraham in vv. 20-21; otherwise all or a portion of this discourse has been added.[7] The spokesman seems also to have been the one originally carrying on the dialogue with Abraham over the fate of Sodom (18.23-32). Since three men appear at the beginning of the story, and only two arrive in Sodom (19.1), we may assume one has remained behind to speak with Abraham (18.22).[8]

---

6. The documentary hypothesis, of course, enjoys no consensus of support at the present time; see Rolf Rendtorff, *The Old Testament: An Introduction* (trans. J. Bowden; London: SCM Press, 1985), p. 160; N. Whybray, *Introduction to the Pentateuch* (Grand Rapids: Eerdmans, 1995), pp. 20-26, 133-38. J. Van Seters retains it in the main, but rejects a tenth-century dating of J; in his view the Sodom story in its present form is nevertheless the work of the Yahwist (J); cf. Van Seters, *Abraham in History and Tradition* (New Haven: Yale University Press, 1975), p. 151; *Prologue to History: The Yahwist as Historian in Genesis* (Louisville, KY: Westminster/John Knox Press, 1992), pp. 258-60. Older scholars attributing Genesis 18–19 to the Yahwist include, J.E. Carpenter and G. Harford-Battersby, *The Hexateuch II* (London: Longmans, Green & Co., 1900), pp. 25-28; J. Skinner, *A Critical and Exegetical Commentary on Genesis* (ICC; Edinburgh: T. & T. Clark, 1910), pp. 298-99, 306; G. von Rad, *Genesis* (OTL; trans. J.H. Marks; Philadelphia: Westminster Press, 1961), p. 199; and E.A. Speiser, *Genesis* (AB, 1; Garden City, NY: Doubleday, 1964), p. 130. S.R. Driver, *An Introduction to the Literature of the Old Testament* (Cleveland: World Publishing Co., 1967), p. 119, considered the present passage to be one of the noteworthy specimens of the Yahwist's style.

7. Since Wellhausen vv. 17-19 have been considered a soliloquy added by the Yahwist; cf. Skinner, *Genesis*, p. 298; von Rad, *Genesis*, p. 204; and Speiser, *Genesis*, p. 135. Van Seters (*Abraham in History and Tradition*, p. 213), however, sees no reason to consider the verses redactional.

8. In 18.22b the text originally read, 'but Yahweh remained standing before Abraham'. Later Jewish tradition altered this reading to 'but Abraham remained standing before Yahweh' (already in the LXX). The reason for the change (a *tiq soph*) was that Abraham, having inferior status, could not show proper respect if Yahweh was said to be standing *before him*; cf. von Rad, *Genesis*, p. 206; Speiser, *Genesis*, p. 134. If, however, an earlier form of the story had a man/messenger standing before Abraham,

He may proceed to Sodom after the dialogue is over (18.33), we cannot say. Also, an earlier form of the story appears to have the men acting as agents of destruction (19.13: 'for *we* are about to destroy this place').

It is unnecessary to posit a pre-Yahwistic version of the story in which three gods visit human beings.[9] Three divine messengers, perhaps, but not three gods. The story now, with its present Yahwistic overlay, has Yahweh speaking to Abraham and Sarah about Sarah bearing a son, Yahweh pondering whether to make Abraham privy to his Sodom plans, and then telling him (18.17-21), and Yahweh carrying on the dialogue with Abraham over Sodom's fate. When all is over, Yahweh is the one who rains fire and brimstone on the wicked cities (19.24). An earlier summary statement has God (הָאֵל)[10] overthrowing the wicked cities (19.25)—another doublet. Here, as elsewhere, the Yahwist brings Yahweh down to earth where he stands before people (18.22 prior to the *tiq soph*), talks to them directly, and goes his way once the conversation is finished (18.33). For other Yahwistic theology see 18.1; 19.13-14, 16, 27.

The story in its final form provides clear evidence of parataxis, for example, the shifts between 'men', 'messengers'. and 'Yahweh'. These strike the modern reader as poor editing, resulting in a narrative that is inconsistent and possibly even incoherent. But from another point of view more background is created. In that background, for example, is the messenger whom Yahweh eclipses by assuming or supplementing the discourse that he carried on. The modern reader loses sight of his presence, but he is there. What the modern reader needs is a hypotactic construction, such as, 'Yahweh, speaking through the messenger, said...'. This, to some extent, is compensated for in later midrash. In *Genesis Rabbah* (50.2)[11] Michael is the messenger announcing the news to Abraham and then departing, Gabriel the messenger sent to destroy Sodom, and Rafael the messenger going down to Sodom to rescue Lot. This Midrash (51.2) also attributes Yahweh's statement about the destruction of Sodom and Gomorrah in 19.24 to Gabriel.

III

Now to the celebrated dialogue, which is our primary concern. Here one finds more parataxis: economy of words and action, thoughts and feelings

---

the problem of respect would likely not have arisen. Van Seters (*Prologue to History*, p. 259) says only two of the three men proceed to Sodom with Yahweh remaining behind to carry on the dialogue with Abraham. But what happens to the third man?

9. J.A. Loader, *A Tale of Two Cities* (Kampen: Kok, 1990), pp. 23-26.

10. Modern English versions, here and in v. 8, emend MT הָאֵל ('the God') to הָאֵלֶה ('these/those').

11. *Midrash Rabbah: Genesis*, I (ed. and trans. H. Freedman; London: Soncino, 1951).

7. Parataxis, Rhetorical Structure, and the Dialogue over Sodom 77

unexpressed, and enumeration that helps to build suspense while at the same time serving to correct Abraham's misperceptions.

The bargaining taking place is for the entire city of Sodom (18.26), even though Abraham speaks only on behalf of the righteous.[12] It is the sort of bargaining carried on today in Near Eastern bazaars.[13] As will be seen more clearly in a moment, it is really kinsman Lot and his family who are uppermost in Abraham's mind, for they are settled in Sodom and a destruction of the city will mean their destruction. Abraham rescued them once before (Genesis 14). Any anxiety over Lot is entirely unexpressed, however, but it is there and must not be overlooked or judged peripheral in the dialogue.[14] The fate of Lot and his household stands behind the very first question Abraham asks of Yahweh, 'Will you indeed sweep away the righteous with the wicked?' (18.23).

Throughout the dialogue Abraham takes the initiative, posing questions that Yahweh in turn answers. Yahweh does not answer every question, only those containing specific numbers for saving the city. Neither of the big questions posed at the beginning of the dialogue is answered (vv. 23, 25b). One at least is rhetorical. Both, in any case, are left for the audience to ponder.

In the sequence of questions about the number of righteous required to save the city we see a rhetorical structure unfolding, one which will assist the audience in making the interpretation the narrator intends. The numbers

---

12. Collective and individualistic thinking in the dialogue is discussed by von Rad, *Genesis*, p. 208. See also von Rad, *Old Testament Theology*, I (trans. D.M.G. Stalker; Edinburgh: Oliver & Boyd, 1962), pp. 394-95; and G. Fohrer, *Introduction to the Old Testament* (trans. D.E. Green; Nashville: Abingdon Press, 1968), p. 151. Van Seters (*Abraham in Tradition and History*, p. 214) recognizes that Abraham is bargaining for the whole of Sodom, but says the emphasis in vv. 23-32 is on individual responsibility, a theme prominent in Ezekiel and at the beginning of the exilic period. His supposition that the verses have in mind 'the specific salvation of the righteous one, Lot', narrows the focus too much; see discussion following.

13. Or 'just another bout of male bargaining'; so P.R. Davies, 'Abraham and Yahweh—A Case of Male Bonding', *BiRev* 11 (1995), p. 32.

14. Hermann Gunkel in *The Legends of Genesis* (trans. W.H. Carruth; New York: Schocken Books, 1964), p. 60, says the narrator, in reporting Abraham's return the next morning to the place overlooking Sodom (19.27-28), wishes to impress upon the hearer that Abraham is there thinking certain thoughts, although he does not tell us what those thoughts are. The same might be said of Abraham prior to the dialogue, a point which has already been made; see L. Turner, *Announcements of Plot in Genesis* (Sheffield: JSOT Press, 1990), pp. 79-81, 109; D.J.A. Clines, *What Does Eve Do to Help? and Other Readerly Questions to the Old Testament* (Sheffield: JSOT Press, 1990), p. 73; and Davies, 'Abraham and Yahweh', p. 32. Von Rad (*Genesis*, p. 207) believed that before the dialogue Abraham was not concerned with saving Lot (nor Sodom).

are reduced from 50 to 45, then to 40, then to 30, then to 20, and then to 10, which Abraham promises will be his final proposal. But to judge from the deferential language and temerity expressed thus far, we wonder if it will be. In bargaining of this sort it is not over until it's over. We know Abraham cannot reduce the number once more by 10, for that would bring him to zero, but he could make a reduction by 5. *Genesis Rabbah* (49.12), in fact, quotes a tradition which says that Abraham wanted to descend from 50 to 5, but God told him, 'Back up!'—that is, do not make so great a jump. From a rhetorical point of view he could end with a decrement of 5 because he began that way. We know Hebrew rhetoric has a proclivity for balancing the end with the beginning. The audience, in fact, might be anticipating precisely this. If he did make such a reduction, the numbers would decrease in the following manner:

```
50 people
            -5
45 people
            -5
40 people
           -10
30 people
           -10
20 people
           -10
10 people
           [-5]
[5 people]
           [-5]
```

Abraham does not reduce the magic number to 5. To do so would be to bargain for a number *lower* than the sum of Lot's household, which consists of 6 people: Lot, his wife, two daughters, and two men engaged to the daughters (called 'sons-in-law'). At 10 it is still possible for everyone in Lot's household to be righteous; at 5 it cannot be. This has to be why Abraham does not go below 10, even though *Genesis Rabbah* gives other reasons, one of which is that Abraham thought Lot's family to consist of 10 people (49.13; 50.9): Lot, his wife, four daughters and four sons-in law—two married and two engaged to be married. The Hebrew of 19.14 will not support such a reading;[15] nevertheless, it is significant that the midrash ties in the final offer with the number of members in Lot's family, which gives support to the idea that Abraham is thinking of them as the righteous for whom all of Sodom should be spared.

    15. The midrash reads 19.14: 'And Lot went out, and spoke to his sons-in-law *and* those who were taking his daughters' (italics mine).

The narrator will go on to tell us just how righteous Lot's household is. Abraham, of course, cannot be expected to anticipate Lot's offer of his virgin daughters to the crazed men of Sodom,[16] jesting sons-in-law who do not want to leave an evil city, Lot's disobedient wife, and the incest carried out later by the daughters with their father (19.30-38). Similarly, he cannot know the mercy Yahweh will show to Lot and members of Lot's household. Nevertheless, the narrator makes it clear to us, the audience, that Abraham has overestimated the righteousness of Sodom, and underestimated the justice and mercy of Yahweh. I say this because I believe the narrator in his sequel wants to tell us that not a soul in Sodom—including Lot—was righteous, and but for Yahweh's mercy neither Lot, his wife, nor his daughters would have been spared (19.16).[17] The summary statement of 19.29 says it was because God remembered Abraham—not particularly high praise for Lot. If no one in Sodom can be said to have been righteous, then the whole of Genesis 18–19 comes into line with Jer. 5.1-8 where just one righteous person is sought in Jerusalem, but not found.

The dialogue breaks off with no resolution, no communiqué announcing that a settlement has been reached.[18] Yahweh's acceptance of Abraham's final proposal is the last thing to be said. After that the text says tersely, 'And Yahweh went his way when he had finished speaking to Abraham; and Abraham returned to his place' (18.33). This lack of resolution and concluding silence means that the audience is left to answer for itself the large questions raised at the beginning of the dialogue, 'Will you indeed sweep away the righteous with the wicked?' and 'Shall not the Judge of all the earth do justice?' Leaving

---

16. This act is said to be a reflection of oriental hospitality, according to which a stranger coming under one's roof is protected at all cost (so Skinner, *Genesis*, p. 307; von Rad, *Genesis*, p. 213; and R. deVaux, *Ancient Israel*, I [New York: McGraw–Hill, 1965], p. 10). Because of his hospitality Lot is considered to be a righteous man (Gunkel, *The Legends of Genesis*, p. 107; J. Morgenstern, *The Book of Genesis* [2nd edn; New York: Schocken Books, 1965], p. 126; T.D. Alexander, 'Lot's Hospitality: A Clue to his Righteousness', *JBL* 104 [1985], pp. 290-91). Nevertheless, the offer of virgin daughters to sex-crazed men would certainly offend the Hebrew sense of morality generally, and that of the Yahwist particularly who is conceded to have an acute consciousness of sin (e.g., Gen. 3). On the former see Turner, *Announcements of Plot in Genesis*, pp. 80-81. The incident here in Genesis 19 is strikingly similar to the one in Judges 19 concerning the Levite, his concubine, and the men of Gibeah who were judged wicked enough and to have created enough of an offense against all Israel that a war between Israel and the Benjaminites was the result (Judg. 20).

17. Van Seters (*Abraham in History and Tradition*, pp. 217-20) says the 'secondary motifs' in 19.17-38 are not independent of the primary theme, and attempts should not be made to isolate them in a now-unified chap. 19.

18. *Contra* von Rad, *Genesis*, p. 209, who says the conversation does not end with an open question.

big questions for the audience to answer is what happens also in Jer. 5.1-8, where the all-important question is whether Yahweh will pardon Jerusalem.[19]

Finding in the whole of Lot's household no one who is righteous forces a re-examination of well-entrenched readings of this story that:

1. focus on the perverted 'men of Sodom' as embodying all that is wicked in the city;
2. heap disproportionate judgment on Lot's wife, whose disobedience is explicit; and
3. single out Lot as Sodom's only righteous inhabitant.

Later Jewish tradition reckoned Lot to be righteous because of his hospitality toward strangers. Already in Wis. 19.17 the hapless men of Sodom are contrasted with 'the righteous man' Lot. Christians too have kept pace in venerating Lot. In 2 Pet. 2.6-8 Lot is said not only to have been righteous himself, but to have been 'vexed in his righteous soul day after day' because of the licentious wicked in the city. A seventh-century monastery and basilica dedicated to Saint Lot was discovered in 1990 at Deir 'Ain 'Abaṭa in Jordan, near the Dead Sea, which archaeologists believe was a site of pilgrimage. A Byzantine Greek inscription, left behind by three pilgrims reads, 'Lot please bless us'.[20] A cave room in the north aisle of the basilica may also have been presented to pilgrims as the actual place where Lot took refuge with his daughters.[21] Generous estimations of Lot continue into the present day,[22] lauding his hospitality and minimizing the immoral treatment of his daughters and intemperate behavior that allowed the daughters to later return the favor. All of this, no doubt, has developed as a result of Auerbach-defined parataxis in the argument and narrative in Genesis 18–19.

---

19. See my article, 'Jeremiah and the Break-away from Authority Preaching', *SEÅ* 56 (1991), pp. 7-28.

20. Reported in *The Chicago Tribune*, December 14, 1992, Section 1 p. 3; see Konstantinos D. Politis, 'Excavations at Deir 'Ain 'Abaṭa', *ADAJ* 34 (1990), pp. 377-88; 35 (1992), pp. 281-90; 'Excavations at the Monastery of Agios Lot at Deir 'Ain 'Abaṭa', *LA* 40 (1990), p. 475; cf. B. MacDonald, *The Southern Ghors and Northeast 'Arabah Archaeological Survey* (Sheffield Archaeological Monographs, 5; Sheffield: J.R. Collins and the University of Sheffield, 1992), pp. 97-104; 'Deir 'Ain 'Abaṭa', in *The New Encyclopedia of Archaeological Excavations in the Holy Land* I, pp. 336-38.

21. K.D. Politis, 'Excavations at the Monastery of Saint Lot at Deir 'Ain 'Abaṭa', *LA* 41 (1991), p. 517; 'The 1992 Season of Excavations and the 1993 Season of Restorations at Deir 'Ain 'Abaṭa', *ADAJ* 37 (1993), p. 506.

22. So e.g., Loader (*A Tale of Two Cities*, pp. 36-38), who overstates the virtue of Lot's hospitality and understates the vice of giving up virgin daughters to gang-rape. To be repulsed by the latter is not pious moralizing; see n. 16.

Chapter 8

SCRIBAL CONTRIBUTIONS TO OLD TESTAMENT THEOLOGY*

The scribes who received such sharp criticism from Jesus (Mt. 23.1-39), and from Jeremiah centuries earlier (Jer. 8.8), possessed, nevertheless, an enviable position within Judaism and enjoyed great reputation, for which reason, no doubt, they lay open to censure. Because of their ability to read and write, scribes in ancient societies generally were entrusted with important matters of temple and state, handling administrative affairs, facilitating international relations, copying texts from antiquity, and giving counsel to kings. In Judaism and early Christianity their role in preparing and transmitting Scripture was crucial—some would say indispensable—whether we cite Baruch ben Neriah (Jer. 36.1-8), Matthew the disciple (Mt. 9.9; cf. 13.52), or Tertius, the amanuensis of Paul (Rom. 16.22). Nameless others up until the invention of printing in the fifteenth-century diligently copied biblical texts by hand—in daylight and by candlelight—so the treasured Word of God might survive to the present day.

Scribes were at their craft over five millennia ago, from the time we first begin to see written texts emerge in Mesopotamia and Egypt. Before then—indeed, a long time before—we have but artwork in caves to look at, animal paintings, mainly, from such places as the Altamira caves in northern Spain and the La Mouthe and Chauvet caves in southern France, the last-named discovery coming as recently as 1994. Ancient Sumer had scribes and scribal schools, called 'tablet houses', around 3000 BCE,[1] and we are now reasonably well informed about scribal practices and scribal schools in Old Babylonia,[2]

---

* *To Hear and Obey* (Essays in Honor of Frederick C. Holmgren; ed. Bradley J. Bergfalk and Paul E. Koptak; Chicago: Covenant Publications, 1997), pp. 42-49.

1. Samuel Noah Kramer, 'Schooldays: A Sumerian Composition Relating to the Education of a Scribe', *JAOS* 69 (1949), pp. 199-215.

2. Benno Landsberger, 'Babylonian Scribal Craft and Its Terminology', in *Proceedings of the Twenty-Third International Congress of Orientalists* (ed. Denis Sinor; London: Royal Asiatic Society, 1954), pp. 123-26; C.J. Gadd, *Teachers and Students in the Oldest Schools* (London: School of Oriental and African Studies, University of London, 1956); Carl H. Kraeling and Robert M. Adams (ed.), *City Invincible*. A symposium on 'Urbanization and Cultural Development in the Ancient Near East' held at the Oriental Institute of the University of Chicago, December 4-7, 1958 (Chicago: University of Chicago Press, 1960), pp. 94-123.

as well as at Ugarit[3] where the first alphabetic writing occurred two or three centuries before Israel's arrival in Canaan. Here a simplified cuneiform script of twenty-two to thirty letters was developed, a precursor to the Semitic alphabet. Scribal activity is also in evidence in Egypt from the early third millennium BCE, beginning with the development of a complex state in the Old Kingdom.[4]

While writing of some sort existed in early Israel,[5] it was not until the time of David that scribes (Heb. סֹפְרִים) began appearing at the royal court as high officials.[6] A central administration was not possible without writing. According to Lipiński,[7] annalistic activity of royal scribes began in Solomon's reign, with the first complete annals of a king probably being compiled by Rehoboam. Mowinckel believed that Solomon founded a school for scribes in Jerusalem.[8] In subsequent years, scribes were the ones who collected, committed to writing, and copied for themselves and generations to come Temple psalms, collections of proverbs (Prov. 25.1), accounts of the creation and flood, stories about the Patriarchs—in short, all of Israel's history and literature, a select portion of which came to be included in our Old Testament. In collecting oral traditions and committing them to writing, these individuals were not unlike the Brüder Grimm in Germany and the Peter Christen Asbjørnsen—Jørgen Moe team in Norway in modern times.

Scribes are seen functioning in the court of King Hezekiah (2 Kgs 18.18 = Isa. 36.3),[9] and the suggestion has been made that possibly Isaiah the prophet was a scribe.[10] Scribes appear as a professional class in the book of Jeremiah (Jer. 8.8), where we also meet up with individual scribes such as Baruch (called 'Baruch, the scribe' in Jer. 36.26, 32),[11] and Baruch's brother, Seraiah, the

---

3. Anson F. Rainey, 'The Scribe at Ugarit', in *Proceedings of the Israel Academy of Sciences and Humanities*, III (Jerusalem: Israel Academy of Sciences and Humanities, 1969), pp. 126-47.

4. See Ronald J. Williams, 'Scribal Training in Ancient Egypt', *JAOS* 92 (1972), pp. 214-21; Kraeling and Adams, *City Invincible*, p. 103, mention a government school for scribes existing c. 1900 BCE.

5. Alan R. Millard, 'In Praise of Ancient Scribes', *BA* 45 (1982), pp. 143-53.

6. Eduard Nielsen, *Oral Tradition* (SBT, 11; Chicago: Alec R. Allenson, 1954), p. 43.

7. E. Lipiński, 'Royal and State Scribes in Ancient Jerusalem', in *VTSup* 40 (1988), pp. 157-58.

8. Sigmund Mowinckel, 'Psalms and Wisdom', in *Wisdom in Israel and in the Ancient Near East* (ed. Martin Noth and D. Winton Thomas; VTSup, 3; Leiden: E.J. Brill, 1955), p. 206.

9. James Crenshaw, 'Education in Ancient Israel', *JBL* 104 (1985), pp. 601-15.

10. Robert T. Anderson, 'Was Isaiah a Scribe?', *JBL* 79 (1960), pp. 57-58.

11. On Baruch, see the article by James Muilenburg, 'Baruch the Scribe', in *Proclamation and Presence: Old Tstament Essays in Honor of Gwynne Henton Davies* (ed. John I. Durham and J.R. Porter; Richmond: John Knox Press, 1970), pp. 215-38.

8. Scribal Contributions to Old Testament Theology

'quartermaster' of Zedekiah (Jer. 51.59-64).[12] Both are cited with patronym or double patronym, 'son of Neriah (son of Mahseiah)' (Jer. 32.12; 36.4; 51.59), which probably indicates that their father and grandfather were also scribes. In Israel, as in neighboring societies, the profession was passed on from generation to generation, resulting in so-called 'scribal families' (cf. 1 Kgs 4.3).[13] Seal impressions with the names of both Baruch and Seraiah have turned up in excavations.[14] Other scribes mentioned in the important chapter 36 of Jeremiah are Shaphan and Elishama (vv. 10-11). Shaphan, a major figure when the lawbook was found in the Temple in 622 BCE (2 Kgs 22.8-14), was probably head of a scribal school in Jerusalem,[15] connected, as was customary, with the Temple.[16] Muilenburg, noting the enormous amount of scribal activity also in Assyria during the same period, calls this 'a scribal age'.[17]

In the present essay I wish to point out a single contribution that scribes have made to the theology of the Old Testament, one not altogether obvious and one whose discovery falls more under a study of rhetoric and composition than under text criticism, the usual hunting ground for insights into scribal practice. On occasion scribes will be seen deliberately juxtaposing materials in the biblical text in order to set up a contrast, much in the way modern journal, magazine, and newspaper editors run contrasting articles in succession or place them side by side on a page. They do not tell you they are doing this; nevertheless, the editing is intentional and an effect on the readership is expected. When statements are made in this manner, we must be alerted to them and appropriate them into our theological understanding, for such statements are as important as those of an explicit nature. The phenomenon of juxtaposition has not gone unnoticed in Jewish tradition. Rabbi Akiba is reported to have said, 'Every section in Scripture in explained by the one that stands next to it' (*Sifre Num.* 131).

Some years ago Robert Gordis pointed out in the book of Proverbs, amidst a collection dealing with 'fools' (26.1-12), these two proverbs in immediate succession:[18]

---

12. Jack R. Lundbom, 'Baruch, Seraiah, and Expanded Colophons in the Book of Jeremiah', *JSOT* 36 (1986), pp. 101-109.

13. W.G. Lambert, 'Ancestors, Authors, and Canonicity', *JCS* 11 (1957), pp. 2-3; Rainey, 'The Scribe at Ugarit', p. 128; Lipiński, 'Royal and State Scribes in Ancient Jerusalem', p. 162.

14. N. Avigad, 'Baruch the Scribe and Jerahmeel the King's Son', *IEJ* 28 (1978), pp. 52-56 [= *BA* 42 (1979), pp. 114-18]; 'The Seal of Seraiah (Son of) Neriah' (Hebrew with English summary), in *H.L. Ginsberg Volume* (Eretz-Israel, 14; ed. Menahem Haran; Jerusalem: Israel Exploration Society, 1978), pp. 86-87, 125.

15. Lundbom, 'Baruch, Seraiah, and Expanded Colophons in the Book of Jeremiah', p. 108.

16. Rainey, 'The Scribe at Ugarit', p. 128.

17. Muilenburg, 'Baruch the Scribe', pp. 216-17.

18. Robert Gordis, 'Quotations in Wisdom Literature', *JQR* 30 (1939–40), p. 137.

> Answer not a fool according to his folly
> > lest you be like him yourself
> Answer a fool according to his folly
> > lest he be wise in his own eyes
>
> (26.4-5)

One proverb says not to answer a fool with foolishness; the other advises precisely that. Each has its reason. The scribe responsible for this juxtaposition knew exactly what he was doing, and most likely wants to teach us something about the limits of wisdom. One can be right doing either. One can also be wrong. It all depends. The contrast takes us beyond the truth embodied in each individual proverb.

In an earlier article[19] I sought to show how the scribe juxtaposing the Tower of Babel story in Gen. 11.1-9 with the call of Abraham in Gen. 12.1-3, before the genealogies of 11.10-32 were added, intended to make an unspoken point about the relative importance of buildings and people to Yahweh. The contrast is embodied in a play on the phrase, 'making a name'. The men of Babel say, 'And *let us make* for ourselves *a name*' (Gen.11.4), by which they mean, 'Let us erect a city within which we will place a grand temple'. The word *tower* in the AV, RSV, and NRSV is misleading; the building is a temple, or ziggurat, perhaps of the type described in *Enuma elish* VI, 60-66 (*ANET*³, pp. 68-69).[20] Yahweh, however, says to Abraham, '*I will make* of you a great nation, and I will bless you, and I will make great *your name*' (Gen. 12.2).

This hubris of humanity is set over against the inestimable grace of Yahweh. But there is more. The men of Babel seek their name by erecting a pretentious temple, whereas Abraham will achieve his name by having a myriad of descendants. The contrast is between imposing, pretentious temples, which Yahweh rejects, and human descendants, which Yahweh promises to give. The same theology—made from a wordplay on 'house' (בַּיִת)—occurs in 2 Samuel 7. Both are early versions of 'the church is not buildings, but people' theme. In 2 Samuel 7 this theology is embodied in a single narrative. In Gen. 11.1-9 and 12.1-3, however, it is derived from the juxtaposition of the passages, which is the work of a theologically minded scribe.

This same juxtaposition technique can be seen in three additional Old Testament passages, another from Genesis and one each from Isaiah and Jeremiah. In all three the contrast is to moralize, or better, to teach behavior that is pleasing to God and, in two of the cases, behavior that is not.

---

19. Jack R. Lundbom, 'Abraham and David in the Theology of the Yahwist', in *The Word of the Lord Shall Go Forth: Essays in Honor of David Noel Freedman* (ed. Carol L. Meyers and M. O'Connor; Winona Lake, IN: The American Schools of Oriental Research and Eisenbrauns, 1983), pp. 203-209.

20. E.A. Speiser, *Genesis* (AB, 1; Garden City, NY: Doubleday, 1964), pp. 75-76.

Genesis 38–39

Chapter 38 of Genesis is agreed by all to be an interpolation into the Joseph story, which is chaps. 37–50 and one of the most homogeneous passages in the entire Bible. At the other end, in chap. 49, the 'Blessing of Jacob' poem is inserted. The Joseph story is sometimes called a novella. The insertion of chap. 38 is credited to a scribe called the 'Yahwist',[21] whose preferred term for God, *Yahweh*, appears only in chaps. 38 and 39 of the narrative.[22]

The story begins with Joseph being sold by his brothers into slavery, arriving in Egypt, and being sold a second time to Potiphar, an officer of the Pharaoh. Chapter 38 then interrupts with a report of what was going on in Canaan, a 'meanwhile back at the ranch' type of interlude.[23] Things actually were not going well. Judah has had an affair with Tamar, his daughter-in-law, which resulted in a child. This would have cost Tamar her life, except that she outwitted her father-in-law, exposing his misdeed. The story by itself relates another important fact. The son born to Tamar became a forefather to King David (1 Chron. 2.4-15, where David descends from Perez).

But why has the Judah episode in chap. 38 been inserted into the Joseph story at precisely this point? The answer, it seems to me, is found by looking ahead to chap. 39. The two chapters juxtaposed set up another contrast. In 38, Judah knowingly commits harlotry and unknowingly is guilty of incest with his daughter-in-law; in 39, Joseph resists the clutches of Potiphar's wife, who, if she had had her way, would have seduced him into an act of adultery. By juxtaposing Judah's affair with Tamar and Joseph's rebuff of Potiphar's wife, this theologically minded scribe quietly moralizes about sexual propriety and impropriety, ironically contrasting Joseph's virtuous behavior in a foreign land with Judah's misadventure back home. The sum is again greater than its individual parts. In the minds of many, things work just the reverse: corruption comes in a foreign land; purity exists at home.

Isaiah 5–6

In the prophetic books, it is commonplace to say that materials are not always arranged in chronological order. A case in point is the early chapters of Isaiah where the prophet's call comes not in chap. 1, but in chap. 6. Earlier scholars assuming chronological order in the book, had to conclude either

---

21. Gerhard von Rad, *Genesis* (OTL; Philadelphia: Westminster Press, 1961), p. 352.
22. In Genesis 37–50 אֱלֹהִים appears thirty-four times and יהוה twelve times. All twelve occurrences of יהוה, with the single exception of 49.18, which is in Jacob's poem of blessing, are found in chaps. 38–39.
23. So Edwin M. Good, *Irony in the Old Testament* (Philadelphia: Westminster Press, 1965), p. 107. It is recognized also as an interlude by von Rad (*Genesis*, p. 352) and Speiser (*Genesis*, pp. 299-300).

that the call took place after Isaiah had been preaching for some time or that chap. 6 was a 'call of renewal' following an inaugural call not recorded. Tannaitic interpreters wanted the call at the beginning of the book,[24] which is where the calls of Jeremiah and Ezekiel are placed. The consensus now is that chap. 6 is the prophet's inaugural call, and that the preaching in chaps. 1–5 came afterwards.[25] The call is commonly explained as a preface to a collection of material reflecting the Syro-Ephraimite crisis, which ends at 9.6.[26] It came earlier than this crisis, for which reason it is written in retrospect, possibly from Isaiah's own memoirs.[27]

Scholars, however, have paid little or no attention to the relationship between chap. 6 and what precedes it. Leon Liebreich connects chaps. 1–5—particularly chap. 5—with chap. 6, citing keywords that refer to Yahweh, the 'Holy One of Israel'.[28] There are other linking terms connecting chap. 5 to chap. 6, suggesting that the scribe who placed the call where he did intended a juxtaposition with the 'woe oracles' of 5.8-22, and another contrast as well. In 5.8-22, Isaiah cries 'woe' (הוֹי) on the rich, the drunks, the liars, the conceited, and the unjust in Jerusalem's elite. But in 6.5 he turns the spotlight on himself, saying: 'Woe is me' (אוֹי־לִי). All together we have seven woes, which is probably significant in that the number seven in Hebrew thought signifies completeness.[29]

---

24. Mordecai Kaplan, 'Isaiah 6.1-11', *JBL* 45 (1926), p. 251.

25. John Skinner, *Isaiah I–XXXIX* (CB; Cambridge: Cambridge University Press, 1930), p. 44. Kaplan, 'Isaiah 6.1-11', argued on other grounds that chap. 6 was not an inaugural vision, but his lead has not been followed.

26. Chapter 6 fits particularly well with chaps. 7–8, since all are biographical prose. B. Duhm, *Das Buch Jesaia* (HAT; Göttingen: Vandenhoeck & Ruprecht, 1902), p. ix, says, 'zuerst die Drohung, zuletzt die Verheissung, in der Mitte die Motivierung der ersteren und die Vermittlung der letzteren'.

27. Scholars usually cite the reference to Uzziah's death in 6.1 as an indication that Isaiah's call was seen in retrospect. See Duhm, *Das Buch Jesaia*, pp. 40-41; R.B.Y. Scott, 'Isaiah 1–39', in *IB*, V (New York: Abingdon Press, 1956), p. 204. Scott is convinced that the call is from Isaiah's memoirs: 'If anything in the book can be said clearly to be Isaiah's own composition, it is the narrative of his call in ch. 6' (p. 157).

28. Leon Liebreich, 'The Position of Chapter Six in the Book of Isaiah', *HUCA* 25 (1954), pp. 37-40. His argument runs as follows: (1) chaps. 1–5 begin and end with verses designating Yahweh as the 'Holy One of Israel' (1.4; 5.24), with Yahweh called this also in 6.3; and (2) chap. 5 mentions Yahweh as a 'holy' God three times in 5.16, 19 and 24, which Liebreich says provides a 'fitting sequel' to the threefold 'holy', in 6.3 (p. 39).

29. This could also explain what some take to be the separation of the two 'woe oracles' beginning in 10.1 and 5 from those in 5.8-22, that is, it was done to make room for Isaiah's 'Woe is me'. Professor D.N. Freedman has suggested to me in personal communication that these separated woe oracles in their present locations could act as a frame around a center interpolation of 6.1–9.6. Different spellings of

The combined message of the two passages is obvious, as more than one sermon has pointed out. The prophet who finds himself capable of making judgments on others is seen to render judgment also on himself, which goes some distance, surely, in humanizing the prophet. But more important, it gives Isaiah his warrant to preach. One who recognizes his own uncleanness can then venture forth to point out uncleanness in others (cf. Mt. 7.1-5). And a scribe provides us with this insight by juxtaposing Isaiah's call with a select number of his oracles of woe.

Jeremiah 34–35

In Jeremiah, a lack of chronological order is documented in the dated prose of chaps. 21–45. Incidents from the reign of Jehoiakim are freely interspersed with those occurring during the reign of Zedekiah, a decade later. In chaps. 34–35 we have a clear case where Zedekiah prose has been placed ahead of Jehoiakim prose. Since chap. 34 also does not fit into a rhetorical structure taking in other Zedekiah prose,[30] an explanation is required as to why it is placed where it is. One can be given if we see chap. 34 intentionally juxtaposed to chap. 35 for the purpose of setting up a contrast between the Rechabites and Judah's last king.

Chapter 34 reports an incident in which Zedekiah reneges on a covenant made with the people to honor a general release of Hebrew slaves, made after failing earlier to honor the sabbatical release of Deut. 15.12-18. For this he receives strong censure from the prophet Jeremiah. Chapter 35 tells about the Rechabites, a marginal group of seminomadic folk presently living in Judah, whom Jeremiah brings into the Temple to give people an object lesson on fidelity and obedience. The Rechabites have taken a vow not to drink wine. Jeremiah therefore sets in front of them jars of wine and tells them to drink. They refuse, and in so doing show fidelity to Jonadab, their father, who had given them the command. The juxtaposition shows the Rechabites to be faithful and obedient in a way Zedekiah was not—another contribution to Old Testament theology by a scribe, in this case perhaps Jeremiah's colleague and friend, Baruch.

Old Testament theology comes through many different types of people and in a variety of literary and rhetorical forms. To the list of inspired prophets and faithful priests, gifted kings and the seasoned wise, must be added theologically minded scribes. Actually the list is greater, including

---

'woe'—אוֹי in 6.5 and הוֹי in the others—point to, though certainly do not prove, editorial work in chaps. 5 and 6.

30. Jack R. Lundbom, *Jeremiah: A Study in Ancient Hebrew Rhetoric* (SBLDS, 18; Missoula, MT: Society of Biblical Literature and Scholars Press, 1975), pp. 109-11 [2nd edn; Winona Lake, IN: Eisenbrauns, 1997, pp. 143-45].

storytellers and a host of plain, ordinary people. We find theology explicitly stated in creeds, liturgies, hymns, stories, wisdom pieces, oracles, narratives, historical writings, and many other genres, but it is present also, less explicitly, in Hebrew rhetoric—in metaphors, similes, repetitions, hyperbole, wordplays, argument, humor, and countless other rhetorical forms. The task of interpretation is therefore varied and complex, and the sensitive biblical interpreter will look not only to what is said in the text, but also to what is not said, for in the latter also are statements that are part and parcel of the revealed Word of God.

Chapter 9

GOD'S USE OF THE *IDEM PER IDEM* TO TERMINATE DEBATE*

Twice in the Book of Exodus where tradition preserves the revelation of the divine name to Moses, God employs a peculiar idiom which S.R. Driver has called the *idem per idem*.[1] In Exod. 3.14 God says:

אהיה אשר אהיה

I will be what I will be[2]

And again in 33.19 he tells his servant:

וחנתי את־אשר אחן
ורחמתי את־אשר ארחם

But[3] I will be gracious to whom I will be gracious
and I will show mercy on whom I will show mercy

The *idem per idem* is a tautology of sorts,[4] which Driver says is employed 'where the means or the desire to be more explicit does not

---

*   *Harvard Theological Review* 71 (1978), pp. 193-201.

1.   S.R. Driver, *The Book of Exodus* (CB; Cambridge: Cambridge University Press, 1911), pp. 362-63; *Notes on the Hebrew Text and the Topography of the Books of Samuel* (2nd edn; Oxford: Clarendon Press, 1966), pp. 185-86.

2.   This translation of the Hebrew Massoretic text—where the verbs are pointed Qal—is the one preferred by William R. Arnold in his detailed paper, 'The Divine Name in Exodus iii. 14', *JBL* 24 (1905), pp. 125-27. See also W. Robertson Smith, *The Prophets of Israel* (London: A. & C. Black, 1895), pp. 386-88; S.R. Driver, *Exodus*, pp. 23-24; and more recently K.-H. Bernhardt, '*hāyāh*', *TDOT*, III, p. 381. In the RSV 'I will be what I will be' appears as an alternative reading in the footnotes. Ancient support for this translation comes from Aquila and Theodotion who rendered the idiom: ἔσομαι ὃς ἔσομαι.

3.   On the translation of the Hebrew *waw* as an adversative, see the discussion following.

4.   On the tautological nature of the idiom, see further C. Perelman and L. Olbrechts-Tyteca, *The New Rhetoric* (Notre Dame/London: University of Notre Dame, 1971), pp. 214-18, and S.I. Hayakawa, *Language in Thought and Action* (2nd edn; New York: Harcourt, Brace & World, 1964), pp. 219-20. I cannot agree with those who take the idiom as paronomastic, e.g., T. C. Vriezen, ''Ehje 'Ašer 'Ehje', in *Festschrift Alfred Bertholet*

exist'.⁵ Driver calls the idiom Semitic,⁶ and indeed it is, as one can see by perusing the many examples from Hebrew and Arabic cited earlier by Paul de Lagarde in his *Psalterium iuxta Hebraeos Hieronymi*.⁷ But it is also found, as we shall see in a moment, in other languages both ancient and modern.⁸

The Bible contains a handful of *idem per idem*s besides those found in Exod. 3.14 and 33.19. All are constructed from verbs:

Gen. 43.14	But if I am bereaved I am bereaved
Exod. 4.13	Send please whomever you will send
Exod. 16.23	What you will bake, bake
	and what you will boil, boil
1 Sam. 23.13	And they went about where they went about
2 Sam. 15.20	I will go where I will go
2 Kgs 8.1	And sojourn where you can sojourn
Ezek. 12.25	For I Yahweh speak the word which I speak
Esth. 4.16	And if I perish I perish

Three other *idem per idem*s have been adduced in Deut. 9.25, 1 Sam. 1.24, and Zech. 10.8, but all remain a matter of dispute.⁹

From the New Testament Lagarde cites Jn 19.22, where Pilate says to the Jews:

> What I have written I have written

(ed. W. Baumgartner *et al.*; Tübingen: J.C.B. Mohr [Paul Siebeck], 1950), pp. 498-512; Bertil Albrektson, 'On the Syntax of אהיה אשר אהיה in Exodus 3.14', in *Words and Meanings* (ed. Peter R. Ackroyd and Barnabas Lindars; Cambridge: Cambridge University Press, 1968), p. 27; Brevard Childs, *The Book of Exodus* (OTL: Philadelphia: Westminster Press, 1974), p. 69. See a similar criticism by Roland de Vaux, 'The Revelation of the Divine Name YHWH', in *Proclamation and Presence* (ed. John I. Durham and J.R. Porter; Richmond: John Knox Press, 1970), p. 67.

    5. Driver, *Exodus*, p. 363.
    6. Driver, *Notes on the Hebrew Text of Samuel*, p. 185.
    7. Paul de Lagarde, *Psalterium iuxta Hebraeos Hieronymi* (Leipzig: B.G. Teubner, 1874), pp. 156-58.
    8. Outside the Bible the oldest example of the idiom is thought to exist in *The Instruction for King Meri-ka-Re*, an Egyptian document from the 22nnd-century BCE. The Egyptian reads *wnn·'i wn·kw'i*, and *ANET*³ (p. 416, line 95) translates 'I am while I am'. This was first cited as a parallel to Exod. 3.14 by Albrecht Alt in his brief note, 'Ein ägyptisches Gegenstück zu Ex 3.14', *ZAW* 58 (1940–41), pp. 159-60, and later picked up by de Vaux in 'The Revelation of the Divine Name YHWH', pp. 68-69, and Walter Bühlmann/Karl Scherer in *Stilfiguren der Bibel* (Fribourg: Schweizerisches Katholisches Bibelwerk, 1973), p. 26. But Professor Leonard Lesko, an Egyptologist at the University of California, Berkeley, has pointed out to me that because the two verb forms are different the translation could just as well be 'I will be (as) I have been'.
    9. Lagarde lists 1 Sam. 1.24 and Zech. 10.8, to which Smith adds Deut. 9.25. Driver accepted all three, but not Arnold; cf. Arnold, 'The Divine Name in Exodus iii. 14', pp. 127-28.

9. *God's Use of the* idem per idem *to Terminate Debate*

There is also an *idem per idem* in 1 Cor. 15.10, where Paul says in his own defense:

> But by the grace of God I am what I am

To quote Driver again, this idiom is said to be employed 'where the means or the desire to be more explicit does not exist'. As a purely descriptive statement this explanation is perhaps adequate, for it is true that all *idem per idem*s contain a certain lack of specificity about what is affirmed, resolved, or commanded. My concern in the present essay, however, will be with rhetorical function. I should like to demonstrate first of all how the *idem per idem* serves as a closure device, more than that how it functions in argumentative discourse to terminate debate. We can see this taking place in ancient human discourse when some of the biblical *idem per idem*s just cited are restored to their contexts.[10] And we can see it also in modern human discourse where speakers use the *idem per idem*. Our focus, however, will be on the divine–human discourse in Exodus 3 and 33. There, I believe, God uses the *idem per idem* both times to terminate a debate he is having with Moses.[11] Once this is recognized, it is possible to go on and engage in fresh exegetical and theological discussion. That we will do in the latter part of the essay.

Let us begin by taking a closer look at how some of the biblical *idem per idem*s function. In Genesis 42–43 Jacob is resisting the idea of sending Benjamin to Egypt with Judah and the other brothers. Joseph is gone and now, more recently, Simeon too. The thought of also losing Benjamin is more than Jacob can stand. But the famine is severe, and Jacob wants them to get more food. Judah knows, however, that they cannot face the Pharaoh's vizier unless Benjamin is with them. Thus they converse back and forth. Finally Jacob relents and is willing to let Benjamin go. The *idem per idem*, 'But if I am bereaved I am bereaved', is Jacob's final word. After it nothing more is said.

The *idem per idem* in Est. 4.16 is also a closure device. Here Mordecai wants Esther to approach the Persian king on behalf of the Jews. Esther knows, however, that to do this without first being invited is to court death. The two communicate back and forth in this case by means of a messenger. Finally Esther agrees to go to the king saying, 'And if I perish I perish'. For

---

10. The examination of figures in their context is particularly stressed by modern rhetoricians, such as Chaim Perelman and William J. Brandt. See Perelman, *The New Rhetoric*, p. 218, and Brandt, *The Rhetoric of Argumentation* (New York: Bobbs–Merrill, 1970), pp. 100, 120.

11. The *idem per idem* is found in the mouth of God only one other time in the Bible, and that is in Ezek. 12.25, where God says, 'For I Yahweh speak the word which I speak'. There the function seems to be strictly one of emphasis. God wants to affirm that his word—once spoken—will indeed be performed (cf. Isa. 55.10-11).

her the *idem per idem* is a resolve, not a word of resignation as was the case with Jacob. But again it constitutes the final statement of the discourse.

In John 19 the discourse is unmistakably argumentative. Pilate has been debating with the Jews about what to do with Jesus. After he has put a sign on the cross which reads, 'Jesus of Nazareth, the King of the Jews', the chief priests object saying, 'Do not write, "The King of the Jews", but, "This man said I am king of the Jews"'. To this Pilate responds, 'What I have written I have written'. That is it. The debate is over and nothing more is said.

In 1 Corinthians 15 the *idem per idem* works a bit differently because Paul is arguing both sides of the debate. At issue is his apostleship. After having made the point that he is least of the apostles (vv. 5-9), he anticipates an opponent who might think he is nothing at all. The *idem per idem*, 'But by the grace of God I am what I am', moves to silence that opponent. Paul, after all is still a 'somebody'. His following remark about working harder than anyone else serves only to further substantiate this claim.

In modern discourse the *idem per idem* very often has a debate-closure function. The husband who says of his marriage, 'What's spoiled is spoiled',[12] wants to terminate any discussion about reconciliation with his wife. The judge who says, 'The law is the law', intends to terminate debate with the defendant in court. And for the student who petitions the dean at school to have some requirement waived, the reply, 'But rules are rules', can mean only one thing: the discussion is over. One will note that these latter *idem per idem*s are for the most part noun formations, the more common type in modern-day English.

Recently in the *Daily Californian*, which is the campus newspaper at the University of California, Berkeley, a front-page article reported a survey which showed that incoming undergraduates to the university were considerably less liberal than their predecessors.[13] But the Director of Student Affairs Research was then quoted as saying that despite this fact, 'Berkeley is still Berkeley'. For him the *idem per idem* served to cap all discussion about conservative trends, and his following remark merely repeats the same idea in different words: 'Kids here are still much more liberal and adventuresome'.

Some years ago two American songwriters took the Spanish proverb, 'Que sera sera', and gave it a closure function in a popular song.[14] In this song a little girl asks her mother questions about the future such as 'Will I

---

12. Cited in Paul Tournier, *The Adventure of Living* (New York: Harper & Row, 1976), p. 120.
13. The issue of January 10, 1977.
14. The song was titled, 'Whatever Will Be Will Be', and was written by Jay Livingston and Ray Evans (North Hollywood: Artists Music, 1955).

be pretty?' and 'Will I be rich?' to which the mother replies, 'Que sera sera, whatever will be will be'. The *idem per idem* here gently seeks to put an end to questions which the mother cannot answer. One could cite many other *idem per idem*s in everyday use which serve as closure devices or which terminate debate. Parents, for example, say to their children in tones that are not always gentle, 'And that's that'.

Let us turn now to Exodus 3 and 33. The *idem per idem*s here are both in argumentative discourse. God on two separate occasions is arguing with his servant Moses. First Exodus 3. This chapter and the one following combine to narrate the call of Moses. God appears to Moses in a burning bush and tells him he intends to deliver his people out of Egypt, after which he will bring them into a land of their own (3.8). Moreover, he wants Moses to go along as the people's leader. Moses' first assignment will be to go to Pharaoh to secure the people's release. But Moses demurs. Martin Buber remarks, 'And now begins the great duologue in which God commands and the man resists'.[15] God promises, 'But I will be with you' (כי־אהיה עמך), and Moses is given a sign (3.12). But Moses says if he goes to the people they will want to know God's name, so he asks, 'What shall I say to them?' God replies, 'I will be what I will be (אהיה אשר אהיה)... Say this to the people of Israel, "I will be (אהיה) has sent me to you"' (3.14). God, it seems, has had enough. The *idem per idem* censors the question, as von Rad and others have pointed out.[16] But it does more. It brings the debate to an end; Moses says no more.

I take v. 14, then, to be the conclusion of the discourse begun in v. 4. According to the source critics, all of chap. 3 is JE; nevertheless, many single out vv. 10-15 as belonging to E.[17] Albright, however, rightly argues that the seam exists rather between 14 and 15.[18] Not only does 15 begin with the supplementary-sounding, 'And God *also* said to Moses' (ויאמר עוד אלהים אל־משה), but vv. 14b and 15 are doublets. Both contain the same introductory words, 'Say this to the people of Israel', with 14b supplying the divine name 'I will be'[19] and 15 'He will be' (Yahweh).

It follows too that all three occurrences of אהיה ('I will be') in v. 14 must be Qal (אֶהְיֶה), which is how they were pointed by the Massoretes. Haupt

---

15. M. Buber, *Moses* (Oxford/London: East & West Library, 1946), p. 46.

16. Gerhard von Rad, *Old Testament Theology*, I (Edinburgh: Oliver & Boyd, 1962), p. 182. Arnold ('The Divine Name in Exodus iii. 14', p. 129) detects 'a tone of resentment and rebuke.' See the similar judgment of W.F. Albright in 'Contributions to Biblical Archaeology and Philology', *JBL* 43 (1924), p. 376.

17. J. Estlin Carpenter and G. Harford-Battersby, *The Hexateuch*, II (London: Longmans, Green, 1900), pp. 82-84; Arnold, 'The Divine Name in Exodus iii. 14', p. 107.

18. Albright, 'Contributions to Biblical Archaeology and Philology', p. 377.

19. While אהיה is not meant to be a proper name in the *idem per idem*, it is a proper name here; cf. Arnold, 'The Divine Name in Exodus iii. 14', p. 124.

and Albright and, more recently, Freedman and Cross have argued that both verb forms (אהיה and יהוה) were originally H-stems, in which case they would have causative meaning.[20] If this were true, the *idem per idem* would translate 'I cause to be what I cause to be', or, following Freedman, 'I create what I create'.[21] The divine names would correspondingly be 'I cause to be' and 'He causes to be', or 'I create' and 'He creates' respectively. Now whether יהוה (Yahweh) is an original H-stem or not I will leave to others to decide.[22] I will insist only that each אהיה in v. 14 be read Qal since the pointing of אהיה is Qal in v. 12. There is deliberate repetition here, and any interpretation of the passage, if it is to be correct, must take this into account.[23]

We turn now to Exodus 33. Here and in the chapter preceding God tests the man whom he has chosen. Once again the two are embroiled in an argument, only this time, interestingly enough, their positions are reversed. Moses now is committed to the journey while God, after the golden calf episode, objects to going along. Instead he offers to send his 'angel' (32.34; 33.2; cf. 4.10-13, where Moses wants God to send someone other than himself). Moses, however, insists that God himself must come. Finally God relents and says his presence (lit. 'face') will go (33.14). But the argument continues.[24] Moses presses this time to see God's 'glory', which here means God's bright, beneficent face. But God answers:

20. Paul Haupt, 'Der Name Jahwe', *OLZ* 12 (1909), cols. 211-14; W.F. Albright, 'Contributions to Biblical Archaeology and Philology', pp. 374-78; *From the Stone Age to Christianity* (2nd edn; Garden City, NY: Doubleday, 1957), pp. 15-16; David Noel Freedmen, 'The Name of the God of Moses', *JBL* 79 (1960), pp. 152-55; Frank Moore Cross, 'Yahweh and the God of the Patriarchs', *HTR* 55 (1962), p. 255.

21. Freedman, 'The Name of the God of Moses', p. 154.

22. Freedman says the original meaning of יהוה (Yahweh) was forgotten ('The Name of the God of Moses', p. 153, n. 6). This now is even more likely if the *Ya* found affixed to personal names at Ebla (3rd millennium BCE) is a form of Yahweh; cf. Giovanni Pettinato, 'The Royal Archives of Tell Mardikh–Ebla', *BA* 39 (1976), p. 48.

23. The amount of literature on this passage is enormous, yet only a few scholars notice and place emphasis upon the repetition of אהיה in vv. 12, 14 and 4.12, 15. Raymond Abba, 'The Divine Name Yahweh', *JBL* 80 (1961), pp. 325-26, is an exception. He translates אהיה 'I will be present' and recognizes that it has the same meaning in 3.12, 14; 4.12, 15. The *idem per idem* for him is 'only a more emphatic affirmation of this assurance', meaning 'I will indeed be present'. Brevard Childs also notes the four occurrences of אהיה in chaps. 3 and 4 and says they provide for 'thematic unity'; cf. Childs, *Exodus*, p. 70. Earlier Smith (*The Prophets of Israel*, pp. 387-88) was influenced in his views—which are different, however, from those expressed here—by a suggestion of R. Jehuda Hallevy that 3.14 should be interpreted in light of 3.12. Driver too (*Exodus*, p. 41 n. 1) cited with approval H. Ewald who connected these two verses, though he rejected Ewald's translation of the *idem per idem*. More recently the connection between 3.12 and 3.14 has been noted and emphasized by Bernhardt in '*hāyāh*', *TDOT*, III, p. 381.

24. James Muilenburg did a careful study of vv. 12-17 in his article 'The Intercession

9. *God's Use of the* idem per idem *to Terminate Debate* 95

> I will make all my goodness pass before you, and I will proclaim before you my name, 'Yahweh'; *but* I will be gracious to whom I will be gracious, and I will show mercy on whom I will show mercy. *Thus* he said, You cannot see my face, for man shall not see me and live (33.19-20).

God will let Moses see only his back after he has passed (vv. 21-22). A second time now Moses has been silenced. The *idem per idem* again terminates their debate. The discourse beginning in 34.1 is to be taken from a latter time when God does fulfill the promise made here (34.6).

In the above translation I have taken the *waw* (ו) of וחנתי (19b) as 'but', and the *waw* (ו) of ויאמר (20a) as 'thus'. The latter might also be just as well rendered 'therefore' or 'and'. In any case the flow of the argument requires that the adversative, which signals the beginning of God's qualifying remarks, be placed prior to the *idem per idem* in v. 19 instead of at the beginning of v. 20, which is where certain modern English translations (RSV, NEB, NAB) would have it. The LXX used καί in both places, and the AV in both places used 'and'. But Luther in his translation of vv. 19-20 seems to give support for the interpretation proposed here:

> Ich wil fur deinem angesicht her alle meine Güte gehen lassen, und wil lassen predigen des HERRN Namen fur dir, Wem ich *aber* gnedig bin, dem bin ich gnedig, und wes ich mich erbarme, des erbarme ich mich. *Und* sprach weiter, Mein Angesicht kanstu nicht sehen. Denn kein Mensch wird leben, der mich sihet.[25]

The final sentence of discourse, 'You cannot see my face; for man shall not see me and live', is again a rearticulation of the *idem per idem*, only in different words. It is also possible, I suppose, that the final sentence is to be taken as editorial. But the point is that 19b and 20 mean to place a limit on the goodness promised in 19a. Moses does have God's overall favor (v. 17), but this does not mean his every request will be granted.[26] God's grace (or favor) is his alone to give and it cannot be presumed upon. Thus Moses cannot see God's face, which means that with respect to this request God's favor is denied him.

The rhetoric of a passage is then a key to meaning and interpretation. In Exodus 3 scholars continue to debate over whether God gives or does not give Moses a name.[27] Obviously there is tension in the text, but must we

---

of the Covenant Mediator (Exodus 33.1a, 12-17)', in *Words and Meanings* (ed. Ackroyd and Lindars), pp. 159-81, but I cannot agree with him that a unit ends at v. 17. The chapter may indeed be a composite as Muilenburg claims, but vv. 12-23 appear to me to be too firmly held together to admit further fragmentization.

25. M. Luther, *WADB*, VIIII, p. 307.
26. Freedman, Lundbom, '*ḥānan*', *TDOT*, V, p. 31.
27. Arnold ('The Divine Name in Exodus iii. 14', p. 129) felt that the *idem per idem* in 14a was a non-answer, so he deleted it as a midrashic gloss on 14b. De Vaux

come down on either one side or the other? Why not rather acknowledge the tension and simply leave it at that? When the *idem per idem* terminates debate there is always tension, because the answer it gives will be perceived at the same time as a non-answer. Anyone who has been on the receiving end of an *idem per idem* used in this manner will attest to the fact that this is more than just an impression.

Theologically it is important that we preserve this tension lest the dynamic quality of biblical revelation be destroyed. God reveals himself while at the same time remaining hidden. Paul Ricoeur in a recent article on the idea of revelation says the following:

> If one thing may be said unequivocally about all the analogical forms of revelation, it is that in none of its modalities may revelation be included in and dominated by knowledge. In this regard the idea of something secret is the limit-idea of revelation. The idea of revelation is a twofold idea. The God who reveals himself is a hidden God and hidden things belong to him. The confession that God is infinitely above human thoughts and speech, that he guides us without our comprehending his ways, that the fact that human beings are an enigma to themselves even obscures the clarity that God communicates to them—this confession belongs to the idea or revelation. The one who reveals himself is also the one who conceals himself. And in this regard nothing is as significant as the episode of the burning bush in Exodus 3. Tradition has quite rightly named this episode the revelation of the divine name. For this name is precisely unnamable.[28]

There was tension also in Exodus 33, as we noted earlier. There God gave and at the same time did not give Moses his favor.

The results of our analysis raise another matter, which from a theological point of view is potentially more problematic. The *idem per idem* culminates debate by cutting it off, and from the point of view of the one being silenced the termination will be abrupt and premature. We must therefore come to terms with the fact that anyone using the *idem per idem* in this manner lies open to the charge of behaving irrationally. If the person is someone in authority—as is most often the case, and is surely the case here in Exodus 3 and 33—that person will be thought of as acting in a 'high-handed'

---

too ('The Revelation of the Divine Name YHWH', pp. 64-65) argued that 14 was a non-answer. For him the answer does not come until v. 15. Abba ('The Divine Name Yahweh', p. 324) thinks both 14b and 15 give a positive answer. This is also the judgment of Childs (*Exodus*, p. 69), though later on (p. 76) he says precisely what we are affirming here: 'The formula is paradoxically both an answer and a refusal of an answer.'

28. Ricoeur, 'Toward a Hermeneutic of the Idea of Revelation', *HTR* 70 (1977), pp. 17-18; published also as Colloquy 27 of the Center for Hermeneutical Studies in Hellenistic and Modern Culture (Berkeley: Center for Hermeneutical Studies, 1977), p. 7.

sort of way. How unlike the Socratic dialogues! And it is of more than just passing interest that nowhere in the classical rhetoric handbooks such as Aristotle's *Rhetoric*, the *ad Herennium*, or Quintilian's *Institutes* do we find *idem per idem* arguments recommended. Greek rhetoric teaches reasoning, especially syllogistic reasoning. But Hebrew rhetoric depends more upon repetition.[29] Yet if repetition is used in such a way that discourse becomes irrational, why does God resort to it? Or are we simply to conclude that because God is God he can act any way he wants?

Happily the problem is not a serious one, at least not within the confines of our present discussion, the reason being that in both Exodus 3 and 33 God acts in a *gracious* capacity. In Exodus 3 he is promising to lead a people out of slavery and be with them on their journey. In Exodus 33 the discussion itself revolves around grace and mercy. This, I believe, makes perfectly acceptable God's use of the *idem per idem* to terminate debate. For we can accept and indeed trust a God who withholds for the present only good from us. And although it may baffle and frustrate us, we can accept a God who at times is irrational in the way he dispenses his goodness. Just so long as God does not behave this way when he metes out judgment. We would feel differently I am sure if we heard God say, 'I will judge whomever I will judge'. That sounds capricious, and would tend to undermine any faith and trust we might have in him.[30]

One can find supporting evidence from the Bible that Yahweh God does indeed act irrationally—if we may use that term—in the dispensation of his grace. His judgments meanwhile are accomplished by reasons and they are valid reasons. Westermann has pointed out in his study of the prophetic speeches that the judgment-speech is almost always accompanied by a reason, whereas in the salvation-speech the reason is conspicuously absent.[31] One can read Second Isaiah in vain to find a reason why God is delivering his people out of exile. In gracious acts God is motivated only by his love and faithfulness (Isa. 43.4; cf. Deut. 7.6-8), and since these qualities originate with him they need no rationale. We observe also that the unconditional covenants given to Noah, Abraham, and David—all of which are mentioned, interestingly enough, in Second Isaiah (54.9-10; 41.8-10; 55.3-5)—likewise rank as gracious acts in that they need no rationale nor do they require any conditions.[32] In the New Testament we see the irrational God

29. James Muilenburg, 'A Study in Ancient Hebrew Rhetoric: Repetition and Style', *Congress Volume Copenhagen* (VTSup, 1; Copenhagen, 1953), pp. 97-111.

30. One will notice, however, that Paul expands upon Exod. 33.19 in Rom. 9.18, saying that God 'hardens the heart of whomever he wills'; but even this falls short of his saying 'I will judge whomever I will judge'.

31. Claus Westermann, *Basic Forms of Prophetic Speech* (Philadelphia: Westminster Press, 1967), pp. 97-98.

32. On the unconditional covenants, see David Noel Freedman, 'Divine Commitment

of grace vividly portrayed in Jesus' parable of the Laborers in the Vineyard (Mt. 20.1-15).

Thus I would conclude that Yahweh God uses the *idem per idem* only to hide from our eyes his infinite grace and unlimited goodness. It is this kind of God who withholds from Moses a full revelation of his name and a complete unveiling of his face.

and Human Obligation', *Int* 18 (1964), pp. 3-15 [repr. in *Divine Commitment and Human Obligation: Selected Writings of David Noel Freedman* I; ed. John R. Huddlestun; Grand Rapids: Eerdmans, 1997, pp. 168-78].

Chapter 10

The Decalogue in the Primary History*

David Noel Freedman, who named Genesis to 2 Kings Israel's 'Primary History', and believed this history to have been a completed work by c. 560 BCE, went on to argue in his last years a brilliant thesis in the book, *The Nine Commandments*,[1] namely, that the scribe (or scribes) compiling the Primary History used nine (not ten) commandments of the Decalogue to create a 'command–violation' structure in this history. It was not transparent, but rather 'hidden' in the scribal work. Freedman noted this 'command–violation' principle being introduced at the very beginning of Genesis, in the stories of Adam and Eve and Cain and Abel.

In the Book of Exodus, where the covenant is ratified and the Ten Commandments are given, this unknown scribe proceeded to go through the Primary History, book by book, all the way to the end of Kings, and include in each book a showcase example of how each of the commandments was violated. The violations and the books in which they occur are the following:

1–2. No other gods and no idols—violated in the golden calf episode (Exod. 32.7-8)
3. No empty use of the Name—violated in a man's blasphemy (Lev. 24.10-17)
4. Observing the Sabbath—violated by a wood-gathering man (Num. 15.32-36)
5. Honoring father and mother—violated by the rebellious son (Deut. 21.18-21)
6. No stealing (# 6 in Jer. 7.9)—violated in Achan's stealing (Josh. 7.20-26)
7. No murder (#7 in Jer. 7.9)—violated with a Levite's concubine (Judg. 20.34-48)
8. No adultery (#8 in Jer. 7.9)—violated by David with Bathsheba (2 Samuel 11)
9. No empty witness—violated by the testimony against Naboth (1 Kings 21)

In order to arrive at this scheme, Freedman combined the 'no other gods' and 'no idols' commandments into one, which finds support in the Jewish, Roman Catholic, Anglican, and Lutheran traditions. The Orthodox and Reformed traditions separate these commands.[2] He also followed the order of commandments 6, 7, and 8 in Jer. 7.9, which is stealing, murder,

---

* Paper read at the International Society of Biblical Literature Meeting in Tartu, Estonia, on July 29, 2010.
1. Freedman, *The Nine Commandments* (New York: Doubleday, 2000).
2. Freedman, *The Nine Commandments*, pp. 15-17.

and adultery.³ In Exodus and Deuteronomy, the order is murder, adultery, and stealing (Exod. 20.13-15; Deut. 5.17-19), which is the order also in 4QDeut^n; Mt. 19.18; Mk 10.19; the Samaritan Pentateuch; the Targums; and Josephus (*Ant* 3.92). The LXX has adultery, stealing, and murder. The Nash papyrus has adultery, murder, and stealing. Other ancient texts sequence these commandments differently, e.g., in Hos. 4.2 the listing is murder, stealing, and adultery. Freedman argues that the sequence of these commandments was not fixed until later.

The Tenth Commandment on coveting is not included in Freedman's scheme. He reasons that this commandment is left out because coveting is not a verifiable crime.⁴ While coveting may well be an impetus for violating certain other commandments, e.g., coveting a neighbor's wife may lead to adultery, and coveting a neighbor's property may lead to theft, it cannot, in Freedman's view, be singled out as a crime in itself.

A scheme in which key ideas are sequenced in a literary work is not that extraordinary, at least in Hebrew compositions of the late pre-exilic and early exilic period. Something similar occurs in Jeremiah and Lamentations, only there it is not key ideas, but key words and phrases that lie 'hidden' in the text. Condamin pointed out many years ago that in Lamentations 1–2, key words embodied in stanzas of the laments form a large chiasmus.⁵ Here, in the fact that the laments in question are also acrostics, we have a control for identifying a rhetorical structure. In Jer. 2.5-9 and 5.1-8 the same thing occurs, where the control in each case is a balanced speaker structure existing simultaneously.⁶ The two structures, that in the Primary History, and that in Lamentations and Jeremiah, are admittedly not the same, but they are similar and lie 'hidden' in the compositions where they occur. All three literary works, Jeremiah, Lamentations, and the Primary History, come from roughly the same period, i.e., the end of the 7th-century and beginning of the 6th-century BCE.

The present essay accepts Freedman's basic thesis, but argues that the Tenth Commandment on coveting should be included in the scheme. This commandment cannot come at the end, but it could come at the beginning, which is where it does come. The showcase example of the coveting command being violated in the Primary History occurs in the Garden of Eden story, where Eve is said to have found the forbidden fruit to be *desirable* (תַאֲוָה) to the eyes *and coveted* (וְנֶחְמָד) to make one wise, so she took of the

---

3. Freedman, *The Nine Commandments*, pp. 85-98.
4. Freedman, *The Nine Commandments*, p. 20.
5. Albert Condamin, 'Symmetrical Repetitions in *Lamentations* Chapters I and II', *JTS* os 7 (1905), pp. 137-40; Jack R. Lundbom, *Jeremiah 1–20* (AB, 21A; New York: Doubleday, 1999; New Haven: Yale University Press, 2009), pp. 81-82.
6. Lundbom, *Jeremiah 1–20*, pp. 82-83, 256-57, 371-73.

fruit and ate it, and then gave it to her husband, and he ate (Gen. 3.6). The wording is precisely what we find in Deut. 5.21: '*And you shall not covet* (וְלֹא תַחְמֹד) the wife of your fellow, *and you shall not desire* (וְלֹא תִתְאַוֶּה) the house of your fellow...'.[7] In Exod 20.17 the commandment is slightly different, in that the verb 'covet' is used in reference to both the wife and the house.

I would argue then that this ingenious scribe compiling the Primary History did not eliminate the Tenth Commandment after all; he simply put the showcase violation of coveting at the beginning of his scheme, which is the only place he could have put it. The advantage of this revision is that the Tenth Commandment and the Book of Genesis, both of which Freedman left out, are now included in the scheme. So according to the revised scheme, the Ten Commandments and their showcase violations in the Primary History are the following:

10. No coveting—violated by Eve in the Garden of Eden story (Gen. 3.6)
1–2. No other gods and no idols—violated in the golden calf episode (Exod. 32.7-8)
3. No empty use of the Name—violated in a man's blasphemy (Lev. 24.10-17)
4. Observing the Sabbath—violated by a wood-gathering man (Num. 15.32-36)
5. Honoring father and mother—violated by the rebellious son (Deut. 21.18-21)
6. No stealing (# 6 in Jer. 7.9)—violated in Achan's stealing (Josh. 7.20-26)
7. No murder (#7 in Jer. 7.9)—violated with a Levite's concubine (Judg. 20.34-48)
8. No adultery (#8 in Jer. 7.9)—violated by David with Bathsheba (2 Samuel 11)
9. No empty witness—violated by the testimony against Naboth (1 Kings 21)

7. Freedman, *The Nine Commandments*, pp. 18-19.

Chapter 11

THE INCLUSIO AND OTHER FRAMING
DEVICES IN DEUTERONOMY 1–28*

The book of Deuteronomy is widely acknowledged to be *the* rhetorical book of the Hebrew Bible. Its prose style, initially, is what pointed to the discourse—or portions of the discourse—being read aloud to an assembled audience. Gerhard von Rad, following the lead of A. Klostermann, said nearly a half century ago:

> Deuteronomy is not divine law in codified form, but preaching about the commandments—at least, the commandments appear in a form where they are very much interspersed with parenesis.[1]

Von Rad thought this to be the most elemental difference between Deuteronomy and the Book of the Covenant (Exodus 20–23). Others earlier had come to a similar conclusion based on D vocabulary and phraseology. S.R. Driver recognized D's rhetorical style in his commentary on Deuteronomy for the ICC, published in 1895.[2] A half century later Robert H. Pfeiffer said, '[Deuteronomy's style] from beginning to end...is that of a pulpit orator'.[3] Recently, Timothy A. Lenchak describes Deuteronomy as 'highly rhetorical'.[4]

Von Rad's desire was to advance the critical study of Deuteronomy from a rhetorical and homiletical standpoint. His method was form criticism, worked out with consummate skill in *Das formgeschichtliche Problem des Hexateuch* (1938) and *Deuteronomium-Studien* (1947), both of

---

* *Vetus Testamentum* 46 (1996), pp. 296-315.

1. Gerhard von Rad, *Studies in Deuteronomy* (London: SCM Press, 1953), p. 15; see also 'The Form-Critical Problem of the Hexateuch', in von Rad, *The Problem of the Hexateuch and Other Essays* (New York: McGraw–Hill, 1966), p. 30. The point had been made earlier by Herbert Breit, *Die Predigt des Deuteronomisten* (Munich: Chr. Kaiser, 1933).

2. S.R. Driver, *A Critical and Exegetical Commentary on Deuteronomy* (ICC; Edinburgh: T. & T. Clark, 1895), pp. ii-iii, lxxvii-xcv.

3. Robert H. Pfeiffer, *Introduction to the Old Testament* (rev. edn; New York: Harper & Bros., 1948), p. 53.

4. Timothy A. Lenchak, *'Choose Life!' A Rhetorical-Critical Investigation of Deuteronomy 28,69–30,20* (AnBib, 129; Rome: Pontifical Biblical Institute, 1993), p. 37.

which were translated into English.⁵ Von Rad believed that Deuteronomy reflected an ancient cultic festival at Shechem, appropriating to this extent the view of Adam C. Welch that the book's provenance was North Israel.⁶ But the preachers behind its sermons were post-701 BCE Levitical priests from the Judean countryside.⁷ Von Rad's views were accepted by and large by G. Ernest Wright,⁸ James Muilenburg,⁹ and others.¹⁰

Already by the mid-1950s, however, the focus of Deuteronomy studies had shifted to the Hittite treaties unearthed at Boghazköy, published two decades earlier (1931). George E. Mendenhall in an important study showed formal similarities between these treaties and the biblical covenants,¹¹ after which Dennis McCarthy made it even more clear that the covenant form in Deuteronomy was the real beneficiary of the new comparison.¹²

Subsequent comparisons were made between Deuteronomy and the Assyrian vassal treaties of Esarhaddon, discovered in 1956. After an examination of these treaties Moshe Weinfeld judged Deuteronomy to be a 'loyalty oath' imposed by a suzerain (Yahweh) on his vassal (Israel), prior to a leadership

---

5. See note 1.

6. Adam C. Welch, *The Code of Deuteronomy: A New Theory of its Origin* (London: James Clarke, 1924); see also W.F. Albright, *From the Stone Age to Christianity* (2nd edn, Garden City, NY: Doubleday, 1957), p. 315.

7. Von Rad, 'The Form-Critical Problem of the Hexateuch', pp. 33-40; *Studies in Deuteronomy*, pp. 14, 41, 45, 66-68; 'Deuteronomy', in *IDB*, I, pp. 835-37. According to 1 Kgs 12.26-31 and 2 Chron. 11.13-17; 13.9-12, northern Levites were disenfranchised at the time of Jeroboam I, after which they came south to Jerusalem. In Jehoshaphat's reign (873–849 BCE) the Levites were lay teachers in the cities of Judah (2 Chron. 17.7-9). On the Levites as teachers, see G.E. Wright, 'The Levites in Deuteronomy', *VT* 4 (1954), pp. 325-30; 'Deuteronomy', in *IB*, II (ed. George A. Buttrick; New York: Abingdon Press, 1953), p. 316.

8. Wright, 'Deuteronomy', in *IB*, II, pp. 315-16.

9. James Muilenburg, 'The Form and Structure of the Covenantal Formulations', *VT* 9 (1959), pp. 348-50.

10. H.W. Wolff suggested Levitical circles in the north in his article, 'Hoseas geistige Heimat', *TLZ* 81 (1956), cols. 83-94; see discussion in E.W. Nicholson, *Deuteronomy and Tradition* (Philadelphia: Fortress Press, 1967), pp. 73-76. A majority of scholars support the 7th-century date of composition (Nicholson, pp. xi-xii). Wright ('Deuteronomy', *IB*, II, p. 324) suggested a date between 740 and 640 BCE. A 7th-century date has been reaffirmed more recently by Moshe Weinfeld, who is impressed by the similarities between Deuteronomy and the vassal treaties of Esarhaddon (672 BCE); cf. Weinfeld, 'Deuteronomy, Book of', in *ABD*, II (New York: Doubleday, 1992), p. 174; *Deuteronomy 1–11* (AB, 5; New York: Doubleday, 1991), p. 9.

11. George E. Mendenhall, *Law and Covenant in Israel and the Ancient Near East* (Pittsburgh: Presbyterian Board of Colportage of Western Pennsylvania, 1955; repr. of two articles in *BA* 17 [1954], pp. 26-46, 49-76).

12. Dennis J. McCarthy, *Treaty and Covenant* (AnBib, 21; Rome: Pontifical Biblical Institute, 1963).

change (Moses to Joshua). Similarities extended even into language, for example, the command in both the treaties and Deuteronomy that the vassal 'love' the suzerain 'with all the heart and all the soul' (cf. Deut. 6.5).[13]

Despite the consuming interest during this time in treaty forms, Muilenburg echoed the sentiments of von Rad in calling for further work in Deuteronomy along rhetorical lines. He said:

> The large and varied terminology associated with covenantal formulations requires closer attention, the composition and rhetoric and structural forms need to be studied more carefully...[14]

Such work was, in fact, already taking place. Roman Catholic scholars at the Pontifical Biblical Institute in Rome were currently applying to the OT a method of rhetorical research practiced earlier in the century by such Scripture scholars as A. Condamin, A. Bea, and H. Galbiati, also the Protestant biblical scholar Nils W. Lund.[15] The method was not unlike Muilenburg's own.[16] The emphasis was on locating in the text keyword, motif, and speaker distributions which formed inclusions and concentric inclusions. The two scholars at the center of the Deuteronomy research were W.L. Moran[17] and Norbert Lohfink.[18] A third, L. Alonso Schökel, was working in Isaiah and more broadly in OT poetry.[19]

In Deuteronomy a concentric inclusion of speakers was observed by Lohfink and Moran in the spy report of 1.6-36,[20] and another of keywords

---

13. Weinfeld, 'Deuteronomy', in *ABD*, I, pp. 169-71; *Deuteronomy 1–11*, pp. 6-9. On the use of the term 'love', in the ancient Near East treaties, see W.L. Moran, 'The Ancient Near Eastern Background of the Love of God in Deuteronomy', *CBQ* 25 (1963), pp. 77-87.

14. Muilenburg, 'The Form and Structure of the Covenantal Formulations', p. 348.

15. See Lohfink, 'Darstellungskunst und Theologie in Dtn. 1,6–3,29', *Biblica* 41 (1960), p. 123 n. 2. Two important works by Condamin were *Le Livre de Jérémie* (Paris: Victor Lecoffre, 1920), and *Poèmes de la Bible* (2nd edn; Paris: Gabriel Beauchesne et ses fils, 1933). Lund's major work was *Chiasmus in the New Testament* (Chapel Hill, NC: University of North Carolina, 1942; repr. Peabody, MA: Hendrickson, 1992).

16. Muilenburg's major work employing rhetorical criticism was his 'II Isaiah' commentary in *IB*, V, pp. 381-773.

17. Moran's class notes at the Pontifical Biblical Institute, *Adnotationes in libri Deuteronomii capita selecta* (Rome, 1963), had limited circulation among his students.

18. Lohfink's class notes at the Pontifical Biblical Institute, *Lectures in Deuteronomy* (trans. S. McEvenue; Rome, 1968), had limited circulation among his students.

19. Alonso Schökel's first major work was *Estudios de poética hebrea* (Barcelona: Juan Flors, 1963).

20. Lohfink, 'Darstellungskunst und Theologie in Dtn. 1,6–3,29', p. 122; see also Moran, 'Deuteronomy', in *A New Catholic Commentary on Holy Scripture* (ed. Reginald C. Fuller; Camden, NJ and London: Thomas Nelson, 1969), p. 261. An abbreviated structure (without Yahweh's speech at the extremities) appears in Lohfink,

and motifs in the superscription of 1.1-5.[21] In his *Das Hauptgebot* (1963), Lohfink found a concentric inclusion of keywords for 'keeping the law' in 5.27–6.3, which argued for breaking the unit at 6.3 instead of at 6.1.[22] Both Lohfink and Moran identified a concentric motif structure in 8.1-20, with Moran finding one of keywords in vv. 7-10.[23] The latter contains the following distribution:

a	*good land*	v. 7
b	*land* of brooks... *hills*	v. 7
c	*land* of wheat...	v. 8
d	*land* of olive...	v. 8
c'	*land* in which... bread	v. 9
b'	*land* whose stones... *hills*	v. 9
a'	*good land*	v. 10

Lohfink also found less-intricate 'inclusions', for example, 3.29 with 1.6 (motif: 'the final camp'); 11.32 with 5.1 (keywords: 'statutes and ordinances'); 14.21 with 14.2 (keywords: 'holy people'); 26.16 with 12.1 (keywords: 'statutes and ordinances'); etc.[24] These and the others did not lead him to conclude with von Rad that the style of Deuteronomy was necessarily 'preaching style', for the treaties too possessed a rhetorical cast and were meant to be read aloud.[25]

With respect to Deuteronomy's final composition, Lohfink followed P. Kleinert (1872) in arguing that the book was an 'archive', its main divisions marked by the headings in 1.1; 4.44; 28.69 [29.1]; and 33.1.[26] Lohfink did not entirely abandon the idea that Deuteronomy embodied traditions from the north; however, the accent now was on a written document of Jerusalem origin, not an oral document of northern provenance.[27]

Lectures in Deuteronomy, p. 15.

21. Lohfink, 'Der Bundesschluss im Land Moab: Redaktionsgeschichtliches zu Dt. 28,69–32,47', *BZ* N.F. 6 (1962), p. 32; also Lohfink, *Lectures in Deuteronomy*, p. 11; and Moran, 'Deuteronomy', in *New Catholic Commentary*, p. 260.

22. Lohfink, *Das Hauptgebot: Eine Untersuchung literarischer Einleitungsfragen zu Dtn 5–11* (Rome: Pontifical Biblical Institute, 1963), p. 67; *Lectures in Deuteronomy*, p. 23.

23. Lohfink, *Höre, Israel! Auslegung von Texten aus dem Buch Deuteronomium* (Düsseldorf: Patmos, 1965), p. 76; Moran, *A New Catholic Commentary*, p. 266.

24. Lohfink, *Lectures in Deuteronomy*, pp. 15, 20, 24.

25. Lohfink, 'Die Bundesurkunde des Königs Josias', *Biblica* 44 (1963), pp. 261-88, 461-98.

26. Lohfink, 'Der Bundesschluss im Land Moab', pp. 32-34; *Lectures in Deuteronomy*, pp. 7-9.

27. Lohfink, 'Die Bundesurkunde des Königs Josias'.

Weinfeld continued the move away from von Rad. He agreed that Deuteronomy contains material of northern provenance, but it is not surviving oral torah from preaching Levites. What we have rather is a written document compiled by Jerusalem scribes.[28] Such a conclusion, says Weinfeld, is supported by wisdom elements in the book. At the same time, rhetorical work has continued with tangible results.[29] The present writer has found a chiastic (= concentric) keyword structure of 'law...words...song' / 'song...words...law' in Deut. 31.24-30 and 32.44-47, the prose surrounding the Song of Moses, also a framing method of composition for the whole of Deuteronomy 31–34.[30]

The present article will follow von Rad and others who have sought to advance the critical study of Deuteronomy along rhetorical and homiletical lines, with the one difference that the method used will be that of rhetorical criticism. Our focus will be on framing devices, particularly the inclusio, whose employment can be seen throughout Deuteronomy 1–28. The term 'inclusio' will be used in its restrictive sense to mean, 'keyword balance at the beginning and end of a discourse unit, where the balance usually—but not always—is a repetition'. This excludes keywords that do not effect closure, and avoids structures alleged solely on the basis of conceptual categories. Many of the latter exist only in the imagination of the modern scholar who finds them. While there is evidence to indicate that the inclusio—and the chiasmus—are thought patterns,[31] the sum of existing research supports the general rule that rhetorical structures are more likely to be truly present in the text if the same build on keyword repetition or keyword balance.

Deuteronomy 1.1-5
The superscription to the book of Deuteronomy, 1.1-5, is framed by a keyword inclusio:

---

28. Weinfeld, 'Deuteronomy—The Present State of Inquiry', *JBL* 86 (1967), pp. 249-62 [repr. in Duane L. Christensen (ed.), *A Song of Power and the Power of Song: Essays on the Book of Deuteronomy* (Winona Lake, IN: Eisenbrauns, 1993), pp. 21-35].
29. See, e.g., Gottfried Seitz, *Redaktionsgeschichtliche Studien zum Deuteronomium* (BWANT, 93; Stuttgart: W. Kohlhammer, 1971), pp. 167-78.
30. Lundbom, 'The Lawbook of the Josianic Reform', *CBQ* 38 (1976), pp. 293-302; 'Scribal Colophons and Scribal Rhetoric in Deueronomy 31–34', in *Haim M.I. Gevaryahu Memorial Volume* (ed. Joshua Adler and B.Z. Luria; Jerusalem: World Jewish Bible Center, 1990), pp. 53-63. Georg Braulik, 'Die Ausdrücke für "Gesetz" im Buch Deuteronomium', *Biblica* 51 (1970), p. 66 n. 1, sees a chiastic keyword repetition of תּוֹרָה and דְּבָרִים in 31.26, 28 and 32.46.
31. Lund, *Chiasmus in the New Testament*, p. 34, argued that the chiasmus was a 'thought pattern'.

These are the *words*
 that *Moses spoke* to all Israel
  beyond the Jordan... (v. 1)

 beyond the Jordan, in the land of Moab,
  Moses undertook *to explain*
this *law* saying... (v. 5)

The return in v. 5 repeats keywords from v. 1, and, for the sake of variation, rounds out completion with conventional synonyms. In this context, then, 'words' and 'law' have roughly equivalent meaning. The audience is told that the words (הַדְּבָרִים) following—which constitute a law or teaching (הַתּוֹרָה)—were given by Moses 'beyond the Jordan'. Intervening verses (vv. 2-4) summarize the trek from Horeb to settlement in trans-Jordan, a more full report of which is given in the historical prologue of chaps. 1–4. The introduction then, taken as a whole, looks ahead both to the prologue and to the teaching beginning in chap. 5.

It is not therefore entirely accurate to say with Noth that Deuteronomy 1–3 (4) does not introduce the Deuteronomic law, but is directly related only to the Deuteronomistic history.[32] 1.1 and 1.5 are quite explicit in presenting the law promulgated on the Moabite plains. The same is true for 4.44, about which more will be said in a moment. This does not necessarily vitiate Noth's theory, for 1–4 may well preserve two functions: (1) a narrow function, which originally introduced the Deuteronomic law; and (2) a broad function, which later introduced the Deuteronomic history.

We see the same thing happening with colophons, which originally had the function of concluding texts for which they were explicitly written, but later in expanded compositions were made to assume a broader function not envisioned at first. In the book of Jeremiah the colophon of Baruch, MT 45.1-5 [= LXX 51.31-35], originally concluded the first edition—very likely chaps. 1–20. In the LXX it now concludes a book comprising chaps. 1–51. The same is true with Seraiah's colophon, MT 51.59-64. Originally it concluded only the oracles to Babylon (MT 50–51), but in the MT it now concludes another book comprising chaps. 1–51.[33] The same phenomenon can indeed be observed with single words or phrases anywhere in the biblical

---

32. Martin Noth, *The Deuteronomic History* (JSOTSup, 15; Sheffield: JSOT Press, 1981), pp. 12-17. Noth (p. 13) also considers Deuteronomy 31–34 as part of this Introduction, since 31.1-13 and parts of chap. 34 contain elements making a direct link to Joshua 1.

33. Lundbom, 'Baruch, Seraiah, and Expanded Colophons in the Book of Jeremiah', *JSOT* 36 (1986), pp. 99-109.

text where expansion has taken place. We can point, for example, to the תּוֹרָה said to be written by Moses in Deut. 31.24. In the original prose frame to the Song of Moses (Deuteronomy 32), this torah referred simply to the Song. Later, however, it came to denote the whole of Deuteronomy, and finally the entire Pentateuch.[34]

In the closing component (v. 5) keywords are articulated in reverse order, making this a chiastic (or concentric) inclusio. Lohfink and Moran, as was pointed out, found a more elaborate concentric inclusion comprised of balancing thought categories in the center of 1.1-5, where also expansion was believed to have taken place. But their center categories of 'place' and 'time' are too subjective, and it is best to see the present rhetorical structure as a less intricate keyword inclusio. The center material has another balancing function, as we shall see shortly.

Deuteronomy 1–4

The historical and geographical summary of 4.44-49 is widely taken to be an introduction to the presentation of law beginning in 5.1. Looked at in this way it is a superscription. S.R. Driver noted similarities to the summary in 1.1-5, saying 4.44-49 was 'superfluous' after 1.1-5.[35] Subsequent scholars have agreed, most taking 1.1-5 and 4.44-49 as two introductions to the book.[36] Wellhausen earlier held the view that chaps. 1–4 and 5–11 in their entireties were two introductions to Deuteronomy proper, that is, chaps. 12–26.[37] But Noth rendered the first of these unnecessary by taking those chapters as the introduction to the Deuteronomic history concluding at 2 Kgs 25.30. This view is now widely accepted, in spite of arguments by Driver and G.A. Smith that 1–4.40 is by the same hand as 5ff.[38]

With 4.44-49 so similar in content to 1.1-5, it is surprising the former has not been judged a subscription, in which case the repetition, instead of being 'superfluous', would take on rhetorical significance. Its function would be to close a unit of discourse, namely, chaps. 1–4, thus another inclusio. The two summaries read as follows:

---

34. Lundbom, 'Scribal Colophons and Scribal Rhetoric in Deuteronomy 31–34', pp. 62-63.
35. Driver, *Deuteronomy*, p. 79.
36. So, e.g., G.E. Wright, 'Deuteronomy', in *IB*, p. 314; Lohfink, *Lectures in Deuteronomy*, p. 7; Weinfeld, *Deuteronomy 1–11*, pp. 233-34.
37. Julius Wellhausen, *Prolegomena to the History of Israel* (Cleveland: World, 1965), p. 369.
38. Nicholson, *Deuteronomy and Tradition*, p. 20 n. 2.

11. *The Inclusio and Other Framing Devices in Deuteronomy 1–28*

Deut 1.1-5

These are the words *which Moses spoke* to all *Israel beyond the Jordan* in the wilderness, in the *Arabah* over against Suph, between Paran and Tophel, Laban, Hazeroth, and Dizahab. It is eleven days' journey from Horeb by the way of Mount Seir to Kadesh-barnea. And in the fortieth year, on the first day of the eleventh month, *Moses* spoke to the people of Israel according to all that Yahweh had given him in commandment to them, after he had *defeated Sihon the king of the Amorites, who lived in Heshbon*, and *Og, the king of Bashan*, who lived in Ashtaroth and in Edrei. *Beyond the Jordan*, in the land of Moab, Moses undertook to explain *the law, this* one, saying…

Deut. 4.44-49

This is *the law* which Moses set before the children of Israel; these are the testimonies, the statutes and the ordinances, *which Moses spoke* to the children of *Israel* when they came out of Egypt, *beyond the Jordan* in the valley opposite Beth-peor, in the land of *Sihon the king of the Amorites, who lived in Heshbon*, whom *Moses* and the children of Israel *defeated* when they came out of Egypt. And they took possession of his land, and the land of *Og the king of Bashan*, the two kings of the Amorites, who lived to the east *beyond the Jordan*; from Aroer, which is on the edge of the valley of the Arnon, as far as Mount Sirion (i.e., Hermon), together with all the *Arabah* on the east side of the Jordan as far as the Sea of the Arabah, under the slopes of Pisgah.

When the keywords are separated out one can see how some in 4.44-49 nicely invert from 1.1-5:

Deut. 1.1-5

beyond the Jordan
which Moses spoke…Israel

Arabah

Moses…defeated
Sihon the king of the Amorites
who lived in Heshbon

Og, the king of Bashan

beyond the Jordan

the law/this

Deut. 4.44-49

This/the law
which Moses spoke…Israel
beyond the Jordan

Sihon the king of the Amorites
who lived in Heshbon
Moses…defeated

Og, the king of Bashan

beyond the Jordan

Arabah

While the content is not precisely the same in each—we should not expect it to be—it is similar enough to see that 4.44-49 is a summary of chaps. 2–3. Its focus is not on what lies ahead. Only 'this law' with its embellishment in 4.44-45 is forward-looking. 4.44-49 prepares the audience for the giving of the law no more or less than the summary of 1.1-5, and no more or less than all of chaps. 1–3. It therefore has no preeminent claim to being the introduction to 5–28. The entire prologue—the first part being a historical summary of the wilderness wanderings (1.6–3.29), the second part consisting of a sermon on what lies ahead for Israel (4.1-40)—forms the introduction to 5–28.

The function of 4.44-49 is to bring the prologue to a close. The chapter division is therefore correctly placed at the end of v. 49, not at 4.44, which is where the majority of modern scholars would have it.

Deuteronomy 5–11
Chapters 5–11 form another acknowledged unit within Deuteronomy, following the prologue and preceding the main legal code in 12–26. Chapter 5 begins with the 10 commandments, which are interspersed with a parenesis (5.1-33). Chapter 11 ends with a blessing and a curse (11.26-31). The structure here betrays influence of the treaty form, with the blessing and curse seemingly playing a role in bringing about closure. In the center of the unit are sermons about the importance of keeping the commandments (6.1–11.25).

The controlling structure for chaps. 5–11, however, is a keyword inclusio appearing at the limits of the unit warning about being careful to do the covenant demands. This has already been noted by Lohfink.[39] The initial admonition is in 5.1, the repetition coming in 11.32. The whole is also chiastic:

> And Moses summoned all Israel, and said to them, Hear, O Israel, *the statutes and the ordinances* which I speak to your hearing *today*, and you shall learn them *and be careful to do them* (5.1).

> ... *you shall be careful to do* all *the statutes and the ordinances* which I set before you *today* (11.32).

Framing the center sermons is yet another call for covenant obedience, this one a tightly knit injunction which appears in 6.6-9 and 11.18-20. Its first recitation follows the Shema. One might say, as Driver did about the historical summary in 4.44-49, that the injunction of 11.18-20 is 'superfluous' after 6.6-9, but again this would be to miss the significance of repetition, which, in oral discourse is done intentionally and for a purpose. Here in chaps. 5–11 the injunction comes after the 10 commandments and

---

39. Lohfink, *Lectures in Deuteronomy*, p. 20; the keywords 'statutes and ordinances' are repeated also in 12.1 and 26.16, which may be another inclusio.

before the blessing and curse. Its repetition in 11.18-20 does not effect closure, which comes with the inclusio statement of 11.32. But it assists, as do the blessing and curse. The primary function of the injunction in 6.6-9 and 11.18-20 seems to be to frame the center sermons.

The two injunctions, which vary only slightly in terminology and contain another reversal in the center, are the following:

Deut. 6.6-9	Deut. 11.18-20
And *these words* which I command you this day shall be upon *your hearts*	You shall therefore lay up *these words* of mine in *your heart* and in your soul
And you shall teach them diligently to your children, and shall talk of them when you sit in your house, and when you walk by the way, and when you lie down and when you rise	*And you shall bind them as a sign upon your hand, and they shall be as frontlets between your eyes*
And you shall bind them as a sign upon your hand, and they shall be as frontlets between your eyes	*And you shall teach them to your children, talking of them when you sit in your house, and when you walk by the way, and when you lie down, and when you rise*
And you shall write them on the doorposts of your house and on your gates.	*And you shall write them on the doorposts of your house and on your gates.*

Just preceding the injunction in 6.3, and following its repetition in 11.22, come more warnings about being careful to do the covenant. These make another frame within chaps. 5–11:

> Hear, therefore, O Israel, and *be careful to do them*; that it may go well with you... (6.3).

> For if *you will be careful to do* all this commandment which I command you to do... (11.22).

Deuteronomy 12

Within chaps. 12–26, which contain the main legal code of the book, are some nicely-structured discourses in 12–18. Individually or in compilation all are held together by the inclusio except 16.1-17, which is a sermon on the three-yearly feasts: Passover, Weeks, and Booths. It is given closure by a repeating of the three feasts in summary fashion at the end (vv. 16-17).[40]

---

40. It is interesting to note that the parallel passage in the Covenant Code, Exod. 23.14-17, does have an inclusio: 'Three times in the year... Three times in the year' (vv. 14, 17).

Chapter 12 is a rambling homily on the single sanctuary, but with effort one can identify in the center instructions regarding: (1) tithes and offerings (vv. 4-14); and (2) clean and unclean foods (vv. 15-28). Each is discussed in more detail two chapters hence: 14.1-21 is on clean and unclean foods, and 14.22–15.23 is on tithes and offerings. In this later discussion the topics appear in reverse order from their introduction.

Creating an inner frame for the instructions here in chap. 12 are admonitions, in vv. 2-3 and vv. 29-31, which warn the audience to 'beware of *other gods*', a subject elaborated more fully in chap. 13.[41] An outer frame consisting of v. 1 and 13.1 [Eng. 12.32] contains more warnings about the importance of doing the commandments. These apply to what lies ahead in chaps. 13–26. Keywords in the outer frame make clear the preacher's intent to close his homily with an inclusio:

> These are the *statutes and ordinances* which *you shall be careful to do* in the land… (12.1).
>
> *Every word* that I command you, *you shall be careful to do*; you shall not add to it or take from it (13.1 [Eng. 12.32]).

The 'statutes and ordinances' of 12.1 are balanced by 'every word' in 13.1, with both verses containing the phrase, 'you shall be careful to do'. Most English Bibles (AV, RSV, NEB, NIV, NRSV, REB) disregard the MT and LXX and follow the Vulgate, which takes the closing verse as 12.32. In the MT and the LXX this verse begins chap. 13. The JB and the NAB follow this division. While the verse does seem to close the homily of chap. 12, it also shares keywords with the closing verse of chap. 13 (13.19 [Eng. 18]), which means it could make an inclusio in chap. 13. This apparent dual function likely accounts for the uncertainty whether the verse closes 12 or begins 13.

Despite its rambling nature the whole of chap. 12 has the following rhetorical structure:

> These… *statutes and ordinances*… *you shall be careful to do* (12.1)
>   Beware of *other gods* (12.2-3)
>   Instructions on tithes and offerings (12.4-14)
>   Instructions on clean and unclean food (12.15-28)
>   Beware of *other gods* (12.29-31)
> *Every word* that I command you *you shall be careful to do* (13.1 [Eng. 12.32])

Deuteronomy 13

This chapter is a rhythmic sermon admonishing the listening audience not to follow 'other gods'. It focuses on three categories of people: (1) prophets

---

41. See also J.G. McConville, *Law and Theology in Deuteronomy* (JSOTSup, 33; Sheffield: JSOT Press, 1984), pp. 64-67.

11. *The Inclusio and Other Framing Devices in Deuteronomy 1–28* 113

(vv. 2-6 [Eng. 1-5]); (2) family members and close friends (vv. 7-12 [Eng. 6-11]); and (3) certain base fellows (vv. 13-18 [Eng. 12-17]). All are a threat to Yahweh worship if they entice people to follow other gods. The sermon is polemical, putting into the mouths of individuals words they would not likely say: 'Let us go after other gods and serve them, which you (and your fathers) have not known' (vv. 3, 7, 14 [Eng. 2, 6, 13]). The audience is told not to follow such individuals because 'Yahweh your God is testing you, to know whether you love Yahweh your God with all you heart and with all your soul' (v. 4 [Eng. 3]). Individuals leading people in the direction of other gods are to be put to death.

Closure comes at the end of v. 19 [Eng. 18], which repeats the key verb 'command' from v. 1 [Eng. 12.32]. The beginning and end thus make another inclusio:

> Everything that *I command you* you shall be careful to do; you shall not add to it or take from it (13.1 [Eng. 12.32]).

> ... keeping all the commandments which *I command you* this day, and doing what is right in the sight of Yahweh your God (13.19 [Eng. 18]).

As was pointed out above, 13.1 [Eng. 12.32] also makes an inclusio with 12.1, which may explain why the Vulgate, the AV, and other modern English versions put these words at the close of chap. 12. The verse has a dual function. The present inclusio, however, justifies the Masoretic and LXX division at 13.

Deuteronomy 14.1-21
The next sermon on dietary laws is delimited to 14.1-21. It too divides into three sections—in this case, three categories of food declared to be clean and unclean: (1) animals (vv. 3-8); (2) water fowl (vv. 9-10); and (3) birds (vv. 11-20). At the beginning (vv. 1-2) and at the end (v. 21), making a frame for the whole, are miscellaneous prohibitions related and unrelated to the dietary laws. Included also are statements about Israel's election. This election statement at the beginning is more full; at the close it is simply, 'for you are a people holy to Yahweh your God'. These words, which are centered in the two component parts, form an inclusio.[42] The frame consists of the following:

> You are the children of Yahweh your God; you shall not cut yourselves or make any baldness on your foreheads for the dead. *For you are a people holy to Yahweh your God*, and Yahweh has chosen you to be a people for his own possession, out of all the peoples that are on the face of the earth (14.1-2).

---

42. Noted also by Lohfink, *Lectures in Deuteronomy*, p. 24.

> You shall not eat anything that dies of itself; you may give it to the alien who is within your towns, that he may eat it, or you may sell it to a foreigner. *For you are a people holy to Yahweh your God.* You shall not boil a kid in its mother's milk (14.21).

The repetition here is neither fortuitous nor a redundancy.[43] The preacher of Deuteronomy, in good rhetorical style, simply announces closure of his sermon. Since the framework is made up of miscellaneous prohibitions, the prohibition about not boiling a kid in its mother's milk should be kept with the rest of v. 21. Modern English translations (RSV, NRSV, NEB, REB, JB, NAB, NIV, NJV) all separate it out. The rhetorical form here has simply opted for variation: at the beginning, the miscellaneous laws are grouped together; at the close they are split up.

Deuteronomy 14.22–15.23

The next sermonic discourse on tithes and offerings is delimited to 14.22–15.23. The organizing principle here is the calendar:

> Duties which come up *year by year* (14.22-27)
> > Duties which come up every three years (14.28-29)
> > Duties which come up every seven years (15.1-18)
> Another duty which comes up *year by year* (15.19-23)

The preacher here reworks material from Exodus 21 and 23. Cultic duties are presented in logical order—those required year by year, those required every 3 years, and those required every 7 years, until we get to the final regulation regarding the offering of first-born animals, which comes up *year by year*. Why is this regulation placed here and not at the beginning? The answer seems to be that the preacher wants a tie-in between end and beginning, in which case we have another inclusio. This has been noted already by Lohfink.[44]

Deuteronomy 13–18

The sermons concluding chaps. 12–18 set forth regulations concerning the four major office-holders in Israelite society: (1) the judge (16.18–17.13);[45] (2) the king (17.14-20); (3) the priest (18.1-8); and (4) the prophet (18.9-22). The prohibitions against planting Asherahs and erecting pillars in 16.21-22, and against sacrificing blemished animals in 17.1, have no obvious connection to their contexts and are probably intrusive.

The list of community officials concludes with the prophet. If this is intentional, a tie-in is made with the beginning of chap. 13, where the

---

43. The JB for some reason leaves out the repeated phrase in 14.21; NJB restores.
44. Lohfink, *Lectures in Deuteronomy*, p. 26.
45. The priests assist the judges in some legal matters (17.9, 12).

prophet heads the three categories of individuals capable of leading people in the direction of other gods. We then have an inclusio for chaps. 13–18. The outer frame for this rhetorical unit consists of the following:

prophets who lead people astray (13.2-6 [Eng. 1-5])
    family and friends who lead people astray (13.7-12 [Eng. 6-11])
        base fellows who lead people astray (13.13-18 [Eng. 12-17])

        laws concerning the judges (16.18–17.13)
    laws concerning the king (17.14-20)
laws concerning the priests (18.1-8)
laws concerning the *prophets* (18.15-22)

For scholars looking to quantify thought units, the 3 + 4 pattern appearing here may have significance. Casper Labuschagne has found such a scheme, supported by keywords, in chaps. 1–3.[46]

The passages on the prophets merit closer examination. Both are concerned with identifying false prophets, and are the only guidelines of their kind in the Old Testament. The two presuppose different realities and offer different tests for authenticity. These may be summarized as follows:

Deut. 13.2-4 [1-3]	Deut. 18.20-22
Assumed Reality	
Prophets of Yahweh and prophets of other gods are both giving signs and wonders which are coming to pass.	Prophets of Yahweh—all of them—are speaking in Yahweh's name, but their words contradict one another.
Question	
How does one know the false prophet?	
Answer	
It is the prophet who is not a Yahweh prophet.	It is the prophet whose word does not come to pass.

Except for the difference that prophets in chap. 13 are performing signs and wonders, and prophets in chap. 18 are speaking the divine word, the assumed reality in the one situation is the test for the other, and vice versa. Deuteronomy 13.2-4 [Eng. 1-3] presupposes a reality in which there are prophets of Yahweh, prophets of Baal, prophets of Asherah, and prophets

46. Casper Labuschagne, 'Divine Speech in Deuteronomy', in Christensen, *A Song of Power and the Power of Song*, p. 380.

with other portfolios—all in competition with one another. All, moreover, are enjoying a measure of success, that is, their signs and wonders are coming to pass. In such a situation how is one to know false (and true) prophets? The answer given is that prophets who are not Yahweh prophets are not genuine, and must be put to death. It makes no difference whether their signs and wonders come to pass. These individuals—like the magicians of Egypt—are given their day in the sun only so that Yahweh can test his people for loyalty. Prophets who are not Yahweh prophets are false, and must not be followed.

Deuteronomy 18.20-22 presupposes a different reality entirely. The prophets here are all Yahweh prophets, but their prophecies are contradictory. How is one to know false (and true) prophets in this situation? The answer: see whether their word comes to pass—the precise reality *mutatis mutandis* assumed in 13.2-4 [Eng. 1-3]. If it does not, the prophet is false and under sentence of death. How long one must wait for fulfillment is not stated. Presumably, prophesies of doom are at issue, since mention is made about not having to be afraid of prophets whose word goes unfulfilled (v. 22). It should also be noted that v. 20, which puts presumptuous prophets under sentence, adds, for the sake of inclusiveness, 'or [the prophet] who speaks in the name of other gods'. This is carried over from chap. 13. The basic test being applied here is what 13.2-4 [Eng. 1-3] assumes, namely, that prophetic acts or words have come to pass.

These guidelines for establishing inauthentic prophets are likely a legacy of Israel's experience with prophets during the reign of Ahab. In these years two individuals stand out amidst a host of inauthentic prophetic colleagues: Elijah the Tishbite, and Micaiah ben Imlah.

Elijah appears on the stage at a time when prophets of Yahweh are in eclipse in North Israel, thanks to Tyrian Jezebel who resides in Samaria's royal palace. Most Yahweh prophets, in fact, are hiding in caves (1 Kgs 18.13). Enjoying unrivaled success are prophets of Baal and Asherah, who number 850 when all are present and accounted for at the queen's table (1 Kgs 18.19). The contest on Mt Carmel, in which Elijah is the central figure, is told therefore with great relish in 1 Kings 18. It is the consummate victory for the Yahweh prophets, an event from which the legislation in Deut. 13.2-7 [Eng. 1-6] can well be imagined to have come. The death of the Baal and Asherah prophets, at Elijah's hands no less (1 Kgs 18.40), is precedent enough for the death sentence proscribed in Deut. 13.6 (Eng. 5).

Elijah's victory over the indigenous prophets of Canaan appears to have been successful, for at the end of Ahab's reign none is present when the king is preparing war against the king of Syria (1 Kings 22). All the prophets speaking to the king's foreign policy are Yahweh prophets—now a reduced company of 400 (1 Kgs 22.6). They are predicting victory, at which point Micaiah, another Yahweh prophet, is brought in. The king is dismayed, for he anticipates a contrary word. That in fact is what he gets, which means we now have a situation where all the prophets are Yahweh prophets but two contrary words have been spoken—the precise situation presupposed in Deut. 18.20-22. How is one to know the false prophet (or prophets)? And how is one to know which prophet (or prophets) is true? The answer: see whose word comes to pass. Micaiah's parting word when being led away squares well with Deut. 18.22: 'If you [the king] return in peace, *Yahweh has not spoken by me*' (1 Kgs 22.28). The wait was not long. Ahab died in battle, which vindicated Micaiah and showed the other 400 Yahweh prophets to be inauthentic.

If the guidelines for determining false prophets in Deut. 13.2-7 [Eng. 1-6] and 18.20-22 have these dramatic events as background, support is increased for the view that Deuteronomy's provenance is North Israel. A *terminus a quo* for these sermons would be c. 850 BCE, the death of Ahab. A *terminus ad quem* would be c. 600 BCE when both sermons appear to be known and used to vindicate Jeremiah (Jeremiah 26–28). In one confrontation the guidelines in 18.20-22 discredit the Yahweh prophet Hananiah.[47]

Deuteronomy 1–28
One final inclusio binds together the whole of chaps. 1–28, supporting the view that 1–28 is the essential Deuteronomy, with 29–34 being later addenda. About chap. 27 scholarly opinion remains divided; many argue that it is a later interpolation.[48] The inclusio binding together what may well be the first edition of Deuteronomy consists of the opening and closing words of the superscription in 1.1-5, and the words of 28.69 [Eng. 29.1], which I take to be a subscription:

> *These are the words* that *Moses* spoke to *all Israel* beyond the Jordan… beyond the Jordan, *in the land of Moab*, Moses undertook to explain *this law* … (1.1-5).

> *These are the words of the covenant* which Yahweh commanded *Moses* to make with *the people of Israel in the land of Moab*, beside the covenant which he made with them at Horeb (28.69 [Eng. 29.1]).

Keywords repeat, with variation provided by the terms 'covenant' (בְּרִית) and 'law' (תּוֹרָה), both synonyms or near-synonyms to the preferred Deuteronomic term 'words' (דְּבָרִים). The terms 'law' and 'words' are made

---

47. See my article, 'Jeremiah and the Break-Away from Authority Preaching', *SEÅ* 56 (1991), pp. 18-22.

48. Wright, 'Deuteronomy', in *IB*, pp. 315, 317; Lohfink, *Lectures in Deuteronomy*, p. 18; Nicholson, *Deuteronomy and Tradition*, pp. 19, 36. Noth, *The Deuteronomic History*, p. 16, said that 4.44–30.20 had to include 27.1-8. Weinfeld, *Deuteronomy 1–11*, pp. 9-13, also has a more complex view of composition.

synonymous in the prose frame to the Song of Moses in Deuteronomy 32, and 'law' and 'covenant' are synonyms in the phrases 'book of the law' and 'book of the covenant' in 2 Kgs 22.8–23.25.[49]

The MT, which takes 28.69 as a subscription, is followed by the JB, NAB, and NJV. The LXX and Vulgate take the verse as 29.1, and are followed by the AV, RSV, NEB, NIV, NRSV and REB. Lohfink, as we noted earlier, takes the verse as beginning chap. 29, supporting his archival view of the book's final compilation. He notes that the word 'covenant', which appears twice in 28.69 [29.1], recurs in 29.8 [9], 11 [12], and 13 [14],[50] suggesting to him that the verse must at least introduce 29.1-14 [Eng. 13]. But the argument has also been made of late that the verse in question is a subscription concluding Deuteronomy 1–28,[51] which I believe is correct. It is of course possible that in the present text, which contains the addenda in 29–34, the verse assumes a dual function of subscription/superscription,[52] which is what was said earlier about 12.32 [13.1].

Conclusions

The foregoing confirms much of what has been previously thought about the nature and compostition of Deuteronomy, while at the same time leading to some fresh conclusions. The law in this book is unquestionably sermonic, as von Rad and others have pointed out, with repetition playing an even greater role in structuring discourse than was previously imagined. The inclusio is seen to be the pre-eminent closure device in chaps. 1–28. Other repetitions—large and small—assist in discourse closure even when they do not actually effect it. Many repetitions employ inversion, further substantiating rhetorical intention. Confirmed then seems to be the view that the present book is made up of originally independent discourses, also compilations of discourses, the main ones of which are those generally recognized: 1–4, 5–11, 12–18, 19–26 or 28.

The first identifiable book of Deuteronomy is 1–28, which I have called the first edition. Chapters 29–34 are addenda. Of particular significance is the recognition that 4.44-49 and 28.69 [Eng. 29.1] are subscriptions, each of which makes a tie-in with the superscription of 1.1-5. The final book then is

---

49. Lundbom, 'The Lawbook of the Josianic Reform', pp. 299-301; 'Scribal Colophons and Scribal Rhetoric in Deuteronomy 31–34', pp. 55-56.

50. Lohfink, 'Der Bundesschluss im Land Moab', p. 36; *Lectures in Deuteronomy*, p. 29; 'Dtn. 28,69—Überschrift oder Kolophon?', *BN* 64 (1992), pp. 40-52.

51. H.F. Van Rooy, 'Deuteronomy 28, 69—Superscript or Subscript?', *JNSL* 14 (1988), pp. 215-22.

52. So A.D.H. Mayes, 'Deuteronomy 4 and the Literary Criticism of Deuteronomy', *JBL* 100 (1981), p. 44 [= Christensen, *A Song of Power and the Power of Song*, p. 217].

not an 'archive' as Lohfink maintains. The treaty form is seen to have some impact upon 5–11 and 12–28; however, in neither has it become the controlling structure. The controlling structures in Deuteronomy 1–28 are all rhetorical, dictated by canons of Hebrew rhetoric well known and widely practiced in the 7th-century BCE.

With the recognition that 4.44-49 is a subscription, not a superscription, we can abandon the 'two introductions' theory, which is a legacy from Wellhausen. In this earlier school of biblical criticism repetition was taken to be evidence of separate written sources, not viewed as a rhetorical device whose function might be to embellish oral discourse and bring about discourse closure. Chapters 1–4 then, with or without 4.1-43, constitute a *bona fide* rhetorical unit.

Regarding Noth's theory that 1–3(4) introduces the larger Deuteronomic History, nothing from my research calls this into question, except to point out from the keywords in 1.1-5 and 4.44-49 that the introduction as it stands gives no indication of an expanded function; it purports only to introduce the law/covenant given by Moses in the plains of Moab. Further substantiation of a more limited function for 1–4 comes from 28.69 [Eng. 29.1], which ties-in with 1.1-5. Chapters 1–28, then, with or without chap. 27, constitute another *bona fide* rhetorical unit—expanded later to include chaps. 29–34. A comparison with biblical colophons suggests, however, that 1–4 could easily have taken on the expanded function which Noth claims, once either book had become integrated into the larger Deuteronomic History.

The whole debate whether the authors of Deuteronomy were Levites (von Rad, Wright) or scribes (Weinfeld) may well fade into insignificance if, as 2 Chron. 34.13 says, 'some of the Levites were scribes'. The Chronicler writes later, to be sure, but his statement is made in the context of the lawbook's finding in 622 BCE. Also, in Nehemiah 8—a text of which von Rad made considerable use—Ezra is called both 'Ezra the priest' and 'Ezra the scribe' (Neh. 8.1, 9). If then these overlaps of terminology correspond to reality in pre-exilic times, which is not hard to envision,[53] Weinfeld's argument that Deuteronomy is authored by scribes, not Levites, loses much of its force. The authors of Deuteronomy may have been both Levites and scribes. Priests, scribes and even prophets during the 8th- to 6th-centuries BCE all shared in a common rhetorical tradition fully capable of producing the speaking voice in Deuteronomy. There is nothing, in any case, to preclude our calling the discourse of Deuteronomy 'preaching about the commandments' (von Rad).

---

53. See S. Mowinckel, 'Psalms and Wisdom', in *Wisdom in Israel and in the Ancient Near East* (ed. M. Noth and D.W. Thomas; VTSup, 3; Leiden: E.J. Brill, 1955), p. 206, and my comments in 'Baruch, Seraiah, and Expanded Colophons in the Book of Jeremiah', pp. 102-103.

More at issue is Deuteronomy's provenance. My study points to Deuteronomy 1–28 having an oral provenance. Individual sermons and larger rhetorical units make liberal use of the inclusio, which is at home in oral discourse. Our analysis of the 'prophet passages' in chaps. 13 and 18 point to prophetic activity in the north—during the reign of King Ahab. But whether these or any other sermons in Deuteronomy 1–28 were ever preached in the north it is not possible to say.

Provisionally we may say the following about Deuteronomy. The essential book, which I have called the first edition, consists of chaps. 1–28. The sermons therein may have been preached as early as 750–700 BCE in the north, otherwise preached and re-preached in the south in conjunction with the reforms of Hezekiah and Josiah. The first edition was put into writing some time during the 7th-century BCE.

Chapters 29–34 are addenda. First came 29–30, which is brought to a close by the 'two ways' sermon of 30.15-20. This was added sometime before Jeremiah parodied that sermon in Jer. 21.8-10. Chapters 31–34 manifest a framing mode of composition, with the Song of Moses in Deuteronomy 32, which I believe was the lawbook of 622 BCE, serving as the core. This was added sometime after the finding of the lawbook. Thus in general terms: Deuteronomy 1–28 is a legacy of Hezekiah's reign; Deuteronomy 29–34 a legacy of the reign of Josiah. The entire book, except for additions here and there, can well have been completed before the fall of Jerusalem in 587 BCE.

Chapter 12

THE LAWBOOK OF THE JOSIANIC REFORM*

Current research in Deuteronomy—indeed in the entire Pentateuch—rests upon the thesis of de Wette (1805) that Deuteronomy was the lawbook found in the temple during the reign of King Josiah (2 Kgs 22.8).[1] In the years subsequent to de Wette a quest began for *Urdeuteronomium*[2] since it was thought that the scroll of 622 BCE could not possibly contain all the material now found in our present book of Deuteronomy.[3]

We have, of course, nothing explicit from the Deuteronomic Historian (DH)[4] telling about the contents of the scroll. Nevertheless, scholars have seemed to agree that the DH inadvertently left us a clue. Josiah's great purge, which is described in 2 Kgs 23.4-20, is purported to have taken place immediately following the finding of the scroll, and since the specific acts of this purge correlate so well with the prohibitions outlined in Deuteronomy 5–26, 28[5]—not only in content but in vocabulary and

---

* *Catholic Biblical Quarterly* 38 (1976), pp. 293-302.

1. W.M.L. de Wette, *Dissertatio critica* (Jena, 1805); see further O. Eissfeldt, *The Old Testament: An Introduction* (New York: Harper and Row, 1965), p. 173; M. Noth, *The Laws in the Pentateuch* (Philadelphia: Fortress Press, 1966), p. 41. H.H. Rowley in *Men of God* (London: Nelson, 1963), p. 161 says: 'That Josiah's Law Book was Deuteronomy in some form, though not wholly identified with the present book of Deuteronomy, seems to be one of the most firmly established results of Old Testament scholarship'. Some of the early Church Fathers, viz., Athanasius, Chrysostom, Jerome, and Theodoret, also identified the lawbook with Deuteronomy; cf. Eb. Nestle, 'Das Deuteronomium und II Könige 22', *ZAW* 22 (1902), pp. 170-71, 312-13.

2. J. Wellhausen, *Die Composition des Hexateuchs und der historischen Bücher des Alten Testaments* (Berlin: Georg Reimer, 1889), p. 191.

3. G. Fohrer, *Introduction to the Old Testament* (Nashville: Abingdon Press, 1968), pp. 169-70; Eissfeldt, *The Old Testament: An Introduction*, pp. 173-74.

4. The term is not wholly satisfactory, but we use it here to refer to the principal author of 2 Kings 22–23.

5. Chapters 1–4 are taken by Noth to be the introduction to the entire Deuteronomic History (cf. D.N. Freedman, 'Pentateuch', *IBD*, III, p. 716), which may in fact be the case; nevertheless, I have argued in my dissertation, *Jeremiah: A Study in Ancient Hebrew Rhetoric* (SBLDS, 18; Missoula, MT: Society of Biblical Literature and Scholars Press, 1975), p. 141 n. 155 [2nd edn; Winona Lake, IN: Eisenbrauns,

phraseology[6]—it is assumed that *Urdeuteronomium* must lie somewhere within these chapters.

But here scholarly agreement ends. Some think the scroll contained only the core of the legal material (12–26), while others insist that the parenesis found in 5–11 must be included. Wellhausen and Eissfeldt are in the former group,[7] and S.R. Driver is in the latter.[8] More complex proposals have also been put forward which we need not go into at the present time. Discussion has for the most part subsided and in my judgment things have reached a dead end. At the present time we know nothing more about the contents of *Urdeuteronomium* than was purportedly known at the turn of the century.[9]

This would be reason enough to propose that we take a new look at the problem. But another development has already taken place that puts things into a different perspective. I refer to the shift in our evaluation of the Chronicler's History *vis-à-vis* the history of the DH. At the turn of the century the Chronicler was thought to be inaccurate because he was late,[10] which meant that any variation in the two histories would be settled by giving more weight *a priori* to the DH. All this has changed. The Chronicler today has a 'better press' and we no longer begin with the assumption that he is merely writing 'tendentious history'.[11]

This matter bears directly on our problem because the two accounts of Josiah's reform are markedly different. According to the DH the reform began in the 18th year of Josiah and was the immediate response of the king to the finding of the scroll (2 Kings 22–23). The Chronicler, on the other hand, states that Josiah began in his 8th year to seek Yahweh, but more important, that the reform proper was begun in his *12th year* (2 Chron.

1997, pp. 28-29, n. 155], that 28.69 forms an inclusio with 1.1-5, a fact which then makes 1–28 the first identifiable *book* of Deuteronomy. Chapter 27 may still be a later insertion, as most take it.

6. Lewis B. Paton, 'The Case for the Post-Exilic Origin of Deuteronomy', *JBL* 47 (1928), pp. 325-26; Artur Weiser, *The Old Testament: Its Formation and Development* (New York: Association, 1961), pp. 127-28; E.W. Nicholson, *Deuteronomy and Tradition* (Philadelphia: Fortress Press, 1967), p. 3.

7. Wellhausen, *Die Composition des Hexatuechs*, pp. 193-95. According to Fohrer (*Introduction to the Old Testament*, p. 170) and S.R. Driver (*Deuteronomy* [ICC; Edinburgh: T. & T. Clark, 1895], p. lxv), Eissfeldt too held this position originally. Yet in Eissfeldt's latest edition of the *Introduction* he is cautious and noncommittal; cf. Eissfeldt, *The Old Testament: An Introduction*, pp. 174-76, 231-32.

8. Driver, *Deuteronomy*, pp. lxv-lxvii.

9. See Fohrer, *Introduction to the Old Testament*, pp. 169-72; Nicholson, *Deuteronomy and Tradition*, pp. 18-36.

10. Robert Pfeiffer, 'Chronicles, I and II', *IDB*, I, p. 577.

11. Werner E. Lemke, 'The Synoptic Problem in the Chronicler's History', *HTR* 58 (1965), pp. 349-63; cf. J. Bright, *A History of Israel* (2nd edn; Philadelphia: Westminster Press, 1972), p. 225; Nicholson, *Deuteronomy and Tradition*, p. 7.

34.3). The Chronicler compresses what he has taken from the DH about the purge (compare 2 Chron. 34.3-7 with 2 Kgs 23.4-20),[12] since he is more concerned to describe the later Passover celebration (compare 2 Chron. 35.1-19 with 2 Kgs 23.21-23). But what is crucial to notice is that the purge is placed very clearly by the Chronicler *before* the discovery of the scroll rather than after it. It is thus impossible, at least at this point, to harmonize the two accounts.

What happens then if we begin out inquiry with the Chronicler instead of the DH? Assuming that the purge took place before the scroll was found, we are faced, I believe, with two possible alternatives:

(1) *Either* Deuteronomy 5–26, 28 (or 12–26, 28) had *no influence* upon the reform (since it had not yet been found), in which case the reform was primarily a response to the change which was taking place on the international scene (Assyria was on the decline, and the time was ripe for repudiating Assyrian suzerainty and Assyrian worship),[13]

(2) *or* Deuteronomy 5–26, 28 *did influence* the reform, in which case it was *not* the lawbook found in the temple.

I see no possibility of having it both ways if the Chronicler's account is to be taken seriously.

The way to a correct solution lies in taking the second alternative. Deuteronomy 5–26, 28—or in my opinion Deuteronomy 1–28[14]—*did* influence the reform, but was *not* the temple scroll either in full or in part. Incidentally, I take Deuteronomy 1–28 to be the reform document from *Hezekiah's* time;[15] while this reform lapsed and perhaps died altogether under Manasseh (687–642 BCE), I do not think this document was ever lost. It is very difficult to believe that a document of this size and importance could possibly get lost in the temple archives.

What then was found by Hilkiah in the temple? Was it not Deuteronomy after all? The question is wrongly put. It was not all or part of Deuteronomy 1–28. If we are to find the lawbook we must look rather within the so-called appendix of Deuteronomy, namely, chaps. 29–34. My thesis is that the lawbook is the Song of Moses in Deuteronomy 32.[16]

---

12. Frank M. Cross and David Noel Freedman ('Josiah's Revolt against Assyria', *JNES* 12 [1953], p. 57) think that the material in 2 Chron. 34.3b-7 was derived entirely from an independent source. It looks to me, however, as if the Chronicler has simply compressed 2 Kgs 23.4-20 and made minor alterations, which of course would not preclude his making use of other sources.

13. This is the position of Cross and Freedman.

14. See n. 5 above.

15. See Freedman, 'Pentateuch', p. 715.

16. William Holladay, in 'Jeremiah and Moses: Further Observations', *JBL* 85 (1966),

Two lines of evidence point to the same conclusion. The first is this: two stanzas of Deuteronomy 32 (viz., vv. 15-22) compare very closely *in content* to a portion of Huldah's oracle in 2 Kgs 22.16-20. Huldah was the prophet living in Jerusalem to whom Hilkiah and other leading temple persons went at Josiah's behest to obtain a divine oracle. There she was apparently given the scroll to read, or else someone read the scroll to her.[17] She then obliged with a very nicely structured two-part oracle,[18] the first part being directed to the nation (vv. 16-17) and the second part to the king (vv. 18-20). Our interest is only in the first part, which we now want to compare with the two stanzas from the Song of Moses. Let us look at the respective texts:

Deut. 32.15-22

15וַיִּשְׁמַן יְשֻׁרוּן וַיִּבְעָט   שָׁמַנְתָּ עָבִיתָ כָּשִׂיתָ
וַיִּטֹּשׁ אֱלוֹהַּ עָשָׂהוּ   וַיְנַבֵּל צוּר יְשֻׁעָתוֹ
16יַקְנִאֻהוּ בְּזָרִים   בְּתוֹעֵבֹת יַכְעִיסֻהוּ
17יִזְבְּחוּ לַשֵּׁדִים לֹא אֱלֹהַּ   אֱלֹהִים לֹא יְדָעוּם
חֲדָשִׁים מִקָּרֹב בָּאוּ   לֹא שְׂעָרוּם אֲבֹתֵיכֶם
18צוּר יְלָדְךָ תֶּשִׁי   וַתִּשְׁכַּח אֵל מְחֹלְלֶךָ

19וַיַּרְא יְהוָה וַיִּנְאָץ   מִכַּעַס בָּנָיו וּבְנֹתָיו
20וַיֹּאמֶר אַסְתִּירָה פָנַי מֵהֶם   אֶרְאֶה מָה אַחֲרִיתָם
כִּי דוֹר תַּהְפֻּכֹת הֵמָּה   בָּנִים לֹא־אֵמֻן בָּם
21הֵם קִנְאוּנִי בְלֹא־אֵל   כִּעֲסוּנִי בְּהַבְלֵיהֶם
וַאֲנִי אַקְנִיאֵם בְּלֹא־עָם   בְּגוֹי נָבָל אַכְעִיסֵם
22כִּי־אֵשׁ קָדְחָה בְאַפִּי   וַתִּיקַד עַד־שְׁאוֹל תַּחְתִּית
וַתֹּאכַל אֶרֶץ וִיבֻלָהּ   וַתְּלַהֵט מוֹסְדֵי הָרִים

2 Kgs 22.16-17

16כֹּה אָמַר יְהוָה
הִנְנִי מֵבִיא רָעָה אֶל־הַמָּקוֹם הַזֶּה וְעַל־יֹשְׁבָיו
אֵת כָּל־דִּבְרֵי הַסֵּפֶר אֲשֶׁר קָרָא מֶלֶךְ יְהוּדָה
17תַּחַת אֲשֶׁר עֲזָבוּנִי וַיְקַטְּרוּ לֵאלֹהִים אֲחֵרִים
לְמַעַן הַכְעִיסֵנִי בְּכֹל מַעֲשֵׂה יְדֵיהֶם
וְנִצְּתָה חֲמָתִי בַּמָּקוֹם הַזֶּה וְלֹא תִכְבֶּה

p. 26, suggests that perhaps Deuteronomy 32 was part of *Urdeuteronomium* because of the strong echoes of the Song in Jeremiah's diction.

17. 2 Kgs 22.14-15 says nothing about Huldah reading the scroll; it says only that Hilkiah and other officials talked with her. Huldah refers in her oracle to a reading of the scroll by the king (v. 16), but we cannot be sure whether or not *she* read it. Nevertheless, we assume that somehow the substance of the scroll was made available to her before she formulated her oracle.

18. The oracle as a whole is framed by an inclusio: 'Behold I will bring evil upon this place…'/'…all the evil which I will bring upon this place' (16a, 20b).

Deut. 32.15-22

¹⁵But Jeshurun grew fat and kicked
  you grew fat, you became thick, you were gorged
Then *he forsook the God* who made him
  and scoffed at the Rock of his salvation
¹⁶They stirred him to jealousy with strangers
  with abominations *they provoked him to anger*
¹⁷*They sacrificed* to demons which were *no gods*
  gods they had never known
New ones recently come in
  your fathers never feared them!
¹⁸*The Rock* that begot you *you neglected*
  and *you forgot the God* who gave you a beginning.

¹⁹Yahweh saw and rejected
  the provocation of his sons and daughters
²⁰And he said, 'I will hide my face from them
  I will see what their end will be
For they are a perverse generation
  children in whom is no faithfulness
²¹They have stirred me to jealousy with a no-god
  they have provoked me to anger with their idols
So I will stir them to jealousy with a no-people
  with a foolish nation I will provoke them to anger
²²For *a fire is lit in my anger*
  and *it burns to the depths of Sheol*
It devours the earth and its increase
  and sets ablaze the foundations of the mountains.'

2 Kgs 22.16-17

¹⁶Thus says Yahweh:
Behold I will bring evil upon this place and upon its inhabitants—all the things of the book which the king of Judah has read. ¹⁷Because *they have forsaken me* and *have burned incense to other gods*, that *they might provoke me to anger with all the work of their hands*. Therefore *my wrath will be kindled* against this place and *it will not be quenched*.

One will immediately see that while the vocabularies are for the most part quite different, the substance of the two passages is the same. In both we note (1) that Israel is indicted because it has *forgotten* Yahweh and *made him angry* by *sacrificing to other gods*; and (2) that Yahweh's *wrath* is promised to *burn* in judgment like an *unquenchable fire*. Drawn together the parallel vocabularies are as follows:

2 Kgs 22.17	Deut. 32.15-22
עֲזָבוּנִי	וַיִּטֹּשׁ אֱלוֹהַ
	צוּר...תֶּשִׁי
	וַתִּשְׁכַּח אֵל
	יַכְעִיסֻהוּ
	מִכַּעַס
הִכְעִסֵנִי בְּכֹל מַעֲשֵׂה יְדֵיהֶם	כִּעֲסוּנִי בְּהַבְלֵיהֶם
וַיְקַטְּרוּ לֵאלֹהִים אֲחֵרִים	יִזְבְּחוּ...לֹא אֱלֹהַּ
וְנִצְּתָה חֲמָתִי	אֵשׁ קָדְחָה בְאַפִּי
וְלֹא תִכְבֶּה	וַתִּיקַד עַד־שְׁאוֹל תַּחְתִּית

Only the verb כעס appears in both; otherwise Huldah translates the vocabulary of the song into the current idiom,[19] immediately recognizable as the standard prose of the 7th–6th centuries found throughout the Deuteronomic writings.[20] The account given by the Chronicler is not significantly different.[21]

19. It is of course also possible that Huldah's speech has been stylized by the DH, but we lack the controls necessary for making such a judgment. Yet regardless of how one decides this matter our basic thesis remains unaffected.

20. אלהים אחרים and מעשה ידים/מעשה ידך are both listed by S.R. Driver and J.E. Carpenter–G. Harford Battersby as standard D phrases. Driver (*Deuteronomy*, p. lxxxii) lists מעשה ידים as phrase #55; Carpenter–Battersby (*The Hexateuch* [London: Longmans, Green, 1900], p. 207) lists מעשה ידך as phrase #119. מעשה ידיחם occurs elsewhere in Jer. 25.14; 32.30; and Lam. 3.64. אלהים אחרים is phrase #2 in Driver (*Deuteronomy*, p. lxxviii) and #85 in Carpenter-Battersby (*The Hexateuch*, p. 205). This latter phrase is commonly found in the Deuteronomic prose, e.g., 1 Kgs 17.7, 35, 37, 38; 22.17; Jer. 1.16; 7.6, 9, 18; etc. The remaining terms—including כעס—appear in the Deuteronomic writings (Deuteronomy, Kings) and in Jeremiah as follows:

עזב—in the sense of 'forsaking Yahweh/his covenant/his law/his commandments':
   Deut. 28.20; 29.24 [Eng. 25]; 31.16; 1 Kgs 9.9; 11.33; 18.18; 19.10, 14: 2 Kgs 17.16; 21.22; 22.17; Jer. 1.16; 5.19; 9.12 [Eng. 13]; 16.11; 19.4; 22.9.
כעס—in the sense of 'provoking Yahweh to anger': Deut. 4.25; 9.18; 31.29 (במעשה ידכם);1 Kgs 14.9, 15; 15.30; 16.2, 7 (במעשה ידיו), 13, 26, 33; 21.22; 22.54 [Eng. 53]; 2 Kgs 17.11, 17; 21.6, 15; 22.17; 23.19, 26; Jer. 7.18, 19; 11.17; 25.6 (במעשה ידכם), 7 (במעשה ידכם); 32.29, 30 (במעשה ידיהם), 32; 44.3, 8 (במעשי ידיכם).
קטר—in the sense of 'burning (incense) on the high places/to other gods': 1 Kgs 3.3; 11.8; 12.33; 13.1, 2; 22.44 [Eng. 43]; 2 Kgs 12.4 [Eng. 3]; 14.4; 15.4, 35; 16.4, 13, 15; 17.11; 22.17; 23.5, 8; Jer. 1.16 (לאלהים אחרים);| 7.9; 11.12, 13, 17; 19.4 (לאלהים אחרים), 8 (לאלהים אחרים), 5 (לאלהים אחרים), 13; 32.29; 44.3 (לאלהים אחרים), 15 (לאלהים אחרים), 17, 18, 19, 21, 23, 25.

12. *The Lawbook of the Josianic Reform*

Since this exact combination of ideas is not to be found elsewhere in the OT in quite the way that it appears in these two passages (Deut. 29.24-26 [Eng. 25-27] lacks the provocation of Yahweh to anger; Jer. 7.17-20 and 44.3-6 lack the forsaking of Yahweh or his covenant), we have already a case for our thesis that Huldah drew the substance of her indictment against Israel from the Song of Moses.

The second line of evidence comes as the result of a rhetorical analysis of the prose frame to the Song. The question might well be raised at this point whether a 'song' could be construed as a 'lawbook'. 2 Kings 22.8 says quite clearly that a 'book of the law' (סֵפֶר הַתּוֹרָה)[22] was found in the temple. We know that *torah* need not always be translated 'law' (it can mean 'teaching' or 'instruction'), but can a *torah* be a song? The answer fortunately is already given us in the prose of Deuteronomy 31–32. There, as some scholars have already noted, the song is referred to precisely as a *torah* (31.24, 26; 32.46). Eissfeldt says the song 'at a later date was regarded as a summarizing of the Deuteronomic law', but he adds with some puzzlement, 'it is remarkable that the two terms *law* (תּוֹרָה) and *song* appear together'.[23] What has apparently gone unnoticed, however,—at least so far as I am aware—is the deliberate ordering of the terms. If the immediate frame of 31.24-30 and 32.44-47 is analyzed, a nice inversion appears with תּוֹרָה at the extremes:[24]

Deuteronomy 31–32

אֶת־דִּבְרֵי הַתּוֹרָה הַזֹּאת	31.24
(אֵת סֵפֶר הַתּוֹרָה הַזֶּה)[25]	26
אֵת הַדְּבָרִים הָאֵלֶּה	28
אֶת־דִּבְרֵי הַשִּׁירָה הַזֹּאת	30
אֶת־כָּל־דִּבְרֵי הַשִּׁירָה הַזֹּאת	32.44
אֶת־כָּל־הַדְּבָרִים הָאֵלֶּה	45
אֶת־כָּל־דִּבְרֵי הַתּוֹרָה הַזֹּאת	46

This I take to be deliberate. The creation of such a structure subtly makes a שִׁירָה into a תּוֹרָה, with דְּבָרִים—a good Deuteronomic term—mediating

---

יצת N Stem with הָמָה as subject—2×: 2 Kgs 22.13, 17. In the H Stem the verb is used commonly by Jeremiah with אֵשׁ as subject, e.g., Jer. 17.27; 21.14; etc.

ולֹא תכבה—Jeremiah only; 7.20 (with חמתי); 17.27 (with הצתי אש); אין מכבה appears in Jer. 4.4 and 21.12.

21. The Chronicler substitutes ותתך (will be poured out) for ונצתה (will be kindled); more significant perhaps is the substitution of אלות (curses) for דברי (words) in v. 16 (cf. 2 Chron. 34.24).

22. The construct term in a construct chain is usually taken to be definite, but not always, e.g., 2 Sam. 23.11: חֶלְקַת הַשָּׂדֶה, 'a plot of ground' (cf. GKC, §127e).

23. Eissfeldt, *The Old Testament: An Introduction*, p. 227.

24. N. Lohfink has discovered similar patterns in Deuteronomy 5–11; see his *Das Hauptgebot* (Rome: Pontifical Biblical Institute, 1963), pp. 67, 181-83.

25. סֵפֶר הַתּוֹרָה in 2 Kgs 22.8; see below.

between the two.[26] So whatever the more precise meaning of each term might have been, it is clear that in this context the author would have us take all three terms as being interchangeable. The only intrusion in the system is סֵפֶר הַתּוֹרָה in 31.26. Is this meant to be a direct link to the סֵפֶר הַתּוֹרָה in 2 Kgs 22.8? I think so, in which case the identification is then complete: *Deuteronomy 32 is the scroll that Hilkiah found in the temple.*

We have thus found a way out of our impasse. By locating the scroll in Deuteronomy 32 we are free to see the prohibitions in Deuteronomy 1–28 influencing the activity of 628 BCE, which according to the Chronicler was the year the purge took place. The only casualty, of course, is the scheme given by the DH. We must therefore return to 2 Kings 22–23 to see what explanation, if any, can be given for the misplacement of the purge in DH's sequence of events.

The passage out of order is 23.4-20. The purge there described took place six years earlier (2 Chron. 34.3-7). It appears then that 23.4-20 is a separate document or the rewriting of a separate document which the DH has incorporated into his larger narration.[27] This becomes a good working assumption, since we can then go on to discover the DH's intended structure for the whole even if we remain unable to judge his knowledge or lack of knowledge of the facts.

The DH intends to make the purge the *center* and *climax* of his narrative. We know that it is the climax just because of the space he gives it: a total of 17 verses compared to 5 by the Chronicler. But it is also the center. An analysis of the immediate context shows that it has been framed in the same way Deuteronomy 32 is framed. We note the distribution of key words:

2 Kings 22–23

סֵפֶר הַתּוֹרָה מָצָאתִי בְּבֵית יְהוָה	22.8
אֶת־דִּבְרֵי סֵפֶר הַתּוֹרָה	11
אֶת־כָּל־דִּבְרֵי סֵפֶר הַבְּרִית הַנִּמְצָא בְּבֵית יְהוָה	23.2
אֶת־דִּבְרֵי הַבְּרִית הַזֹּאת הַכְּתֻבִים עַל־הַסֵּפֶר הַזֶּה	3
Account of the Purge	4-20
כַּכָּתוּב עַל סֵפֶר הַבְּרִית הַזֶּה	21
אֶת־דִּבְרֵי הַתּוֹרָה הַכְּתֻבִים עַל־הַסֵּפֶר אֲשֶׁר מָצָא...בֵּית יְהוָה	24
כְּכֹל תּוֹרַת מֹשֶׁה	25

26. I say 'subtly' because in 31.9 it appears that Moses has written an earlier *torah*, which is referred to variously throughout chaps. 29–30. This *torah* is described as a covenant with curses in 29.20 [Eng. 21]. It is obvious, I think, that our editor(s) are not aiming for clarity here but rather ambiguity.

27. Lohfink likewise assumes earlier sources here; cf. 'Die Bundesurkunde des Königs Josias', *Biblica* 44 (1963), p. 265.

12. *The Lawbook of the Josianic Reform* 129

In the outer material the newly found scroll is called a תּוֹרָה or סֵפֶר הַתּוֹרָה (22.3-20; 23.24-25), while in the material immediately surrounding the purge it is called a סֵפֶר הַבְּרִית (23.1-3, 21-23).[28] Comparing this with Deuteronomy 31–32 we note that while the inner בְּרִית (covenant) is new,[29] the outer תּוֹרָה is the same. Does this suggest a single author for both 2 Kings 22–23 and Deuteronomy 31–32? Possibly, but we cannot of course be sure. What is clear is that the same kind of rhetoric is being employed in the framing of the two compositions.

We should note too that positioning the climax at the center instead of at the end is commonly done in literature of this period. It can be seen in the Jeremianic speeches,[30] and also in the book of Lamentations.[31] One has only to look at the Chronicler's account of the Josianic Reform to see the more conventional method of bringing things to a climax. As we mentioned earlier, the climax for him is the celebration of the Passover, and it comes at the end.

Norbert Lohfink has argued that there is yet another structure controlling this material in which the action of the king is central.[32] In 22.3-11 the king does penance; in 12-20 he is pardoned by Huldah; in 23.1-3 the king renews the covenant; and in 21-23 he celebrates the Passover in accordance with the renewed covenant. This also appears to be deliberately conceived, although the narrative must, in my judgment, be concluded at 23.25.[33] Verse 25 closes the account in much the same way that Deut. 34.10 closes the appendix of Deuteronomy:

2 Kgs 23.25   And *like him* (וְכָמֹהוּ) there was no king before him who turned to Yahweh with all his heart and with all his soul and with all his might, according to all the law of Moses, *nor* after him *did any arise* (לֹא־קָם) *like him* (כָּמֹהוּ).

Deut. 34.10   And there has not arisen (וְלֹא־קָם) a prophet since in Israel *like Moses* (כְּמֹשֶׁה) whom Yahweh knew face to face.

---

28. 'Die Bundesurkunde des Königs Josias', pp. 285-88.
29. Lohfink ('Die Bundesurkunde des Königs Josias', p. 280) calls the scroll 'die alte Bundesurkunde'. Note in addition references to 'my covenant' in Deut. 31.16, 20 and 'ark of the covenant' in 31.9, 25-26.
30. Lundbom, *Jeremiah: A Study of Ancient Hebrew Rhetoric*, pp. 69, 86, 89, 95 [1997, pp. 92, 114, 118. 126].
31. Norman K. Gottwald, 'Lamentations', *Int* 9 (1955), p. 330.
32. 'Die Bundesurkunde des Königs Josias', pp. 267-71.
33. Lohfink (p. 267) takes 23.22-23 to form an inclusio with 22.3 on the basis of the repetition of 'in the eighteenth year of King Josiah'. Admittedly this is plausible, but I opt instead for 23.25 being the close because vv. 24-25 refer to the scroll as *torah* and round out our rhetorical structure. Also v. 25 concludes very much like Deut. 34.10; see discussion to follow.

It seems clear that the DH is using criteria other than chronology in the structuring of his account. This appears to be about all we can say. Whether he broke chronology knowingly or unknowingly remains unanswerable. But we do at least know how he structured his work and where he meant the emphasis to lie.

It would be tempting to speculate further about the dates of the respective compositions, but that will take more research. I might say, however, that the appendix of chaps. 29–34 appears to me to be a contribution to Deuteronomy from the Josianic Reform. And by calling the newly-found scroll a 'torah', the editor can claim to rank this appendix with the rest of Deuteronomy 1–28, which is also Moses' 'torah' (Deut. 1.5; 4.44).

One final point. The identification of Deuteronomy 32 with the temple scroll clears up to some extent the problematic relationship between the Josianic Reform and Jeremiah. We have always wanted to establish a more direct connection between the two, and that is now possible. William Holladay has shown that Deuteronomy 32 had a great influence on the poetry of Jeremiah,[34] which means that the prophet was influenced precisely by the scroll that was found in the temple.[35]

---

34. Holladay, 'Jeremiah and Moses: Further Observations', pp. 18-21.

35. In my view Jer. 15.16 contains a recollection of the finding of the scroll: 'Thy words were found and I ate them...' (cf. 'Jeremiah and Moses, Further Observations', p. 23). I do not, however, accept Holladay's low chronology (call = 609 BCE), which implies a 13 year gap between the finding and the eating. It appears rather that Jeremiah's feelings of inner joy and social isolation *occur immediately after* the scroll has been discovered (vv. 16b-17). Also, since Deut. 18.18 is no longer to be taken as part of the lost *Urdeuteronomium*, there is less need to posit a low chronology; Deut. 18.18 was easily accessible to Jeremiah in 627 BCE (cf. Holladay, 'The Background of Jeremiah's Self-Understanding: Moses, Samuel, and Psalm 22', *JBL* 83 [1964], pp. 154-61).

Chapter 13

STRUCTURE IN THE SONG OF MOSES
(DEUTERONOMY 32.1-43)*

The modern view that the Song of Moses (Deut. 32.1-43) is poetry finds support in the medieval codices (M^A, M^L) where the text is written stichometrically. This is not the case with the Blessing of Moses (Deuteronomy 33), which appears in normal three-column prose (33.2-8 also in 4QpaleoDeut^r).[1] The Song has also turned up in stichometric formatting in some Qumran fragments (4QDeut^b, 4QDeut^c, 4QpaleoDeut^r, 4QDeut^q), indicating that already in antiquity it was taken to be poetry, or discourse akin to poetry. Josephus (*Ant.* 4.8.44), wanting to commend the composition to a Greek audience, said the Song was written in hexameter verse. George Adam Smith[2] noted in the Song many instances of *qina* (3.2) rhythm, e.g., in vv. 11, 14, 16, 21, 23(?), 24-25, 29, 30-32, 34, 36, 39, 41. *Biblia hebraica*, as well as all the modern English Versions, print the Song as poetry.

Early critical scholars were not much interested in finding a structure in the Song of Moses, focused as they were on questions of date, authorship, and provenance. Kampenhausen,[3] however, did identify vv. 1-3 as an introduction. Hebrew Bibles of the time contained no section markings, which were later found to be present in M^L, M^A, and also in the Qumran fragments. M^L lacks sections in other Old Testament poetry, e.g., Exodus 15; Numbers 23–24; and Judges 5. M^L and M^A delimit the Song only in its entirety, having a *petuḥah* before v. 1 and another *petuḥah* after v. 43.

S.R. Driver called vv. 1-3 of the Song an exordium, taking v. 43 to be a corresponding conclusion.[4] Subsequent scholars have largely agreed,

---

* Shorter version of a paper read at the Biblical Colloquium West in San Diego, CA, on February 18, 2006, published in my *Deuteronomy* commentary (Eerdmans, 2013).

1. Patrick W. Skehan *et al.*, *Qumran Cave 4. IV* (DJD, 9; Oxford: Clarendon Press, 1992), p. 148.

2. George Adam Smith, *The Early Poetry of Israel in its Physical and Social Origins* (London: Henry Frowde, Oxford University Press, 1912), p. 22.

3. Adolf Kamphausen, *Das Lied Moses Deut. 32, 1-43* (Leipzig: F.A. Brockhaus, 1862), p. 1.

4. S.R. Driver, *A Critical and Exegetical Commentary on Deuteronomy* (ICC; Edinburgh: T. & T. Clark, 1895), pp. 348-49, 80.

some recognizing the proclivity of ancient Hebrew poets to balance the end with the beginning.[5] However, most stop short of identifying stanzas in the Song, making their divisions only for the sake of convenience.[6] Many divide the Song—if they divide it at all—on the basis of content, which can be done reasonably well since the flow of thought is not in any real doubt.

A modest advance in finding additional structure in the Song—more than simply introduction and conclusion—must be credited once again to S.R. Driver, who, as Deuteronomy editor for the 1905 edition of *Biblia hebraica* (BH^1), is presumably the one responsible for indenting lines at vv. 4, 7, 10, 15, 19, 23, 28, 34, 39, and 43. This created de facto units, suggesting indirectly, if not directly, that the Song contained an introduction, a body of 8 stanzas, and a conclusion. The RSV, for whom James Muilenburg was poetry editor,[7] delineated the same units as *Biblia hebraica*, with one exception: it did not break between vv. 6 and 7, taking vv. 4-9 to be a single unit. The Song, then, according to the RSV, can be said to contain the following structure:

Introduction	vv. 1-3
Stanza I	vv. 4-9
Stanza II	vv. 10-14
Stanza III	vv. 15-18
Stanza IV	vv. 19-22
Stanza V	vv. 23-27
Stanza VI	vv. 28-33
Stanza VII	vv. 34-38
Stanza VIII	vv. 39-42
Conclusion	v. 43

Subsequent English Versions have more or less followed the lead of *Biblia hebraica* and RSV in marking internal divisions, which are indicated by blank lines left between verses. But there are variations. The following chart shows where breaks are made *after* the verse in BH^1 and a select number of modern English Versions. The NEB and NAB, because they have gone their own way, are not included:

---

5. James Muilenburg, 'Form Criticism and Beyond', *JBL* 88 (1969), p. 9.
6. G.A. Smith, *The Book of Deuteronomy* (CBSC; Cambridge: Cambridge University Press, 1918), 343; G.E. Wright, 'The Lawsuit of God: A Form-Critical Study of Deuteronomy 32', in *Israel's Prophetic Heritage* (Essays in Honor of James Muilenburg; ed. Bernhard W. Anderson and Walter Harrelson; New York: Harper & Bros., 1962), p. 34.
7. Muilenburg, 'The Poetry of the Old Testament', in *An Introduction to the Revised Standard Version of the Old Testament* (ed. Luther A. Weigle; New York: Thomas Nelson and Sons, 1952), pp. 62-70.

13. Structure in the Song of Moses (Deuteronomy 32.1-43)

	BH¹	RSV	JB	NJV	NIV	NRSV	REB	NJB
v. 2					x		x	
v. 3	x	x	x	x		x		x
v. 4					x		x	
v. 6	x			x	x			
v. 7							x	
v. 9	x	x	x	x	x	x	x	x
v. 11								x
v. 12				x	x		x	
v. 14	x	x	x	x	x		x	x
v. 18	x	x		x	x	x	x	
v. 22	x	x			x		x	
v. 27	x	x		x	x	x	x	
v. 31				x				
v. 33	x	x			x	x		
v. 35				x	x	x		
v. 36							x	
v. 38	x	x			x	x		
v. 39							x	
v. 42	x	x	x	x	x	x	x	x

The units delineated in RSV can be confirmed and refined by rhetorical analysis, which consists in paying attention to climactic and ballast lines, repeated words and particles in strategic collocations, chiasms, partial chiasms, inclusios, rhetorical questions, and shifts to direct address. Then a syllable count of the units, which will be carried out following the rhetorical analysis, points to a poem having an introduction, 8 stanzas balanced in 4 pairs, and a conclusion. This structure will be seen to correlate well with the thematic development in the song. First, the rhetorical analysis.

Rhetorical Analysis

Climactic and Ballast Lines

Muilenburg noted that lines of Hebrew poetry often appear in well-defined clusters, each possessing their own identity, integrity, and structure. These he called 'strophes' or 'stanzas'.[8] Stanzas sometimes conclude with 'climactic' or 'ballast' lines, which are weighty bicolons or tricolons bringing the discourse to a dramatic conclusion. Muilenburg learned about ballast lines from George Adam Smith, who in his *Schweich Lectures* of 1910 called attention to 'a longer, heavier line, generally at the end of a strophe...similar to what the Germans call the "Schwellvers" in old German ballads'.[9] Smith found instances of this heavy line in the Song of Deborah and the Song of Moses, noting also that such lines may correspond to a change in theme.

---

8. Muilenburg, 'Form Criticism and Beyond', pp. 9-12.
9. Smith, *The Early Poetry of Israel*, pp. 20-21, 77.

In Deuteronomy 32, Smith identified the tricolon in v. 14, which ends a stanza, as a ballast line:

> *sons of Bashan and he-goats*   v. 14b
>   *with the choicest grains of wheat*
>   *yes, blood of the grape, you drank wine!*

Two other ballast lines in the Song of Moses were the final bicolons of vv. 42 and 43, both of which end stanzas. In the case of v. 43b, the bicolon concludes the entire Song:

> *From the blood of slain and captive*   v. 42b
>   *from the long-haired head of the enemy*
>
>   *yes, he will return vengeance to his adversaries*   v. 43b
> *And atone for his land, his people.*

In the poetry of Second Isaiah, Muilenburg delineated stanzas on the basis of climactic lines that lifted up the name of Yahweh.[10] The stanza in Isa. 47.1-4, he said, reaches its climax in these words:

> *Our redeemer—Yahweh of hosts is his name—*   Isa. 47.4
>   *is the Holy One of Israel.*

Other stanzas in Second Isaiah conclude with a climactic 'Yahweh of hosts is his name' (Isa. 48.2; 54.5, 15). In Isa. 44.23, the prophet concludes a stanza with a shout:[11]

> *For Yahweh has redeemed Jacob*   Isa. 44.23c
>   *and in Israel will glorify himself.*

Climactic lines naming Yahweh occur frequently in other OT poetry, e.g., in Exod. 15.3; Amos 4.13; 5.8; 9.6; Hos. 12.6 [Eng. 12.5]; Jer. 10.16 = 51.19; and Isa. 51.15-16.

Here in the Song of Moses, some of the bicolons naming Yahweh appear to be climactic lines coming at the end of stanzas. Concluding the exordium is this confident affirmation:

> *For the name of Yahweh I proclaim*   v. 3
>   *ascribe greatness to our God!*

Another climactic bicolon naming Yahweh and his covenant partner occurs in v. 9:

---

10. Muilenburg, 'Isaiah', in *IB*, V (ed. George A. Buttrick; New York: Abingdon Press, 1956), pp. 544-635.
11. Muilenburg, 'Isaiah', pp. 392, 510.

13. *Structure in the Song of Moses (Deuteronomy 32.1-43)* 135

> *Indeed Yahweh's portion is his people*   v. 9
>   *Jacob, his alloted inheritance.*

Yahweh is named also in v. 27, again at the conclusion of a stanza in the Song:

>   *lest they say: Our hand is raised up*   v. 27b
> *And not Yahweh has done all this.*

If we read the first colon of v. 37 with 4QDeut^q and the LXX, we have another occurrence of 'Yahweh' beginning a stanza in the Song that functions as a conclusion (vv. 37-38). The cohortatives in v. 38b, which disparage the no-gods, close the stanza and are its climax:

> *Then Yahweh will say: Where is his god*   vv. 37-38
>   *the rock in whom they took refuge?*
> *Choice portions of his sacrifices they ate*
>   *they drank wine of their libations*
> *Let them arise and let them help you*
>   *let it be your protection!*

Muilenburg did not believe that climactic lines always come at the end of stanzas. He said they 'may indeed appear at several junctures within a pericope'.[12] Here in the Song, we find that sometimes Yahweh is named climactically at midpoint in the stanza:

> *Do you repay Yahweh thus?*   v. 6a
>   *O people foolish and unwise!*

> *Yahweh alone guided him*   v. 12
>   *and no foreign god was with him.*

> *unless indeed their Rock had sold them*   v. 30
>   *and Yahweh had delivered them up?*

> *Indeed Yahweh will vindicate his people*   v. 36
>   *and feel sorry over his servants.*

In v. 19 a bicolon naming Yahweh begins a stanza:

> *So Yahweh saw and spurned*   v. 19
>   *because of the provocation of his sons and daughters.*

At the beginning of the Song's final stanza (vv. 39-42), Yahweh names himself. Here the string of divine asseverations are strengthened by five occurrences of the first-person pronoun:

12. Muilenburg, 'Form Criticism and Beyond', p. 9.

> *See now indeed I, I* (אֲנִי אֲנִי) *am he*   vv. 39-40
>   *and there is no god with me*
> *I* (אֲנִי), *I kill, and I make alive*
>   *I wound, and I* (אֲנִי), *I heal*
>   *and none can rescue from my hand*
> *Indeed I lift up my hand to heaven*
>   *and I say: As I* (אָנֹכִי) *live forever.*

Muilenburg noted that in Second Isaiah emphatic personal pronouns ('I', 'you', etc.) often begin and end stanzas. Beginning (and throughout) the grand poem of Isa. 44.24–45.13 is the divine asseveration, 'I am Yahweh', also the first-person pronouns אֲנִי and אָנֹכִי that emphasize the divine person and divine action. These pronouns occur no fewer than ten times in the divine speech.[13] Looking here in the Song at the distribution of the divine name 'Yahweh', also at the divine asseverations in vv. 39-40, we see that all 10 occurrences appear in significant collocations: at the beginning, in the middle, or at the end of stanzas.

Repetitions in Strategic Collocations

Appearing in strategic collocations within the Song are repeated words and particles. Muilenburg said with reference to literary compositions of ancient Israel: 'Repeated words or lines do not appear haphazardly or fortuitously, but rather in rhetorically significant collocatiions'.[14] He noted as particularly striking threefold repetitions in a single stanza, citing the thrice-repeated 'come' (לְכוּ) in Isa. 55.1, and the thrice-repeated 'shame' (בוֹשׁ) in Ps. 25.1-3. Both occur at the beginning of stanzas. Sometimes threefold repetitions come at midpoint in the stanza, e.g., the repeated 'again' (עוֹד) in Jer. 31.4-5, which functions as anaphora.[15]

Muilenburg believed that even little words take on importance in Hebrew poetry and Hebrew rhetoric. In Exodus 15, a repeated 'till' (עַד) creates anaphora in the poem's final refrain,[16] where also Yahweh is named:

> ***till*** *your people, Yahweh, pass by*   Exod. 15.16cd
>   ***till*** *the people pass by whom you have purchased.*

---

13. Muilenburg, 'Isaiah', pp. 391-93, 516-28.
14. Muilenburg, 'Form Criticism and Beyond', pp. 16-17.
15. Jack R. Lundbom, *Jeremiah 21–36* (AB, 21B; New York: Doubleday, 2004), p. 412.
16. Muilenburg, 'A Liturgy on the Triumphs of Yahweh', in *Studia biblica et semitica Theodoro Vriezen in dedicata* (ed. W.C. van Unnik and A.S. van der Woude; Wageningen: H.V. Veenman en Zonen, 1966), p. 248.

13. *Structure in the Song of Moses (Deuteronomy 32.1-43)* 137

Here in the Song, a repeated 'from' (מִ) creates anaphora in the final stanza:

> ***From*** *the blood of slain and captive*   v. 42
>   ***from*** *the long-haired head of the enemy.*

This same kind of repetition occurs in Jer. 4.26b; 9.18b [Eng. 9.19b]; and 25.38b.[17] In Jer. 4.26b Yahweh is named.

In his celebrated lecture, 'Form Criticism and Beyond', Muilenburg said this about particles:

> Particles play a major role in all Hebrew poetry and reveal the rhetorical cast of Semitic literary mentality in a striking way. Chief among them is the deictic and emphatic particle כִּי, which performs a vast variety of functions and is susceptible of many different renderings, above all, perhaps, the function of motivation where it is understood causally. It is not surprising, therefore, that it should appear in strategic collocations, such as the beginnings and endings of the strophes.[18]

Muilenburg found כִּי beginning poetic stanzas in Isa. 34.2a, 5a, 6c, and 8a.[19] Sometimes the particle concluded stanzas or entire poems, assuming what Muilenburg calls a motivational function, e.g., Ps. 1.6. The particle כִּי closes stanzas and entire oracles in Jeremiah, e.g., Jer. 4.6b, 8b; and 5.5b, 6c.[20]

The particle כִּי occurs 15 times in the Song of Moses, some usages of which appear to have the rhetorical function Muilenburg attributes to it. It begins ballast lines in vv. 3 and 9, the former concluding the introduction (vv. 1-3), and the latter concluding a stanza of the Song (vv. 4-9). The particle also begins a double bicolon that concludes another stanza (vv. 19-22):

> ***For*** (כִּי) *a fire is kindled in my anger*   v. 22
>   *and it will burn to the depths of Sheol*
> *Yes, it will consume the earth and its yield*
>   *and set ablaze the mountains' foundations.*

In two cases, the particle כִּי begins or appears near the beginning of a stanza:

---

17. Lundbom, *Jeremiah 1–20* (AB, 21A; New York: Doubleday, 1999; New Haven: Yale University Press, 2009), pp. 356, 558; *Jeremiah 21–36*, p. 277.
18. Muilenburg, 'Form Criticism and Beyond', pp. 13-14.
19. Muilenburg, 'The Linguistic and Rhetorical Usages of the Particle כִּי in the Old Testament', *HUCA* 32 (1961), pp. 148-49; 'Form Criticism and Beyond', p. 14.
20. Lundbom, *Jeremiah 1–20*, pp. 332, 334, 372, 374.

> **For** (כִּי) *a nation bereft of counsel are they* v. 28
> *and there is no understanding in them.*
>
> *See now* **indeed** (כִּי) *I, I am he* v. 39a
> *and there is no god with me...*
> **Indeed** (כִּי) *I lift up my hand to heaven* v. 40
> *and I say: As I live forever.*

More striking is a threefold repetition of כִּי occurring at midpoint in the stanza of vv. 34-38:

> *unless* **indeed** (כִּי) *their Rock had sold them* v. 30b
> *and Yahweh had delivered them up?*
> **Indeed** (כִּי) *their rock is not like our Rock* v. 31
> *even our enemies being assessors*
> **Indeed** (כִּי) *their vine is from the vine of Sodom* v. 32a
> *and from the terraces of Gomorrah.*

At midpoint in the very next stanza, vv. 34-38, another כִּי repeats three times:

> **Indeed** (כִּי) *the day of their disaster is near* v. 35b
> *and things prepared are hastening to him*
> **Indeed** (כִּי) *Yahweh will vindicate his people* v. 36
> *and feel sorry over his servants*
> **Indeed** (כִּי) *he will see that support is gone*
> *and none remains bond or free.*

So out of the 15 occurrences of כִּי in the Song, 11 manifest a rhetorical function, and should be taken as contributing to the Song's structure.

Nils Lund discovered that balancing repetitions and amplifications frequently occur at the center of large chiastic structures, where they have a climactic function.[21] This phenomenon is now amply documented in the poetry of Jeremiah, for example, in Jer. 2.5-9, 5.1-8, and 51.34-45.[22] Here in the Song, the balanced repetitions, correlative terms, and entire colons at the center of vv. 19-22 are noted by all commentators:

> *They, they made me jealous with a no-god* v. 21
> *they provoked me with their nothings*
> *So I, I will make them jealous with a no-people*
> *with a foolish nation I will provoke them.*

---

21. Nils W. Lund, *Chiasmus in the New Testament* (Chapel Hill, NC: University of North Carolina Press, 1942 [reprint: Peabody, MA: Hendrickson Publishers, 1992]), pp. 40-41, 44.

22. Lundbom, *Jeremiah 1–20*, pp. 256-57, 371-73; *Jeremiah 37–52* (AB, 21C; New York: Doubleday, 2004), pp. 469-72.

13. *Structure in the Song of Moses (Deuteronomy 32.1-43)* 139

Chiasms, Partial Chiasms, and Inclusio

According to Muilenburg,[23] it is the 'diversities which give [Hebrew] poetry its distinctive and artistic character'. One of these diversities is chiasmus, which most commonly consists of inverted syntax or inverted keyword structures. Chiasms vary the monotony of repetition and parallelism, the two dominant characteristics of Hebrew poetry.[24]

Here in the Song, the climactic bicolon closing a stanza in v. 9 contains a keyword chiasmus:

> *Indeed Yahweh's portion is/his people*   v. 9
>   *Jacob/his alloted inheritance.*

A syntactic chiasmus in v. 18 closes another stanza:

> *The Rock that begot you/you neglected*   v. 18
>   *and you forgot/the God who bore you in travail.*

Concluding the entire Song in v. 43 (MT), is this keyword chiasmus:

> *Give **his people** ringing acclaim, O nations*   v. 43
>   *for the blood of his servants **he will avenge***
>   *yes, **he will return vengeance** to his adversaries*
> *And atone for his land, **his people**.*

The longer reading of v. 43 in 4QDeut^{q}[25] has the same keyword chiasmus:

> *Give **his people** ringing acclaim, O heavens*   v. 43
>   *and worship him, all you gods!*
> *For the blood of his sons **he will avenge***
>   *yes, **he will return vengeance** to his adversaries*
> *And to those who hate him he will requite*
>   *and atone for the land of **his people**.*

Chiastic bicolons close segments in other OT poetry, e.g., Gen. 4.24 (The Song of Lamech),[26] Jer. 2.9, 13, and 4.22c.[27]

A partial chiasmus concludes a stanza of the Song in v. 27. Here, at the center of a double bicolon, a repeated particle also creates anaphora:

---

    23. Muilenburg, 'Form Criticism and Beyond', p. 10.
    24. Muilenburg, 'A Study in Hebrew Rhetoric: Repetition and Style', in *Congress Volume Copenhagen* (VTSup, 1; Leiden: E.J. Brill, 1953), pp. 97-111; 'Form Criticism and Beyond', p. 10.
    25. Eugene Ulrich *et al.*, *Qumran Cave 4 IX* (DJD, 14; Oxford: Clarendon Press, 1995), p. 141.
    26. Robert Alter, *The Art of Biblical Poetry* (New York: Basic Books, 1985), p. 7.
    27. Lundbom, *Jeremiah 1–20*, pp. 262, 266, 355.

> *Except I feared the provocation of the enemy*   v. 27
>   *__lest__ his adversaries should misjudge*
>   *__lest__ they say: Our hand is raised up*
> *And not Yahweh has done all this.*

Similar structures effect closure in Jer. 5.10b-11, 9.21 [Eng. 9.22], and 46.23.[28] In Jer. 6.8, 8.13, and 17.1, partial chiasms begin poetic units.[29]

Two stanzas of the Song conclude with a keyword inclusio, which is a repetition occurring only at the beginning and end of a unit. The stanza in vv. 4-9 concludes with this inclusio:

> *When the Most High gave the nations an __inheritance__*   v. 8
>   *when he separated the sons of man*
> *He fixed the boundaries of peoples*
>   *to the number of the sons of God*
> *Indeed Yahweh's portion is his people*   v. 9
>   *Jacob, his allotted __inheritance__.*

The stanza in vv. 28-33 concludes with a keyword inclusio in a double bicolon:

> *Its grapes are grapes of __poison__*   v. 32b
>   *its clusters are bitter*
> *Their wine is the venom of serpents*   v. 33
>   *yes, the cruel __poison__ of vipers.*

A similar keyword inclusio concludes a stanza in Jer. 8.7.[30]

All throughout the Bible are larger keyword chiasms,[31] many of which occur in the prose and poetry of Jeremiah.[32] Two fine examples are in Jer. 2.5-9 and 5.1-8 where, in both cases, the chiasmus is coterminous with the limits of the literary unit.[33]

Here in the Song, a large keyword chiasmus takes in all but 15a of the stanza in vv. 15-18. Keywords name Israel's God at beginning and end, and the no-gods in the center. Then in the final bicolon, as we noted earlier, a syntactic chiasmus brings closure. In this final bicolon, 'Rock' and 'God' invert from 'God' and 'Rock' in v. 15b:

---

28. Lundbom, *Jeremiah 1–20*, pp. 387, 559; *Jeremiah 37–52*, p. 220.
29. Lundbom, *Jeremiah 1–20*, pp. 421-22, 521, 775.
30. Lundbom, *Jeremiah 1–20*, p. 506.
31. Nils W. Lund, 'The Presence of Chiasmus in the Old Testament', *AJSL* 46 (1930), pp. 104-26; 'Chiasmus in the Psalms', *AJSL* 49 (1933), pp. 281-312; *Chiasmus in the New Testament*.
32. Lundbom, *A Study in Ancient Hebrew Rhetoric* (SBLDS, 18; Missoula, MT: Society of Biblical Literature and Scholars Press, 1975), pp. 61-112 [2nd edn; Winona Lake, IN: Eisenbrauns, 1997, pp. 82-146]
33. Lundbom, *Jeremiah 1–20*, pp. 256-57, 371-73.

a	*Then he abandoned the **God** who made him*	v. 15b
	*and took to be foolish the **Rock** of his salvation*	
	b *They made him jealous/with **strangers***	v. 16
	*with **abominations**/they provoked him*	
	c *They sacrificed to demons/**no-gods***	v. 17
	gods/they had not known	
	b' ***New ones** recently come in*	
	*your fathers were not awed by **them***	
a'	*The **Rock** that begot you/you neglected*	v. 18
	*and you forgot/the **God** who bore you in travail.*	

Rhetorical Questions

Rhetorical questions also occur in strategic collocations,[34] beginning a discourse unit, ending a unit, or coming in the middle. Rhetorical questions—sometimes a pair—begin psalms and stanzas of psalms (Pss. 2.1; 10.1; 15.1; 35.17; 49.6 [Eng. 49.5]; Ps. 52.3 [Eng. 52.1]; 58.2 [Eng. 58.1]; and elsewhere). They also begin oracles and stanzas of oracles in Jeremiah (Jer. 2.5a, 29; 5.7a). In Jer. 4.21, a rhetorical question ends a unit of poetry. In Jer. 5.7a, the question, 'Why then will I pardon you?', is the conclusion to which the entire oracle has been building.

The Song contains four rhetorical questions, all of which come at the beginning, in the middle, or at the end of stanzas. The rhetorical question in v. 34 begins a stanza:

Is not this stored up with me	v. 34
sealed in my storehouses?	

In vv. 6 and 30 rhetorical questions occur in the middle of stanzas:

Do you repay Yahweh thus?	v. 6
O people foolish and unwise!	
Is not he your father? he created you!	
He, he made you and he established you!	

How could one chase a thousand	v. 30
and two put thousands to flight	
unless indeed their Rock had sold them	
and Yahweh had delivered them up?	

And in vv. 37-38a, a rhetorical question concludes the stanza:

Then Yahweh will say: Where is his god	vv. 37-38a
the rock in whom they took refuge?	
Choice portions of his sacrifices they ate	
they drank wine of their libations.	

34. Muilenburg, 'Form Criticism and Beyond', p. 16.

Shift to Direct Address

In Jeremiah one sometimes observes at the end of an oracle, or in other discourse, a shift from the third person to the second person, making the discourse more direct. This occurs in Jer. 2.9, 5.31b, 12.13b, and 48.46. Jeremianic preaching manifests a 'rhetoric of descent', that is, it begins at a distance, and comes in close at the end.[35]

In the Song of Moses, a shift to the second person occurs at the end of the stanza in vv. 10-14, driving home the point that the Israelites became fat after their settlement in the land:

> *Curds of the herd and milk of the flock*   v. 14
>   *with the choicest of lambs and rams*
> *sons of Bashan and he-goats*
>   *with the choicest grains of wheat*
>   *yes, blood of the grape,* **you** *drank wine!*

At the end of the next stanza, vv. 15-18, is another shift to the second person:

> *New ones recently come in*   vv. 17b-18
>   **your** *fathers were not awed by them*
> *The Rock that begot* **you,** **you** *neglected*
>   *and* **you** *forgot the God who bore* **you** *in travail.*

Here second-person speech ending the stanza ties-in with second-person speech beginning the stanza, which is the tricolon lying outside the large chiasmus:

> *So Jacob ate and became sated*   v. 15a
>   *yes, Jeshurun got fat and kicked*
>   **you** *got fat,* **you** *grew thick,* **you** *became gorged.*

Another shift from third to second person concludes the stanza of vv. 34-38:

> *Let them arise and let them help* **you**   v. 38b
>   *let it be* **your** *protection!*

Von Rad said these shifts to the second person 'make the whole appear as a prophetic indictment'.[36]

---

35. Lundbom, *Jeremiah: A Study in Ancient Hebrew Rhetoric*, p. 116 [1997, p. 150].

36. Gerhard von Rad, *Deuteronomy* (OTL; London: SCM Press, 1966), p. 198.

Metrical Analysis

A structure in the Song of Moses consisting of an introduction, 8 stanzas, and a conclusion, well supported by rhetorical analysis, can now be corroborated and refined by metrical analysis carried on along the lines of David Noel Freedman's work in OT poetry. Freedman used syllable counting to analyze Exodus 15,[37] Psalms, Lamentations, and other biblical laments,[38] Deuteronomy 33,[39] and poems in Isaiah, Job, and elsewhere.[40] In his work on the 'Song of the Sea' in Exodus 15, he credited Muilenburg for having discovered refrain-like dividers, agreeing that they served as structural markers within the poem. Freedman then went on to do his own analysis, using a syllable counting method.

Freedman was not interested simply in counting syllables of colons, bicolons, and tricolons, although he did that. He believed something could be learned about Hebrew poetic composition by looking at syllable totals in larger units, where, not infrequently, symmetries turn up and internal structures can be seen with greater clarity. He noted that the Shakespearean sonnets have a total length of 140 syllables, plus or minus a syllable or two.

---

37. D.N. Freedman, 'The Song of the Sea', in *A Feeling of Celebration* [In Honor of James Muilenburg] (San Anselmo: San Francisco Theological Seminary, 1967); 'Strophe and Meter in Exodus 15', in *A Light unto My Path* (Essays in Honor of Jacob M. Myers; ed. Howard N. Bream *et al.*; Philadelphia: Temple University Press, 1974), pp. 163-203.

38. D.N. Freedman, 'The Structure of Psalm 137', in *Near Eastern Studies in Honor of William Foxwell Albright* (ed. Hans Goedicke; Baltimore: The Johns Hopkins University Press, 1971), pp. 187-205; 'Acrostics and Metrics in Hebrew Poetry', *HTR* 65 (1972), pp. 367-92; 'The Refrain in David's Lament over Saul and Jonathan', in *Ex orbe religionum*, I (Studia Geo Widengren; Leiden: E.J. Brill, 1972), pp. 115-26; 'Divine Names and Titles in Early Hebrew Poetry', pp. 55-107; 'Psalm 113 and the Song of Hannah', in *H.L. Ginsberg Volume* (Eretz Israel, 14; ed. Menahem Haran; Jerusalem: Israel Exploration Society, 1978), pp. 56-70; 'Acrostic Poems in the Hebrew Bible: Alphabetic and Otherwise', *CBQ* 48 (1986), pp. 408-31; 'Another Look at Biblical Hebrew Poetry', in *Directions in Biblical Hebrew Poetry* (ed. Elaine R. Follis; JSOTSup, 40; Sheffield: Sheffield Academic Press, 1987), pp. 11-28; 'Patterns in Psalms 25 and 34', in *Priests, Prophets and Scribes* (ed. Eugene Ulrich *et al.*; JSOTSup, 149; Sheffield: Sheffield Academic Press, 1992), pp. 125-38.

39. D.N. Freedman, 'The Poetic Structure of the Framework of Deuteronomy 33', in *The Bible World* (ed. Gary Rendsburg *et al.*; New York: Ktav and The Institute of Hebrew Culture and Education of New York University, 1980), pp. 25-46.

40. D.N. Freedman, 'The Structure of Job 3', *Biblica* 49 (1968), pp. 503-508; 'Early Israelite History in the Light of Early Israelite Poetry', in *Unity and Diversity: Essays in the History, Literature and Religion of the Ancient Near East* (ed. H. Goedicke and J.J.M. Roberts; Baltimore: The Johns Hopkins University Press, 1975), pp. 3-35; 'The Structure of Isaiah 40.1-11', in *Perspectives on Language and Text* (ed. Edgar W. Conrad and Edward G. Newing; Winona Lake, IN: Eisenbrauns, 1987), pp. 167-93.

This is because they have 14 lines in iambic pentameter, which means regular lines adding up to a predictable total. But, he says:

> What is different about Hebrew poetry is that, while the sum-total is predictable within a very narrow range, the total is not based upon the repetition of lines of the same length, as in the case of the English sonnet. Unless we engage in wholesale emendation and improvement of the text, we must recognize it as a basic fact of Hebrew poetry that individual lines (and stanzas) very considerably in length.[41]

Freedman found that larger, fixed syllable totals turn up also in Japanese poetry.

In counting syllables in the Song of Moses I follow Freedman[42] in using the vocalized Hebrew of MT with the following exceptions: (1) segholates are taken to be monosyllabic; (2) the *furtive pataḥ* is not counted; and (3) the compound *shewa* after laryngeals is not counted. There is one occurrence of the relative pronoun אֲשֶׁר in the poem, beginning v. 38a. It probably does not belong there, but the question is, where does it belong? Relative pronouns are rare in Hebrew poetry, although they do occur, for example, in Jer. 20.14-18.[43] Here in this poem, it could simply be excised, which is what Freedman does with a lone אֲשֶׁר in Deut. 33.29b.[44] My own preference is to relocate it after צוּר ('rock') in the prior line, where it makes sense in a colon that appears to be truncated. Support for this transfer comes from both 4QDeutᑫ and the LXX. In 4QDeutᑫ an אשר actually appears at this point in the text,[45] and the LXX has ἐφ' οἷς. This change, it should be noted, will have no effect on the total syllable count, since the אֲשֶׁר in MT is counted only once.

In four instances I have not followed the readings of MT. The first is in v. 8b, where I adopt the 4QDeutʲ reading 'sons of God' (בני אלוהים) over MT 'sons of Israel' (בְּנֵי יִשְׂרָאֵל). This presents no problem for a syllable count, since בני אלוהים and בְּנֵי יִשְׂרָאֵל are both 5 syllables. The LXX's 'angels of God' (ἀγγέλων θεοῦ), if it in fact translated the Hebrew מַלְאֲכֵי אֱלֹהִים, would be 6 syllables instead of 5. I also adopt, as most scholars do, the additional colon of Sam and LXX beginning v. 15a, 'So Jacob ate and became sated' (LXX καὶ ἔφαγεν Ιακωβ καὶ ἐνεπλήσθη). Its Hebrew equivalent, וַיֹּאכַל יַעֲקֹב וַיִּשְׂבַּע, adds 9 syllables to the count of MT. This colon was probably lost in MT due to haplography (homoeoarcton: ו...ו). I also adopt the readings of 4QDeutᑫ and LXX that add יהוה as a subject in v. 37. This

---

41. Freedman, 'Another Look at Biblical Hebrew Poetry', p. 19.
42. Freedman, 'Acrostics and Metrics in Hebrew Poetry', p. 369; 'The Poetic Structure of the Framework of Deuteronomy 33', p. 30.
43. Lundbom, 'The Double Curse in Jeremiah 20.14-18', *JBL* 104 (1985), pp. 591-92
44. Freedman, 'The Poetic Structure of the Framework of Deuteronomy 33', pp. 31-32.
45. Ulrich *et al.*, *Qumran Cave 4 IX*, p. 139.

increases the syllable count of the first colon by 2. Then, in the conclusion of v. 43, for the sake of argument, I adopt the LXX reading, which is 8 colons compared to 4 colons in MT, and 6 colons in 4QDeut^q. This gives an 8 colon conclusion, balancing the 8 colon introduction in vv. 1-3. Syllable counts of the 8 stanzas in the Song are then as follows:

	I		II
4	6 : 7	10	8 : 9
	8 : 6		10 : 9
5	8 : 7	11	6 : 7
6	8 : 7		9 : 8
	9 : 10		
		12	7 : 7
7	6 : 7		
	10 : 9	13	9 : 8
8	7 : 8		10 : 6
	7 : 8	14	8 : 8[46]
9	7 : 7		8 : 7 : 8
	———		———
	152		152

	III		IV
15	8 : 9 : 9	19	7 : 9
	8 : 9	20	10 : 7
16	7 : 8		7 : 6
17	9 : 7	21	7 : 7
	8 : 8		8 : 7
18	7 : 9	22	8 : 8
	7 : 9		
	———		———
	107		107

	V		VI
23	7 : 6	28	8 : 7
24	9 : 5	29	7 : 8
	9 : 8	30	7 : 9
25	6 : 7		8 : 6
	7 : 6	31	8 : 8
26	6 : 7	32	7 : 7
27	8 : 7		7 : 8
	9 : 8	33	7 : 7
	———		———
	115		119

46. The term וְאֵילִים ('and rams') beginning the next line in *BHS* is taken at the end of this line with most commentators.

	VII		VIII
34	8 : 7	39	10 : 8
35	6 : 6		7 : 8 : 7
	6 : 7	40	9 : 1111
36	7 : 8	41	8 : 8
	8 : 7		7 : 7
37	10 : 6[47]	42	6 : 7
38	9 : 6[48]		7 : 6
	8 : 7		
	116		116

The syllable count supports a poem consisting of 8 stanzas, indicating that the stanzas should be taken as 4 pairs. Paired stanzas have different totals from other paired stanzas, but each pair has identical or near-identical totals, which cannot be accidental. And with an 8-colon conclusion in v. 43 of the LXX, balancing an 8-colon introduction in vv. 1-3, the poem is seen to be entirely symmetrical.

The Song of Moses, with rhetorical features italicized and/or put in bold type, and its stanzas arranged in pairs, contains the following structure:

INTRODUCTION

¹Give ear, O heavens, and I will speak
    and let the earth hear the speech of my mouth
²Let my teaching drop like the rain
    let my speech distil like the dew
like raindrops upon grass
    and like showers upon green plants
³*For the name of* **Yahweh** *I proclaim*
    ascribe greatness to our God!

I

⁴The Rock, his work is perfect
  indeed all his ways are just
A God of faithfulness, and without wrong
  righteous and upright is he
⁵It acted corruptly toward him
    Is not their blemish his children's
      a generation perverted and crooked!
⁶*Do you repay* **Yahweh** *thus?*
    O people foolish and unwise!
Is not he your father? he created you!
    He, he made you and he established you!

II

¹⁰He found him in a wilderness land
  yes, in a howling desert waste
He encircled him, he took care of him
  he guarded him as the pupil of his eye
¹¹As an eagle who stirs up his nest
  over his young ones he hovers
he spreads out his wings, he takes him up
  he lifts him upon his pinion
¹²**Yahweh** *alone guided him*
  and no foreign god was with him
¹³He made him ride on earth's high places

47. Adding יהוה after the verb in the first colon with 4QDeutq; the LXX has κύριος. In the second colon the relative pronoun אֲשֶׁר is added after צוּר with 4QDeutq and the LXX.

48. Eliminating the initial אֲשֶׁר in MT as a reinsertion from v. 37.

13. Structure in the Song of Moses (Deuteronomy 32.1-43)

⁷Remember the days of old
    consider the years of many generations
Ask your father and he will inform you
    your elders, and they will tell you
⁸When the Most High gave the nations an *inheritance*
    when he separated the sons of man
He fixed the boundaries of peoples
    to the number of the sons of God
⁹*Indeed* **Yahweh's** *portion is/his people*
    Jacob/his alotted inheritance

and he ate the produce of the high country
    and he made him suck honey from the crags
    and oil from the flinty rock
¹⁴Curds of the herd and milk of the flock
    with the choicest of lambs and rams
sons of Bashan and he-goats
    with the choicest grains of wheat
    yes, blood of the grape, **you** *drank wine!*

III

¹⁵So Jacob ate and became sated
    yes, Jeshurun got fat and kicked

you got fat, **you** grew thick, **you** became gorged
Then he abandoned the **God** who made him
    and took to be foolish the **Rock** of his salvation
¹⁶They made him jealous/with **strangers**
    with **abominations**/they provoked him
¹⁷They sacrificed to demons/**no-gods**
    gods/they had not known
New ones recently come in
    your fathers were not awed by **them**
¹⁸*The* **Rock** *that begot* **you**/**you** *neglected*
    and **you** *forgot/the* **God** *who bore* **you** *in travail*

IV

¹⁹*So* **Yahweh** *saw and spurned*
    because of the provocation of his sons and daughters
²⁰And he said: I will hide my face from them
    I will see what their end will be
For a generation of perversities they are
    children in whom is no faithfulness
²¹*They, they made me jealous with a no-god*
    they provoked me with their nothings
So I, I will make them jealous with a no-people
    with a foolish nation I will provoke them
²²*For* a fire is kindled in my anger
    and it will burn to the depths of Sheol
Yes, it will consume the earth and its yield
    and set ablaze the mountains' foundations

V

²³I will heap evils upon him
    my arrows I will exhaust against them
²⁴Smiting famine
    and burning plague
        and bitter pestilence
and the teeth of beasts I will send against them
    with venom of crawlers in the dust
²⁵Outside a sword shall bereave
    and in the chambers terror
both young man and maiden
    nursing child with the gray-haired man
²⁶I thought: I will strike them down
    I will make their memory cease from humankind
²⁷*Except I feared provocation of the enemy*
    lest his adversaries should misjudge
    lest they say: Our hand is raised up
And not **Yahweh** *has done all this.*

VI

²⁸*For* a nation bereft of counsel are they
    and there is no undertanding in them
²⁹If they were wise, they would consider this
    they would discern their end

³⁰*How could one chase a thousand*
    and two put thousands to flight
unless indeed their Rock had sold them
    and **Yahweh** *had delivered them up?*
³¹*Indeed* their rock is not like our Rock
    even our enemies being assessors
³²*Indeed* their vine is from the vine of Sodom
    and from the terraces of Gomorrah
Its grapes are grapes of *poison*
    its clusters are bitter
³³Their wine is the venom of serpents
    yes, the cruel *poison* of vipers

VII	VIII
³⁴*Is not this stored up with me*	³⁹*See now indeed I, I am he*
sealed in my storehouses?	*and there is no god with me*
³⁵Vengeance is mine, and repayment	*I, I kill, and I make alive*
for the time when their foot shall slip	*I wound, and I, I heal*
Indeed the day of their disaster is near	*and none can rescue from my hand*
and things prepared are hastening to him	⁴⁰*Indeed I lift up my hand to heaven*
³⁶*Indeed **Yahweh** will vindicate his people*	*and I say, As I live forever*
and feel sorry over his servants	⁴¹If I sharpen my gleaming sword
Indeed he will see that support is gone	and my hand takes hold on judgment
and none remains bond or free	I will return vengeance to my adversaries
³⁷*Then **Yahweh** will say: Where is his god*	and to those who hate me, I will repay
the rock in whom they took refuge?	⁴²*I will make my arrows drunk from blood*
³⁸Choice portions of his sacrifices they ate	*and my sword shall consume flesh*
they drank wine of their libations	*From the blood of slain and captive*
*Let them arise and let them help **you***	*from the long-haired head of the enemy*
*let it be **your** protection!*	

CONCLUSION

⁴³*Rejoice, O heavens, with him*
   let all the sons of God worship him
Rejoice, O nations, with his people
   and let all the angels of God confirm for him
For the blood of his sons he avenges
   and he will avenge and repay judgment to his enemies
And those who hate he will repay
   and the Lord will purify the land of his people

The question may be asked why the stanzas of the Song are grouped in pairs. Is such a structure crafted for antiphonal singing, such as we may have indicated in Deut. 27.11-14, where six Israelite tribes bless the people from Mount Gerizim, and six tribes speak curses from Mount Ebal? There the Levites are apparently at the center, in the Shechem plain, directing the recitation. We do not know. What may be pointed out, however, is that 'pairing' of a similar nature occurs elsewhere in the Hebrew Bible. It has long been noted that in the P account of Creation, the first three days of creation are paired with the second three days, with the seventh day standing alone as a day of rest.[49] Also, in the Decalogue, Commandments 1 and 2, 3 and 4, 6 and 7, and 8 and 9 go together, with 5 and 10 standing apart.[50] Here in the Song, what we appear to have is a symmetrical composition: 8 stanzas in 4 pairs, and an introduction and conclusion making a split 5th pair, framing the whole.

49. John Skinner, *A Critical and Exegetical Commentary on Genesis* (ICC; Edinburgh: T. & T. Clark, 1930), pp. 8-9.
50. D.N. Freedman, *The Nine Commandments* (New York: Doubleday, 2000), pp. 168-73.

13. *Structure in the Song of Moses (Deuteronomy 32.1-43)*   149

Content

In all literature of a high order, form and content go hand in hand. The structure exhibited here correlates well with the Song's thematic development, which is the following:

Introduction (1-3)

I Yahweh Great/Israel is his Adversary (4-9)	II Prior Salvation of Israel (10-14)
III Indictment of Unfaithful Israel (15-18)	IV Sentence on Unfaithful Israel (19-22)
V Extent of Israel's Punishment (23-27)	VI Israel's Punishment in Retrospect (28-33)
VII Future Salvation of Israel (34-38)	VIII Yahweh Great/Enemy is his Adversary (39-42)

Conclusion (43)

We now discern a thematic inversion in the Song as a whole. The last pair of stanzas (VII and VIII) invert the balancing themes of the first pair (I and II). Stanza I acclaims the greatness of Yahweh, seen in his perfect creation, his just ways, and his faithfulness to the covenant, contrasted with a corrupt and perverse adversary: Israel. Stanza VIII again acclaims the greatness of Yahweh, seen now in his infinite and incomparable power, contrasted with a hateful enemy who remains unnamed. Also, Yahweh's prior salvation of Israel in Stanza II balances Yahweh's future salvation of Israel in Stanza VII. The other stanzas balance in more normal fashion: Israel's indictment for unfaithfulness in Stanza III balances Israel's sentence for unfaithfulness in Stanza IV, and the extent of Israel's punishment in Stanza V balances Israel's punishment in retrospect in Stanza VI.

Chapter 14

ELIJAH'S CHARIOT RIDE*

One event about which the Old Testament keeps strangely silent is the death of the prophet Elijah. Mentioned only is a dramatic departure from earth in 2 Kings 2, where he ascends by fiery chariot into heaven, from which he will later return, according to the prophet Malachi, to usher in the coming Day of Yahweh (Mal. 4.5-6). Josephus says that 'Elijah disappeared (ἠφανίσθη) from among humans and, to this day, no one knows his end'.[1] Josephus continues by noting that the Scriptures reserve euphemistic language for both Enoch and Elijah—that they became invisible (γεγόνασιν ἀφανεῖς). No doubt these traditions were widespread in the New Testament era with all the speculation we read of in the New Testament about Elijah's return,[2] as well as the statement in Heb. 11.5 that Enoch 'did not see death' (μὴ ἰδεῖν θάνατον).

Actually, we must go again to the New Testament to find any suggestion of Elijah's death. In Jn 8.51-53 Jesus is involved in a dispute with some opponents[3] over immortality. Admittedly there is some misunderstanding over what Jesus means when he speaks of 'never see[ing] death', still, the opponents make an important concession worth noting:

> Now we know that you have a demon. Abraham died, as did the prophets; and you say, 'If anyone keeps my word, he will never taste death'. Are you greater than our father Abraham, who died? And the prophets died! Who do you claim to be? (Jn 8.52-53 [RSV]).

Jesus is set over against Abraham and the prophets, the best of Yahweh's chosen men, all of whom died. And we must assume that *all* the prophets are meant, else the argument loses its force. Thus we can conclude that Elijah is referred to implicitly, since any such list of prophets would certainly include Elijah.

---

* *Journal of Jewish Studies* 24 (1973), pp. 39-50.
1. Josephus, *Ant.* 9.2 (Loeb).
2. Mt. 11.14; 16.14; 17.10-13; etc.
3. Whether the reference to the 'Jews' in the immediate context (v. 48) means the Pharisees or not is unclear. The Pharisees are explicitly named earlier (v. 13) as Jesus' opponents in the Temple, yet this type of argument sounds more like one put forth by the Sadducees, who did not believe in resurrection. In the Pseudepigrapha (*T. Abr.* 8.9; *OTP*, p. 886) it says: 'Not one of the prophets escaped death'.

How then is this to be explained? Was there also a tradition about Elijah's death available at that time which is now lost to us? We simply cannot say. Instead we shall go on to propose in this paper that a new look be taken at the text of 2 Kings 1–2, where, I believe the results of a rhetorical analysis will take us further than we may get from employing other types of literary criticism in shedding light on the question just raised.[4] Rofé has recently called attention to the inadequacy of form-critical criteria in dealing effectively with these prophetical legends.[5] Hence a new methodology is called for. By observing patterned repetitions of vocabulary and phraseology we shall be able to discover what in all probability the ancients understood full well, namely, that structure and rhetorical style are a key to meaning and interpretation. In the case of 2 Kings 1–2 we will provide some new observations concerning the events that marked the final days of the prophet Elijah.

Form and Composition in 2 Kings 1–2

The text of 2 Kings 1–2 contains four legendary episodes about Elijah and Elisha. Included also is a historical note about Moab's rebellion after the death of Ahab (1.1), and the stereotyped obituary for Ahaziah (1.17-18), which completes the Deuteronomic formula begun in 1 Kgs 22.51-53. These legends, and we shall refer to them as separate legends even though our subsequent analysis will show them to be a unity, are delineated as follows: (1) Elijah's denunciation of Ahaziah and his servants for seeking help from Baalzebub[6] in curing the king's sickness (1.2-16); (2) Elijah's final walk with his disciple Elisha, followed by Elijah's departure in a fiery chariot (2.1-18); (3) Elisha's cleansing of the water at Jericho (2.19-22); and (4) Elisha's cursing of the rude boys on the road to Bethel (2.23-24).

As the text now stands before us, these legends are placed within a framework set up by the editor(s) of our present book of Kings. The

---

4. This methodology has found its clearest formulation in James Muilenburg's 'Form Criticism and Beyond', *JBL* 88 (1969), pp. 1-18. See also Muilenburg's earlier article, 'A Study in Hebrew Rhetoric: Repetition and Style', in *Congress Volume Copenhagen* (VTSup, 1; Leiden: E.J. Brill, 1953), pp. 97-111.

5. Alexander Rofé, 'The Classification of the Prophetical Stories', *JBL* 89 (1970), pp. 427-40. See another article in the same *JBL* volume by David Greenwood entitled 'Rhetorical Criticism and Formgeschichte: Some Methodological Considerations', pp. 418-26, which puts the matter very clearly.

6. This is evidently an intentional corruption of Baalzebul (so J. Montgomery, *The Book of Kings* [ICC; Edinburgh: T. & T. Clark, 1951], p. 349), now known to us from the Ras Shamra texts and appearing frequently in the NT (Mt. 10.25; 12.24, 27; etc.).

events of chap. 1 quite clearly took place during the reign of Ahaziah, Ahab's son and successor; thus the completion of the obituary in vv. 17-18, begun earlier in 1 Kgs 22.51-53. As for the events in chap. 2, Jehoram is most probably king, although we have here a well-known chronological problem, the solution of which lies beyond the scope of our present discussion.[7]

Looking to a stage prior to their inclusion within the royal history, scholars have generally grouped the tales of Elijah and Elisha into separate cycles, each of which grew up around the individual prophet and then circulated independently for a time. Both cycles had their origin in the North[8] where the prophets had been active. Our pericope of 2 Kings 1–2, while focusing at least as much upon Elijah as Elisha, is nevertheless included in the Elisha cycle and serves as its introduction. This cycle is distinguished from the Elijah cycle (1 Kings 17–19, 21) by its unrealistic view of the miraculous,[9] a general lack of ethics or concern for humanity,[10] and the crude way in which reverence for the prophet is instilled.[11]

We can now go a step further. There is evidence—at least in our pericope—that legendary material was cast into deliberate structural forms as it was collected and preserved. If we plot the geographic points mentioned in the text, we can see that the controlling structure is a chiasmus that binds all four legends together. It depicts a circuitous journey which begins in Samaria (1.2), moves to the Trans-Jordan, where Elijah is taken away (2.9-12), and then returns to Samaria again (2.25).[12]

---

7. The problem is created by the note in 1.17, where the death of Ahaziah and the ascension of his brother Jehoram is said to have taken place in the second year of Jehoram of Judah, who was Jehoshaphat's son. The Deuteronomic scheme of 1 Kgs 22.51 (cf. v. 42) and 2 Kgs 3.1, on the other hand, places the ascension of Jehoram of Israel in the 18th year of Jehoshaphat. This can perhaps best be explained as a co-regency of Jehoshaphat with his son Jehoram; cf. Edwin R. Thiele, *The Mysterious Numbers of the Hebrew Kings* (rev. edn; Grand Rapids: Zondervan, 1983), p. 61, and John Gray, *1 and 2 Kings* (OTL; 2nd rev. edn; London, SCM Press), p. 66.

8. So N.H. Snaith, 'I and II Kings', in *IB*, III (ed. George A. Buttrick; New York: Abingdon Press, 1954), p. 12.

9. Montgomery, *Kings*, p. 348.

10. S. Szikszai, 'Elijah the Prophet', in *IDB*, II, p. 89; see also Montgomery, *Kings*, p. 348, and Gray, *1 and 2 Kings*, p. 416.

11. Snaith, 'I and II Kings', pp. 190-91.

12. A geographic chiasmus has been found in Luke by M.D. Goulder; see Goulder, 'The Chiastic Structure of the Lucan Journey', in *Studia evangelica II* [Papers of the Second International Congress on New Testament Studies, Oxford, 1961] (ed. F.L. Cross; TU, 87; Berlin: Akademie-Verlag, 1964), pp. 195-202; *Type and History in Acts* (London: SPCK, 1964), pp. 135-38.

14. *Elijah's Chariot Ride*

A   Samaria (1.2)
    B   Unidentified Mountain (1.9)
       C   Gilgal (2.1)
          D   Bethel (2.2-3)
             E   Jericho (2.4-5)
                F   Jordan River (2.6-8)
                    G   Trans-Jordan (2.9-12)
                F'   Jordan River (2.13-14)
             E'   Jericho (2.15-22)
          D'   Bethel (2.23-24)
       C'   ....
    B'   Mount Carmel (2.25)
A'   Samaria (2.25)

As is always true in a chiastic form, the climax comes not at the end, but at the center.[13] This is certainly the case here, where the departure of Elijah and the transfer of the prophetic office to Elisha serve admirably as a point of climax.

Before going on to draw some implications from this structure, we should call attention to those parts of the chiasmus that are not perfect. As the diagram makes clear, Gilgal (C) has no counterpart in C'. If we accept, though, the site of Jiljulieh, which is usually linked with this Gilgal,[14] then it fits in very well with the basic course of the journey. Another less obvious imperfection can be noted. At the end of the first legend in chap. 1, Elijah comes down to meet the king (1.15), who, unless he is now up and around, would still be confined to his bed in Samaria. Samaria is not mentioned by name, it

---

13. This was pointed out in the classic study of chiasmus in the biblical literature by Nils W. Lund, *Chiasmus in the New Testament* (Chapel Hill, NC: University of North Carolina, 1942 [repr. Peabody, MA: Hendrickson, 1992], p. 40. Unfortunately for Old Testament studies, this book suffers from a misnomer. Lund believed that chiasmus was a Semitic form originally, and devoted no less than 86 pages of his first section to examples from the Old Testament.

14. Jiljulieh is about 7 miles north of Bethel on the high road to Shechem, and is identified with this Gilgal by George Adam Smith, *Historical Geography of the Holy Land* (London: Hodder & Stoughton, 1931; originally 1894), p. 494, also James Muilenburg, 'Gilgal', in *IDB*, II, p. 398. It is also interesting to note that Wellhausen suggested we emend v. 25 to read 'Gilgal', in accordance with v. 1, but this was rejected by Montgomery (*Kings*, p. 356) and J. Skinner, *I and II Kings* (CB; Edinburgh and London: T.C. & E.C. Jack, 1908), p. 282.

is true, but still our structure builds on the course of a journey. Neither deviation would seem, however, to seriously challenge what is quite obviously a deliberate structure. We said earlier that these were originally separate legends, and their collocations in concluding the first legend and beginning the second serve only to point out the overall authenticity of the composition. A new unity has been created without violating the marks of its individual parts.

Now we can move on to show how at least two implications can be drawn from the discovery of this structure. The first concerns what I have called the 'unidentified mountain' in B. Balanced with Mount Carmel in B', we immediately suspect that this too is Mount Carmel. Elijah's encounter with the messengers of Ahaziah would then take place at the same location where Elijah had an earlier more famous contest with the legions of Baal (1 Kings 18). The sanctuary of Baalzebul would also be on Carmel, and it is to there that the messengers of the king go, not to Ekron. (The text says only that they went to inquire of Baalzebub, god of Ekron; it doesn't imply that they necessarily went to Ekron.) Additional support for this contention comes in that the site is designated in 1.9 as הָהָר. This cannot be translated 'a hill' (RSV) or a 'a hilltop' (NEB); the definite article necessitates either 'the hill' or 'the mountain'. It is a specific site with which we are expected to be familiar, therefore 'the mountain' must be correct. The term הַנָּהָר was commonly used to refer to the Euphrates;[15] likewise הָהָר must have been another name for Carmel,[16] the largest and probably best-known mountain in the area.[17]

The other implication is that the מַלְאַךְ יהוה of chap. 1 is none other than Elisha. Whereas from 2.1 on he is explicitly named, here he remains incognito for reasons we will discuss later. Although the function of the

---

15. Gen. 31.21; Exod. 23.31; Josh. 24.2, 3, 14, 15; etc.

16. As far as I know, the only other commentator to make this suggestion was William Barnes (*The Two Books of the Kings* [CBSC; Cambridge: Cambridge University Press, 1908), p. 185, who simply said, 'perhaps Carmel is meant'.

17. I would assume, of course, the traditional site for Mount Carmel on the coast near Haifa (cf. Josh. 19.26; Jer. 46.18); nevertheless, an interesting alternative has come to my attention that would fit nicely with the course of our journey. H. Neil Richardson thinks that since כַּרְמֶל is a general term meaning 'garden' or 'orchard', and serves elsewhere in the OT as a place-name (Josh. 15.55; 1 Samuel 25), being not necessarily the mountain by the sea, it may well be another name for Gerizim (modern Tell el Ras). This is certainly possible, since Gerizim later became the site of the Samaritan Temple (see the latest excavation reports in *BA* 31 [1968], pp. 58-72). Its proximity to Samaria would make it a more convenient site than Carmel by the sea for a sanctuary to Baalzebul. Moreover, it would enhance our chiastic scheme, since Gerizim lies precisely at the Shechem junction where the east–west road from Samaria meets the north–south road to Gilgal, Bethel, and Jerusalem.

prophet as Yahweh's messenger is well established,[18] it may be questioned as to whether or not the מַלְאַךְ יהוה is really another prophetic name at this period. It is true that neither Elijah nor Elisha are anywhere explicitly referred to as a מַלְאַךְ יהוה. The term does appear one other time in the Elijah–Elisha cycles, namely, at 1 Kgs 19.7, where the context is quite similar to our own, and thus not decisive. Sometime later, Haggai is called a מַלְאַךְ יהוה (Hag. 1.13). We should also note that in both Genesis 18–19 and Judges 13 the terms מַלְאַךְ or מַלְאַךְ יהוה are used interchangeably with אִישׁ, אִישׁ הָאֱלֹהִים, and מַלְאַךְ הָאֱלֹהִים, all designations for the prophet. Thus I see no reason to prevent מַלְאַךְ יהוה from being another name for Elisha. This places him at the side of Elijah in 2 Kings 1. Since 2 Kings 1 was originally independent, it has retained its distinctive vocabulary even after being joined with the legends of chap. 2. We can also see why Elisha returned (שָׁב) to Samaria via Mount Carmel (2.25): it was not only because he had a home there, but because he wanted to re-visit those places where he and Elijah had been so recently.

To sum up then our discussion on the overall composition of 2 Kings 1–2, we have seen that the four legends of this pericope were drawn into a pre-Deuteronomic structure which bound them together into a new unity. Exactly how and when these legends came together we cannot say. This structure may be the work of some editor, and if so, it displays a remarkable measure of artistry on his part. On the other hand, it is also possible—and maybe even more probable—that we are here confronted with a form dating to an early period of oral transmission. The chiasmus in this case not only enhances the story as it is told, but more importantly serves as a mnemonic device to aid retention.

Congruence of Style and Literary Motifs in the Elijah Legends

Having now shown 2 Kings 1–2 to be a structural unity, we shall press on to a closer scrutiny of the two larger legends featuring Elijah (1.2-16; 2.1-18). By examining rhetorical features common to both legends, we can go on to argue for a relation between the events described, where indeed the one serves to explain the other.

---

18. See E. Jacob, *Theology of the Old Testament* (trans. Arthur W. Heathcote and Philip J. Allcock; London: Hodder & Stoughton, 1958), pp. 75-77, and James F. Ross, 'The Prophet as Yahweh's Messenger', in *Israel's Prophetic Heritage* [Essays in Honor of James Muilenburg] (ed. Bernhard W. Anderson and Walter Harrelson; New York: Harper & Bros., 1962), pp. 98-107. Additional bibliography can be found in J. Limburg, 'The Root ריב and the Prophetic Lawsuit Speeches', *JBL* 88 (1969), p. 304 n. 41.

To begin with, both legends embody a three-fold rhythmic cycle common in both ancient[19] and modern[20] folk literature. This rhythm is produced by repetitive statements of the principal figures together with those of the narrator. In chap. 1 the cycles depict the three visits of the king's messengers to Elijah and the judgment that came upon two of the companies.

A	Captain:	'O man of God, the king says, "Come down!"' (1.9)
B	Elijah:	'If I am a man of God, let fire come down...' (1.10a)
C	Narrator:	'Then fire came down...' (1.10b)

A'	Captain:	'O man of God, thus says the king: "Come down quickly!"' (1.11)
B'	Elijah:	'If I am a man of God, let fire come down...' (1.12a)
C'	Narrator:	'Then fire came down...' (1.12b)

A"	Captain:	'O man of God, please let my life...be precious before you...' (1.13-14)
B"	Messenger:	'Go down with him...' (1.15a)
C"	Narrator:	'So he arose and went down...' (1.15b)

In chap. 2 the cycles are larger, containing verbal exchanges between Elijah and Elisha on the one hand, and Elisha and the sons of the prophets on the other. Here the narration comes in the center instead of at the end like chap. 1.

A	Elijah:	'Stay here, please, for Yahweh has sent me as far as Bethel' (2.2a)
B	Elisha:	'As Yahweh lives...I will not leave you' (2.2bα)
C	Narrator:	'So they went down to Bethel' (2.2bβ)
D	Narrator:	'And the sons of the prophets who were in Bethel came out...' (2.3a)
E	Prophets:	'Do you know that today Yahweh will take away your master...?' (2.3bα)
F	Elisha:	'Yes I know it, be still!' (2.2bβ)

---

19. Montgomery (p. 348) calls this 'good oriental style'; Gray (p. 409) says, 'The repetitive style of the narrative is characteristic of saga'. The most important study of repetitions in folk literature was done by the Danish folklorist, Axel Olrik, who formulated a 'trinary law' showing that saga had a predilection for the number three: three persons, three things, three successive incidents of the same kind, etc. See Olrik, 'Episke love i folkedigtningen', *Danske studier* 5 (1908), p. 81, and a later version entitled, 'Die epischen Gesetze der Volksdichtung', *ZDA* 51 (1909), pp. 1-12 [Eng. 'Epic Laws of Folk Narrative', in A. Dundes (ed.), *The Study of Folklore* (Englewood Cliffs, NJ: Prentice–Hall, 1965), pp. 129-41]. Following Olrik, Alfred Bock accumulated over 600 examples of threefold repetitions in Icelandic folk sagas; cf. Bock, 'Die epische Dreizahl in den Islendinga sogur', *Arkiv för nordisk filologi* 37 (1920–21), pp. 263-313; 38 (1921–22), pp. 51-83.

20. One only need be reminded of *The Three Bears* and *The Little Engine That Could*, in which repetition is important.

A'	Elijah:	'Stay here please, for Yahweh has sent me to Jericho' (2.4a)
B'	Elisha:	'As Yahweh lives...I will not leave you' (2.4bα)
C'	Narrator:	'So they came to Jericho' (2.4bβ)
D'	Narrator:	'The sons of the prophets who were at Jericho drew near...' (2.5a)
E'	Prophets:	'Do you know that today Yahweh will take away your master...?' (2.5bα)
F'	Elisha:	'Yes I know it, be still!' (2.5bβ)
A"	Elijah:	'Stay here please, for Yahweh has sent me to the Jordan' (2.6a)
B"	Elisha:	'As Yahweh lives...I will not leave you' (2.6bα)
C"	Narrator:	'So the two of them went on' (2.6bβ)
D"	Narrator:	'Fifty men of the sons of the prophets also went and stood...by the Jordan' (2.7)
E"	....	....
F"	....	....

The repetitions are striking and give the stories their rhythm; yet there is just enough variation to insure movement. In chap. 1 the captain of the second cycle is more insistent and urgent in his demand. Instead of 'the king says' (הַמֶּלֶךְ דִּבֶּר), we have the formulaic 'thus says the king' (כֹּה־אָמַר הַמֶּלֶךְ). Elijah is told not merely to 'come down' (רְדָה) but to 'come down quickly' (מְהֵרָה רְדָה). The third cycle is significantly modified, with the captain now imploring Elijah to save his life and the lives of his men. In Elijah's place the messenger speaks, telling Elijah to go down, which they then do.

In chap. 2 the same is true. The first two cycles are almost identical except for what appears to be a subtle increase in intensity. The narrator shifts from וַיֵּצְאוּ in D to וַיִּגְּשׁוּ in D', which could be mere stylistic variation, but more likely a deliberate change. The exchange between Elisha and the sons of the prophets reveals some underlying tension and the narrator could well be calling attention to the actual *space* between them—a gap that narrows in the second cycle. Elisha is clearly not anxious to discuss his master's imminent departure. He tells them to 'be quiet!' (הֶחֱשׁוּ), the verb sometimes having the meaning 'to be silent in the face of iniquity'.[21] Like the third cycle in chap. 1, the third cycle here is also significantly modified. The prophets do not continue their dialogue with Elisha. Instead we picture them quietly trailing behind with their 50 men, lurking somewhere in the background by the river's edge as Elijah and Elisha walk alone towards the Jordan.

In addition to this similarity of rhythmic style, we have three dominant motifs appearing in both episodes, motifs which cannot help but force associations in our minds between the two. They are, (1) the skilful interplay of the 'up and down'; (2) the repeated appearances of the '50 men'; and (3) the use of 'fire' as a sign of divine intervention.

---

21. BDB, *s.v.* חשה (p. 364).

First the interplay of the 'up and down'. In chap. 1 Ahaziah is lying sick in his 'upper chamber' (עֲלִיָּתוֹ). Elijah's word to him is literally, 'the bed to which you have ascended (עָלִיתָ), you shall not descend (תֵרֵד) from it' (vv. 4, 6, 16). Elijah then ascends the mountain to act out the prophecy symbolically. By refusing to come down, he is saying that Ahaziah will in fact not come down from his upper chamber. He counters the captain's command to 'come down' (רְדָה) with 'If I am a man of God, let fire come down' (תֵרֵד).

Balancing this in chap. 2 is the 'upgoing' (הַעֲלוֹת) of Elijah into heaven (v. 1; cf. v. 11). Preceding this *ascension* is a long journey of *descent* to the lowest point on earth, namely, the Jordan Valley at the Dead Sea.

The second motif is that of the '50 men'. In chap. 1 the three groups of 50 sent to fetch Elijah seem clearly enough to be standard units of the king's army.[22] Echoing this in chap. 2 is another group of '50 men' (vv. 7, 16, 17), whose identity remains ambiguous. Commentators generally consider them to be part of the בְּנֵי־הַנְּבִיאִים.[23] Yet there are compelling reasons for believing otherwise. In the first place, the prefixed מ in מִבְּנֵי הַנְּבִיאִים (v. 7) could imply separation, which would mean that the '50' are a group distinct from the prophets. Also in v. 16, when the prophets ask Elisha if a search party may be sent out to look for Elijah, they say, *'there are with your servants* (יֵשׁ־אֶת־עֲבָדֶיךָ) fifty strong men'. Note the plural עֲבָדֶיךָ, which again suggests that there are two groups: prophets and 50 strong men.

In the second place, the designation of the 50 in v. 16 as בְּנֵי־חַיִל suggests that these were men trained for war, that is, soldiers. The Old Testament usage of this term is almost exclusively with this meaning. This, of course, does not preclude prophets from being soldiers. Samuel and Elijah were both capable of bearing arms (cf. 1 Sam. 15.33; 1 Kgs 18.40). Yet the term nowhere refers specifically to prophets in the Old Testament, and only once is it used to designate a group of priests (2 Chron. 26.17). Thus we are forced to conclude, I think, that this group of 50 looks very much like the groups of 50 in chap. 1. They are soldiers, who provide a striking thread of continuity with the soldiers in chap. 1. No doubt they *are* the 50 whom Elijah spared when they pleaded for their lives. What their role was in this context will be discussed in a moment.

The third motif to appear in both episodes is that of the divine 'fire'. In chap. 1 Elijah calls down fire from heaven to consume the first two groups of 50. In this instance, the fire is clearly a sign of divine judgment, whatever set of historical facts it is meant to conceal. In the second instance, the narrator speaks of a chariot and horses of fire that carries Elijah away. Here also the fire is a sign of divine intervention, and if there is any hint of judgment,

---

22. So Gray, *1 and 2 Kings*, p. 414.
23. Montgomery, *Kings*, p. 354; this also seems to be the assumption of Snaith, 'I and II Kings', p. 192.

it is clearly subordinate to the controlling idea that Yahweh has taken his faithful servant to be with him in heaven.

These parallel features argue, I believe, for more than a casual connection between the two stories. Their juxtaposition is a silent testimony to a relationship of the events they describe—a relationship in which Elijah's chariot ride comes in direct response to his conquest of the 100 men in Ahaziah's army. About this we must say more.

'My Father, my Father, the Chariots of Israel and its Horsemen!'

Our rhetorical analysis has suggested a connection between the Elijah–Elisha legends, but in order that we may find out what that connection is, we must go to Elisha's final words in 2.12 as he sees his master being whisked away. Elisha is quoted as saying, 'My father, my father, the chariots of Israel and its horsemen!' This is indeed a problematic line; nevertheless, it provides the final clue as to what actually took place. The אָבִי אָבִי causes no real difficulty; it is directed to Elijah as an honorific title, although T.H. Gaster has suggested to me that it could be an interjection expressing shock, like the Italian, 'mamma mia!' What causes the problem for interpretation is the phrase, 'chariots of Israel and its horsemen'. What does this mean? The usual explanation is that these words are an appellation for Elijah. Skinner says, Elijah was a 'greater strength to his nation than all its chariots and horsemen'.[24] Montgomery says, 'Elijah was worth a whole fighting army to Israel'.[25] The Targum to this verse reads: רבי רבי דטב להון לישראל בצלותיה מרתיכין ופרשין ('Rabbi, Rabbi, who was better for Israel by his prayer than chariots and horsemen'[26]). This has its ambiguity also, but it does seem to compare Elijah with a fighting host and may be the source of our current confusion. I maintain that all these explanations are unnecessarily opaque. So also is von Rad's idea that this is an old shout reflecting a coalescence of prophecy and Holy War, which first appeared in 2 Kgs 13.14, and only later was associated with Elijah's ascension.[27] The words

---

24. Skinner, *I and II Kings*, pp. 279-80.

25. Montgomery, *Kings*, p. 354. It is interesting to note that Gunkel interpreted it the same way, only he recognized that such a designation was not really suitable for Elijah. In commenting upon this phrase, Gunkel said, 'For Elisha it meant the loss of a father, for Israel the loss of its great wall of defense. This conception of Elijah as the champion of Israel is not in keeping with the rest of the tradition regarding him. Elijah did not come prominently forward to help Israel in its battles. All his life he was in opposition to his nation. It was otherwise with Elisha...'; see Gunkel, 'Elisha—The Successor of Elijah (2 Kings ii. 1-18)', *ET* 41 (1929–30), pp. 184-85.

26. This is the English translation of David Daube, *The New Testament and Rabbinic Judaism* (London: Athlone, 1956), p. 25.

27. Gerhard von Rad, *Der heilige Krieg im alten Israel* (ATANT, 20; Zürich:

are well suited in their present context and are in all probability the *ipsissima verba* of Elisha. If its meaning is elusive it is because it is too obvious. Elisha is describing nothing more or less than what appears before his very eyes: *the chariots of Israel and its horsemen*. Elijah has been kidnapped in one of the king's chariots and taken away to meet his death. This was the original meaning of the expression, and when we hear it later on the lips of Joash when Elisha is about to die, then it takes on figurative meaning (2 Kgs 13.14). The imminent death of the central figure provides the constant. Joash now speaks words that were well known to Elisha, words that will revive associations with the context in which Elisha spoke them. There is one main difference, in that here the king is weeping before Elisha—no doubt very much unlike the emotional state of Jehoram who stood behind Elijah's abduction.

Summary and Reconstruction

Let us now summarize the results of our analysis and proceed to a reconstruction of the historical situation that lies behind these legends. We began by showing that 2 Kings 1–2 contained the vestiges of a pre-Deuteronomic form embodying four originally separate legends into a larger compilation. The unifying principle was a chiasmus marking the route of a journey. A geographic chiasmus such as this is artificial only in the sense that chronological time is markedly compressed. Thus it is a 'journey' that extended over a period of months, or possibly even a year or two. Whether this form originated in oral tradition or whether it came instead from a writing scribe who left his own mark on the material, is best left an open question. In either case, it is sufficiently clear that we have before us a cluster of stories that have been deliberately made into a larger unity.

The identification of this structure has aided us in interpretation. The mountain of chap. 1 was Carmel, evidently a popular site for confrontations between Yahweh and Baal. Since Elijah's first encounter with those hostile forces (1 Kings 18), the worship of Yahweh has enjoyed something of a revival. We see, for example, in 1 Kings 22 that the large group of prophets advising the king against Micaiah were nonetheless prophets of Yahweh. Now after Ahab's death, the cult of Baalzebul has gained a foothold on Carmel, and Elijah's ministry ends much in the way it began—by violence and death to those not faithful to Yahweh. Yet one cannot help but be sympathetic towards the soldiers of Ahaziah who seem merely to have been carrying out orders in trying to bring Elijah down. Maybe there was some widespread disgust with Elijah's actions. This would then explain

Zwingli-Verlag, 1951), p. 55 [Eng. *Holy War in Ancient Israel* (trans. Marva J. Dawn; Grand Rapids: Eerdmans, 1991), p. 100].

why Elisha remains incognito in the story. Were he identified, he would certainly share some responsibility for this massacre. Being also legends in the Elisha cycle, we would expect that Elisha remain in as good a light as possible. Thus our interpretation of Elisha as the מַלְאַךְ יהוה is plausible, and another implication drawn from a recognition of the structure.

The parallel featuring of the two large legends about Elijah link the events they describe. As punishment for the slaughter of 100 of Ahaziah's soldiers, Elijah is kidnapped in a chariot of the king, who is now Jehoram, Ahaziah's brother.[28] For him it was easily rationalized as blood revenge. And we can be quite sure that it was done with the blessing of the Queen Mother, Jezebel, if not with some active prodding on her part (cf. 1 Kgs 19.2). The 50 soldiers in chap. 2 were those spared earlier by Elijah in chap. 1. Together they follow the course of events, making ready for a possible ambush. We can assume that all were aware of Elijah's imminent capture. The repeated question, 'Do you know that today Yahweh will take away your master from over you?', is another way in which the prophets ask if they can be of any help. Elisha, though, is every bit as resigned to what is coming as is Elijah, and bids the world-be helpers to be still.[29] They are left to watch the abduction from the hidden confines of the jungle that lined the west bank of the Jordan River.

The story was of course not remembered as a defeat for Elijah. The picture Elisha had of his master disappearing up one of the Judean or Moabite hills in a cloud of dust was preserved in legend as a chariot ride into heaven. It was out of death and apparent defeat that Yahweh wrought a great victory. Such an explanation would show that theology is not here drawn from mythology; its prototype is a very 'earthy' picture of Elijah's abduction and death.

In conclusion, let us take one final look at Elisha. After his master is taken away, he journeys back to Carmel and Samaria, and in so doing retraces the steps that he and his departed master had taken together. For him it was undoubtedly a catharsis—a way of working out his grief by re-visiting the places and re-living the fellowship from a journey that was still very vivid in his mind.[30]

---

28. Elisha's intense dislike of Jehoram expressed shortly thereafter (2 Kgs 3.14) is no doubt because of this evil deed.

29. Gray (p. 461) commenting on the 'horses and chariots of fire' in 2 Kgs 6.17 agrees that such imagery comes from saga, but considers an ambush to figure in the historical basis for the tradition.

30. A first draft of this article was read at the annual meeting of the Society of Biblical Literature in Toronto, 1969. The writer would like to express thanks to Professor David Daube for his criticisms and helpful advice.

The Prophets

Chapter 15

RHETORICAL DISCOURSE IN THE PROPHETS*

Rhetoric in the Ancient Near East

If the classic prophets emanate from ancient Israel, the classic orators and teachers of rhetoric hail from ancient Greece and Rome. The names of Aristotle, Cicero, and Quintilian spring immediately to mind, but there were others, many others. Rhetoric in the modern West is therefore conceptualized and measured in large part against what we know about classical rhetoric, and many do not even think of looking at cultures predating the Greeks and Romans to find a rhetorical tradition more ancient than the one they know best.

We have, of course, the Hebrew Old Testament, and teachers in church, synagogue, and academy have long noted a rhetorical excellence in this document of Holy Writ. Its excellence was carried over into the New Testament, and not infrequently, better explains the richness of discourse there than classical rhetoric taught in Hellenistic schools of the time. Today, Hebrew rhetoric is being much studied, and we are learning a considerable amount by simply reading the biblical text with an eye for the rhetorical nature of its discourse. But we have no textbook on the subject. As a result, we must depend on classical handbooks for definitions and functions of rhetorical figures. Research is also being carried on in the broader field of ancient Near Eastern rhetoric, inasmuch as we have at our disposal thousands of excavated texts from the ancient Near East. Decipherment and translation of these texts have gone on for 150 years, opening up a whole new world more ancient than the classical world of Greece and Rome. The rediscovery of this ancient Near Eastern world is nothing short of a new renaissance.

Hebrew Rhetoric

Hebrew rhetoric developed from an ancient pre-classical rhetorical tradition going back to the beginning of recorded history. Sumerian scribal schools, called 'tablet houses', produced a literate class that has left behind a rich legacy of rhetorical discourse from early Mesopotamian society (c. 3000 BCE).

* First published in *The Hebrew Prophets* (Minneapolis: Fortress Press, 2010), pp. 165-207.

The Sumerians wrote poetry having repetition, parallelism, epithets, and similes.[1] Cuneiform texts of the third and second millennia show that this rhetorical tradition survived in Old Babylonia, Assyria, and Ugarit. A rhetorical tradition doubtless developed during the same period in Egypt, where scribal schools are known to have existed from the early third millennium, and where poetry also was written, but about this tradition little is known.

Israel's oldest literature, to judge from its earliest poems (Exodus 15; Deuteronomy 33; Judges 5) and other writings, contains works of fine art. A simplified twenty-two- to thirty-letter alphabet introduced at Ugarit two to three centuries before Israel's entry into Canaan (thirteenth-century), which is the prototype of the Hebrew alphabet, created new possibilities for oral and written discourse as words began replacing older cuneiform signs. Ancient Hebrew rhetoric survives largely in the Hebrew Bible/Old Testament, from which it may be concluded that during the eighth- to sixth-centuries BCE it experienced its 'golden age', a full three centuries and more before the art achieved classical expression by Aristotle in Greece, and much later by Cicero, Quintilian, and others in Rome.

Hebrew rhetorical tradition produced no theoretical work the like of Aristotle's *Rhetoric* (322–320 BCE), nor handbooks such as the *ad Herennium* (c. 86–82 BCE) and Quintilian's *Institutes* (c. 90 CE). Nevertheless, in the Bible are to be found an array of figures of speech performing the same or similar functions as in classical rhetoric, as well as modes of argumentation known and classified by later Greek and Roman authors. Prophets embellish their discourse with metaphor, simile, comparison, euphemism, epithet, chiasmus, asyndeton, alliteration, rhetorical question, hyperbole, paronomasia, and irony both dramatic and verbal. Amos is the prophet of the rhetorical question; Hosea is the prophet of vivid metaphors and oracles with split bicolons (i.e., bicolons split so that one colon begins the oracle and one colon ends it), also the prophet with an extraordinary capacity for expressing pathos; Isaiah is the master of verbal irony; and Ezekiel is the prophet of the extended metaphor, or allegory. But the prophet possessing the greatest rhetorical skill is unquestionably Jeremiah, who can hold rank with the best of the Greek and Roman rhetors, anticipating them as he does in style, structure, and modes of argumentation. His indebtedness is to Hosea and the sermonic prose of Deuteronomy. The latter might be expected, since Deuteronomy is a seventh-century book, and Jeremiah a prophet of the late seventh and early sixth-century. Moreover, Deuteronomy is widely conceded to be the rhetorical book par excellence of the Old Testament.

1. Samuel Noah Kramer, 'Sumerian Similes: A Panoramic View of Some of Man's Oldest Literary Images', *JAOS* 89 (1969), pp. 1-10; *The Sacred Marriage Rite* (Bloomington, IN: Indiana University Press, 1969), pp. 23-48 (Chapter 2, 'The Poetry of Sumer: Repetition, Parallelism, Epithet, Simile').

The preachers of Deuteronomy appear to have been Levitical priests, some of whom were trained scribes and went by the name of 'scribe' (2 Chron. 34.13). How they received their schooling is not known, but it is reasonable to assume that they attended a Jerusalem school where writing and rhetorical skills were taught. Isaiah, Jeremiah, Ezekiel, and other Judahite prophets would have attended this school, receiving the same training as the Levitical priests before venturing forth as heralds of the divine word. Although we know nothing of a Jerusalem school, one would have been required in the time of David and Solomon (10th-century BCE), when scribes first began appearing at the royal court as high officials.[2] In Jeremiah's time, this school would have been headed by Shaphan the scribe and would have been attached to the palace or the temple, as in neighboring societies (cf. 2 Kgs 22.8-10).

Prophetic Rhetoric

In this essay I want to provide a window into the world of Hebrew rhetoric as it appears in oracles and other discourse emanating from the prophets. Particular attention will be paid to rhetorical moves in the discourse of Jeremiah. Although Israel's prophetic movement began with Samuel, who, together with Nathan, Elijah, Micaiah ben Imlah, and others, burst in early upon the scene and delivered Yahweh's word with a power that still commands our admiration, the real rhetors of preexilic Israel were the so-called 'writing prophets', that is, Amos and Hosea in northern Israel, and Micah, Isaiah, perhaps Joel, Nahum, Habakkuk, Obadiah, Zephaniah, and Jeremiah in Judah a century and a half later. Ezekiel was born and reared in the Judah, but his prophecies were given in Babylon to Judahites who were taken there in the exile of 597 BCE. The great prophet of the exile is a nameless individual we call Second Isaiah, the one responsible for the lofty poetry in Isaiah 40–66. Postexilic prophets are Haggai, Zechariah, and Malachi, all of whom possessed rhetorical skills that are worthy of our attention.

Repetition

Repetition is the single most important feature of ancient Hebrew rhetoric,[3] being used for emphasis, wordplays, expressing the superlative, creating pathos, and structuring both parts and wholes of prophetic discourse. Its

---

2. Sigmund Mowinckel, 'Psalms and Wisdom', in *Wisdom in Israel and in the Ancient Near East: Presented to Professor Harold Henry Rowley by the Society for Old Testament Study in Association with the Editorial Board of Vetus Testamentum, in Celebration of His Sixty-fifth Birthday, 24 March 1955* (ed. M. Noth and D. Winton Thomas; VTSup, 3; Leiden: E.J. Brill, 1955), p. 206.

3. James Muilenburg, 'A Study of Hebrew Rhetoric: Repetition and Style', in *Congress Volume Copenhagen* (VTSup, 1; Leiden: E.J. Brill, 1953), pp. 97-111.

importance can hardly be overestimated. Repetitions can be sequential or placed in strategic collocations to provide balance. In both they can also bring about closure: repeated terms can be intentionally broken at the end of a series, and repeated words and/or split bicolons can form a tie-in between beginning and end (*inclusio*).

The Superlative. Repeated words can function as a paraphrasis for the superlative:

Isa. 6.3	*holy, holy, holy*
Joel 3.14	*multitudes, multitudes*

Isaiah is acclaiming Yahweh to be 'the holiest'; Joel means 'multitudes upon multitudes'.

Geminatio. Many repetitions are simply for emphasis (*geminatio*), for example:

Jer. 4.19	*my innards, my innards*
Jer. 6.14 [= 8.11]	*peace, peace*
Jer. 7.4	*the temple of Yahweh, the temple of Yahweh, the temple of Yahweh*
Jer. 22.29	*land, land, land*
Ezek. 21.27	*ruin, ruin, ruin*

An echo effect is created when repetitions occur in succession:

Jer. 46.20	*A beautiful, beautiful* heifer was Egypt a horsefly from the north *came, came*.

Anaphora. Anaphora is the repetition of a word or words at the beginning of two or more successive colons, lines, or poetic verses. This figure serves to heighten pity, disdain, fear, joyful anticipation, or other emotional state. This type of repetition often creates *onomatopoeia*.

In Jer. 5.15-17 a fourfold repetition of 'nation' is answered by a fourfold repetition of 'it/they shall consume', where the latter simulates an enemy who eats without stopping. The initial stanza has *epiphora* in the center ('it is'), and predications in the latter stanza form a chiasmus:

> Look! I will bring upon you
>   *a nation* from afar, house of Israel…
>   *a nation* well established **it is**
>   *a nation* from antiquity **it is**
>   *a nation* whose language you do not know
>   and what it says you will not understand.

> *It shall consume* your **harvest** and your **food**
>   *they shall consume* your **sons** and your **daughters**
>   *it shall consume* your **flocks** and your **herds**
> *It shall consume* your **vines** and your **fig trees**
> It will beat down your fortified cities—
>   in which you trust—by the sword.

In Jer. 50.35-38 a fivefold repetition of 'sword' simulates the repeated stabbing of victims, but at the end is a climactic *paronomasia* with the similar-sounding 'drought':

> *A sword* (חֶרֶב) upon Chaldeans...and to the inhabitants of Babylon...
> *A sword* (חֶרֶב) to the diviners, that they become foolish
> *A sword* (חֶרֶב) to her warriors, that they be broken
> *A sword* (חֶרֶב) to his horses and to his chariots, and to all the mixed races...
>   that they become women
> *A sword* (חֶרֶב) to her treasures, that they become booty
> *A drought* (חֹרֶב) to her waters, that they be dried up.

In Jer. 51.20-23 a ninefold repetition of 'with you I smashed' simulates the sense by creating the sound of a hammering club (onomatopoeia). The tedium of repetition is lessened with the terms of predication, naming the hapless war victims, arranged into a chiasmus:

> You were a club for me, a weapon of war:
>   *with you I smashed* **nations**...and **kingdoms**
>   *with you I smashed* **horse** and **his rider**
>   *with you I smashed* **chariot** and **its rider**
>   *with you I smashed* **man** and **woman**
>   *with you I smashed* **old** and **young**
>   *with you I smashed* **young man** and **maiden**
>   *with you I smashed* **shepherd** and **his flock**
>   *with you I smashed* **farmer** and **his team**
>   *with you I smashed* **governors** and **commanders**.

In Jer. 31.4-5, Jeremiah simulates the resumption of city life in Zion with this anaphora:

> *Again* I will build you, and you shall be built
> *Again* you'll deck yourself with your hand-drums
>   and go forth in the dance of merrymakers
> *Again* you'll plant vineyards on Samaria's mountains
>   planters shall plant and eat the fruit.

Zephaniah is particularly fond of anaphora:

Zeph. 1.2-6   *I will utterly sweep away* everything
                   from the face of the earth, says Yahweh
               I will sweep away man and beast
               I will sweep away the birds of the air
                   and the fish of the sea

               those who bow down on the roofs
                   to the hosts of heaven
               those who bow down and swear to Yahweh
                   and yet swear by Milcom
               those who have turned back from following Yahweh
                   who do not seek Yahweh or inquire of him.

The repetitions in vv. 5-6 echo the repetitions of vv. 2-3 (cf. Jer. 5.15-17). There is also deviation in that the final line uses another verb.

Zeph. 1.15   *A day* of wrath is that day
                   a day of distress and anguish
               a day of ruin and devastation
               a day of darkness and gloom
               a day of clouds and thick darkness
                   a day of trumpet blast and battle cry
                       against the fortified cities
                       and against the lofty battlements.

This poetry compares structurally with Jeremiah's chaos vision in Jer. 4.23-26. More anaphora occurs in Zeph. 2.2: *before...before...before*. The 'woe... therefore' structure of Isa. 5.8-25 and the 'woe' structure of Hab. 2.6-17 are anaphora on a large scale.

Epiphora. Epiphora (Lat: *conversio*) is the repetition of a word or words at the end of two or more successive colons, lines, or poetic verses. In Jeremiah:

Jer. 4.19   My innards, my innards, let me writhe
                   the walls of *my heart*
                   it roars to me, *my heart*
               I cannot be still

In one of his three-stanza poems, Jeremiah shifts from epiphora to anaphora:

Jer. 8.22–9.2 Is there no balm in Gilead?
                   Is there no healer there?
               Indeed so why has it not arisen
                   healing for *my dear people?*

               Who can make my head waters
                   and my eyes a well of tears
               So I might weep day and night
                   for the slain of *my dear people?*

15. *Rhetorical Discourse in the Prophets* 171

> *Who* can make for me in the desert
> a traveler's lodge
> So I might forsake my people
> and go away from them?

A large-scale epiphora occurs in Amos 7.14-15, where the fivefold repetition of 'yet you did not return to me' becomes a virtual refrain.

Alliteration. Alliteration is the repetition of consonants in succession, usually occurring at the beginning of two or more consecutive words, or in words near to one another. This is a figure of sound, not meaning. Quite often there will also be *paronomasia*. In Jeremiah:

Jer. 17.12-13a	The consonant *k* (כ) begins two words, and immediately following are five successive words beginning with the *m* (מ) consonant
Jer. 48.15	The combination *bḥ* (בח) repeats three times (paronomasia)
Jer. 49.15	The *b* (ב) consonant repeats three times.

Inclusio. The inclusio structures poetic and prose discourse by repeating at the end of a given discourse, or portion of discourse, words or phrases occurring at the beginning. Sometimes the end terms will be synonyms or fixed equivalents of the beginning terms. Classicists call this figure 'ring composition'. The inclusio commonly functions to effect closure, although it can simply give emphasis and have other functions. This inclusio appears in Amos:

Amos 2.9	Yet I destroyed *the Amorite* before them
	Whose height was like the height of the cedars and who was as strong as the oaks I destroyed his fruit above and his roots beneath Also I brought you up out of the land of Egypt and led you forty years in the wilderness
	To possess the land of *the Amorite*.
Amos 5.2	Fallen, no more to *rise* is the virgin Israel Forsaken on her land with none to *raise her up*.

Other inclusios occur in Amos 5.10-12 (*gate...gate*) and Amos 8.9-10 (*day... day*).

Hosea crafts oracles with split bicolons containing keyword repetitions, for example:

Hos. 4.11-14   New wine takes away the mind of *my people*

They inquire of their thing of wood
   and their staff gives them oracles
For a spirit of whoredom has led them astray
   and they have gone a-whoring out from under their God
On the tops of the mountains they sacrifice
   and on the hills they burn offerings
Under oak, poplar, and terebinth
   because their shade is good!
Therefore your daughters play the whore
   and your sons' brides commit adultery
I will not punish your daughters when they play the whore
   nor your sons' brides when they commit adultery
For those men over there go aside with whores
   and sacrifice with sacred prostitutes

A people without sense will be thrust down!

Hos. 8.9-13   For *behold they* have gone up to Assyria

A wild ass off by himself
   Ephraim has hired lovers
Even though they hire among the nations
   now I will gather them up
So that they soon writhe under the burden
   of the officials' king
Indeed, Ephraim has multiplied altars
   he uses them for sinning
     altars for sinning
Though I write for him multitudes of my laws
   they are regarded as something strange
Sacrifices they love, so they sacrifice
   flesh, and they eat
     Yahweh takes no delight in them
Now he will remember their iniquity
   and punish their sins.

Behold they will return to Egypt!

Another keyword inclusio in Hosea:

Hos. 5.3-4   *I know* Ephraim
   and Israel is not hid from me
for now, Ephraim, you have played the harlot
   Israel is defiled
Their deeds do not permit them
   to return to their God
For the spirit of harlotry is within them
   and *they know not* Yahweh.

15. *Rhetorical Discourse in the Prophets*

The prophetess Huldah framed her celebrated Josiah oracle with an inclusio:

> 2 Kgs 22.16-20 *I will bring/evil/upon this place*
> ...*all the evil/that I will bring/upon this place*

Nahum's preaching contains this inclusio:

> Nah. 1.9-11 What do you *plot against Yahweh?*
> He will make a full end
> he will not take vengeance twice on his foes
> Like tangled thorns they are consumed
> like dry stubble
> Did one not come out from you
> who *plotted* evil *against Yahweh*
> and counseled villainy?

Jeremiah makes liberal use of the inclusio, reflecting as one might expect the rhetoric of Deuteronomy where the inclusio is the controlling rhetorical structure of the First Edition (chaps. 1–28). A single word creates this inclusio in a double bicolon:

> Jer. 5.21 *Hear* this, would you please
> stupid people without heart
> They have eyes but do not see
> they have ears but do not *hear*.

There is also irony here: The prophet asks a people to hear who cannot hear.

Jeremiah points up one of many incongruities with this inclusio, where also epiphora occurs at the center:

> Jer. 4.22 For my people are fools
> me *they do not know*
> stupid children are **they**
> not discerning are **they**
> wise are they to do evil
> but to do good, *they do not know*.

Jeremiah's three Temple Oracles all make use of the inclusio:

> Jer. 7.3-7 *and I will let you dwell in this place...*
> *then I will let you dwell in this place*
>
> Jer. 7.8-11 *Look*
> *Look!*
>
> Jer. 7.12-14 *my place...in Shiloh...*
> *the place...to Shiloh*

Jeremiah's defense before the court begins and ends:

> Jer. 26.12-15 *Yahweh sent me...all the things...*
> ...*Yahweh sent me...all these things*

Entire poems in Jeremiah have inclusio structures (3.1-5; 10.6-7; 20.7-10, 14-18; 51.11-14).

In Joel is this inclusio:

> Joel 1.19-20
>
> *For fire has devoured*
>   *the pastures of the wilderness*
> and flame has burned
>   all the trees of the field
> Even the wild beasts cry to you
>   because the water brooks are dried up
> *Yes, fire has devoured*
>   *the pastures of the wilderness.*

Chiasmus. Chiasmus is an inversion of words, word cognates, fixed pairs, syntactic units, and even sounds in the bicolon, the verse, and the larger composition. In larger structures, the center of the chiasmus is the turning point, also frequently the climax.[4] This figure occurs in both the poetry and prose of the prophets. These keyword chiasms from Amos:

> Amos 2.11-12
>
> And I raised up some of your sons for *prophets*
>   and some of your young men for *Nazirites*
>   Is it not indeed so, O people of Israel?
>   but you made the *Nazirites* drink wine
> and commanded the *prophets*: 'You shall not prophesy'.

> Amos 5.4-6a
>
> *Seek me and live*
>   but do not seek *Bethel*
>   and do not enter into *Gilgal*
>   or cross over to *Beersheba*
>   for *Gilgal* shall surely go into exile
>   and *Bethel* shall come to nought
> *Seek Yahweh and live.*

Another keyword chiasmus occurs in Amos 2.14-16.

From the prophet Hosea:

> Hos. 12.4-5a
>
> In the womb he took his brother by the heel
>   and in his manhood *he strove* with God
>   yes *he strove* with an angel and prevailed
> He wept and sought his favor.

Here keywords in the center repeat the account of Jacob's wrestling at the Jabbok (Gen. 32.22-32); the first and last colons recount Jacob's relationship with brother Esau.

---

4. Nils W. Lund, *Chiasmus in the New Testament* (Chapel Hill, NC: University of North Carolina Press, 1942). p. 40 [repr. Peabody, MA: Hendrickson, 1992].

An entire keyword chiasmus in Hosea is the following:

> Hos. 13.14　　　Shall I ransom them from the power of *Sheol*?
> Shall I redeem them from *Death*?
> O *Death*, where are your plagues?
> O *Sheol*, where is your destruction?

Isaiah makes a keyword chiasmus with fixed word pairs:

> Isa. 5.7　　　For the *vineyard* of Yahweh of hosts
> is the *house of Israel*
> and the *men of Judah*
> are his *pleasant planting*.

This keyword chiasmus turns up in the preaching of Micah:

> Mic. 3.2-3　　　who tear the *skin* from off my people
> and their *flesh* from off their bones
> who eat the *flesh* of my people
> and flay their *skin* from off them.

Jeremiah crafts an array of chiastic structures. This one is laden with irony:

> Jer. 2.27b-28a　　　But *in the time of their trouble* they say
> '*Arise and save us*'
> but where are your gods which you made for yourselves?
> Let them *arise* if they can *save* you
> *in your time of trouble*.

At the center Yahweh interrupts the peoples' cry to pose a question of his own.

This keyword chiasmus in Jeremiah has long been noted:

> Jer. 9.4　　　Each person beware of his *fellow*
> and every *brother* do not trust
> for every *brother* is a 'Jacob'
> And every *fellow* goes about slandering.

Large keyword chiasms in whole poems occur in Jer. 2.5-9; 5.1-8; 8.13-17; and 51.34-45.

From the prophet Joel is this chiasmus using both repetition and fixed word pairs:

> Joel 2.28-29　　　And it shall be afterwards: *I will pour out my spirit* on all flesh
> your *sons* and your *daughters* shall prophesy
> your *old men* shall dream dreams
> and your *young men* shall see visions
> even upon the *menservants* and *maidservants*
> In those days, *I will pour out my spirit*.

Peter quotes this prophecy at Pentecost (Acts 2.17-18), but inverts the center colons.

Zechariah crafts this keyword chiasmus:

> Zech. 9.5 *Ashkelon* shall see it, and be afraid
> *Gaza* too, and shall writhe in anguish
> *Ekron* also, because its hopes are confounded
> The king shall perish from *Gaza*
> *Ashkelon* shall be uninhabited.

Another type of chiasmus is made by inverted syntax. From Isaiah:

> Isa. 11.1 It shall come/a shoot from the stump of Jesse
> and a branch from his roots/it shall grow.

Jeremiah's poetry teems with syntactic chiasms, where verbs are typically placed at the extremes. A few examples:

> Jer. 2.19 It will chasten you/your wickedness
> and your apostasy/will reprove you
>
> Jer. 4.7 It has gone up/a lion from the thicket
> and a destroyer of nations/has gone forth
>
> Jer. 4.9 And they shall be appalled/the priests
> and the prophets/shall be astounded
>
> Jer. 20.6 You shall go/into captivity
> and Babylon/you shall enter.

Only rarely does Jeremiah place verbs in the center:

> Jer. 2.36 So by Egypt/you will be shamed
> as you were shamed/by Assyria
>
> Jer. 51.38 Together like lions/they shall roar
> they shall growl/like lion's whelps.

Multiclinatum. *Multiclinatum* is the repetition of verbal roots in succession, occurring often in Jeremiah where it is a virtual signature of the prophet:

> Jer. 11.18 Yahweh made me know, and I knew
>
> Jer. 15.19 If you return, then I will let you return
>
> Jer. 17.14 Heal me, Yahweh, and I shall be healed
>
> Jer. 20.7 You enticed me, Yahweh, and I was enticed.

Accumulation

The celebrated rhetorical prose in Jeremiah and the Deuteronomic literature is largely accumulation (*accumulatio*). It is heavy and stereotyped, with nouns heaping up in twos, threes, and fours, and longer phrases balancing

15. *Rhetorical Discourse in the Prophets* 177

rhythmically in parallelism. Accumulation is found also in poetry. Hebrew rhetoric, says Muilenburg, strives after totality.[5]

Accumulatio. Accumulatio turns up most often in the Jeremiah prose. Some examples:

> *the cities of Judah...the streets of Jerusalem* (Jer. 7.17, 34; 11.6; 33.10; 44.6, 17, 21)
> *the voice of joy and the voice of gladness, the voice of groom and the voice of bride* (Jer. 7.34; 16.9; 25.10; 33.11)
> *the(ir) dead bodies...will be food for the birds of the skies and the beasts of the earth* (Jer. 7.33; 16.4; 19.7; 34.20)
> *disgrace, proverb...taunt and curse* (Jer. 24.9; and variously in Jer. 19.8; 25.9; 29.18; 44.12)

Often nouns appear in triads:

> *into a fortified city, and into an iron pillar, and into walls of bronze, against its princes, against its priests, and against the people of the land* (Jer. 1.18)
> *by sword, and by famine, and by pestilence* (Jer. 14.12; 21.9; 24.10; 27.8)

Some examples of accumulatio in the Jeremianic poetry:

Jer. 1.10
> *to uproot and to break down*
> *and to destroy and to overthrow*
> *to build up and to plant*

Jer. 12.7
> *I have forsaken my house*
> *I have abandoned my heritage*
> *I have given the beloved of my soul*
> *into the hand of her enemies.*

Accumulatio turns up also in the poetry of Joel:

Joel 2.19   *grain, wine, and oil*

Asyndeton. Asyndeton is the rapid accumulation of verbs, with or without connectives, in both prose and poetry. Classical authors used asyndeton to heap up praise or blame. Jeremiah uses the figure to heap up blame (7.9), press home a message of divine judgment (51.20-23), or emphasize the joy attending Israel's future salvation (31.4-5). Other examples:

Jer. 4.5   *Blow...cry out, pour it out, and say:*

Jer. 5.1   *Go back and forth in the streets of Jerusalem, look please, and take note, and search her squares.*

---

5. Muilenburg, 'A Study in Hebrew Rhetoric', p. 99.

From Jeremiah's Foreign Nation Oracles:

Jer. 46.3-4	*Ready* buckler and shield!
	    and advance to battle!
	Harness the horses!
	    and *rise up*, O horsemen!
	Stand ready with helmets!
	    Polish lances.
	        Put on scale armor!

Jer. 49.8	*Flee! Be gone! Go deep to dwell*
Jer. 49.30	*Flee! Wander all about! Go deep to dwell!*

Chain Figure. This figure, which lacks a better name, occurs in Joel's locust parade:

Joel 1.4	What the *cutting locust* left
	    the *swarming locust* has eaten
	What the *swarming locust* left
	    the *hopping locust* has eaten
	And what the *hopping locust* left
	    the *destroying locust* has eaten.

The function of this figure is to express totality. It is not to be confused with the *sortie*, which came with the infusion of Greco-Roman rhetoric into postexilic Jewish life in the fourth century BCE.[6] The sortie (Gk. *climax*; Lat. *gradatio*) appears in the Jewish writings of *Pirqe Aboth* (1.1) and the Wis. Sol (6.17-19). It, too, is a catalogue of statements, each word picking up from a preceding word, but its function is to lead to a climax. The sortie was used often by Paul, for example, in Rom. 5.3-5: 'More than that we rejoice in our *sufferings,* knowing that *suffering* produces *endurance*, and *endurance* produces *character*, and *character* produces *hope*, and *hope* does not disappoint us'; and in Rom. 8.29-30: 'For those whom he foreknew he also *predestined* to be conformed to the image of his Son...and those whom he *predestined* he also *called*; and those whom he *called* he also *justified*; and those whom he *justified* he also glorified'.

Tropes
Tropes are words or expressions used to mean something other than what they normally mean, yet having a connectedness to normal meanings—sometimes through a link term—so as to give an idea freshness or emphasis.[7]

---

6. Henry A. Fischel, 'The Use of Sorties (Climax, Gradatio) in the Tannaitic Period', *HUCA* 44 (1973), pp. 119-51.
7. William J. Brandt, *The Rhetoric of Argumentation* (New York: Bobbs-Merrill, 1970), pp. 135-37.

15. *Rhetorical Discourse in the Prophets*

Prophets, like all good orators, embellished their oracles and other speeches with tropes, which strengthened the discourse and kindled audience imagination. Common tropes are the metaphor, simile, allegory, metonymy, synecdoche, abusio, epithet, and irony, all of which are well represented in discourse of the prophets.

Metaphor. Metaphors are tropes in which figurative terms or descriptions are superimposed over literal terms or descriptions, creating a vivid mental likeness of objects or ideas. In lowering the level of abstraction, metaphors make ideas more concrete. At the same time, they appeal to the imagination. Prophetic discourse teems with metaphors, some of the more common drawing from the family, animals, sex, the wilderness, the hunt, cooking, agriculture, and the military. Animal metaphors occur very often. Amos, Hosea, and Jeremiah sometime combine metaphors with similes or literal equivalents, which, according to modern tastes, weaken the figure.

One of the most striking metaphors in the Old Testament is Amos' use of 'lion' for God:

> Amos 3.8　　*The Lion has roared*
> 　　　　　　　who will not fear?
> 　　　　　　　Yahweh God has spoken
> 　　　　　　　who will not prophesy?

'Lion' here is a pure metaphor for God, a coinage without parallel in the Hebrew Bible. Another striking metaphor from Amos:

> Amos 4.1　　Hear this word, you *cows of Bashan*.

Here the prophet follows with a clarifying word, identifying the 'cows of Bashan' as the women of Samaria who oppress the poor and whine to their husbands for something more to drink.

Some of the most memorable metaphors emanate from Hosea, who describes the covenant as a relationship between 'father and son' or between 'husband and wife' (Hosea 2; 11.1, 3). Other metaphors from Hosea:

> Hos. 7.8　　*Ephraim is a cake not turned*
>
> Hos. 10.1　　*Israel is a luxuriant vine*
>
> Hos. 10.11　　*Ephraim was a trained heifer that loved to thresh*

In the following examples, Hosea combines metaphors with literal equivalents:

> Hos. 8.9　　*A wild ass wandering alone*
> 　　　　　　Ephraim has hired lovers
>
> Hos. 9.16　　Ephraim is stricken
> 　　　　　　　*their root is dried up*
> 　　　　　　　*they shall bear no fruit*

Hos. 12.7   *A trader in whose hands are false balances*
             he loves to oppress

Hos. 13.12-13   The iniquity of Ephraim is bound up
                 his sin is kept in store
                 The pangs of childbirth come for him
                 but he is a dumb son
                 for now he does not present himself
                 at the mouth of the womb.

Jeremiah's preaching owes a great debt to the preaching of Hosea. His metaphors describe Yahweh, the false gods, kings, the nation, the enemy, and even the prophet himself. One of his more memorable metaphors for God:

Jer. 2.13   they have forsaken me, *the fountain of living waters*

The false gods, says Jeremiah, are

broken cisterns, which do not hold water

Jeremiah's most disparaging metaphors are reserved for his own nation:

Jer. 2.20   *you broke your yoke*
             you tore away your straps

Jer. 2.23-24   *a swift young camel crisscrossing her tracks*
                a wild ass..in her desirous craving sniffing the wind

Jer. 5.8   *well-endowed early-rising horses.*

Like Hosea, Jeremiah will sometimes combine a metaphor with a clarifying statement:

Jer. 3.3   The *brow of a whore-woman* you have
            you refuse to be disgraced

Jer. 4.7   *A lion has come up from the thicket*
            a destroyer of nations set out.

Simile. The simile is a metaphor with 'as' or 'like', resulting in an imaginative comparison.

Hosea's preaching contains an abundance of similes.

Hos. 4.16   *Like a stubborn heifer, Israel is stubborn*

Hos. 5.14   *For I will be like a lion to Ephraim*
             and like a young lion to the house of Judah

Hos. 6.4   *Your love is like a morning cloud*
             like the dew that goes early away

Hos. 7.11   *Ephraim is like a dove*
             silly and without sense

Hos. 7.16   *They are like a treacherous bow.*

15. Rhetorical Discourse in the Prophets

Similes, like metaphors, are sometimes combined with clarifying statements:

| Hos. 7.7 | *All of them are hot as an oven* |
| | *and they devour their rulers* |

Jeremiah's similes cover much the same ground as his metaphors:

Jer. 4.13	*Look, like clouds he comes up*
	and like the whirlwind his chariots
Jer. 4.17	*like keepers of a field they are against her round about*
Jer. 4.31	*distress like one bearing her first child*
Jer. 6.24	*pain like a woman in labor*
Jer. 8.6	Everyone turns into their course
	like a horse plunging headlong into battle
Jer. 9.22	*The human corpses shall fall*
	like dung in the open field
	like grain stalks after the reaper

Second Isaiah uses a simile that compares God to a mother:

| Isa. 42.14 | *Now I will cry out like a woman in travail* |
| | *I will gasp and pant.* |

Abusio. One of the harsher tropes is the abusio, which is an implied metaphor. This type of metaphor behaves somewhat extravagantly, in that a word is taken from one usage and put to another. Abusios can be made from either nouns or verbs.

This abusio occurs in both Amos and Joel:

| Amos 1.2 | Yahweh *roars* from Zion |
| Joel 3.16 | Yahweh *roars* from Zion. |

In Hosea are these *abusios*:

Hos. 8.7	They *sow* the wind
	and they shall *reap* the whirlwind
Hos. 10.13	You have *plowed* iniquity
	you have *reaped* injustice
	you have *eaten* the fruit of lies
Hos. 12.1	Ephraim *herds* the wind.

Jeremiah's most memorable images are abusios:

Jer. 4.4	Remove the foreskins of *your hearts*
Jer. 5.8	each man *neighing* for his neighbor's wife
Jer. 7.28	truth *perished, it was severed* from their mouth
Jer. 18.18	Come, let us smite him with *the tongue*
Jer. 51.44	nations no longer *stream* to him

In the following example, Jeremiah combines an abusio with a clarifying statement:

> Jer. 6.10   Look! *their ear* has foreskin
> they are unable to take heed.

Euphemism. Another example of 'language at a stretch' is the euphemism, which is the substitution of a milder term or one with adjunct meaning for a term deemed too harsh or too explicit. In Jeremiah:

> Jer. 13.22   For your great sin, *your skirts* were exposed
> *your heels* were violated

He really means the 'private parts' of a personified nation. The same indelicacy is alluded to in another euphemism:

> Jer. 13.26   Your *disgrace* was seen.

Parable. Jesus, like the rabbis generally, taught in parables, but some can be found also in the Old Testament. Hosea says: 'I spoke to the prophets; it was I who multiplied visions, and through the prophets *I give parables*' (Hos. 12.10).

Nathan uses a parable to trap King David regarding his sin against Uriah the Hittite:

> There were two men in a certain city, the one rich and the other poor. The rich man had very many flocks and herds; but the poor man had nothing but one little ewe lamb, which he had bought. And he brought it up, and it grew up with him and with his children; it used to eat of his morsel, and drink from his cup, and lie in his bosom, and it was like a daughter to him. Now there came a traveler to the rich man, and he was unwilling to take one of his own flock or herd to prepare for the wayfarer who had come to him, but he took the poor man's ewe lamb, and prepared it for the man who had come to him (2 Sam. 12.1-4).

Then Nathan points the finger saying: 'You are the man!' (v. 7), after which the parable is given an explanation.

An unnamed prophet traps King Ahab in similar fashion with a disguise and a parable:

> Your servant went out into the midst of the battle; and behold a soldier turned and brought a man to me, and said, 'Keep this man; if by any means he be missing, your life shall be for his life, or else you shall pay a talent of silver' (1 Kgs 20.39).

Ahab concurred with the judgment, at which point the prophet threw off the bandage on his eye and applied the judgment to the king. Isaiah's well-known 'Song of the Vineyard' (Isa. 5.1-7) is a parable with a built-in interpretation.

Allegory. An allegory is an extended metaphor in which a series of actions is symbolic of other actions, and in which the symbolism frequently—but not always—involves personification.

Jeremiah's oracle on the 'Fallen Sisters' is an allegory:

> And Yahweh said to me in the days of Josiah the king:
> Have you seen what she did, Rebel Israel, that woman going up on every high hill and under every leafy tree and whoring there? And I thought, After she has done all these things she will return to me, but she did not return. And Faithless, her sister Judah, saw it. And she saw that precisely because Rebel Israel committed adultery I sent her away—handed her a bill of divorce. Yet Faithless Judah, her sister, was not afraid, and went and played the whore—she too! And she took her whoring casually, polluted the land, and committed adultery with the stone and with the tree. And yet for all this Faithless, her sister Judah, did not return to me wholeheartedly, but falsely—oracle of Yahweh.
>
> And Yahweh said to me:
> Rebel Israel is herself more righteous than Faithless Judah! (Jer. 3.6-11).

Ezekiel is the prophet of the allegory, as we know best from his 'faithless wife' allegory in chap. 16 and his 'Oholah and Oholibah' allegory in chap. 23. Zechariah, too, gives us an allegory, on 'Grace and Union' (Zech. 11.4-14).

Epithet. An epithet is an honorific or disparaging title giving character to a name. Isaiah and Jeremiah are particularly fond of epithets:

Isa. 30.7	Egypt is called 'Rahab Who Sits Still'
Jer. 3.23	Baal is called 'Noise of the Mountain'
Jer. 17.13	Yahweh is called 'The Hope of Israel'
Jer. 30.17	Jerusalem is called 'The Zion Whom No One Cares about'
Jer. 46.17	Pharaoh is called 'Loud Noise, Who Lets the Deadline Pass'
Jer. 50.7	Yahweh is called 'The Righteous Pasture' and 'Hope of their Fathers'

Metonymy. Metonymy is the substitution of a word for another it suggests, usually the abstract for the concrete. From Jeremiah:

Jer. 4.29	*every city* is fleeing

'Every city' here means 'the people of every city'.

Jer. 26.2	*all the cities of Judah* who come to worship in the house of Yahweh

'All the cities of Judah' means 'all the people of the cities of Judah'.

> Jer. 32.24   Look, the *siege ramps* have come to the city to take it

'Siege ramps' means 'the Babylonian army that has built the siege ramps'.

> Jer. 33.4   toward the *sword*

'Sword' here means 'the Chaldeans wielding the sword'.

> Jer. 50.6   *mountains* led them astray

'Mountains' refer in this case to the 'fertility worship taking place on the mountains'.

Synecdoche. Synecdoche is a type of metonymy in which a part is substituted for the whole, or the whole for a part. From Jeremiah:

> Jer. 4.20   suddenly my tents are devastated
> in a moment *my curtains*

'My curtains' represents all the home furnishings.

> Jer. 14.12   [Judah's] *gates* languish

Judah's 'gates' are Judah's cities.

> Jer. 32.4   *his mouth* shall speak with *his mouth*

Nebuchadnezzar and Zedekiah will meet personally.

Merismus. A form of synecdoche, in which a totality is expressed by contrasts or extremes:

> Jer. 51.22   *old and young*

Reference here is to 'everyone'.

Comparison

Speech that carries over elements of likeness from one thing to another thing yields a comparison (Lat. *similitudo*). The figure is used to clarify or reprove. Metaphors are commonly expanded into comparisons, being more general and less vivid than similes. Jeremiah contains the following comparisons using כְּ...כֵּן and אַף...כֵּן constructions:

> Jer. 2.26   *like* the shame of a thief when found out
> *so* the house of Israel is deeply shamed
>
> Jer. 3.20   *Surely as* a woman faithless to her companion
> *so* you have been faithless to me, house of Israel
>
> Jer. 5.27   *as* a cage is full of birds
> *so* their houses are full of loot

Jer. 6.7	*as* a well keeps fresh its water *so* she has kept fresh her evil
Jer. 18.6	*like* clay in the hand of a potter *so* are you in my hand, house of Israel

Second Isaiah compares God to a comforting mother:

Isa. 66.13	*as* one whom his mother comforts *so* I will comfort you.

Contrast

Prophets also make contrasts, a figure in classical rhetoric called the *antithesis*. The antithesis is an opposition created by contrasting words, phrases, or ideas. From Isaiah comes this well-known contrast:

Isa. 1.3	The ox knows its owner and the ass its master's crib But Israel does not know my people does not understand

Jeremiah's preaching is filled with contrasts, most of them with rhetorical questions used as a foil. The following example does not use rhetorical questions but is nevertheless a contrast of the 'But my people' type:

Jer. 8.7	Even the stork in the skies knows her seasons The turtledove, swift, and swallow keep the time of their coming But my people do not know the order of Yahweh

See also the contrast between the 'cursed and blessed man' in Jer. 17.5-8, and the contrast of the 'two ways' in Jer. 21.8-9.

Oxymoron. An oxymoron is the juxtaposition of incongruous or contradictory terms. From Jeremiah:

Jer. 25.9	Nebuchadrezzar, the king of Babylon, *my servant*

'My servant' in the mouth of Yahweh is otherwise a term of endearment.

Argument

While prophets speak with divine authority, they also use argument, particularly Jeremiah, whose rhetoric comes closer to Greek dialectic than that of any other prophet, including Haggai, Zechariah, and Malachi, who use question and answer to great effect.

Authority. In Hebrew rhetoric the driving force behind the assertive discourse of one speaking for God is *authority*, which substitutes for *ethos* in classical rhetoric. Elijah speaks thus to Ahab:

> 1 Kgs 17.1   As Yahweh the God of Israel lives, before whom I stand, there shall be neither dew nor rain these years, except by my word.

Enthymeme. The enthymeme, as was pointed out earlier, is a syllogism lacking one premise, usually the major premise. In prophetic preaching, the major premise can be supplied from Deuteronomic preaching. In Jeremiah, the enthymeme often takes the form:

> [A Judah not listening to Yahweh's word will be punished]
> Judah—or its king, priests, prophets, people—has not listened to Yahweh's word
> Judah—or its king, priests, prophets, people—will be punished.

Protasis–Apodosis. The protasis–apodosis form ('If...then...') is at home in legal discourse, but one finds it in the preaching of Jeremiah:

> Jer. 4.1-2   *If* you return, Israel—oracle of Yahweh
>   to me you return
> *And if* you remove your wretched things from me
>   and do not waver about
> *Then* you can swear 'By Yahweh's life'
>   in truth, in justice, and in righteousness
> *Then* nations shall bless themselves in him
>   and in him they shall boast.
>
> Jer. 31.36-37   *If* these statutes depart
>   from before me—oracle of Yahweh
> *Then* the seed of Israel shall cease
>   from being a nation before me—all the days.
>
> *If* the heavens above can be measured
>   and the foundations of the earth explored to the depths
> *Then* I, I will reject all the seed of Israel
>   because of all that they have done—oracle of Yahweh.

Arguments a minori ad maius. The argument *a minori ad maius* (Hillel: *qal vechomer*) is from the lesser to the greater. In the New Testament, it is expressed with the phrase 'how much more'. In Jeremiah we encounter these examples of the *a minori ad maius* argument:

> Jer. 3.1   *Look! [if]* a man sends away *his wife*
>   and she goes from him
>   and becomes wife to another man
>   will he return to her again?
> Would not that land
>   be greatly polluted?

> *But* you, you have whored with *many companions*
> and would you return to me?

Jer. 12.5
> *If* with men on foot you have run and they wearied you
> *how then* will you fare in a heat with horses?
> And [*if*] in a peaceful land you have fallen down
> *how then* will you do in the jungle of the Jordan?

Jeremiah uses this same argument in addressing the nations:

Jer. 25.29
> For look, *if* I am beginning to work evil in the city upon which my name is called, *then* for you, shall you assuredly go unpunished?

In one case, Jeremiah poses the argument and then answers it:

Jer. 49.12
> Look, [*if*] those for whom there is no judgment to drink the cup must surely drink, are you *then* one who will surely go free? You will not go free, for you will surely drink!

Haggai uses an argument *a minori ad maius* in order to get the Temple rebuilt:

Hag. 1.4
> Is it time for you yourselves to dwell in your paneled houses, while this house lies in ruins?

Rhetorical Question. This is a question posed for which there is only one answer, but because the answer is self-evident or self-condemnatory, the addressee will not give it. Rhetorical questions function as emphatic statements and are often used to intimidate. All the prophets employ the rhetorical question. One comes to Saul from Samuel, which the prophet then answers:

1 Sam. 15.22
> Has Yahweh as great delight in burnt offerings and sacrifices
> as in obeying the voice of Yahweh?
> Look! to obey is better than sacrifice
> and to hearken than the fat of rams.

Prophets used rhetorical questions as foils for preferred subjects. Nothing quite matches the string of rhetorical questions in Amos 3.3-8:

> Do two walk together
> unless they have made an appointment?
> Does a lion roar in the forest
> when he has no prey?
> Does a young lion cry out from his den
> if he has taken nothing?
> Does a bird fall in a snare on the earth
> when there is no trap for it?
> Does a snare spring up from the ground
> when it has taken nothing?

>   Is a trumpet blown in the city
>   and the people are not afraid?
>   Does evil befall a city
>   unless Yahweh has done it?
>   ....
>   The Lion has roared
>   who will not fear?
>   Yahweh God has spoken
>   who will not prophesy?

Isaiah follows up these rhetorical questions with a bit of irony:

Isa. 10.15	Shall the axe vaunt itself over him who hews with it
	   or the saw magnify itself against him who wields it?
	As if a rod should wield him who lifts it
	   or as if a staff should lift him who is not wood!

Jeremiah uses rhetorical questions as much as Amos does, but they are not as mechanical. His set-up questions in almost every case contain a word or thought link to the preferred subject, which comes next. Jeremiah puts the rhetorical question to two specialized uses, both aimed at exposing an incongruity. In one, a single or double question lifts up some paradigmatic behavior, a common happening, or something built into the natural order, which the prophet then contrasts to the nation's behavior, judged to be scandalous:

Jer. 2.11	Has a nation exchanged gods
	   even though they are no-gods?
	But my people has exchanged its glory
	   for No Profit!

Jer. 2.32	Can a maiden forget her ornaments
	   a bride her knotted cords?
	But my people have forgotten me
	   days without number

Jer. 18.14-15	Can it leave the mountain highland
	   the snow of Lebanon?
	Can foreign waters dry up
	   the cool flowing streams?
	But my people have forgotten me
	   they burn incense in vain.

The second type is a threefold question in the הַ...אִם...מַדּוּעַ... (commonly 'Is...is...so why?' or 'If...if...so why?') form, which is a signature of this prophet. Here two rhetorical questions are a foil for the third, which states the troubling vexation Jeremiah really wants to address. Some examples:

15. *Rhetorical Discourse in the Prophets* 189

Jer. 2.14	Is Israel a slave? Is he a house-born? So why has he become plunder?
Jer. 2.31	Have I become a wilderness to Israel? or a land of thick darkness? So why do my people say, 'We are free to roam we will no longer come to you?'
Jer. 8.4-5	If [people] fall down, do they not get up? If one turns away, does he not return? So why has this people turned away, Jerusalem, the rebel perpetual?
Jer. 8.22	Is there no balm in Gilead? Is there no healer there? Indeed, so why has it not arisen healing for my dear people?

Hypophora. Sometimes Jeremiah will answer his own rhetorical question, which in the classical rhetorical handbooks was given the name *hypophora*:

Jer. 6.20	Why is it frankincense comes to me from Sheba
	    and the good cane from a distant land?
	Your offerings are not acceptable
	    your sacrifices are not pleasing to me

Jer. 31.20	Is Ephraim my dear son?
	    the child of my delight?
	For as often as I speak of him
	    I certainly remember him still

Jer. 46.7-8	Who is this that rises like the Nile
	    like the great river, its waters swell?
	Egypt rises like the Nile
	    and like the great river, the waters are swollen

Jer. 49.7	Is there no longer wisdom in Teman?
	    counsel has perished from people of understanding
	    their wisdom stinks!

Surrender. 'Surrender' (Gk. *epitropē*; Lat. *permissio*) is a veiled argument in which one yields a matter to the will of another. This argument was commonly used in court cases. An example from the *ad Herennium*:

> Since only soul and body remain to me, now that I am deprived of everything else, even these, which alone of many goods are left me, I deliver up to you and to your power. You may use and even abuse me in your own way as you think best; with impunity make your decision upon me, whatever it may be; speak and give a sign—I shall obey (*ad Herennium* 4.29; LCL).

In his celebrated trial of 609 BCE, Jeremiah spoke thus to the court:

> But as for me, look! I am in your hands. Do with me as seems good and right in your eyes. Only know for sure that if you put me to death you will bring innocent blood upon yourselves and on this city and its inhabitants; for in truth Yahweh sent me to you to speak in your ears all these things (Jer. 26.14-15).

Descriptio. In classical rhetoric, *descriptio* was an argument used by either the prosecution or the defense to describe adverse consequences of possible court action. The *ad Herennium* proposes this descriptio for a defense:

> For if you inflict a heavy penalty upon the defendant, men of the jury, you will at once by a single judgment have taken many lives. His aged father, who has set the entire hope of his last years on this young man, will have no reason for wishing to stay alive. His small children, deprived of their father's aid, will be exposed as objects of scorn and contempt to their father's enemies. His entire household will collapse under this undeserved calamity. But his enemies, when once they have won the bloody palm by this most cruel of victories, will exult over the miseries of these unfortunates, and will be found insolent on the score of deeds as well as of words (*ad Herennium* 4.39; LCL).

Jeremiah in his defense before the court says:

> Only know for sure that if you put me to death, then you will bring innocent blood upon yourselves and to this city and to its inhabitants; for in truth Yahweh sent me to you to speak in your ears all these things (Jer. 26.15).

Distributio. A speaker will sometimes say, 'Not this…but that…', which is an argument classical rhetoricians called the *distributio*. This figure does more than compare; it apportions. Jeremiah used a *distributio* in his exchange with the prophet Hananiah:

> Jer. 28.8-9   The prophets who were before me and before you, from ancient times, yes, they prophesied to many lands and against great kingdoms of war and evil and pestilence. The prophet who prophesies peace, when the word of that prophet comes to be, the prophet whom Yahweh has truly sent will be known.

A 'broken distributio' destroys a distinction widely held to be true, arguing for inclusiveness. These turn up in successive Jeremiah oracles:

> Jer. 23.23-24   Am I a God nearby
> oracle of Yahweh
> and not a God far off?

> If a person hides himself in secret places
>   do I myself not see him?
>   oracle of Yahweh
>
> The heavens and the earth
>   do I not fill?
>   oracle of Yahweh

Exaggerated Contrast. Hebrew rhetoric contains a type of distributio to which has been given the name 'exaggerated contrast'. This idiom juxtaposes statements solely to emphasize the one occurring second, having the practical effect of making the second statement more important than the first. The first statement negates an idea, but the speaker does not really mean to deny it, for it is otherwise valid or true. If the negation were to stand alone, it would be false. Some modern examples of the exaggerated contrast:

> You're not getting older, you're getting better (greeting card)
> The church is not a building; the church is people (theology)
> Not he who has died is dead
>   dead is rather the dead among the living (Arab proverb)
> Discrimination is not unfair; it is illegal (civil rights slogan)

Prophets use the exaggerated contrast in argument. From Amos and Jeremiah:

Amos 7.14	I am no prophet, nor a prophet's son, but I am a herdsman and a dresser of sycamore trees
Jer. 7.22-23	For I did not speak to your fathers nor did I command them in the day of my bringing them out of the land of Egypt about such things as burnt offerings and sacrifices. But this word I commanded them: Hear my voice, and I will be for you God; as for you, you will be to me a people
Jer. 22.10	Do not weep for the dead, and do not condole for him; weep bitterly for him who goes away, for he will not return again to see the land of his birth.

Humor and Irony
Humor is difficult—some would say impossible—to define, yet we know it when we hear it. Correction: Some people know it when they hear it. Prophets in both relaxed and stressful contexts were playful with their audiences, sharing with them sudden flashes of insight and quick wit by the use of wordplay, hyperbole, and understatement, all of which would doubtless have put smiles on the faces of their hearers. It is widely conceded that irony was well known in ancient Israel. In ancient Greek culture, of

course, it was developed into a fine art. Irony there was conceived originally as feigned ignorance or agreement meant to provoke one's antagonist (Socratic irony); an *eirōn* was someone who said less than what they meant. More commonly, irony was saying with sublety or ambiguity the opposite of what one meant (verbal irony). Irony addresses a double audience: one that hears but does not understand; and another that perceives more than what meets the ear, as well as the outsider's incomprehension. All the prophets possessed a sense of humor, and there is evidence aplenty that they were skilled in the use of irony. Wordplays emphasize and threaten; hyperbole is a countermeasure for audience resistance; and irony is but another way of telling the truth.

Paronomasia. Broadly defined, paronomasia is either a play on multiple meanings of identical or cognate words, or else a play on different words close enough in sound so as to make *assonance* (near-rhyme) or puns. Paronomasia more generally is called 'wordplay'. Paronomasia of both sound and meaning is everywhere present in the Old Testament, even in laments. The prophets used it to enliven discourse and facilitate audience attention.

Nathan, in an oracle to King David, conveys an important theological message by playing on the word 'house':

> Thus said Yahweh, Would you build me a *house* to dwell in? I have not dwelt in a *house* since the day I brought up the people of Israel from Egypt to this day... Moreover Yahweh declares to you that Yahweh will make you a *house* (2 Sam. 7.5-11).

David wanted to build Yahweh a house of cedar and stone, that is, a temple, but Yahweh comes back with a promise to build David a permanent 'house' of descendants.

From the later prophets we have an array of wordplays:

Amos 8.1-2	'summer fruit' (קָיִץ) and 'the end' (הַקֵּץ)
Mic. 1.10	'Tell it not in Gath, weep not at all' (בְּגַת אַל־תַּגִּידוּ בָּכוֹ אַל־תִּבְכּוּ)
Jer. 1.11-12	'almond' (שָׁקֵד) and 'watching' (שֹׁקֵד)
Jer. 2.12	'Be appalled, Heavens' (שֹׁמּוּ שָׁמַיִם)
Jer. 2.20	'high hill' (גִּבְעָה גְבֹהָה)
Jer. 5.13	'wind' (רוּחַ) meaning both 'spirit' and 'hot air'
Jer. 22.22	'all your shepherds (רֹעַיִךְ) the wind shall shepherd (תִּרְעֶה)'
Jer. 49.30	'Flee! Wander all about!' (נֻסוּ נֻּדוּ)
Jer. 51.44	'Bel in Babylon' (בֵּל בְּבָבֶל)

Like the classical poets, the Hebrew prophets enjoyed playing on both personal names and place names:

15. *Rhetorical Discourse in the Prophets*

Amos 5.5	'Gilgal shall surely go into exile' (הַגִּלְגָּל גָּלֹה יִגְלֶה)
Zeph. 2.4	'Gaza shall be deserted' (עַזָּה עֲזוּבָה תִהְיֶה)
Jer. 4.15	'the voice of one declaring from Dan' (קוֹל מַגִּיד מִדָּן)
Jer. 6.1	'in Tekoa blow the trumpet' (בִּתְקוֹעַ תִּקְעוּ שׁוֹפָר)
Jer. 9.4	'a supplanting Jacob' (עָקוֹב יַעְקֹב)
Jer. 48.2	'in Heshbon they planned' (בְּחֶשְׁבּוֹן חָשְׁבוּ)

Hyperbole. Hyperbole is a deliberate exaggeration of the truth where something is represented as greater or less, better or worse, than is possible. Its purpose is to magnify or minimize before an audience disinclined to listen. Rabbi Simeon ben Gamaliel (early 2nd century CE) noted exaggerated language in Deut. 1.28, where the returning spies said: 'The people are greater and taller than we; the cities are great and fortified up to heaven; and moreover we have seen the sons of the Anakim there' (*Sifre Deuteronomy* §25). Heschel says of the prophets: '[They] were unfair to the people of Israel. Their sweeping allegations, overstatements, and generalizations defied standards of accuracy. Some of the exaggerations reach the unbelievable'.[8]

An example of hyperbole in Isaiah:

Isa. 10.19	The remnant of the trees of the forest will be so few that a child can write them down.

Jeremiah uses hyperbole to heighten divine affirmations and respond to gross evil. In the case of the latter, he must address audiences who are unwilling to listen, exhibit shame, or repent.

Jer. 1.5	Before I formed you in the belly I knew you
	  and before you came forth from the womb I declared you holy
	  a prophet to the nations I made you.

Jer. 2.20	Indeed, on every high hill and under every leafy tree you bend backward, you whore.
Jer. 2.28	For as many as your cities are your gods, O Judah.
Jer. 3.2	Lift up your eyes to the bare heights and see where have you not been laid?

Jer. 4.13	Look, like clouds he comes up
	  and like the whirlwind his chariots
	His horses are swifter than eagles
	  woe to us, for we are devastated!

---

8. Abraham J. Heschel, *The Prophets* (New York: Harper and Row, 1962), p. 13.

| Jer. 37.10 | Even if you should strike down the entire army of the Chaldeans who are fighting against you, and there remained among them only wounded men, each man in his tent, they would rise up and burn this city with fire. |
| Jer. 50.20 | In those days and at that time…iniquity shall be sought in Israel and there shall be none, and sins in Judah, and they shall not be found. For I will pardon those whom I left remaining. |

Jeremiah follows up this hyperbole with a clarifying statement:

| Jer. 5.3 | They have made their faces harder than rock they refuse to repent. |

Litotes. Understatement for rhetorical effect was called *litotes* by the classical rhetoricians. This figure does not occur often in the Old Testament, as Hebrew rhetoric is more given to overstatement than understatement. But prophetic discourse does contain a few litotes.

In one Hebrew manuscript, Elijah is quoted by the king's messenger as having said to those who came to him: 'Go back to *the man* who sent you, and say to him' (2 Kgs 1.6), whereas the Masoretic Text reads: 'Go back to the king who sent you, and say to him'. To refer to the king as simply a 'man' is understatement, and this may be the better and original reading.

Huldah similarly substituted 'man' for 'king' in 2 Kgs 22.15, clearly an understatement.

From Jeremiah are these examples of litotes:

| Jer. 8.14 | let us be silent (= let us die) |
| Jer. 18.23 | their counsel (= their murderous plots) |

Dramatic Irony. The prophet Micaiah used dramatic irony when summoned by Jehoshaphat and Ahab to prophesy the outcome of a battle upon which the kings were about to embark. A company of four hundred prophets had already predicted success, but a contrary word was anticipated from Micaiah, who did not like Ahab. In order to defuse the situation, Micaiah begins by feigning agreement with the four hundred prophets: 'Go up and triumph; Yahweh will give it into the hand of the king' (1 Kgs 22.15). But Ahab is not fooled, and he tells the prophet to speak the truth, which he then proceeds to do.

Jeremiah in his encounter with the prophet Hananiah acted similarly. Knowing that Hananiah and some in the audience were hostile to Jeremiah's message calling for subservience to Nebuchadnezzar, Jeremiah at first feigned agreement with his opposite number. He said:

> Amen! So may Yahweh do! May Yahweh confirm your words that you have prophesied—to bring back the vessels of the house of Yahweh and all the exiles from Babylon to this place!

15. *Rhetorical Discourse in the Prophets* 195

But then the prophet followed with these words:

> But do hear this word that I speak in your ears and in the ears of all the people: The prophets who were before me and before you, from ancient times, yes, they prophesied to many lands and against great kingdoms of war and evil and pestilence. The prophet who prophesies peace, when the word of the prophet comes to be, the prophet whom Yahweh has truly sent will be known (Jer. 28.6-9).

Verbal Irony. Speakers resort to irony when straight talk fails, making ironic language desperate and extravagant. Isaiah is said to be the master of verbal irony. Irony appears early in the account of his call, in which a keyword chiasmus appears also:

Isa. 6.9-10
Go say to this people:
Hear and hear, but do not understand
  see and see, but do not perceive
Make the **heart** of this people fat
  and their **ears** heavy
    and shut their **eyes**
    lest they see with their **eyes**
  and hear with their **ears**
and understand with their **hearts**
and turn and be healed.

Isaiah uses irony in describing how to teach people given to hard drink:

Isa. 28.10, 13
For it is precept upon precept, precept upon precept
  line upon line, line upon line
    here a little, there a little.

On another occasion Isaiah advocates something worse than drunkenness, then explains:

Isa. 29.9-10
Stupefy yourselves and be in a stupor
  blind yourselves and be blind!
Be drunk, but not with wine
  stagger, but not with strong drink
For Yahweh has poured out upon you
  a spirit of deep sleep
and has closed your eyes, O prophets
  and covered your heads, O seers.

Jeremiah is every bit Isaiah's equal in this subtle art, using irony to address incongruities with razor sharpness. The great incongruity for Jeremiah is Israel's abandonment of Yahweh and the covenant, while at the same time showing enormous devotion to idols and idol worship:

Jer. 2.33
How well you make your way
  to seek love
So even you can teach
  your wicked ways.

Jer. 5.30-31   A frightful and horrible thing
                   has happened in the land
                The prophets, they prophesy by The Lie
                   and the priests, they rule at their sides
                And my people, they love it so!
                   But what will you do at the end of it?

Jer. 14.10   *So they have loved to wander*
                   their feet they did not restrain.

Sexual preferences are mocked when Jeremiah reverses the sexes in Baal fertility worship, making the tree masculine and the stone feminine:

Jer. 2.27   ...Who say to a tree, 'You are my father'
                   and to a stone, 'You gave me birth.'

Epitrophe. Epitrophe is the granting of permission for an action of which one disapproves. It is advice given 'tongue in cheek'. Some examples:

Elijah   Cry aloud, for he is a god; either he is musing, or he has gone aside, or he is on a journey, or perhaps he is asleep and must be awakened (1 Kgs 18.27).

Amos   Come to Bethel and transgress
               to Gilgal and multiply transgressions (Amos 4.4-5).

Hosea   Ephraim is joined to idols, let him alone (Hos. 4.17).

Micah   If a man should go about and utter winds and lies, saying,
               'I will preach to you of wine and strong drink',
                   he would be the preacher for this people! (Mic. 2.11)

Jeremiah   Your burnt offerings add to your sacrifices, and eat meat (Jer. 7.21).

Jeremiah   Whoever is to death—to death, and whoever is to the sword—to the sword, and whoever is to famine—to famine—and whoever is to captivity—to captivity (Jer. 15.2).

Jeremiah   Go up to Lebanon and scream
               and in the Bashan raise your voice!
            And scream from Abarim
               because all your lovers are broken (Jer. 22.20).

Jeremiah   Well then confirm your vows! Go ahead and perform your vows! (Jer. 44.25)

Drama

Drama is also found aplenty in prophetic preaching. The Foreign Nation Oracles of Amos, Isaiah, Obadiah, Nahum, Jeremiah and Ezekiel are all dramatic actions, in that they address audiences too distant to hear. Amos' oracles to the nations (Amos 1–2) have even more drama because of his strategy of circumlocution. Eight nations are addressed in all. Here the prophet will have no difficulty bringing his audience along as he thunders judgment on Damascus, Gaza, Tyre, Edom, Ammon and Moab. A northern Israelite audience might also assent to the next judgment, on Judah. But when Amos comes to indict and judge Israel, which is what he really wants to do, the audience, having given hearty assent to judgments on six or seven other nations, will find it difficult to stop the momentum and refrain from judging Israel. The prophet has trapped his audience into making a judgment they are disinclined to give, and his object has been achieved.

Jeremiah's preaching contains much drama. He uses simulated dialogue, also employing the classical figures of onomatopoeia, aposiopesis, apostrophe, personification, pathos and diminution, which is a rhythmic device.

Simulated Dialogue. Jeremiah alternates voices in his poetry, which simulates dialogue. This real or imagined speech occurs between the prophet and others, among other people, or between others—including the prophet—and God. Sometimes Jeremiah is heard speaking to himself (4.19; 5.4-5).

In Jer. 6.4-5 words of the enemy frame the frightened cry of besieged Jerusalem:

Enemy	Sanctify war against her
	up, let us attack at noon
Jerusalem	Woe to us, for the day has turned away
	for the shadows of evening have stretched out
Enemy	*up, let us attack at night*
	let us destroy her citadels.

Jeremiah 8.18-21 is a poem with an elaborate speaker chiasmus:

Jeremiah	My joy is gone
	grief is upon me
	my heart is sick
People	Listen! a voice…
	'Is Yahweh not in Zion?'
	'Is her king not in her?'
Yahweh	So why have they provoked me to anger with their images
	with their foreign nothings?
People	The harvest is past
	the summer is ended
	and we are not saved!
Jeremiah	For the brokenness of my dear people
	I am broken, I mourn
	desolation has gripped me.

The climax comes at the center, where Yahweh interrupts the questions of the people with a more important question of his own.

Open-ended Conclusions. Two speeches of Jeremiah are left open-ended, containing questions from Yahweh that the audience must answer for itself. In Jer. 3.1-5, the pressing question is posed at the beginning:

Jer. 3.1	But you, you have whored with many companions and would you return to me?

In Jer. 5.1-8, it is posed at the end:

Jer. 5.7	Why then will I pardon you?

Onomatopoeia. Onomatopoeia is the sound of a word or its repetition imitating natural sounds or simulating the sense. Jeremiah contains numerous examples of this figure, as we saw earlier in Jer. 5.17; 50.35-38; and 51.20-23.

Aposiopesis. In classical rhetoric aposiopesis (Lat. *praecisio*) is the sudden and intentional breaking off of discourse in mid-sentence. There seems to be evidence of this figure in Jeremiah:

Jer. 10.18	Jeremiah stops short of stating what effect the impending distress will have on the people, saying simply, 'so they may find out…'
Jer. 46.5	Jeremiah leaves unfinished a vision of Egyptians being overrun by Babylonians on the battlefield, saying, 'so why have I seen…?'

Apostrophe. Apostrophe is a turning away from one's audience to address a person, city, nation, or other inanimate object. It is used to emphasize a point, heighten grief, or express indignation. This figure often includes personification. The person may also be purely imaginary, absent, or dead.

Jer. 2.12	Jeremiah addresses the heavens, which cannot hear
Jer. 15.10	Jeremiah addresses his mother, who is absent
Jer. 22.29	Jeremiah addresses the land, which cannot hear
Jer. 22.30	Jeremiah addresses an imaginary scribe
Jer. 31.16-17	Jeremiah addresses Rachel, who is long dead
Jer. 47.6	Jeremiah addresses the sword, which cannot hear

Pathos. Pathos in Greek rhetoric is an emotional appeal to awaken feelings of pity and sorrow. Hebrew rhetoric only occasionally appeals to the emotions, but one does find it in the preaching of Hosea and Jeremiah:

15. *Rhetorical Discourse in the Prophets*   199

Hos. 11.1-4
    When Israel was a child, I loved him
        and out of Egypt I called my son
    The more I called them
        the more they went from me
    They kept sacrificing to the Baals
        and burning incense to idols
    Yet I, I taught Ephraim to walk
        taking them up by his arms
            and they did not know that I healed them
    I led them with cords of human kindness
        with the bands of love
    And I became to them like those
        who lift infants to their cheeks
            yes, I bent down to them and fed them.

Hos. 11.8-9
    How can I give you up, O Ephraim!
        How can I hand you over, O Israel!
    How can I make you like Admah!
        How can I treat you like Zeboiim!
    My heart recoils within me
        my compassion grows warm and tender
    I will not execute my fierce anger
        I will not again destroy Ephraim
    For I am God and no mortal
        the Holy One in your midst
            and I will not come in wrath.

Jeremiah combines 'father-son' and 'husband-wife' imagery in this moving oracle:

Jer. 3.19-20
    And I, I said to myself
        How will I treat you among the children?
    I will give you a fine land
        a heritage—beauty of beauties—among the nations
    And I said, You will call me 'My Father'
        and will not turn back from following me
    Surely as a woman faithless with her companion
        so you have been faithless to me, house of Israel
            oracle of Yahweh.

Even more moving is this confession in which Jeremiah curses the day of his birth. He says:

Jer. 20.14-15
    Cursed be the day
        on which I was born
            the day my mother bore me
    Let it not be blessed
    Cursed be the man
        who brought my father the news:
    'A male child is born to you'
        making him very glad

>   Let that man be like the cities
>   which Yahweh overthrew and did not pity
>   Let him hear a cry in the morning
>   and an alarm at noontime
>   [................................]⁹
>   because he did not kill me in the womb
>   So my mother would have been my grave
>   and her womb eternally pregnant
>   Why this: from the womb came I forth
>   to see hard times and sorrow
>   and my days end in shame?

Other examples in Jeremiah:

> Jer. 31.15   The voice of lament is heard in Ramah
>   bitterest weeping
>   Rachel is weeping over her sons
>   she refuses to be comforted over her sons
>   because they are not
>
> Jer. 31.16-17   Restrain your voice from weeping
>   and your eyes from tears
>   For there is a reward for your labor
>   oracle of Yahweh
>   and they shall return from the land of the enemy
>   And there is hope for your future—
>   oracle of Yahweh—
>   and sons shall return to their territory.
>
> Jer. 31.18-19   I can indeed hear
>   Ephraim rocking in grief
>   You disciplined me, and I was disciplined
>   like a young bull not trained
>   Bring me back so I can come back
>   for you are Yahweh my God
>   For after my turning away
>   I repented
>   And after I came to understand
>   I hit upon my thigh
>   I was ashamed and also disgraced
>   for I bore the reproach of my youth
>
> Jer. 31.20   Is Ephraim my dear son?
>   Is he the child of my delight?
>   For more than all my speaking against him
>   I will assuredly remember him still

---

9. A colon appears to be missing here; see my article, 'The Double Curse in Jeremiah 20.14-18', *JBL* 104 (1985), pp. 589-600.

> Therefore my innards moan for him
> I will assuredly have mercy on him
> oracle of Yahweh.

Diminution. Jeremiah decreases colon length in his moving chaos vision, simulating a cessation of life in the entire creation:

Jer. 4.23-26
> I saw the earth, and look! It was waste and void
> and the heavens, their light was not there
> I saw the mountains, and look! They were quaking
> and all the hills were tossing about
> I saw, and look! The human was not there
> and all the birds of the sky had fled
> I saw, and look! The garden land was a desert
> and all its cities were ruined
> before Yahweh
> before his burning anger.

Chapter 16

THE LION HAS ROARED: RHETORICAL STRUCTURE IN AMOS 1.2–3.8*

Mark Rose, in a study on the Shakespearean plays, has shown that before acts came into being plays were structured by design, not plot, and as a result were symmetrical.[1] The division into acts came later. Something similar has occurred in the text of the Hebrew Bible. Scribal additions of various descriptions—introductions, summaries, and explanatory supplements—have served to obscure pre-existing rhetorical structures made by repeated or balancing vocabulary and phraseology, keyword inversions, speaker alternations, and symmetries of a numerical, rhythmic, or thematic nature. These structures emanate from the biblical preachers and writers or from scribes who collected and compiled inspired discourse for representation to later audiences. Chapter numbers from a still-later date obscure these structures even more when they follow the scribal additions, which they often do.

Some years ago I argued that King Ahaziah's obituary in 2 Kgs 1.17-18, which completes the Deuteronomic formula begun in 1 Kgs 22.51-53, breaks up and obscures a pre-existing rhetorical structure taking in four originally separate legends from the Elisha cycle in 2 Kings 1–2.[2] The structure here is a controlling chiasmus depicting a circuitous journey that begins in Samaria (1.2), moves south and east into the Transjordan, where Elijah is taken into heaven, and then returns again to Samaria, where it concludes (2.25). The climax of the journey is in the center (2.9-13), where Elijah's mantle falls to Elisha, and Elijah ascends into heaven in a fiery chariot. With the elimination of the obituary, the two main legends—legend one reporting Elijah's denunciation of Ahaziah and his servants for seeking help from Baal-zebub (Baal-zebul) in curing the king's sickness (1.2-16), and legend two reporting Elisha's final walk with his master and Elijah's departure in a fiery chariot (2.1-18)—are seen in a new light. Elijah's chariot ride, which

---

* First published in *Milk and Honey* (ed. Sarah Malena and David Miano; Winona Lake, IN: Eisenbrauns, 2007), pp. 65-75.
1. Mark Rose, *Shakespearean Design* (Cambridge, MA: Harvard University Press, 1972).
2. Jack R. Lundbom, 'Elijah's Chariot Ride', *JJS* 24 (1973), pp. 39-50.

is also a ride to death, comes in response to the prophet's conquest of 100 men in Ahaziah's army. The 50 men watching from a distance with the sons of the prophets when Elijah and Elisha have their parting words at the Jordan (2.7) are Ahaziah's third contingent of 50 who were spared (1.13-15) and who are now beholden to Elijah and allied with him. Legend two also aids in clarifying unspecified details in legend one: the 'messenger of Yahweh' (מלאך יהוה) in 1.3 and 1.15 is Elisha, and 'the mountain' (ההר) in 1.9 is Mount Carmel.

At the beginning of the book of Amos, a pre-existing rhetorical structure in 1.2–3.8 has similarly been broken up and obscured by the scribal introduction to Yahweh's weighty pronouncement in 3.2. This introduction, 'Hear this word that Yahweh has spoken against you, O children of Israel, against the whole family that I brought up from the land of Egypt' (3.1), is a later addition, providing another 'Hear this word…' beginning (שמעו [את] הדבר הזה) similar to the sayings in 4.1 and 5.1. In 4.1, 'Hear this word' is a bona fide beginning to a poetic oracle; but in 5.1, as here, it is a prosaic addition betrayed by the *nota accusativi*, a recognized prose particle, which occurs in both texts. This particle is not present in 4.1. Chapter numbers, not surprisingly, have been guided by the 'Hear this word' beginnings in 3.1; 4.1; and 5.1; and in the present passage, commentators take 3.1 as the beginning of a new unit extending through either v. 6 or v. 8.[3]

Condamin, however, correctly saw that the literary unit was in fact 1.2–3.8,[4] and some recent commentators have moved modestly in this direction by noting that Yahweh's roar in 1.2 connects in some fashion with the lion's roar in 3.8.[5] Andersen and Freedman, though not entirely clear about the delimitation of units in these verses,[6] nevertheless call 1.2 and 3.8 an inclusio. The verses read:

---

3. W.R. Harper, *A Critical and Exegetical Commentary on Amos and Hosea* (ICC; Edinburgh: T. & T. Clark, 1905), p. 12; R.S. Cripps, *A Critical and Exegetical Commentary on the Book of Amos* (London: SPCK, 1929), p. 149; J.L. Mays, *Amos* (OTL; Philadelphia, PA: Westminster Press, 1969), pp. 58-59; H.W. Wolff, *Joel and Amos* (trans. Waldemar Janzen *et al.*; Hermeneia; Philadelphia, PA: Fortress Press, 1977), p. 181 (= *Dodekapropheton II: Joel und Amos* [BK 14/2; Neukirchen–Vluyn: Neukirchener Verlag, 1969]); F.I. Andersen and D.N. Freedman, *Amos* (AB, 24A; New York: Doubleday, 1989), pp. 206, 384; S.M. Paul, *Amos* (Hermeneia; Minneapolis, MN: Fortress Press, 1991), p. 100.

4. A. Condamin, *Poèms de la Bible* (Paris: Gabriel Beauchesne, 2nd edn, 1933), pp. 59-71.

5. Mays, *Amos*, p. 62; Wolff, *Joel and Amos*, p. 118; Andersen and Freedman, *Amos*, pp. 17, 219-26.

6. E.g., they accept the break at 3.1 and state also that '2.9–3.8 can be viewed as a unit with internal continuity, in spite of the break between 2.16 and 3.1', *Amos*, p. 378.

1.2 *Yahweh* from Zion *roars*   יהוה...ישאג
      and from Jerusalem *he utters his voice*   יתן קולו
      and the pastures of the shepherds mourn
      and the top of Carmel withers.

3.8 *The Lion has roared*   אריה שאג
      who will not fear?
    Lord Yahweh has spoken   אדני יהוה דבר
      who will not prophesy?

Some have suggested that Yahweh's roar in 1.2 is the roar of thunder, because the parallel expression about Yahweh 'uttering his voice' has this reference elsewhere (Ps. 18.14 [13] = 2 Sam. 22.14; Isa. 30.30).[7] But thunder would not issue forth in a drought, which is what v. 2b envisions.[8] The roar (שאג) must be the roar of a lion, as most commentators agree.

The thesis to be put forth in the present essay is that 1.2–3.8, excluding the supplemental 3.1, shows itself to be a single discourse with a developed rhetorical structure, some portions of which may at one time have been self-standing, but which in their present configuration are intended to be heard as part of a unified prophetic utterance. In this discourse the prophet begins by announcing Yahweh's roar from Zion (1.2), and concludes by arguing that he is therefore left no choice but to prophesy (3.8). In between there is full and irrevocable judgment on all the nations of the world. The foreign nations are judged because of gross inhumanity toward one another; Judah and Israel are judged for covenant violation, stated again succinctly and climactically at the center of the discourse (3.2).

It is generally agreed that 1.2 is a self-standing verse of poetry introducing the oracles to the nations; some take it to be a titular summary in hymnic style of the whole of Amos' preaching.[9] That it does not connect with the first oracle in 1.3-5 is clear from the *petuḥah* after v. 2, as well as the 'Thus said Yahweh' messenger formula beginning the first oracle. Yahweh is the speaker in all the oracles following, but not in 1.2.

In the opening oracles of the book, Yahweh announces irrevocable punishment on eight nations or their capital cities: Damascus, Gaza, Tyre, Edom, Ammon, Moab, Judah and Israel (1.3–2.16). All the oracles begin with a stereotyped indictment:

     For three transgressions of _____
         and for four, I will not revoke it

---

7. Cripps, *Amos*, p. 157; Mays, *Amos*, pp. 21-22; J.A. Soggin, *The Prophet Amos* (trans. John Bowden; London: SCM Press, 1987), p. 28; cf. Job 37.4; Rev. 10.3.

8. Wolff, *Joel and Amos*, p. 119.

9. Harper, *Amos and Hosea*, p. 12; Cripps, *Amos*, p. 115; Mays, *Amos*, p. 21; Wolff, *Joel and Amos*, p. 119.

They conclude—all except the oracle against Israel—with variations of a stereotyped judgment:

> So I will send/kindle a fire against (the wall/the house of) _____
> and it will consume the strongholds of _____/her strongholds.

The lack of a stereotyped judgment against Israel can be explained as a deliberate deviation from an established pattern,[10] here replaced by a different type of judgment oracle (2.13-16).

The question has been raised whether these oracles should be taken separately or together. All have their own messenger formulas; in fact, all have both opening and closing formulas except the oracles against Tyre, Edom and Judah, which lack a concluding 'oracle of Yahweh'. Some have therefore argued that these three oracles are later additions.[11] The *petuḥah* section markings after 1.5, 8, 10, 12, 15; 2.3, 5 and 16 delimit eight units. So one must reckon with the possibility that all eight oracles could at one time have been delivered separately, but in their present configuration they doubtless belong together. Sigmund Mowinckel in discussing these oracles gave customary lip service to the form-critical maxim of brief units but then went on to conclude that the eight oracles make much more sense when taken as a unity.[12]

Shalom Paul has also shown that the six oracles addressing the foreign nations are linked together by catchphrases, which once again supports the argument that these oracles, at least, have been crafted into a larger unity.[13] Because only the foreign nation oracles are linked, however, might the oracles against Judah and Israel be later additions? Andersen and Freedman think the list of eight nations is complete as it stands, mainly because of a 7 + 1 pattern known to be conventional in both Canaanite and Israelite literature.[14] The numbers 3, 3 + 1, 7, and 7 + 1 all signify completeness. Here in each of the foreign nation oracles is the stereotypical: 'For three transgressions…and for four' (3 and 3 + 1 totals 7). For the numbers 7 and 8 (= 7 + 1) in parallelism, see Mic. 5.4 [5]. In our day we cite the baseball maxim, 'three strikes and you're out', to indicate completeness or finality.

---

10. D.N. Freedman, 'Deliberate Deviation from an Established Pattern of Repetition in Hebrew Poetry as a Rhetorical Device', in *Proceedings of the Ninth World Congress of Jewish Studies (Jerusalem, August 4-12, 1985), Division A: The Period of the Bible* (Jerusalem: World Union of Jewish Studies, 1986), pp. 45-52 (repr. in *Divine Commitment and Human Obligation* II [ed. John R. Huddlestun; Grand Rapids, MI: Eerdmans, 1997], pp. 205-12).

11. Mays, *Amos*, pp. 25-26; Wolff, *Joel and Amos*, p. 140.

12. S. Mowinckel, *Prophecy and Tradition* (Oslo: Dybwad, 1946), pp. 56-57.

13. S.M. Paul, 'Amos 1.3–2.3: A Concatenous Literary Pattern', *JBL* 90 (1971), pp. 379-403; Paul, *Amos*, pp. 13-15.

14. Andersen and Freedman, *Amos*, p. 206.

Enumerations in a 7 or 7 + 1 pattern occur with particular frequency in the book of Amos.[15] Gordis cites the list of seven nations in chaps. 1–2, after which Amos' preferred nation comes up for review: Israel (= 7 + 1). Other examples in the book:

1. The 7 transgressions of Israel in 2.6-8 (selling the righteous; selling the needy; tamping the earth with the head of the poor; thrusting aside the afflicted; gang-raping a young girl; sleeping on garments taken in pledge; drinking wine of those fined).
2. The 7 acts of punishment for Israel in 2.14-16 (the swift cannot flee; the strong will lose strength; the mighty will not escape with their lives; the bowman will not stand; the swift of foot shall not escape; the horseman will not escape with his life; the stout-hearted will flee away naked).
3. The 7 + 1 series of rhetorical questions in 3.3-8, about which I will say more below.
4. The 7 verbs calling ironically for sanctuary worship in 4.4-5 (come; transgress; multiply; bring; make smoke; proclaim; publish).
5. The 7 prior calamities cited by Yahweh in 4.6-12 (I gave you cleanness of teeth and lack of bread; I withheld the rain from you; I smote you with blight and mildew; I sent among you a pestilence; I slew your young men with the sword; I made the stench of your camp go up into your nostrils; I overthrew you).
6. The 7 verbs in the hymnic fragment of 5.8-9 (he who makes the Pleiades and Orion; turns deep darkness into morning; darkens the day into night; calls for the waters of the sea; pours them out upon the face of the earth; makes destruction burst upon the strong; brings destruction upon the fortress).
7. The 7 things Yahweh hates in 5.21-24 (your festivals; your sacred assemblies; burnt offerings; your meal offerings; peace offerings; noise of your songs; the melody of your lutes).
8. The 7 verbs calling for woe in 6.4-6 (lie; sprawl; eat; improvise; compose; drink; anoint).
9. The 7 damning quotes from the merchants in 8.5-8 (When will the new moon be over so we may sell grain; and the sabbath so we may open to sell wheat; to make the ephah small; and to make the shekel great; and to cheat with deceitful scales; to buy the poor with silver and the needy with a pair of sandals; and sell the refuse of the wheat).

15. R. Gordis, 'The Heptad as an Element of Biblical and Rabbinic Style', *JBL* 62 (1943), pp. 17-26 (repr. in R. Gordis, *Poets, Prophets and Sages: Essays in Biblical Interpretation* [Bloomington, IN: Indiana University Press, 1971], pp. 97-103); M. Weiss, 'The Pattern of Numerical Sequence in Amos 1–2', *JBL* 86 (1967), pp. 416-23; J. Limburg, 'Sevenfold Structures in the Book of Amos', *JBL* 106 (1987), pp. 217-22.

16. *The Lion Has Roared*

Various attempts have also been made to find a logic or fixity in the ordering of these oracles, such as geographical, historical, or cultic ritual order. But these have not been particularly successful, with one exception. Nils Lund proposed a number of years ago that the eight oracles in sequence form a simple crosswise pattern that follows the points of the compass.[16] The first four locations, more distant from the prophet addressing them, make an 'X'; the four remaining locations are then addressed in clockwise fashion, beginning with Ammon and ending with Israel, at which point the climax is reached, the drama ends, and the audience is shocked to learn the outcome. The four nations of the inner ring, located on either side of the Jordan, complete the 'X' figure:

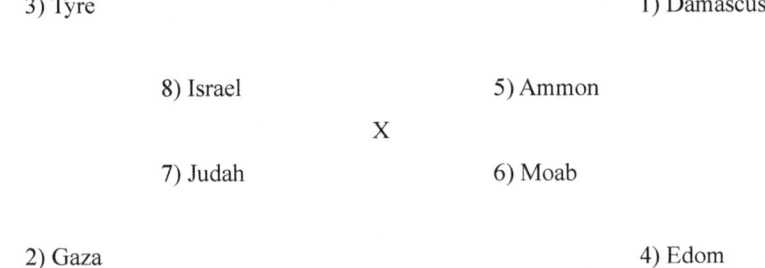

If Amos can be imagined standing somewhere between Jerusalem and Samaria (the 'X' in the diagram)—perhaps at Bethel, the one location where he is known to have preached (Amos 7.10-13)—his recitation of oracles while facing each nation would constitute drama of a high order. Amos first faces the Aramean city of Damascus to the northeast, then turns 180 degrees to face the Philistine city of Gaza to the southwest. The prophet then faces northwest to address the Phoenician city of Tyre, after which he makes another 180 degree turn to address Edom in the southeast. In the sweep of nations closer to home, Amos first addresses Ammon in the near northeast, then Moab in the near southeast. Turning west, he then addresses Judah in the near southwest, and finally Israel in the near northwest. The masterful survey ends right where the prophet intends: with Israel. If the audience has given hearty assent to the judgment on seven nations, which doubtless it has, it cannot now stop the momentum and refrain from judging Israel, the eighth, which it would like to do. This audience—presumably Northern Israelite—has been trapped, and the prophet's object has been achieved.

We must also ask whether the Israel prophecy has undergone subsequent expansion. Wolff takes the historical recital and shift to direct address in 2.10-12 as a later Deuteronomic supplement, judging the verses also to be

---

16. Nils W. Lund, *Chiasmus in the New Testament* (Chapel Hill, NC: University of North Carolina Press, 1942), pp. 87-88 (repr. Peabody, MA: Hendrickson, 1992).

prosaic.[17] Andersen and Freedman also note a broadening at 2.9, where the focus is now on Israel, the nation as a whole, but they still want to maintain the unity and integrity of 1.2–2.16.[18] Here we get no help from section markings, which delimit only the unit 2.6-16. Messenger formulas in the verses indicate two oracles: (I) vv. 9-12; and (II) vv. 13/14-16. Oracle I continues the prior indictment; Oracle II announces the judgment. Both have nice keyword structures, the first of which argues against Wolff's view that vv. 10-12 are secondary. The two stanzas of Oracle I contain these repetitions and balancing keywords:

1	*And I, I destroyed* **the Amorite** *before them*	2.9
	....	
	....	
	And I, I brought you up from the land of Egypt	2.10
	....	
	to possess the land of **the Amorite**	
2	And I raised up some of your sons to be **prophets**	2.11
	and some of your choice men to be **Nazirites**	
	..........................said Yahweh	
	But you made **the Nazirites** drink wine	2.12
	and **the prophets** you commanded:	
	'You shall not prophesy!'	

Stanza 1 has parallelism and a keyword inclusio; stanza 2 has a keyword chiasmus. In stanza 2 we see also that the messenger formula comes at the center (v. 11), not at the end, as in the judgment oracle following (v. 16) and in prophetic oracles generally.

Oracle II may also be two poetic stanzas, although there is uncertainty about the nature of v. 13. With its problematic verb עוק ('press down'), it can be tentatively translated:

1	**Look I** am *pressing (you) down* in your place	2.13
	just as the cart *presses down*	
	the one that is full of sheaves.	

The prosaic כאשר ('just as') may be an indication that this verse is a later addition. Andersen and Freedman label it 'a transitional statement'. On the other hand, כאשר makes a simile in other Amos poetry (5.19). So far as 'Look I' (הנה אנכי) with a participle is concerned, this turns up later in Jeremiah as the most common beginning to the prophetic oracle, in both prose and poetry.[19] So here in v. 13 we may well have a genuine poetic bicolon

---

17. Wolff, *Joel and Amos*, pp. 112-13, 141-42.
18. Andersen and Freedman, *Amos*, pp. 206, 378.
19. Jack R. Lundbom, *Jeremiah 1–20* (AB, 21A; New York: Doubleday, 1999), p. 242 (repr. New Haven, CT: Yale University Press, 2009).

belonging to an oracle composed of vv. 13-16. If so, the bicolon should probably be delimited as a separate stanza, because vv. 14-16 have their own rhetorical structure, as we shall see presently. In any case, v. 13 must be joined with vv. 14-16 because it is part of the judgment, not the indictment.

The remainder of Oracle II has keyword repetitions that form an inclusio and an inverted sequence in the center. It can be taken as a second stanza of the oracle:

> 2 **Flight** (מנוס) shall vanish from the swift 2.14
> ....
> **and the mighty shall not escape with his life**
> 2.15
> and he who is swift of foot **shall not escape**
> and the rider of the horse **shall not escape with his life**
> and he who is stout of heart among **the mighty** 2.16
> **shall flee away** (ינוס) naked in that day
> said Yahweh

We must conclude, then, that 2.9-16 contains two self-standing oracles that are now part of the prophecy against Israel and are integral to the prophecy. This is because without them there is no judgment on the nation, which there must be. Most commentators concur, seeing 2.16 as a conclusion to the Israel prophecy and the prophecies to all the nations.[20] The end of a unit is indicated also by an 'oracle of Yahweh' formula concluding v. 16, after which comes a *petuḥah* section marking.

In the larger rhetorical structure of 1.2–3.8, the center is occupied by the divine word in 3.2, commonly agreed to be the weightiest prophecy uttered by the prophet from Tekoa and one of the weightiest prophecies in the entire Hebrew Bible. In this word Yahweh affirms his special covenant relationship with Israel, but then to the great surprise of this Northern Israelite audience, he says that because of this relationship, not in spite of it, he intends to punish the nation for all its iniquities:

> Only you have I known 3.2
>   of all the families of the earth
> therefore I will punish you
>   with all your iniquities.

There are no messenger formulas or section markings in 3.1-8, which means for the interpreter less certainty about delimiting units in the verses. Nevertheless, v. 2 is generally taken to be a self-standing prophecy, introduced by the prosaic v. 1, about which I remarked above. The rhetorical questions in vv. 3-8 are a different literary genre entirely, and the speaking voice there

---

20. Harper, *Amos and Hosea*, p. 47; Mays, *Amos*, pp. 44-45; Wolff, *Joel and Amos*, pp. 127-73; Soggin, *The Prophet Amos*, p. 46; Paul, *Amos*, pp. 43-99.

is doubtless that of the prophet. In v. 2 it is Yahweh addressing the people directly. Most commentators therefore combine the divine word in v. 2 with its introduction in v. 1, taking the two as a single unit. But Andersen and Freedman identify both verses as prose,[21] which v. 2 does not seem to be. Admittedly, this verse begins its last colon with את, but this may simply be to balance אתכם ('you') in colon one. The modern English versions follow *Biblia hebraica* and scan the verse as poetry, which it gives every indication of being.

What follows is a string of rhetorical questions that is unparalleled in prophetic literature (3.3-8). If Amos is the prophet of the heptad, he is also the prophet of the rhetorical question. These questions are not prophecy per se but an exercise in disputation betraying unmistakable grounding in Israelite wisdom tradition. The series begins with a single question ('Do two walk together…?'), after which come six more questions in pairs: (1) Does a lion roar… Does a young lion lift up his voice…? (2) Does a bird fall upon a trap…Does a trap spring up…? and (3) If a trumpet is blown in a city… If evil befalls a city…? The setup questions number seven, preparing for the concluding double question of v. 8 (7 + 1). The double question at the end once again traps the audience into engagement with the prophet. By having made seven 'no' responses to the setup questions, the audience must now answer 'no one' to the final questions about who on earth can remain quiet once Yahweh has roared. These final questions indirectly validate the call Amos has received to become Yahweh's prophet.

Because a prose statement in v. 7 interrupts the full number of rhetorical questions, and because v. 8 departs from the ה and אם interrogative particles in vv. 3-6 and uses the interrogative מי instead, some commentators argue that the original unit ended at v. 6, and vv. 7-8 are said to be fragments of a separate discourse.[22] It has been noted also that v. 8 departs from the *qina* (3.2) meter of vv. 3-6. But none of these changes in vv. 7-8 materially affects the conclusion most everyone reaches, that v. 8 is the end toward which everything moves, except to say that the statement in v. 7 may have been inserted later, as some commentators allege (Harper; Baumgartner; Mays; Wolff). Andersen and Freedman, however, argue that v. 7 is authentic and an integral part of the discourse.[23] The rhetorical strategy, in any case, is the same as in the parade of oracles against the nations, where seven prophecies were a foil for the prophecy on which the accent was meant to fall.[24] Here seven questions in very mechanical fashion become foil for a double question that is infinitely more important, leaving us with another

21. Andersen and Freedman, *Amos*, pp. 378-79.
22. W. Baumgartner, 'Amos 3.3-8', *ZAW* 33 (1913), p. 79; Cripps, *Amos*, pp. 150-53.
23. Andersen and Freedman, *Amos*, pp. 391-92.
24. Paul, *Amos*, p. 105.

7 + 1 pattern in the book.²⁵ It may also be that this double question at the end intends to return the hearer to the single question that begins the series, which would make an inclusio for 3.3-8. The two walking together would then be Yahweh and Amos, who have been brought together by divine plan.

This preexisting rhetorical structure in 1.2–3.8 can be outlined as follows:

a		**Amos** hearing the voice of Yahweh: *Yahweh from Zion roars...*		1.2
	b	Oracles against the nations in **a scheme of 7**		1.3–2.5
		Oracle against Israel with supplements		2.6-16
		c	**Yahweh** stating to Israel terms of the covenant	3.2
			Only you have I known...	
			therefore I will punish you...	
	b'	Setup rhetorical questions in **a scheme of 7**		3.3-6
		Supplemental word authenticating the prophets		3.7
a'		**Amos'** double question validating his call: *The Lion has roared*		3.8
			who will not fear?	
			Lord Yahweh has spoken	
			who will not prophesy?	

With a strengthening of the view that 1.2 and 3.8 begin and end a single rhetorical discourse, our interpretation of these verses can be clarified at two points. First, because Amos is the speaker in 3.8, he should be taken also as the speaking voice in 1.2. The initial 'And he said' beginning 1.2 indicates as much, connecting as it does the superscription naming Amos (1.1) with the opening prophecy of the book.²⁶ This opening prophecy then need not be assigned to a later Judaic redactor or explained in some other way as being of anonymous origin.

Second, the linking of 1.2 and 3.8 points to the synonymous parallelism in 3.8 being exact; that is, the lion said to have roared in v. 8a is Lord Yahweh, said to have spoken in v. 8b.²⁷ The reference here is not to just any beast in the forest, which effectively rules out a connection, implied or otherwise, to the lion mentioned in 3.4.²⁸ The lion in v. 8a is also not a metaphor for the coming Assyrian army,²⁹ despite future renderings of the verb

---

25. Limburg, 'Sevenfold Structures', pp. 220-21; Andersen and Freedman, *Amos*, p. 391.
26. Paul, *Amos*, p. 37.
27. Andersen and Freedman, *Amos*, p. 400.
28. Wolff, *Joel and Amos*, p. 125; Paul, *Amos*, p. 113.
29. Harper, *Amos and Hosea*, pp. 73-74.

('a lion shall roar') in the LXX and Vulg. The term here is employed as a pure metaphor for God, a coinage found nowhere else in the Bible. Only in the NT is the resurrected and exalted Jesus called 'the Lion of the tribe of Judah' (Rev. 5.5). However, the portrayal itself of Yahweh as a lion is not a rarity in the Hebrew Bible. The expression 'Yahweh roars' in 1.2 (also Jer. 25.30 and Joel 4.16 [3.16]) is an implied metaphor, which was called an *abusio* by the classical rhetoricians.[30] And we often meet up with similes such as the one in Hos. 5.14, where Yahweh says, 'For I will be like a lion to Ephraim, and like a young lion to the house of Judah'. See also Hos. 11.10; 13.7-8; Isa. 38.13; Jer. 25.38; 49.19. With 'lion' in v. 3.8a as a pure metaphor for God, the term should then be made definite and capitalized ('The Lion has roared'), which none of the modern English versions does. Andersen and Freedman make the term definite, but do not capitalize.[31]

---

30. *Rhetorica ad Herennium* 4.33.
31. Andersen and Freedman, *Amos*, p. 383.

Chapter 17

DOUBLE-DUTY SUBJECT IN HOSEA 8.5*

The first bicolon of Hos. 8.5 has long been a *crux*. The MT reads:

זָנַח עֶגְלֵךְ שֹׁמְרוֹן חָרָה אַפִּי בָּם

The difficulty lies with the verb זנח, which the Masoretes pointed as a 3ms affix (perfect) form: זָנַח, 'he has rejected', or 'he has cast off'. The verb with the exact same pointing appears in v. 3 where the meaning is clear: זנח ישראל טוב, 'Israel has rejected the good'. But v. 5 is problematic because it lacks a suitable subject. The translations of the Versions, ancient and modern, as well as those of the commentators, bear this out. The LXX, Aquila, and Theodotion presuppose a Hebrew imperative: LXX: ἀπότριψαι; Aquila: ἀπώσθησον; Theodotion: ἀπόρριψαι. The imperative is accepted by Wolff: 'Verstoße deinen Jungstier, Samaria!'[1] Other ancient readings assume עגלך to be the subject, which would then require a passive form of the verb. This would have to be the past participle זָנֻח, although it should be noted that this form is not otherwise attested in the OT. The Greek Versions 'E and Symmachus (ἀπεβλήθη) support such a reading, as does the Vulgate: 'projectus est vitulus tuus, Samaria'. They are in turn followed by Rudolph[2] and Mays[3] in their commentaries. The AV is of no help. It too makes 'calf' the subject, but adds an indirect object, 'thee', as a bonus: 'Thy calf, O Samaria, hath cast thee off' (cf. BDB: 'Samaria's calf rejects *her*').[4]

Other commentators have proposed emendations that would make Yahweh the subject. Wellhausen emends to אָזְנַח,[5] and *BHK*³ to זָנַחְתִּי. The RSV follows this lead—'I have spurned your calf, O Samaria'—and the reading of JB is similar. Contextually this has much to recommend itself since Yahweh has been the primary speaker from v. 1. An attempt of a different sort

---

* First published in *VT* 25 (1975), pp. 228-230.
1. H.W. Wolff, *Hosea* (BK; Neukirchen–Vluyn: Neukirchener Verlag, 1961), pp. 168-70 (= *Hosea* [Hermeneia; Philadelphia, PA: Fortress Press, 1974], pp. 132, 140-41).
2. W. Rudolph, *Hosea* (KAT; Gütersloh: Gerd Mohn, 1966), pp. 156-57.
3. J.L. Mays, *Hosea* (OTL; Philadelphia, PA: Westminster Press, 1969), p. 113.
4. BDB, p. 276, italics mine.
5. J. Wellhausen, *Die kleinen Propheten* (Berlin: Georg Reimer, 3rd edn, 1898), p. 120.

to retain Yahweh as subject, yet without changing the consonantal text, has been made by Father Huesman.⁶ Huesman suggests we read an infinitive absolute, זָנֹחַ (he finds support from the LXX if he takes ἀπότριψαι to be a 1 aorist active infinitive instead of a 1 aorist middle imperative), which he says is one of several examples in Hebrew where the infinitive absolute is used in a finite sense. He then says the first person subject would be understood. The NEB takes an independent course, assuming here another root, זנח, meaning 'to stink' (cf. KB³ and BDB), otherwise known only from Isa. 19.6: 'Your calf-gods stink, O Samaria'.

All these proposals, I submit, are unnecessary. The MT yields excellent sense once it is realized that the poet has delayed the subject of the entire line until the second colon, where it then performs a double-duty function.⁷ The subject for *both* cola is אַפִּי. Not only does Yahweh's אף burn against the people; this same אף rejects the detestable calf enthroned in Samaria. The bicolon is not the usual *parallelismus membrorum*, despite the presence of some balancing terms. The overall effect is to focus attention in two different directions, first on the calf, and then on the people. And the play on אפי helps to achieve this end. In the second colon, used with חרה, אף means 'anger' (in all the texts of the OT where this combination appears—and there are many—this is its meaning), i.e., Yahweh's *anger burns hot*. But in the first colon, where, by ellipsis, אפי is understood, the literal meaning 'nose' is intended. No doubt Yahweh is also angry with the calf, but the primary meaning must be something more like 'turning up one's nose'. אף is not otherwise subject for זנח in the OT, but this presents no difficulty. זנח is used in parallelism with the cognate verb, אנף, in Ps. 60.3, and יעשן אפך parallels זנחת in Ps. 74.1. Yet the particular idea of Yahweh rejecting the calf with his nose appears to be uniquely expressed by Hosea (cf. Exod. 32.10, 11, 19, 22 where אף is subject for חרה in the calf episode at Sinai).

This reading solves the main problems faced by the translators. The speaker in v. 5 is Yahweh, and his 'nose' is the subject throughout. Moreover, the bicolon in v. 5 now becomes an admirable counterpart to the line in v. 3: Israel rejects the good; now Yahweh (with his nose) rejects both Israel and the calf. Hosea throughout uses language that maintains a high level of abstraction. Despite the fact that an intimate relationship has been broken—indeed one which Hosea characterizes as a marriage—there is a studied avoidance of 'I-thou' terminology. Israel rejects טוב, 'the good', and Yahweh's אף, 'nose', not Yahweh himself, conveys to Israel the rejection of her and her idol.

6. *Biblica* 37 (1956), p. 294.
7. For a list of Hebrew terms (including suffixes) doing double-duty service in OT poetry, see Dahood, *Psalms III* (AB, 17A; Garden City, NY: Doubleday, 1970), pp. 429-44.

From a rhetorical standpoint, the level of abstraction appears intentional. It is done for the same reason which prompts Hosea to delay his subject. Both create *distance* between Hosea and his audience. Remembering that these words were originally spoken to a live audience, which was no doubt hostile to words of harsh judgment, we should not be surprised to find the prophet employing devices which partially obscure the thrust of his indictment. To a hostle audience one often chooses not to be blatantly straightforward. If the message remains partially hidden, only those with ears to hear will be able to perceive it fully.

Chapter 18

CONTENTIOUS PRIESTS AND CONTENTIOUS
PEOPLE IN HOSEA 4.1-10*

In chap. 4 of Hosea the enormous burden which the prophet carries for his nation begins to be unloaded. In chaps. 1–3 he unloaded his personal burden. The two of course cannot be separated—either for him or for us—still there is no mistaking the change that comes with the beginning of chap. 4. All that follows is but an amplification of its initial words: 'For Yahweh has a controversy with the inhabitants of the land' (v. 1).

As the message unfolds, this controversy is seen to be with the priests and the people. That of course could mean everybody, and it virtually does in vv. 1-10. Nevertheless, it is the categories of 'people' and 'priest' which the text presents for special consideration. F.I. Andersen and D.N. Freedman in their recent *Hosea* commentary consider the words of v. 9a, 'like the people, like the priest', thematic for the whole of 4.1–5.7.[1]

The balance between people and priest is delicate and subtle in Hosea's preaching, so much so that it is easily upset by commentators who want the emphasis on one or the other. Calvin weighted interpretation heavily against the people. Modern scholars go to the other extreme and find in vv. 4-8 a focused attack on the priesthood, an attack that controls virtually everything else of an unfavorable nature said against the people.

It will be the task of this article to use rhetorical criticism in the study of Hos. 4.1-10. That means looking carefully at who the audience is, what structures are discernible in the text, and what precisely is going on in the way of a prophetic argument. Commentators over the years have of course done all these things, but more often than not their judgments are random, and seldom are the rhetorical data well integrated into the larger interpretative process.

The Crux: 4b

Much of the controversy over the interpretation of vv. 1-10 centers around 4b, which, like 9a, mentions both people and priest. But there is a difference.

---

* First published in *VT* 36 (1986), pp. 52-70.
1. F.I. Andersen and D.N. Freedman, *Hosea* (AB, 24; Garden City, NY: Doubleday, 1980), p. 320.

Verse 9a is perfectly clear; 4b is not. From ancient times there have been uncertainties about the translation and interpretation of 4b, and for modern scholars these difficulties are compounded by a perceived tension between the phrase and its immediate context, namely vv. 5-6. The Hebrew reads וְעַמְּךָ כִּמְרִיבֵי כֹהֵן, which can be translated either:

(a) and your people are like the contentions of a priest

or

(b) and your people are like those who contend with a priest[2]

In the first instance כִּמְרִיבֵי is taken as the plural noun מְרִיבִים in the construct state from the root רִיב meaning 'to contend' or 'to strive with', preceded by the preposition כְּ, 'as' or 'like'.[3] Thus the translation: 'like the contentions'. The plural noun is unattested in the Bible, but a singular noun מְרִיבָה meaning 'contention' is found in Gen. 13.8 and Num. 27.14. In order for this rendering to make good sense an ellipsis would have to be presupposed: 'and your people (and their contentions) are like the contentions of a priest'. What does this mean? Are the 'contentions of a priest' contentions which priests by virtue of their office have the right to initiate and carry out? Rashi, Ibn Ezra, and David Kimchi all note in discussing 4b that the priests were called upon to teach and reprove Israel, with Rashi and Kimchi citing for support Deut. 33.10.[4] Other texts supporting the priests' right to reprove are Deut. 17.8-13; 19.16-19; 21.5; Ezek. 44.23-24; and 2 Chron. 19.8-11.

Hosea may, however, have in mind unwarranted contentions. That priests could bring the privilege of their office into disrepute is demonstrated by the rebellion of Korah (Numbers 16), which Kimchi says is taken by some to be in the background here, and it is suggested also by the LXX translation of 4b and by quotations of 4b found in the Talmud. The LXX reads, ὁ δὲ λαός μου ὡς ἀντιλεγόμενος ἱερεύς, 'but my people are like an accused priest'. Here 'your people' is changed to 'my people' (influence coming perhaps from 'my people' in 6a and 8a), and כִּמְרִיבֵי is translated with ἀντιλεγόμενος, the

---

2. These are the two translations given by Andersen and Freedman (*Hosea*, p. 347), though in the case of (b) they use 'strive' instead of 'contend'.

3. Kimchi took the כְּ as asseverative. Calvin (*Commentaries on the Twelve Minor Prophets I: Hosea* [Grand Rapids, MI: Baker, 1979], p. 145) rejects this meaning as do most other commentators, yet recently an asseverative meaning has been argued by R. Gordis in 'Quotations as a Literary Usage in Biblical, Oriental, and Rabbinic Literature', *HUCA* 22 (1949), p. 172 (= *Poets, Prophets and Sages* [Bloomington, IN: Indiana University Press, 1971], p. 113). This is accepted by Andersen and Freedman (*Hosea*, pp. 348-50).

4. Besides their commentaries in the Rabbinic Bible, see also Solomon ben Isaac (Rashi), *Parschandatha* (ed. I. Maarsen; Amsterdam: Hertsberger, 1930), and David Kimchi, *The Commentary of Rabbi David Kimhi on Hosea* (ed. H. Cohen; New York: Columbia University Press, 1929).

present passive particle (nom. masc. sg.). An 'accused priest' is at the very least a priest under criticism. At most he is one already judged guilty. Either way he is likely on the defensive,[5] in which case he will be perceived as being unnecessarily contentious. The Babylonian Talmud cites the phrase twice (Shab. 149b; Kid. 70b), and while it has two entirely different points to make about the priests—not the people—it renders כִּמְרִיבֵי כֹהֵן along much the same lines: 'your people are like quarrelsome priests'.[6]

In the second instance the hi. participle (masc. pl. cst.) of ריב is read: 'like those who contend/strive with'. The H stem participle is commonly read in the difficult יהוה יֵחַתּוּ מְרִיבָו of 1 Sam. 2.10, and further on in Hos. 5.10 we have not the same verb but a similar construction nevertheless in כְּמַסִּיגֵי גְּבוּל, 'like those who remove the landmark'. In this translation the party of reference is not the priest but a group of people contending with the priest. Yet again we cannot be sure whether the paradigmatic people are contending rightly or wrongly.

The problem here is a fundamental one for religion. The priesthood—like any institution invested with authority, only more so—has a kind of built-in protection against criticism, that is, it is thought that respect should be due the priest regardless of whether he is right or wrong. The suggestion has been that Hosea faced this very problem.[7] At the same time it is usually conceded just as readily that priests, no matter how high their station, are sometimes deserving of criticism.

The Old Testament in a number of its traditions defends the priest when people contend against him. Moses, who among other things is a priest, twice meets with unlawful contentions from the people during the Wilderness trek. The first is just after the Exodus from Egypt (Exod. 17.1-7); the second is after the death of Miriam when he and Aaron both come under attack (Num. 20.1-13). These confrontations lived on in 'Meribah' ('Contention'), the name given to the place or waters where the people contended. According to the Blessing of Moses, Meribah is where the priestly tribe was tested (and found worthy) by Yahweh (Deut. 33.8). The rebellion of Korah mentioned earlier in connection with translation (a) could also fit here, for, while it was a dispute within the priesthood, it involved not just Korah but a group of people in league with him. Kimchi says, 'And there

---

5. Calvin, though he has already moved in his discussion to the people for whom the comparison with the priest is made, captures the sense perfectly. He says, 'And we see that froward men become thus insolent when they are reproved; for instantly such an objection as this is made by them, "Am I to be treated like a child? Have I not attained sufficient knowledge to understand how I ought to live?"' (*Hosea*, p. 145).

6. See also A. Cohen, *The Twelve Prophets* (London: Soncino, 1948), p. 14.

7. S. Coleman, *Hosea Concepts in Midrash and Talmud* (Bloemfontein: Stabilis, 1960), p. 119, says, 'The dignity of the priesthood was such that even an insolent one could not be criticized.' Cf. Acts 23.1-5.

18. *Contentious Priests and Contentious People in Hosea 4.1-10* 219

are those who interpret כמריב כהן as the *followers* of Korah who contended and undermined the priesthood' (italics mine) (ויש לפרש כמריבי כהן כעדת קרח שהריבו וערערו על הכהונה).

A host of older commentators in the Modern Era saw in 4b a reference to Deut. 17.12, a law prescribing the death penalty for anyone disobeying the priest.[8] For them the Vulgate provided support. It reads: *populus enim tuus sicut hi qui contradicunt sacerdoti*. According to this reading, Hosea likens people of his day to individuals who contend unreasonably with the priest.

Many commentators, however, have serious problems with any interpretation that provides the priest with an *apologia*. This is what creates the tension most modern critical scholars are talking about when they say the MT of 4b cannot be read with vv. 5-6. An early group of these scholars emended כְּמְרִיבֵי to כְּמָרָיו, 'its idol-priests' (cf. 10.5), and read כֹּהֵן as a vocative beginning v. 5[9] for the simple reason that כֹּמֶר is always used in a bad sense.[10]

It would certainly make more sense if we could assume the priest was getting criticism he deserved. The context supports such a view. So also does Hos. 6.9 and numerous passages of a similar tone from Jeremiah (2.8; 5.31; 20.1-6; etc.). We must not suppose that Hosea (likewise Jeremiah) stands alone in criticizing the priesthood of the day. Ibn Ezra and Kimchi say that the people, who under normal circumstances accept reproof from the priest, have turned to reprove him. Ibn Ezra is explicit in saying that the priest has become evil,[11] an unhappy fact acknowledged also by the Rabbis much earlier.[12]

There is then sufficient ambiguity of meaning and interpretation surrounding כְּמְרִיבֵי כֹהֵן. But what about עַמְּךָ, 'your people'? This word is clear. It must also be taken as the preferred subject. Not only is it the first term of the phrase, which for Hebrew commonly indicates emphasis, but the assumption is a fair one that Hosea is concerned not ultimately with paradigmatic priests or a paradigmatic people but rather with a people currently contentious. Because this is a judgment speech we can expect

---

8. See M. DeRoche, 'Structure, Rhetoric, and Meaning in Hosea iv 4-10', *VT* 33 (1983), p. 187.
9. W.R. Harper, *A Critical and Exegetical Commentary on Amos and Hosea* (ICC; Edinburgh: T. & T. Clark, 1905), p. 252; S.L. Brown, *The Book of Hosea* (London: Methuen, 1932), p. 40.
10. G.A. Smith, *The Book of the Twelve Prophets I* (New York: Harper & Bros., rev. edn, 1928), p. 273; Harper, *Amos and Hosea*, p. 253.
11. ומשפט הכהנים היה להוכיח לישראל ועתה שבו הם להוכיח הכהן כי גם הוא רע מעללים כאשר יפרש וזהו ועמך כמריבי כהן, 'And the tradition of the priests was to reprove Israel but now they have turned to reprove the priest for he also is evil in his deeds, according to which it is explained. This is what ועמך כמריבי כהן means.'
12. Coleman, *Hosea Concepts in Midrash and Talmud*, pp. 117-21.

that these people are contentious in a bad sense, and that seems to be confirmed by the line immediately preceding, in which everyone is admonished to keep silent. It says, 'But let no one contend, and let none accuse' (4a). So if Hosea is building on the idea that priests are sometimes contentious to a fault, his point is that people behave this way too. Should he be assuming that priestly contentions are legitimate, the people's in any case are not. On the other hand, if כִּמְרִיבֵי כֹהֵן means people contending with a priest, Hosea's point is that people currently are contending the way people do when they contend with a priest. Here again it does not really matter whether the people of reference contend with justification or without, for, as I have said, 4a precludes all people from contending. In the present context, at least, that statement would seem to control whatever 4b intends to say. We of course still desire a more precise understanding of 4b, but that will have to wait until later when a study of the larger structure will uncover an additional control on meaning.

The discussion here may be concluded simply by noting that the MT reading of 4b intends to pass judgment on the people. This comes as no surprise in Hosea, but, since the verses following indict the priest or appear to indict the priest, a tension is immediately felt.[13] The tension, as I have said, is particularly acute if we choose translation (b) and see in it an *apologia* for the priest.

The Context of 4b

Verse 5 has no textual problems, but lacks specification in the words 'you shall stumble'. Calvin thought it was the refractory people who would stumble. J. Wellhausen, though not emending away 'people' in 4b as many following him did, set a trend nevertheless when he decided that this verse addresses the priest. In his view, the priest is to stumble with the prophet who is mentioned next.[14] Almost everyone since has taken the verse in this way. The condemned mother is likewise thought to be either the priest's mother[15] or else

---

13. Andersen and Freedman comment thus on their two translations of כִּמְרִיבֵי כֹהֵן: 'Neither of the obvious possibilities—"contentions of a priest", or "those who contend against a priest"—seems to fit' (*Hosea*, p. 349).

14. J. Wellhausen, *Prolegmena zur Geschichte Israels* (Berlin: Georg Reimer, 3rd edn, 1886), p. 139 (= *Prolegomena to the History of Israel* [New York: World, 1965], p. 137); J. Wellhausen, *Die kleinen Propheten* (Berlin: Georg Reimer, 1898), p. 110.

15. H. Junker, 'Textkritische, Formkritische und Traditionsgeschichtliche Untersuchung zu Os 4, 1-10', *BZ* 4 (1960), pp. 168-69; N. Lohfink, 'Zu Text und Form von Os 4, 4-6', *Biblica* 42 (1961), pp. 305-308; H.W. Wolff, *Hosea* (BK; Neukirchen–Vluyn: Neukirchener Verlag, 1961), p. 94 (= *Hosea* [Hermeneia; Philadelphia, PA: Fortress Press, 1974], p. 77); Andersen and Freedman, *Hosea*, p. 351.

the priesthood collectively.[16] Some, however, think that the entire nation is meant (cf. 2.4 [2]).[17]

Verse 6 is without ambiguity. Here the priest is explicitly named as the one responsible for the people's lamentable state. They lack knowledge because he has rejected knowledge and forgotten also the תּוֹרָה of his God. Calvin, however, reminds us that the people are still blamed indirectly.

Verse 7 again lacks specification. Calvin thought it was back to amplifying the wickedness of the people, though he recognized that others took the verse as a continuation of the indictment against the priest. Modern commentators for the most part interpret it as a continuation of v. 6, only a shift to the plural indicates that the larger priesthood is now under attack, a priesthood grown large during the reign of Jeroboam II.

Verse 8 continues the soliloquy begun in v. 7, lamenting sins reminiscent of those committed by the infamous sons of Eli (1 Samuel 2). This verse seems to confirm the priestly interpretation of v. 7. So if vv. 5-8 judge the priest and his fellow priests, 4b becomes a source of conflict by putting judgment on the people. This is the dilemma as modern commentators see it.

In vv. 1-3 there is broad condemnation of the 'inhabitants of the land' (v. 1), but the consensus is that these verses form a separate unit. Yet 4a is also a broad statement, commonly translated, 'But let no one contend, and let none accuse'. Here a restrictive meaning for the particle אַךְ helps to set this line off from vv. 1-3 (so Wolff and others). But an asseverative meaning is also possible. Thus we could just as well read, 'Surely let no one contend, and let none accuse'. This is the way Kimchi takes it.[18] The broad character of the statement is clearly a problem for many, and for that reason it has been suggested that perhaps the verbs should be read as passives,[19] or that someone other than Yahweh is the speaker of the line.[20] These various adjustments

16. W.R. Smith, *The Prophets of Israel* (London: Adam and Charles Black, 1882), p. 405; Smith, *The Book of the Twelve Prophets I*, p. 274; Harper, *Amos and Hosea*, p. 254; D.J. McCarthy, 'Hosea', in the *Jerome Biblical Commentary* (Englewood Cliffs, NJ: Prentice–Hall, 1968), p. 258.

17. T.W. Crafer, *The Book of Hosea* (Cambridge: Cambridge University Press, 1923), p. 35; Brown, *The Book of Hosea*, p. 41; Cohen, *The Twelve Prophets*, p. 15; DeRoche, 'Structure, Rhetoric, and Meaning in Hosea iv 4-10', p. 191.

18. אך זה אינו למעט אלא לאמת הדבר, 'This אַךְ is not to diminish but to confirm the matter.' He then cites for support אך עצמי ובשׂרי אתה, 'Surely you are my bone and my flesh' (Gen. 19.14); אך לשׁקר שׁמרתי, 'Surely in vain have I guarded...' (1 Sam. 25.21); and אך טוב לישׂראל אלהים, 'Surely God is good to Israel' (Ps. 73.1). See also J.L. Mays, *Hosea* (OTL; Philadelphia, PA: Westminster Press, 1969), p. 65.

19. K. Budde, 'Zu Text und Auslegung des Buches Hosea', *JBL* 45 (1926), p. 284; Wolff, *Hosea* (Hermeneia), p. 70.

20. Gordis, in 'Quotations as a Literary Usage', p. 172 (= *Poets, Prophets, and Sages*, p. 113), argues that 4a is a quotation from the people who object to what the

enable 4a to fit what follows rather than what precedes. And what follows is Yahweh's judgment on the priest. The opinion then is widespread among modern scholars that at some point between vv. 1-3 and v. 6 the focus must narrow so as to make the priest the sole target of Yahweh's anger.

For some early critical scholars who emended 4b but retained 'your people', v. 4 was transitional. Wellhausen, for example, remarks, 'V. 4 kann nicht gegen das Volk gerichtet sein, der Vers muss vielmehr die Anknüpfung für v. 5 bieten und den Übergang machen vom Schelten gegen das Volk (4, 1-3) zum Schelten gegen die Priester (4,5ss)'.[21]

Others, however, thought the focus narrowed more immediately beneath a corrupt 4b, where also the solution to this double problem of an uncertain Hebrew text and an uncertain context lay hidden. These commentators emended the MT of 4b more radically and did away entirely with 'your people', preferring instead 'and with you' (וְעִמְּךָ). There is not room here to review all the proposals for 4b that have been made; they can be found in the commentaries.[22] The reading most commonly chosen builds on two or three emendations: 'with you (indeed) is my contention O priest' (Th. Hermann;[23] Budde; Lohfink; Wolff; *BHS*; Mays; Andersen and Freedman). This secures the focus on the priest and the notion is reinforced that Hosea, after a broad condemnation of the people in vv. 1-3, aims his judgment immediately at those who bear primary responsibility, namely, the priests. Wolff, for whom v. 4 begins a new 'kerygmatic unit' or new 'rhetorical unit', says, 'But the people who were condemned in vv. 1-3 for their crimes against the community are now pardoned and the priest in charge of the cult is held responsible'.[24]

In the most recent discussions of our passage questions have been raised about this exclusive focus on the priest, particularly since it rests at least in part on a heavily emended 4b. Andersen and Freedman finally follow the consensus and emend; nevertheless, they are still able to see a reason for including the people in the indictment.[25] In a study by M. DeRoche[26] the pendulum swings back to Calvin and goes even further. DeRoche returns first of all to the MT of 4b, which he translates, 'And your people are like those who contend with the priest' (translation [b]). Then in vv. 5-6 he completely reverses the thrust of modern interpretation, finding at every turn a

prophet has said in 1-3. Andersen and Freedman (*Hosea*, pp. 345-46) adopt this view with some changes.

21. *Die kleinen Propheten*, p. 109.
22. See Harper, *Amos and Hosea*, p. 252; also Andersen and Freedman, *Hosea*, pp. 347-48.
23. Th. Hermann, 'Exegetisch-kritische Bemerkungen zu einigen Stellen aus Hosea', *TSK* 52.3 (1879), p. 516.
24. Wolff, *Hosea* (Hermeneia), p. 74.
25. Andersen and Freedman, *Hosea*, p. 350.
26. DeRoche, 'Structure, Rhetoric, and Meaning in Hosea iv 4-10', pp. 190-92.

reference to the people (i.e., Israel). The words 'you shall stumble' beginning v. 5 are addressed to Israel; the prophet is Israel; the mother to be destroyed is Israel; even the priest in v. 6 is Israel; and the children in v. 6 are the children of Israel.

As one can see, the thesis of a 'people-oriented' oracle is pushed too far. This causes problems too, not only whether the prophet, mother, priest, and children can all be designations for Israel, but whether in vv. 4-6 the people can simultaneously be subject and audience.[27] In 4b, for example, if we read, 'And your people are like those who contend with the priest', how can the people be addressed? Does Yahweh speak about 'your people' when talking to the people? DeRoche may perhaps have in mind a subgroup within some larger group, but if so he says nothing of this. In v. 5 a reading which assumes that the people are the audience while at the same time also the prophet and the mother makes no sense. Verse 6 has similar exegetical problems. So in the end we are faced with precisely the problem we have hoped to be rid of. When vv. 4-6 were addressed to the priest, the MT reading of 4b (i.e., 'your people') was disallowed. Now with the people addressed the MT of 4b is again disallowed, and for the same reason: 'your people' does not fit. So while DeRoche is intent on preserving the MT of 4b, his interpretation of vv. 4-6 will not allow it. We must therefore return to a restatement of the problem.

The Problem

We have not merely one problem but three problems which are separate but nevertheless related: (1) can the MT of 4b be read with its context in some meaningful way? (2) Who is the audience for vv. 4-6? Or, who are the audiences if there are more than one? (3) Can we delimit the larger literary unit into which vv. 4-6 fits so as to get a clearer look at the prophetic message? Most commentators assume that a unit begins at v. 4. If this is so, where does that unit end? This last problem is just as difficult as the others, for, as Wolff has pointed out, we have in 4.4-19 no introductory or concluding formulas and no distinctly recognizable transitions from one addressee to another.[28]

Since the MT of 4b is fairly well attested,[29] it is only reasonable that we try to make sense of it. The LXX, the Talmud, the Vulgate, and the leading Jewish

---

27. DeRoche ('Structure, Rhetoric, and Meaning in Hosea iv 4-10', p. 189) says about 4b: 'The whole colon, therefore, addresses the people, and is best translated, "And your people are like those who contend with the priest"'. Perhaps the problem is in his use of the word 'address'. Does he mean 'addressing the subject of' or 'speaking directly to'? In any case, we are still faced with an unresolved audience problem.

28. Wolff, *Hosea* (Hermeneia), p. 74. This was also noted earlier by Calvin.

29. Andersen and Freedman, *Hosea*, p. 346.

medieval commentators all attempt translations of it or else a *Vorlage* that is similar. כִּמְרִיבֵי כֹהֵן remains uncertain, so for now we will consider as possible either of the two translations suggested earlier. Eventually I will express a preference for one over the other, but for the moment it makes no difference which one we choose. Both make eminent sense once the referents in 4b and 5 are clarified. Our first concern has to be with the audience. That, in my view, is the key to a proper interpretation of 4b. A solution of the audience problem will also relieve the tension between 4b and the verses following.

The Audience

Hosea's audience in vv. 4b-5 is neither the people nor the priest; it is the king. So far as I know, this suggestion has not been made before, and that is surprising when one considers that 5.1 addresses the king along with the priests and the people. With the king as the addressee in 4b-5 the MT of 4b reads perfectly well. The phrase 'your people' denotes the king's people, the people of Samaria about whom Hosea has much to say in 10.5, 10 and 14. That chapter, incidentally, speaks also about Samaria's king (vv. 3, 7, 15). But here Hosea says that the king's people are acting either like contentious priests or like contentious people. However we translate כִּמְרִיבֵי כֹהֵן, they are more contentious than they ought to be. Amos spoke about the city's excessively rich (Amos 4.1). Hosea's concern is with those who are excessive in their arguments and recriminations.

The 'you shall stumble' beginning in v. 5 is also addressed to the king. Our predisposition in oracles of judgment has been to pair priest with (false) prophet. Here, however, it is the king who will stumble with the (false) prophet. The alliance of king and prophet is a natural one, for Samaria's kings have had prophets on their payrolls for a century or more. Ahab at the beginning of his reign (869 BCE) had 450 prophets of Baal and 400 prophets of Asherah at his table (1 Kgs 18.19); at the end he was surrounded by 400 prophets of Yahweh (1 Kgs 22.6). There are certainly prophets in Samaria now. In v. 5 it is the king's mother who will be destroyed. Good parallels are found in Jer. 13.18 and 22.26 where the tragic fate in store for King Jehoiachin and his mother is described. So I conclude that vv. 4b-5 address the king of Israel whoever he may have been.

Verse 6 focuses on the priest, as the text clearly indicates. The emphatic כִּי־אַתָּה points the finger directly. It is not necessary to make any changes from the usual interpretation of this verse. The only new insight to come with the present proposal is that Hosea is seen now to be shifting audience without warning. We know already that he shifts from direct to indirect speech without warning, for that takes place between vv. 6 and 7. But we have apparently been unprepared for an audience shift between vv. 5 and 6, and understandably so, for as was mentioned earlier, the signals are missing.

The signals are not missing in Amos 1–2, that famous sermon by Hosea's contemporary to the eight nations. So we know prophetic discourse allows for this sort of thing. Only recently have we learned that Jeremiah alternates speaker without warning (see, e.g., Jer. 8.18-21).[30] But here Hosea shifts his audience after the manner of Amos.

The sequence of speaking first to the king and then to the priest is one that deserves more attention, perhaps, for it occurs elsewhere in prophetic discourse. In Amos 7, a passage to which Hos. 4.4-6 is often compared, the first direct word is spoken against Jeroboam II. He is judged at the very end of vision three (v. 9) and Amaziah the priest perceives that the thrust of Amos' sermon is against him. At least that is what he says (vv. 10-11). The dynamic of the situation is such that Amaziah feels compelled to defend the king. This leads Amos to pass a direct judgment on Amaziah—also on his entire household (vv. 16-17). The king's household likewise receives the judgment given him (v. 9).[31] Throughout, the people of Israel are judged (vv. 8, 11, 17). Prophetic rhetoric strives after totality, which is to say that the prophet more typically delivers the broad message, not the narrow one. It is surely the broad message that Hosea delivers here in chap. 4.

The sequence of speaking first to the king and then to the priest occurs also in Jeremiah. In the sermons dramatized by the yoke (Jeremiah 27–28)[32] the audience sequence is as follows: (1) foreign envoys (27.2-11); (2) Zedekiah the king (vv. 12-15); (3) the priests (vv. 16-22); and (4) Hananiah the prophet (28.1-16). The king and the priests appear in the middle, but it is the king first and then the priests. Hosea's discourse sequence may then be intentional. Yahweh's word of judgment must first go to the king. Then, in anticipation of a defense by the priest, Hosea turns to bring judgment on him.

Poetic Structure and Speech Delimitation

We turn now to the vexed questions of poetic structure and speech delimitation. The former will be dealt with first. I should like to suggest here that there is a structural tie-in between vv. 4b and 9a. Both cola mention people and priest, as was indicated earlier, and similarities between the two have long been noted.[33] Andersen and Freedman suggest that the LXX in

---

30. See my *Jeremiah: A Study in Ancient Hebrew Rhetoric* (Missoula, MT: Society of Biblical Literature and Scholars Press, 1975), pp. 84-86 [1997, pp. 111-14].

31. See Lohfink, 'Zu Text und Form von Os 4, 4-6', pp. 308-11, for a curse scheme that encompasses three generations.

32. W.L. Holladay suggests that Jeremiah wears not the complete yoke bar but merely a collar of thongs and 'yoke pegs'; Holladay, 'The Years of Jeremiah's Preaching', *Int* 37 (1983), p. 155.

33. B. Duhm, *Anmerkungen zu den Zwölf Propheten II. Buch Hosea* (Giessen: Alfred Töpelmann, 1911), p. 21; S. Feigin, 'Hos. 4:4b', *AJSL* 42 (1925), p. 66.

translating 4b was influenced by the comparison of priest and people in 9a.³⁴ Since also 4b and 9a are both taken as single cola in *BHS*,³⁵ they could very well constitute a discontinuous bicolon which Hosea has broken up for rhetorical effect. The cola are strikingly similar when juxtaposed, particularly when translation (a) is read for 4b:

    4b   וְעַמְּךָ כִּמְרִיבֵי כֹהֵן
    9a   וְהָיָה כָעָם כַּכֹּהֵן

    4b   and your *people* are *like* the contentions of a *priest*
    9a   and it shall be *like people like priest*

A type of discontinuous bicolon has been identified in Ugaritic poetry,³⁶ but the best examples of the phenomenon presently being described occur elsewhere in the poetry of Hosea. In 4.11-14 and 8.9-13 discontinuous bicola form an inclusio around 7 bicolic or tricolic lines.³⁷ There separated cola not only contain balancing key terms; they also delimit a literary unit and set up a prophetic argument. We have seen already that 4b and 9a balance keywords, namely, people and priest. Should these cola, however, delimit a literary unit and also set up a prophetic argument, the surrounding context will have to show itself accommodating, and 4b-9a will have to make some independent sense of its own.

First, a look at the context. Our initial concern is with 4a. If 1-3 is a unit as most commentators assume, and 4b-9a is to become the next major unit, 4a will be left by itself. How is this to be explained? Perhaps 4a is a line from another speech inserted into its present position in the compilation process. Or it may be a 'one-liner' for which Hosea was particularly remembered. Its parallelism and syntactic chiasmus make the line ideal as a proverb, except that one is hard pressed to see here any deposit of wisdom. If the line was inserted by an editor at the time of scroll-making it would have

---

34. Andersen and Freedman, *Hosea*, p. 347.
35. Andersen and Freedman (*Hosea*, p. 319) take only 9a as a single.
36. B. Margalit (Margulis) finds a discontinuous bicolon flanking a standard parallel bicolon in RS 24.258 (*UF* 2 [1970] pp. 132, 138). This example, however, does not show nearly the separation which we have here. Also, the discontinuous bicolon does not delimit a unit, though Margalit says it provides strophic termination. Elsewhere in *CTA* 4.I.20-44 and 4.VII.14-19 single cola are found by Margalit at the beginning and end of literary units where they are thought to effect closure. But here the single cola are not separated bicola, and in the case of 4.I.44 it is not clear whether we actually have a single colon; cf. Margalit, *A Matter of 'Life' and 'Death': A Study of the Baal-Mot Epic (CTA 4-5-6)* (Neukirchen–Vluyn: Neukirchener Verlag, 1980), pp. 13-14, 58-59; Margalit, 'Studia Ugaritica I: "Introduction to Ugaritic Prosody"', *UF* 7 (1975), p. 301.
37. J.R. Lundbom, 'Poetic Structure and Prophetic Rhetoric in Hosea', *VT* 29 (1979), pp. 300-308. Andersen and Freedman (*Hosea*, p. 321) argue that 4.6aA and 14bB form a discontinuous bicolon.

to be said that it fits well enough; in fact, the line qualifies as a leit-motif for the whole of vv. 1-10: before Yahweh no one can contend, none can accuse. I am assuming, of course, that there is no narrowing of focus on to the priest or the priesthood and that Hosea is delivering the broad message of judgment.

The possibility of dislocation in the text must also be considered. We know dislocations exist. In Gen. 1.7 the words 'it was so' belong at the conclusion of v. 6 (*BHS*, JB, NAB, GNB, E.A. Speiser in AB,[38] after the LXX); in Exod. 22.3b-4 rearrangement is also necessary (so RSV, NEB, GNB, and somewhat differently in JB and NAB). We could, for example, place Hos. 4.4a after 4b. This would not impair the train of thought; also, the addition of another bicolon between 4b and 9a would bring the poem nicely into line with 4.11-14 and 8.9-13 as far as overall length is concerned. But we have no controls over such a proposal, making this a less desirable solution.

The best explanation, it seems to me, would be to take 4a as the conclusion of 1-3. We may note that Cyprian in one of his treatises delimited 1-4a as his pericope.[39] Taken this way 4a becomes a climax to the thought begun in v. 1, a thought reinforced in the text by the repetition of cognates from ריב. It goes as follows: Yahweh has a *contention* (רִיב) with the inhabitants of the land (1b); they, by contrast, have no right to *contend* (יָרֵב) with anyone (4a). The function of 4a is to effect closure. In the center of the unit are two catalogues, first a catalogue of human sins, and second a catalogue of the non-human inhabitants who will shortly come under Yahweh's condemnation. So, in my judgment, 4a is a suitable conclusion to 1-4a, and 4b is the beginning of the second major speech in the chapter.

Bracketing out 9b-10 does not cause any serious problems for interpretation. These ponderous—not to say platitudinous—words of judgment are intended to make explicit the message of 4b-9a, which is subtle and to certain people surely hidden. I will say more about the subtleties of 4b-9a in a moment. It may be that together with 1-4a these verses form a frame around 4b-9a, for in vv. 2 and 10 there is repetition of the verb פרץ (to break/break away). We still do not know enough about composition in the book of Hosea to be confident in judging speech units from editorial or tradition units. But it is becoming clearer all the time that ancient Hebrew literature does not always conform to canons of modern Western literature, where sequence of thought and logical progression are all-important. Time and again we see the biblical material build from the center outward—in both directions. Therefore the quest for the ancient mode of biblical composition should be made more frequently with two foci: (1) the location of centers; and (2) the location of frames which surround these centers. In this endeavor the identification of an

---

38. E.A. Speiser, *Genesis* (AB, 1; Garden City, NY: Doubleday, 1964).

39. Ad Quirinum III, 47; cf. *Sancti Cypriani Episcopi Opera* (ed. R. Weber; Turnhout: Brepols, 1972), p. 136.

inclusio has great value. The inclusio is no random repetition; nor is it simply a literary 'echo', as some define it.[40] It is a frame, a bracket, a tie-in between beginning and end. In discourse the inclusio is a rhetorical device effecting closure. The prophets used it for this purpose in their preaching; meanwhile, other masters of the rhetorical art pressed the device into a similar service as texts were prepared for public worship. Prophet and scribe are heir to the same rhetorical tradition in ancient Israel. That is to say, Hosea and Amos in the North, and Isaiah, Jeremiah, Ezekiel and other pre-exilic prophets in the South, share precisely the rhetorical tradition which finds expression in Deuteronomy and the so-called Deuteronomic History.[41]

The Prophetic Argument in 4b-9a

Having concluded that a delimited 4b-9a does no violence to the larger context—in fact, the context is surprisingly accommodating—we move on to an examination of these verses as a distinct unit of prophetic discourse. Marking off the discontinuous bicolon only for the purpose of calling attention to it, we read the unit as follows:

[4b]Your people are like the contentions of a priest

[5]You shall stumble by day
   and the prophet also will stumble with you by night
      and I will destroy your mother

[6]My people are destroyed for lack of knowledge
   because you have rejected knowledge
      so I reject you from being priest to me
And since you have forgotten the law of your God
   I will forget your children—even I

[7]The more they increased the more they sinned against me
   I will exchange[42] their glory for shame
[8]They feed on the sin of my people
   they are greedy for their iniquity

[9a]Therefore it shall be like people like priest.

I have omitted the *waws* beginning 4b and 5a for a smoother translation. The *waw* beginning 9a is translated 'therefore' for reasons to be given in a moment. Verse 5, which contains Hosea's judgment on the king, his mother,

---

40. I am thinking here of M. Dahood (AB, *Psalms*) and certain other Roman Catholic scholars who use the term more loosely to refer to a repetition occurring *anywhere* in discourse.
41. Lundbom, *Jeremiah: A Study in Ancient Hebrew Rhetoric*, pp. 113-20. [1997, pp. 147-54]
42. *tiq soph*: They exchanged.

18. *Contentious Priests and Contentious People in Hosea 4.1-10*

and the prophet, is scanned as a lengthy tricolon. Its concluding words, 'and I will destroy your mother', balance the concluding words to the priest in v. 6: 'I will forget your children'. Verse 6, which is 5 cola, is scanned as another long tricolon followed by a bicolon. It is also possible that the middle colon is a 'ballast line' between two bicola. So far as content goes, this colon is climactic within the verse: 'so I reject you from being priest to me'. Verses 7 and 8 are both bicola that speak about the priests in the third person to some unspecified audience.

How is the broken bicolon to be understood? It seems clear by now that כִּמְרִיבֵי כֹהֵן must mean 'like the contentions of a priest' rather than 'like those who contend with a priest'. Here we part company with the more recent defenders of the MT. If we were to take the latter translation, not only would we have two quite different meanings—4b comparing people with people and 9a comparing people with priest—but the cola when read together would leave us without a coherent thought. Verse 9a argues a basic equality between priest and people—both in terms of their guilt and of what their punishment will be.[43] And since 9a is without ambiguity we must work from it to 4b and not in the reverse direction. Good method—indeed also good hermeneutics—requires that one work from the known to the unknown. We may therefore conclude that translation (b) is not correct, which means we can forget about any allusion to Deut. 17.12. This connection rests solely on Jerome and the Vulgate. The LXX and the Talmud here prove to be the better guides to interpretation. I therefore read 4b, 'and your people are like the contentions of a priest', assuming as I have said that the phrase is elliptical and means to convey the basic idea that people with their unwarranted contentions are like the priest and his.

We are now in a position to examine the whole of 4b-9a. These verses do indeed form a coherent piece of discourse. More than that they contain a prophetic argument much like the ones found in 4.11-14 and 8.9-13.[44] The argument here goes as follows. There is a problem with people living in the king's city. They are contentious just like the priests. The elliptical nature of 4b indicates that Hosea does not want to be too clear. In fact, he is probably being deliberately obscure. Though his primary audience is the king, off to the side are others whom the prophet must be careful not to alienate from the start. The king too will be immediately on the defensive if he understands that the people of his city are being attacked. From the prophet's standpoint it is good rhetorical strategy to begin an unpopular subject with ambiguity and wait until the end to clarify, to let it unfold gradually so that the audience may be kept at bay until the final words are

---

43. So Feigin, 'Hos. 4:4b', p. 66; Andersen and Freedman, *Hosea*, pp. 360-61.
44. See Lundbom, 'Poetic Structure and Prophetic Rhetoric in Hosea', pp. 306-308.

spoken.⁴⁵ Hosea's total thought concerning the people cannot come all at once. At the outset it can only be broached. Completion will come in 9a. Verse 5 has a different character. It speaks totally and with painful clarity about Yahweh's judgment, a judgment slated for the king, for his prophet, and for the king's mother. Yet Hosea is still protecting himself by not making any explicit mention of the king. Verse 6 shifts audience but not subject matter. Judgment is still the issue, but now it is the priest who gets it for himself and his children. A reason is given. In 7-8 the entire priesthood is indicted and judged before an audience which remains unspecified. There is no ambiguity here. Because of their sins Yahweh will change the priests' glory into shame. The argument is capped with clarity and finality in 9a. This word sums up the judgment already articulated, but more importantly it clarifies the delicate matter raised at the beginning, which is what to do with Samaria's people. If we did not know it before, we know now that these people are unlawfully contentious and for that reason they must suffer the same fate as the quarrelsome priests. The וְהָיָה is a future as most take it, 'and it shall be', or better 'therefore it shall be' to express causality. The final word is the most difficult Hosea has to deliver: before Yahweh both people and priest are guilty. Modern scholarship has missed this point entirely by placing all the blame on the priest.

The Rhetorical Shape of 4.1-10

Looking at vv. 1-10 we see that this larger section falls into three parts: (1) 1-4a, a speech in which Yahweh announces his רִיב and precludes any other רִיב; also where he enumerates the human sins and the non-human inhabitants of the land upon whom judgment will fall; (2) 4b-9a, a carefully articulated prophetic argument spelling out Yahweh's judgment on the human inhabitants of the land, specifically those living in the royal city; and (3) 9b-10, a supplemental word of judgment on the human inhabitants asserted without subtlety and without argument. The thread tying this larger unit together is the assertion that both leaders and people have broken the bounds in abandoning Yahweh (פָּרִיץ in vv. 2 and 10). The larger unit reiterates in its own way the essential point of 4b-9a, and this confirms the view that Hosea is delivering the broad message. There is no narrowing of focus on to the priest, except as it takes place in v. 6. Rhetorically, the significant moves are from the general to the specific and from the ambiguous to the unambiguous.⁴⁶ The latter we observed within 4b-9a; it operates again (editorially perhaps) when the banal words of 9b-10 are placed after 4b-9a. The

---

45. Lundbom, *Jeremiah: A Study in Ancient Hebrew Rhetoric*, p. 114 (1997 edn, p. 148).

46. For these same rhetorical moves in Jeremiah, see Lundbom, *Jeremiah: A Study in Ancient Hebrew Rhetoric*, pp. 116-17 (1997 edn, pp. 150-51).

18. *Contentious Priests and Contentious People in Hosea 4.1-10* 231

former takes place within 1-4a, where Yahweh's רִיב is announced against the 'inhabitants of the land', after which judgment is specified with regard to the beasts, the birds and the fish. A further move toward specificity takes place when 4b-9a names just about every human inhabitant conceivable: people, king, prophet, king's mother, priest, priest's children, the priesthood, and again people and priest.

A State of Lex Suspensus

One final word about 4a, which I have suggested could be a leit-motif for the whole of 1-10. Andersen and Freedman wonder why Yahweh is precluding all argument when in other places, such as Isa. 1.18, he invites debate.[47] The answer is that all are guilty of wrongdoing. The people have no warrant to speak, nor do the priests. The king may not judge, nor may the prophet. Like the priest, each has failed in the office to which they were called. A corrupt people bears witness to the moral turpitude of its leaders. The point is frequently made that Yahweh here employs the *lex talionis* in meting out his judgments.[48] That is true. But so far as the inhabitants of Samaria are concerned—both people and leaders—Yahweh declares for them a state of *lex suspensus*. The legal process is automatically rendered inoperative whenever those judging are themselves guilty of the crime. Kimchi saw this clearly.[49] The same point precisely is made later on in the chapter where certain men are disqualified from judging their wives and daughters for sexual misconduct when they are doing the same thing (4.14). The suspension of law for hypocritical behavior is a strong biblical theme. We encounter it in the Judah and Tamar story (Genesis 38) and later again in the New Testament account of the woman caught in adultery (Jn 8.2-11; cf. Mt. 7.1-5).

---

47. Andersen and Freedman, *Hosea*, p. 345.
48. Lohfink, 'Zu Text und Form von Os 4,4-6', pp. 311-14; Wolff, *Hosea* (Hermeneia), pp. 74, 79.
49. Kimchi on v. 4a: אמר איש אל ירב ואל יוכח חבירו על רשעו כי לא יועילנו כי גם הוא עושה רעה כמוהו, 'It says, let no one contend and let no one accuse his companion concerning his evil for it will not profit him because he also does evil like him.'

Chapter 19

POETIC STRUCTURE AND PROPHETIC RHETORIC IN HOSEA*

In his *Prolegomenon* to George Buchanan Gray's reissued *The Forms of Hebrew Poetry*,[1] Professor David Noel Freedman proposes that a unit of poetry in Hos. 8.9-13 be isolated on the basis of an inclusio. According to Freedman, the single colon in v. 9:

> For behold they have gone up to Assyria[2]   כִּי־הֵמָּה עָלוּ אַשּׁוּר

balances the single colon in v. 13:

> Behold they will return to Egypt   הֵמָּה מִצְרַיִם יָשׁוּבוּ

Together the two constitute a normal bicolon which the poet has broken up in order to give this unit of poetry a frame. When the two cola are juxtaposed key terms balance each other nicely: הֵמָּה is repeated, the perfect עָלוּ and imperfect יָשׁוּבוּ correspond to each other, while 'Assyria' and 'Egypt' constitute what may very well be a fixed pair.[3] Hosea elsewhere uses 'Assyria' and 'Egypt' in parallel constructions (7.11; 9.3; 11.5, 11; 12.2). We note too that עָלוּ אַשּׁוּר and מִצְרַיִם יָשׁוּבוּ form a chiasmus. Freedman says, 'the two cola complement each other impressively', and so they do.

The recognition that these cola could fit together in parallelism is not new. Duhm, for example, transposed the single colon of v. 13 so that it immediately followed the single colon of v. 9.[4] Freedman's suggestion has the advantage, however, in that it explains the text as it stands. And, if correct, it provides us with important new insights into Hebrew poetry and Hebrew rhetoric.

---

* First published in *VT* 29 (1979), pp. 300-308 (repr. in *Prophecy in the Hebrew Bible* [ed. David E. Orton; Leiden: E.J. Brill, 2000], pp. 139-47).
1. G.B. Gray, *The Forms of Hebrew Poetry* (New York: Ktav, 1972), pp. xxxvi-xxxvii.
2. Freedman translates עָלוּ as a future: 'they will go up'. I take this verb, however, to be a simple past, which is how it would normally be translated.
3. For fixed pairs in Hebrew and Ugaritic poetry, see S. Gevirtz, *Patterns in the Early Poetry of Israel* (Chicago, IL: University of Chicago, 1963), and M. Dahood, *Psalms III* (AB, 17A; Garden City, NY: Doubleday, 1970), pp. 445-56.
4. Bernhard Duhm, *Die Zwölf Propheten* (Tübingen: J.C.B. Mohr [Paul Siebeck], 1910), p. 34.

19. *Poetic Structure and Prophetic Rhetoric in Hosea*

The inclusio is a structural device by which one returns at the end to the point at which they began. It is widely used in both oral and written discourse of today—including poetry[5]—and we find it in ancient discourse as well.[6] In the Old Testament it appears frequently in Deuteronomic sermons, prophetic speeches, and in psalms.[7]

Structures in Deuteronomy 1–28 are of particular interest to us since they reflect the same general period as Hosea, that is, c. 750–700 BCE.[8] We see, for example, the preacher of chap. 12 framing his sermon with an injunction to obedience:

> These are the *statues* and *ordinances* which *you shall be careful to do* in the land...
>
> (12.1)
>
> Every *word* that I command you, *you shall be careful to do*; you shall not add to it or take from it.
>
> (13.1)

In his sermon on clean and unclean foods (14.1-21) he provides a frame by listing miscellaneous regulations at the extremities in the midst of which occur these words:

> *For you are a people holy to Yahweh your God*
>
> (14.2)
>
> *For you are a people holy to Yahweh your God*
>
> (14.21)

The inclusio can also be used to frame a sub-unit of discourse that is much longer. The subscription to the book Deuteronomy contains such an inclusio, which is of the inverted type:

> These are the *words* that *Moses spoke* to all Israel *beyond the Jordan*...
>
> (1.1)
>
> *Beyond the Jordan*, in the land of Moab, *Moses undertook to explain* this law...
>
> (1.5)

---

5. Although she does not call it by this name, Barbara H. Smith recognizes this phenomenon in modern poetry; see her book *Poetic Closure* (Chicago, IL: University of Chicago, 1968), pp. 27, 53-54, 66-67.

6. H. Lausberg, *Elemente der literarischen Rhetorik* (Munich: Max Hueber, 1963), p. 86. For structures larger than the clause or sentence classicists use the term 'ring composition'; see J.A. Notopoulos, 'Continuity and Interconnexion in Homeric Oral Composition', *TAPA* 82 (1951), pp. 81-101.

7. M. Dahood, *Psalms I* (AB, 16; Garden City, NY: Doubleday, 1966), pp. 5 *et passim*; James Muilenburg, 'Isaiah', in *IB* 5 (ed. George A. Buttrick; New York: Abingdon Press, 1956), pp. 385, 392; James Muilenburg, 'Form Criticism and Beyond', *JBL* 88 (1969), pp. 9-10.

8. Deuteronomy 1–28 I date in the reign of Hezekiah; see my article, 'The Lawbook of the Josianic Reform', *CBQ* 38 (1976), pp. 293-302.

Some years after both Hosea and the Deuteronomic preacher, in 622 BCE, the prophet Huldah delivered an oracle to Josiah and the people of Judah in which she employed the inclusio. It too is of the inverted type:

Behold *I will bring/evil/upon this place*...

(2 Kgs 22.16)

...all the *evil*/which *I will bring/upon this place*

(2 Kgs 22.20)

The tradition is maintained by Jeremiah as I have sought to demonstrate in my *Jeremiah: A Study in Ancient Hebrew Rhetoric*.[9]

But to return to Hosea, the inclusio is 8.9-13 is different. First of all, it is created by the break-up of a standard bicolon of poetry. I have seen only one other instance of this, namely, Jer. 51.20-23, where (וְנִפַּצְתִּי בְךָ גּוֹיִם)(הִשְׁחַתִּי בְךָ) מַמְלָכוֹת (20b) balances פַּחוֹת וּסְגָנִים וְנִפַּצְתִּי בְךָ (23c).[10] Otherwise such a phenomenon is rare. Freedman says the structure 'is novel to say the least'.

This inclusio is also different in that the end does not simply repeat the beginning. Freedman speaks of complementation, by which he means that both cola combine to give a more full picture than either of them gives singly. In his view the journey to Assyria lies in the future and will be a parallel experience to the future journey to Egypt, that is, exile will be to both places.[11] But in my view the journey to Assyria lies in the past, and the future journey to Egypt will come about as a result of the former journey. It is *because* messengers have gone to Assyria (instead of to Yahweh) that they will be brought back into slavery (Egypt = slavery). Hosea says virtually the same thing in 5.13-14 and 7.11-12. This is one of many variations of a common prophetic argument. Elijah told the sick Ahaziah that because he sent to Baalzebub instead of to Yahweh he would die (2 Kings 1). Isaiah and Jeremiah likewise advised against foreign alliances when a rejection of Yahweh was implied (Isa. 30.1-7; 31.1-5; Jer. 2.18-19). Such ventures can only bring shame (Jer. 2.36-37). Thus in my opinion the cola do more than complement each other; the final colon advances the thought. The two taken together create a prophetic argument: because you have gone to Assyria you will therefore return to Egypt. Jeremiah puts the inclusio to this same use later on.

Freedman expressed the hope that his lone example might be 'a harbinger of others not yet detected'. We should like then to draw attention to another structure of precisely the same type. It is found in Hos. 4.11-14, where the single colon of vv. 11-12:

---

9. Lundbom, *Jeremiah: A Study in Ancient Hebrew Rhetoric*, pp. 36-60 (1997 edn, pp. 52-81).

10. Lundbom, *Jeremiah: A Study of Ancient Hebrew Rhetoric*, pp. 91-92 (1997 edn, pp. 120-22).

11. Professor Freedman has expressed his views more fully to me in subsequent private correspondence.

New wine takes away the mind of *my people*   תִּירוֹשׁ יִקַּח־לֵב עַמִּי

has its counterpart in the single colon of v. 14:

A people without sense will be thrust down   עָם לֹא־יָבִין יִלָּבֵט

Editorial expansion at the end of 10 and beginning of 11 obscures the upper limit of the opening colon. Our reconstruction follows Elliger in *BHS* and Wolff[12] who omit זְנוּת וְיַיִן וְ from the beginning of 11 and include עַמִּי from 12 (LXX: καρδία λαοῦ μου). Most translators and commentators take עַמִּי to be the subject of 12a. But with our reconstruction the colon becomes 7 syllables, which is the same number of syllables in 14c if the initial *waw* (וְ) is omitted. The syllable count in 8.9-13 is also 7 and 7.[13]

Here too we note that earlier commentators with a feeling for poetry became uneasy at the sight of a single colon. Duhm took 11 and placed it before 14c.[14] W.R. Harper, who made the text of Hosea into strophes, accommodated 11 by omitting part of 12 and placed 14c way back with v. 4.[15] At least Duhm recognized that 11 and 14c go together, but as we can see there is again no need to rearrange the text. This is simply another instance of a bicolon being broken up in order to frame an intervening unit. When juxtaposed these cola are likewise seen to have balancing terms: עָם is repeated and יִקַּח־לֵב corresponds roughly to לֹא־יָבִין. (In Prov. 10.13 לֵב is balanced with the ni. participle נָבוֹן, while in 11.12 and 15.21 it is balanced with תְּבוּנָה/תְּבוּנוֹת.) Hosea describes in both instances a people whose mind has been dulled. We have another chiasmus too: 'takes away the mind/of my people' and 'a people/without sense'.

The statements at the beginning and end of the unit may be independent wisdom sayings as some commentators suggest,[16] but in this context they combine to form another prophetic argument: new wine makes a people drunk, and drunken people can easily be felled.

In both 4.11-14 and 8.9-13 the identification of the inclusio aids in delimiting the poetic unit. In chap. 4 most commentators begin a unit at 11; only Cheyne and Mays, however, end at 14.[17] Edwin M. Good concludes his unit

---

12. H.W. Wolff, *Hosea* (BK; Neukirchen–Vluyn: Neukirchener Verlag, 1961), p. 89 [Eng. Hermeneia; Philadelphia: Fortress Press, 1974, p. 72].

13. Freedman, 'Prolegomenon', p. 37.

14. B. Duhm, *Die Zwölf Propheten*, p. 27.

15. W.R. Harper, *The Structure of the Text of the Book of Hosea* (Chicago, IL: University of Chicago, 1905), pp. 14, 16; W.R. Harper, *Amos and Hosea* (ICC; Edinburgh: T. & T. Clark, 1910), pp. 253, 260.

16. Harper (*Amos and Hosea*, p. 260) cites the earlier opinion of P. Ruben, although Ruben took both 11 and 14c as marginal glosses; see also Mays, *Hosea*, p. 72.

17. T.K. Cheyne, *The Book of Hosea* (CBSC; Cambridge: Cambridge University Press, 1884), *ad loc*; Mays, *Hosea, ad loc.*

at 14, but before the final colon.[18] Wolff extends his unit to 15. In chap. 8 none of the modern commentators begins at v. 9, while v. 14 is thought to be either the conclusion of the unit or else a later addition.[19] Are 4.11-14 and 8.9-13 whole poems or are they sub-units within poems that are larger? It is hard to know. I am inclined to take both as separate and originally independent poems, though I readily concede that the delimitation of poems in Hosea is something about which we still know relatively little.

Having found two poems now with the same rhetorical structure at beginning and end, we will proceed to a closer and more complete comparison. This can be done when the poems are laid out in full:

Hosea 4.11-14

[11]New wine takes away the mind of my people.

[12]They enquire of their thing of wood
    and their staff gives them oracles
For a spirit of whoredom has led them astray
    and they have gone a-whoring out from under their God
[13]On the tops of the mountains they sacrifice
    and on the hills they burn offerings
Under oak, poplar, and terebinth
    because their shade is good!
Therefore your daughters play the whore
    and your sons' brides commit adultery
[14]I will not punish your daughters when they play the whore
    nor your sons' brides when they commit adultery
For those men over there go aside with whores
    and sacrifice with sacred prostitutes.

A people without sense will be thrust down!

Hosea 8.9-13

[9]For behold they have gone up to Assyria.

    A wild ass off by himself
    Ephraim has hired lovers
[10]Even though they hire among the nations
    now I will gather them up

So that they soon writhe under the burden
    of the officials' king[20]

---

18. E.M. Good, 'The Composition of Hosea', *SEÅ* 31 (1966), p. 35.
19. Wolff, *Hosea* (Hermeneia), pp. 136, 146; Mays, *Hosea*, pp. 123-24.
20. The MT here is incomprehensible; translation follows Wolff, *Hosea* (Hermeneia), p. 133.

> ¹¹Indeed Ephraim has multiplied altars
>> he uses them for sinning
>>> altars for sinning
> ¹²Though I write for him multitudes of my laws
>> they are regarded as something strange
> ¹³Sacrifices they love, so they sacrifice²¹
>> flesh and they eat
>>> Yahweh takes no delight in them
> Now he will remember their iniquity
>> and punish their sins.
>
> Behold they will return to Egypt!

It is now possible to see that similarity in structure extends beyond the broken bicolon that opens and closes each poem. The inner bodies of each poem are the same length: 7 bicolic or tricoloic lines. If the broken bicolon is counted as one complete line, then each poem is 8 lines. Of the two 4.11-14 is the more regular. All its lines are bicolic, and with the exception of 13b, all are in good parallelism. In 8.9-13, vv. 11 and 13a are tricola. Earlier scholars deleted מִזְבְּחֹת לַחֲטֹא (v. 11) and יְהוָה לֹא רָצָם (v. 13a), but now most prefer to leave both in the text, which I believe is correct. The parallelism of this poem is not what it is in 4.11-14, but the body still seems to be made up of bicolic and tricolic lines.

The centers of each poem are perhaps worthy of special comment. Verse 13b is the center of 4.11-14, and it is the only bicolon in the poem to lack parallelism. Instead Hosea embellishes his preceding remark with asyndeton: 'oak, poplar, and terebinth'. This emphasizes how many and varied are the places where Israel goes aside to engage in illicit cultic rites. Nils W. Lund in his *Chiasmus in the New Testament* showed how large chiastic structures often contain triplets in the center.²² Here too we have a triplet. There is no triplet in the center line of 8.9-13, which is v. 11, but one does find embellishment of another sort. The phrase מִזְבְּחֹת לַחֲטֹא—which, as we have said, should not be deleted—picks up both לַחֲטֹא in the second colon and מִזְבְּחֹת in the first. This might not be significant except for the fact that the poem does not otherwise build on repetition.²³ There would seem to be at least some indication, then, that Hosea uses the centers of his poems for embellishment. I offer this only as a provisional conclusion which further research can perhaps corroborate. Many of the Jeremanic

---

21. MT again difficult; see Wolff.
22. Nils W. Lund, *Chiasmus in the New Testament* (Chapel Hill, NC: University of North Carolina, 1942; repr. Peabody, MA: Hendrickson, 1992), pp. 57, 199, 201, 274.
23. The repetition in זִבְחֵי הַבְהָבַי יִזְבָּחוּ (13a)—whatever that means—is of a different sort and does not provide the type of embellishment we have in v. 11.

poems have an identifiable center in which balancing techniques are seen to be operative.[24]

That Hosea should compose two poems so much alike certainly deserves our attention. Again, to use Jeremiah for purposes of comparison, I have found the same to be true with some of his poems once the units are properly delimited and the structures are made plain. Poems have the same number of lines, the same rhetorical structure, and sometimes the same words or even the same sounds in identical collocations.[25] We know of course that modern poets and songwriters repeat structures from one composition to another, and so it should occasion no surprise in us to find the ancients doing precisely the same thing. A syllable count of both poems indicates that the overall rhythms, however, are different. The average number of syllables per colon in 4.11-14 is between 9 and 10, while in 8.9-13 it is between 7 and 9. Some cola in the latter have as few as 4 and 5 syllables. Only the opening and closing cola of both poems correspond with a syllable count of 7.

A final word now about prophetic rhetoric. In both poems Hosea has but one objective. He must confront the people with their apostasy and bring to them Yahweh's word of judgment. The indictment in 4.11-14 is for foreign worship—Assyrian perhaps, maybe Canaanite, or a combination of both. Wooden idols and cultic prostitution, regardless of whose influence it comes under, are abominations in the sight of Yahweh. The indictment continues through v. 13. In 14ab, which concludes the body of the poem, Yahweh states whom it is he will *not* judge, namely, the young women. Judgment comes at the end: 'A people without sense will be thrust down!' But even here Hosea speaks only in general terms. He says '*a* people'. Yet when linked up with '*my* people' above, the conviction becomes quite specific.

In 8.9-13 apostasy consists of a political alliance with Assyria together with the cultic practices which this alliance has forced upon the people. The indictment continues through 13a, although we must leave open the interpretation of v. 10, which is corrupt. The important point is that judgment is again saved for the end, coming in 13b where it is stated first in general terms: 'Now he will remember their iniquity, and punish their sins', and then made specific in the final colon: 'Behold they will return to Egypt!' Yet to the end Hosea speaks in partially veiled terms. 'Egypt' most likely refers here to Assyria, which, after all, is where the exile will be. Assyria, he says, will be another 'Egypt'. The inclusio, with its tying together of beginning and end, gives a more precise statement of judgment, which is that the

---

24. They are poems with chiastic structures however; cf. *Jeremiah: A Study in Ancient Hebrew Rhetoric*, pp. 70-96 (1997 edn, pp. 93-127).

25. Lundbom, *Jeremiah: A Study in Ancient Hebrew Rhetoric*, pp. 68, 78-82 (1997 edn, pp. 91, 104-109).

messengers who have gone to Assyria with their tribute money, paying to her the wages of a whore as it were, will later be forced to travel this same road again when Israel is taken into captivity. The end will be like the beginning: the journey into slavery will repeat the journey with the tribute.

Both arguments contain their subtleties and not everyone in Hosea's audience is likely to grasp them. Nevertheless, I think we can still presuppose a measure of sophistication on the part of some. These people, after all, were conditioned to poetic parallelism, which is to say they expected cola to come in twos and threes. If Hosea begins his poem then with a single colon, another will be anticipated. To postpone completion is of course to create expectation. Only when that final colon comes will the attentive listener be satisfied. And if the listener is accustomed to a rhetoric that ties the end in with the beginning, a rhetoric exemplified in passages like those from Deuteronomy, which we saw earlier, they might reasonably be expected to put the two parts of Hosea's argument together.

From Hosea's point of view, breaking up cola in this manner is not done merely for the sake of novelty, although I suppose we cannot rule out this motive entirely. Like the other prophets, Hosea had a difficult message to deliver. The reason he postpones his main point is so that he will not lose his audience. The Deuteronomic preacher, we must remember, had only to admonish and to warn. For him then the inclusio was intended mainly to restore focus and to emphasize key points. But for Hosea the inclusio functioned as an argumentative device, used to convey to the people Yahweh's terrible message of divine judgment.

Chapter 20

Jeremiah and the Break-away from Authority Preaching*

I

One hears today within the major religious communities of the Western world increasing amounts of discourse in the 'assertive mode'.[1] The phenomenon is supported by the perception—rather widespread—that assertions based on authority constitute the sole vehicle whereby revelation, witness, and truth itself are conveyed. On the one level this perception is manifested in notions regarding what constitutes a valid rhetoric for articulating current religious faith. On another level this perception can be observed in notions regarding what sort of rhetoric articulates faith in the authoritative documents of Western religious communities, namely, the Bible, the Koran, the Talmud, and doctrines of the Roman Church.

In public and semi-public forums examples of this modern assertive rhetoric are so numerous as to hardly require mention. Orthodox Jews issue dogmatic statements on 'Who is a Jew?' and how life ought to be regulated in the State of Israel. The Ayatollah Khomeini pronounced in similar fashion on Islamic heresies and Muslim heretics, his edict of death on Salman Rushdie (for *The Satanic Verses*) being the example most widely known. Fundamentalist Muslims continue to speak with authority from 'on high' as they wage *jihad* against Jews, Christians, and others including fellow Muslims over a wide range of religious, political and social issues. Like their late spiritual leader these admit no dialogue with their opponents, no common quest in pursuit of the truth.

In the Roman Church a synonymity between assertive discourse and the language of faith is implied when dogmatic teachings of the magisterium are 'once and for all delivered to the saints' (Jude 1.3).[2] Some bishops and

---

* First published in *SEÅ* 56 (1991), pp. 7-28.
1. The term 'assertive mode' is taken from Chaim Perelman and L. Olbrechts-Tyteca, *The New Rhetoric* (trans. John Wilkinson and Purcell Weaver; Notre Dame, IN: University of Notre Dame Press, 1969), p. 58.
2. See Paul Ricoeur, 'Toward a Hermeneutic of the Idea of Revelation', *HTR* 70 (1977), pp. 1-2.

theologians interpret this, understandably, as an inflexible stand on church doctrine. Protestant Fundamentalists, meanwhile, with Bible in hand preface assertion after assertion with 'The Bible says...' For them dialogue is impossible with modern intellectual thought, also with liberal Protestant groups, most notably the World Council of Churches. Even in Protestant Evangelicalism, 'witness' and 'dialogue' have become mutually exclusive concepts, the latter said to be a concession to religious relativism that destroys Christian integrity, while the former preserves Christian integrity by conveying the 'truths revealed in Scripture'.[3] In each of these religious communities the assumption being made is that revelation, witness, or truth requires the assertive mode of discourse; any other mode yields something less.

In a reflective essay which discuses the training of Christian ministers, Professor Emeritus Paul Holmer of Yale has distinguished between 'language *about* faith' and 'language *of* faith'.[4] Holmer says language *about* faith, which is heard in seminaries and other places where the scholarly temper dominates, is 'incomplete, probable, and dependent on evidence', whereas language *of* faith is 'proclamatory, all-inclusive, and certain'. The scholarly temper, according to Holmer, is 'tentative, hypothetical, and inquisitive, impelled by curiosity'; the Christian temper, on the other hand, is 'declaratory, categorical, and aggressive, urged onward by the need of men for salvation'. Again the assumption—within the Christian tradition—that witness, preaching, and anything else qualifying as the language of faith consist of discourse in the assertive mode—strongly and aggressively in the assertive mode. The model for such is likely the kerygmatic sermons of Acts (2.14-36 *et passim*).

II

This notion about what currently constitutes a valid rhetoric of religious faith in the Judeo-Christian tradition has its reflex in a corresponding notion about the character of biblical rhetoric. George A. Kennedy in his book, *Classical Rhetoric and Its Christian and Secular Tradition from Ancient to Modern Times*,[5] says that the essential rhetorical quality of the Old Testament is its 'assertion of authority'.[6] God's truth, says Kennedy, is enunciated

---

3. Arthur F. Glasser in *Contemporary Theologies of Mission* (ed. Arthur F. Glasser and Donald A. McGavern; Grand Rapids: Baker, 1983), pp. 205-219.

4. Paul Holmer, 'Can We Educate Ministers Scientifically?', in *The Making of Ministers* (ed. Keith R. Bridston and Dwight W. Culver; Minneapolis, MN: Augsburg Publishing House, 1964), pp. 20-21.

5. George A. Kennedy, *Classical Rhetoric and Its Christian and Secular Tradition from Ancient to Modern Times* (Chapel Hill, NC: University of North Carolina Press, 1980), pp. 120-29.

6. Kennedy, *Classical Rhetoric and Its Christian and Secular Tradition*, p. 121.

very simply. Like philosophical rhetoric the rhetoric of the Old Testament is 'uncontaminated by adornment, flattery, or sophistic argumentation'. Yet it differs from philosophical rhetoric in that 'truth is known from revelation or established by signs sent from God, not discovered by dialectic through man's efforts'.

God's direct speech in Genesis 1 contains this assertion of authority. God says, 'Let there be light', and there is light. Later on, when Moses is commissioned as God's messenger, he is unsure of his authority, so God gives him a sign which bolsters his message and becomes, in place of logical argument, the primary mode of persuasion (Exodus 4). Kennedy does recognize, however, that Moses is given the good services of Aaron, who becomes Moses' orator. So in the Hebrew tradition some recognition is given to natural ability. But the ancient Hebrew orator still 'has little need of practice or knowledge of an art'. 'He needs only the inspiration of the Spirit'.[7] In this connection, Kennedy cites another force bearing upon Old Testament rhetoric, namely, the ultimate control which God has over human affairs. 'Persuasion takes place when God is ready', he says, the Exodus event providing our best example. Pharaoh does not listen until God allows him to listen.[8]

Covenant speeches in Deuteronomy 1–4; 5–28; 29–30; Joshua 24; and 1 Samuel 12 all reveal a heightened sense of authority, whether God himself is speaking, or whether it is Moses, Joshua, or Samuel. In the wisdom literature things are no different. Kennedy finds in the speech of Wisdom in Proverbs 1 'no logical argument nor any definition of what is meant by wisdom or knowledge, only assertions delivered with authority'.[9]

About prophetic speech Kennedy says little, save that Ezekiel 24 shows how a covenant speech can be adapted to future circumstances, and that messianic predictions in Isaiah are later converted into a basis of authority for the early Christian preachers. Here the discussion reaches its weakest point, for one would assume that a rhetoric based largely upon authority would finds its greatest expression in the Hebrew prophets. But Kennedy fails to note this.

New Testament rhetoric, according to Kennedy, follows along the same lines. In Jesus' Sermon on the Mount 'the persuasive quality…comes primarily from the authority projected by the speaker'.[10] The same is true in early Christian preaching. It is 'not persuasion, but proclamation, and is based on authority and grace, not on proof'.[11]

---

7. Kennedy, *Classical Rhetoric and Its Christian and Secular Tradition*, p. 122.
8. Kennedy, *Classical Rhetoric and Its Christian and Secular Tradition*, p. 122.
9. Kennedy, *Classical Rhetoric and Its Christian and Secular Tradition*, pp. 124-25.
10. Kennedy, *Classical Rhetoric and Its Christian and Secular Tradition*, p. 126.
11. Kennedy, *Classical Rhetoric and Its Christian and Secular Tradition*, p. 127.

This 'assertion of authority' sets off Judeo-Christian rhetoric from classical rhetoric where arguments involving *logos* (the appeal to reason), *pathos* (the appeal to emotions), and *ethos* (the appeal to the speaker's character) predominate.[12] Kennedy says, 'authority is analogous to ethos in classical rhetoric, but [exists] at a different metaphysical level'.[13] Kennedy does recognize, however, that the Judeo-Christian orator will on occasion use *logos*, *pathos*, and *ethos* on audiences in whom the Spirit once worked, but who now find the life gone from them. Such audiences can be brought back to the truth by rational and emotional means. The character of the speaker can also in such situations affect the success of the speech. So other appeals are made; nevertheless, it is assertions of authority that continue to be the controlling element in Judeo-Christian rhetoric. *Pathos*, for example, is merely a support for authority when past sufferings are recalled or future rewards and punishments are anticipated.

It is unfortunate that these latter insights were not developed further, particularly as they pertain to prophetic rhetoric, for it is the prophets more than anyone who are sent to address 'de-Spirited' audiences. I will return to discuss precisely this subject, arguing that with the prophets authority preaching ascends to its greatest height. Yet at the same time, in the case of Jeremiah, a break-away from authority-based preaching and witness occurs, with the result that Hebrew rhetoric comes surprisingly close to the rhetoric of classical Greece and Rome.

Summing up then Kennedy's description of Hebrew and early Christian rhetoric, let me say simply that it conforms basically to the common perception outlined earlier. Authority statements are statements in the assertive mode. Dialectic is not in evidence, at least so far as Hebrew rhetoric is concerned. Kennedy does concede that Jesus in his encounters with the Pharisees shows some ability at dialectic.[14]

III

Kennedy, it seems to me, has rightly identified the distinguishing feature of Hebrew and early Christian rhetoric. One cannot begin to understand this rhetorical tradition, surely, without recognizing the key role authority and assertions of authority play in conveying God's word to humankind. Having said this, however, it seems equally clear that any assessment of Judeo-Christian rhetoric which recognizes *only* assertions based on authority lies

---

12. Edward P.J. Corbett, *Classical Rhetoric for the Modern Student* (New York: Oxford University Press, 2nd edn, 1971), p. 15; also Quintilian's *Institutes* VI ii 8-20.
13. Kennedy, *Classical Rhetoric and Its Christian and Secular Tradition*, p. 121.
14. Kennedy, *Classical Rhetoric and Its Christian and Secular Tradition*, pp. 126-27.

open to serious challenge, for that amounts to an enormous reduction of what the Bible sets forth as being revelation, witness, and searchings for truth. I would add that the common perception about what today is a valid rhetoric for articulating faith amounts to a reduction of similar magnitude. But that is a subject for another essay. However, before dismissing the modern rhetorical problem I would like to mention an important essay which brings together both modern and biblical thought on the idea of revelation, calling attention to the same sort of 'reductionist' tendency I have just mentioned.

In a 1977 article, 'Toward a Hermeneutic of the Idea of Revelation',[15] Paul Ricoeur argues that our current concept of revelation is too authoritarian and totalitarian, being derived ultimately from speculative philosophy where propositions such as 'God exists', 'God is immutable, omnipotent, etc.', dominate. What we need, says Ricoeur, is a concept that is polysemic and pluralistic, one which gives priority to the modes of discourse that are original to the community of faith. To find these Ricoeur goes to the Old Testament, where the major modes are said to number five: (1) prophetic; (2) narrative; (3) prescriptive (i.e., laws); (4) wisdom; and (5) hymnic. The prophetic mode in Ricoeur's view is 'the original nucleus of the traditional idea of revelation',[16] and this mode serves as a reference term for the other modes, which are analogous to it.[17] The important insight here is that the prophetic mode—which corresponds more or less to what I have called the 'assertive mode'—is taken to be simply one mode of discourse among others, that is, it is not the only vehicle for conveying divine revelation, as the common perception would have it. With five modes of discourse, Ricoeur achieves a concept of revelation that is polysemic and pluralistic.

Ricoeur thus succeeds in wresting the idea of revelation from the grip of speculative philosophy, but his broadened concept remains tied, nevertheless, to the literary categories of prophecy, narrative, law, wisdom, and the psalm. What this amounts to basically, though Ricoeur may not necessarily intend it, is a theological superstructure built upon the foundation of form criticism, for form criticism assumed from the very beginning that genres each possess their own distinctive mode of discourse.[18]

What we need if we intend a more precise evaluation of the *function* of discourse is a different terminology, one enabling us to measure a speaker's persuasive power, the degree of audience involvement, and whether or not any real dialogue is going on. These are the things we must know before

---

15. Ricoeur, 'Toward a Hermeneutic of the Idea of Revelation', pp. 1-37.
16. Ricoeur, 'Toward a Hermeneutic of the Idea of Revelation', p. 3.
17. Ricoeur, 'Toward a Hermeneutic of the Idea of Revelation', pp. 16-17.
18. Hermann Gunkel, 'Die Grundproblem der israelitischen Literatur-geschichte', *DLZ* 29 (1906), pp. 1797-1800; 1861-866.

rendering a judgment on whether or not Hebrew religious discourse consists entirely of assertions based on authority. I suggest therefore the adoption of linguistic terminology in the discussion of discourse modalities. The linguist speaks of four modes of discourse: (1) the assertive; (2) the injunctive (or imperative); (3) the interrogative; and (4) the optative (which is basically the 'wish').[19] Particular attention needs to be given to the interrogative mode, for that mode more than any of the others stimulates audience involvement, and makes dialogue or dialectic a genuine possibility. Question and answer, as is well known, is an important component of Hebrew rhetoric.

IV

Now to my chosen topic, which is prophetic rhetoric, with special attention to the rhetoric of Jeremiah. My thesis, already partially stated, is that authority preaching reaches a high point in the 8th- and 7th-century prophets. It appears also in Jeremiah, who is active in the late 7th- and early 6th-centuries BCE. But with Jeremiah we witness a break-away—not a complete abandonment, let me emphasize, but clear signs of a break-away—with the result that Hebrew rhetoric becomes more dialogical in character, and truth is found not merely in the heavenly regions, but rather on earth by the prophet *and his audience*, who together forge a partnership in pursuit of its discovery. To the extent that this takes place, Hebrew rhetoric can be said to anticipate the later rhetoric of classical Greece and Rome.

In the preaching of the 8th- and 7th-century prophets, one can easily document the sort of rhetoric Kennedy is talking about. What we have there is essentially assertion based on authority, interrupted perhaps only by rhetorical questions, which lie somewhere in between real questions and assertion. Most would agree they lie closer to the latter.

Amos roars like the Lion from Zion, and his audience mourns and withers. The use of the messenger formula, 'thus said Yahweh', is only part of it. All the utterances come across like those of chaps. 1–2, where the prophet announces Yahweh's irrevocable judgment on nations of the world for gross inhumanity towards one another, in the case of Judah—also Israel—on account of covenant violation. Amos shows no real listening power; there is no dialogue between him and his audience, not even as much as between him and Yahweh in the visions of 7.1-9 and 8.1-3, nor indeed between him and Amaziah the priest in 7.10-17, the latter being the only recorded discourse between the prophet and some other person in the book. What we do hear is authority, and plenty of it, from beginning to end. As a consequence, the prophet's message—whether it denounces current evil or announces

---

19. Perelman and Olbrechts-Tyteca, *The New Rhetoric*, p. 158.

future judgment—must be accepted or rejected as given. The following in 4.1-3 is typical Amos preaching:

> **4** ¹Hear this word, you cows of Bashan
>   who are in the mountain of Samaria
> who oppress the poor, who crush the needy
>   who say to their husbands,
>   'Bring, that we may drink!'
> ²The Lord God has sworn by his holiness
>   that, behold the days are coming upon you
> when they shall take you away with hooks
>   even the last of you with fishhooks.
> ³And you shall go out through the breaches
>   every one straight before her
>   and you shall be cast forth into Harmon
>   —oracle of Yahweh.

One finds some audience involvement in Amos' preaching, but it is artificially induced, and if the audience submits, it does so involuntarily. The prophet achieves his end by extensive use of the rhetorical question. The string of seven rhetorical questions in 3.3-6, which is unparalleled in prophetic literature, is nothing more than a 'set-up' for the rhetorical questions of v. 8, which are climactic:

> The Lion has roared, who will not fear?
> Yahweh God has spoken, who can but prophesy?

The audience here is 'trapped' into engagement with the prophet. By answering 'no' seven times it must now say 'no one' two final times to questions aimed at validating the prophet's call.

The same 'trapping technique' occurs in the long opening discourse, where Amos makes a masterful survey of the nations only to come around at the end to his preferred subject, which is Israel. Here again audience involvement—if it occurs—is achieved only by coercion. After having given prior assent to the judgments slated for Damascus, Gaza, Tyre, Edom, Ammon, Moab, and Judah, the audience will have great difficulty in stopping the momentum and refraining from self-judgment when Israel comes up for review. The message from beginning to end—with the possible exception of the rhetorical question in 2.11b—consists of assertions based on authority. One is reminded here of Nathan telling David the parable of the ewe lamb (2 Samuel 12), and David 'involving himself' in the prophet's message by offering a judgment on the man who is consumed by greed, at which point Nathan thunders, 'You are the man!' This is trickery. One can hardly call this persuasion, even if David does, as a consequence, admit his guilt and repent.

Hosea's preaching has a softer tone, more pleading and more pathos, certainly, yet throughout one hears only authoritative assertions from Yahweh

God. Hosea's speeches are difficult to delimit, but some progress has been made. In chap. 4, for example, rhetorical criticism has been able to delimit poetic units, bring arguments into clearer focus, and identify frames that build up the larger composition.[20] Nevertheless, speeches here as elsewhere are essentially authority-based. In 4.1, Yahweh announces a controversy (רִיב) with the people, and what follows is a broad assault on just about everyone in Israelite society. There is no dialogue, no opportunity for rebuttal, only one lone rhetorical question in v. 16b, after which comes more indictment, and a final word of judgment.

Things are no different with Micah and Isaiah, prophets of the southern tradition. Micah 3 and Isa. 5.8-30 give us parade examples of authority preaching, but one finds the same throughout the collected utterances of both prophets. Isaiah, in his celebrated 'song of the vineyard' in 5.1-7, approaches a break-away in authority preaching, but it is no more than an approach. It never really happens. In v. 3 the prophet invites his audience to judge between Yahweh and the vineyard, and rhetorical questions in v. 4 call again for a response. But the audience has little chance to respond, for in vv. 5-6 judgment comes with uncompromising force. And if the audience is not quick enough to interpret Isaiah's metaphor, the prophet reveals it in v. 7, after which he teases them with word plays in the indictment, sealing the case once and for all. Listen to the second half of the song:

5 ⁵And now I will tell you
        what I will do to my vineyard
   I will remove its hedges
        and it shall be devoured
   I will break down its wall
        and it shall be trampled down
   ⁶I will make it a waste
        it shall not be pruned or hoed
            and briars and thorns shall grow up
   I will also command the clouds
        that they rain no rain upon it
   ⁷For the vineyard of Yahweh of hosts
        is the house of Israel
   And the men of Judah
        are his pleasant planting
   And he looked for justice
        but behold, bloodshed!
   For righteousness
        but behold, a cry!

---

20. Jack R. Lundbom, 'Poetic Structure and Prophetic Rhetoric in Hosea', *VT* 29 (1979), pp. 300-308; 'Contentious Priests and Contentious People in Hosea IV 1-10', *VT* 36 (1986), pp. 52-70.

Taking Isa. 5.1-7 to be a self-contained passage, as most do, we are forced to conclude that although an invitation for audience involvement comes in the middle of the speech, nothing of the sort appears after that point. Isaiah throughout is the divine messenger delivering his message with divine authority.

V

Jeremiah is also a divine messenger, and like his predecessors he possesses a strong sense of divine authority. His speeches usually include the messenger formula, but not always; uncompromising judgment can be delivered without it (e.g., 22.20-23 and especially 51.20-23). Jeremiah, in any event, is sufficiently awed by the power of Yahweh's word, comparing it in 23.29 to a consuming fire and a pounding hammer.

Yet with this prophet there is something new and different. Dialogue largely replaces monologue, and truth is looked for down on earth, not thought to exist solely in heaven, where it is received by the prophet in divine council. Yahweh's word may still be uncompromising, but Jeremiah neither receives it nor delivers it in uncompromising fashion. He himself frequently needs to be persuaded by Yahweh. Similarly, in preaching, he tries to persuade an audience rather than blow them off the earth. The Jeremianic preaching contains much argument; some of it is openended to the point where the audience must decide for itself what in fact the message of Yahweh consists of. This new rhetoric, in my view, represents a clean break from earlier authority preaching. It also represents a clean break from authority-based witness, which lies interspersed at various points within prophetic preaching (e.g. Amos 3.8; 7.14-15). Perhaps it is saying too much, but I believe Jeremiah comes surprisingly close to Socrates in making his audience a partner in the discovery of truth.

There is, of course, nothing new in stating that Jeremiah is a prophet of dialogue. Even the most cursory reading of his book leaves one with this impression. In the speech material, for example, Jeremiah repeatedly quotes what people have said (2.20, 23, 25, 27, 31, 35; 5.12; 6.14 [= 8.11], 16-17; 11.19; 17.15; 20.10), what they have not said (2.6, 8; 5.24), and what they ought to be saying, or one day in the future will end up having to say (4.2, 5, 31; 5.19; 51.35). Allowing for exaggeration and the likelihood that discourse derives in large part from the prophet's imagination, behind the dramas is certainly a dialogical reality existing somewhere among real people in the real world. Whatever its precise nature, the Jeremianic discourse betrays a degree of listening power otherwise unknown among heralds of the divine word.

Progress in the delimitation of speeches has revealed carefully crafted dialogues and trialogues, with Yahweh, Jeremiah, the people, and even Judah's enemy speaking in turn (4.19-22; 5.1-8; 6.1-7, 8-12; 8.13-17, 18-21; 17.13-16a). Jeremiah has, in addition, a lively dialogue going on within himself (4.19; 5.4-5; 10.19; 20.9). This alternation of voice stimulates listening, and brings the audience actively into the communication process.

Then, of course, there are the dialogues found in the so-called Jeremianic 'confessions' (chaps. 11–20). From these we learn that Jeremiah is anything but passive in accepting Yahweh's word. He complains, accuses, argues, and questions, yet communication with Yahweh remains open. In some cases, Yahweh answers with corrective word (e.g., 15.15-21), or, if Yahweh has acted on Jeremiah's behalf, the prophet follows his complaint with a song deliverance (e.g., 20.7-13). If the confessions are taken to be liturgical pieces—which they may well be, and which would not, in my view, preclude their being also genuine dialogues between Yahweh and Jeremiah—the audience again is an active participant in the divine–human dialogue. Some in the audience will identify with the prophet's inner anguish, because they have anguish of their own; some will identify with Yahweh's corrective word, because they too wish to correct the good messenger; all—except those plotting Jeremiah's demise—will rejoice to hear of Yahweh's deliverance, for in deliverance lies Israel's hope.

Dialogues between Yahweh and Jeremiah occur in the call and commission of chap. 1, also after Jeremiah's purchase of the field in chap. 32. Throughout the prose one finds, in addition, numerous dialogues between Jeremiah and people living in and around Jerusalem. From the prose perspective, Jeremiah is seen to be in continual conversation with kings, priests, prophets, leading citizens, and plain ordinary people (19.1–20.6; 21.1-10; 26-29; 34-45).

Now for a look at a few passages up close. There are two speeches in the poetry, 3.1-5 and 5.1-8, which clearly show the break-away from authority preaching I have described. But before turning to these, I want first to have a look at a couple of well-known dialogues in the prose, which are prophetic witness, not preaching per se. In each there is a decided break-away from authority-based rhetoric, and like the speeches to be looked at later, both prophet and people are seen to be engaged in a common quest for truth.

Chapter 26 reports Jeremiah's famous 'Temple sermon' delivered in Jehoiakim's accession year (609 BCE). After a scathing indictment of shallow religiosity, and the people's duplicity before Yahweh, which Jeremiah says will bring down the Temple in the same way Shiloh was brought down, the prophet is hastily summoned into court at the New Gate. The priests and the prophets, apparently the ones who were most offended, make up the prosecution. They demand that Jeremiah be put to death. Royal officials in attendance seem allied with the defense. They, in any event, will decide the case, as the king is not present. In his defense Jeremiah says to the court:

> **26** ¹²Yahweh sent me to prophesy against this house and this city all the words you have heard. ¹³Now therefore amend your ways and your doings, and obey the voice of Yahweh your God, and Yahweh will repent of the evil that he has pronounced against you. ¹⁴But as for me, behold, I am in your hands. Do with me as seems good and right to you. ¹⁵Only know for certain that if you put me to death, you will bring innocent blood upon yourselves and upon this city and its inhabitants, for in truth Yahweh sent me to you to speak all these words in your ears.

Jeremiah begins by affirming that Yahweh sent him to prophesy, after which he repeats the warning part of his sermon. Attention then turns to judgment, which now concerns not only Jerusalem's inhabitants, but Jeremiah as well, for he is charged with a capital offense. The real issue, as Jeremiah correctly perceives, has to do with true and false prophets. Authority statements cease; the truth Jeremiah looks for on earth—before and together with the audience that is now gathered round about him. The remarks that follow have clear echoes in classical rhetoric. When Jeremiah says, 'Behold, I am in your hands, do with me as seems good and right to you', his move is what classical rhetoricians later call 'surrender' (Greek ἐπιτροπή; Latin *permissio*).²¹ Surrender is a veiled argument in which one submits to the will of the court. According to the *ad Herennium*, surrender 'is especially suited to provoke pity', and it cites as an example the following:²²

> Since only soul and body remain to me, now that I am deprived of everything else, even these, which alone of many goods are left me, I deliver up to you and to your power. You may use and even abuse me in your own way as you think best; with impunity make your decision upon me, whatever it may be; speak and give a sign—I shall obey.

In the next verse Jeremiah describes the consequences of possible court action. He says, 'Only know for certain that if you put me to death, you will bring innocent blood upon yourselves and upon this city and its inhabitants'. This too has argumentative value. Classical rhetoricians called such a move *descriptio,* which they said could be used both in prosecution and in defense. In the former, it would work to provoke indignation; in the latter, pity.²³ The *ad Herennium* cites the following *descriptio* used as a defence:²⁴

> For if you inflict a heavy penalty upon the defendant, men of the jury, you will at once by a single judgment have taken many lives. His aged father, who has set the entire hope of his last years on this young man, will have no reason for wishing to stay alive. His small children, deprived of their father's aid, will be exposed as objects of scorn and contempt to their

---

21. *ad Herennium* IV xxix.
22. *ad Herennium* IV xxix.
23. *ad Herennium* IV xxxix.
24. *ad Herennium* IV xxxix.

father's enemies. His entire household will collapse under this undeserved calamity. But his enemies, when once they have won the bloody palm by this most cruel of victories, will exult over the miseries of these unfortunates, and will be found insolent on the score of deeds as well as of words.

Jeremiah's final words, 'for in truth Yahweh sent me to you to speak all these words in your ears', simply repeat what was said at the beginning, in good Hebrew rhetorical style. The opening and closing words form an inclusio.[25]

Jeremiah's defence then leaves the decision in the lap of the court. They must decide what is good and right; they must decide whether Jeremiah should be put to death; they must decide the question of innocent blood; and most important, they must judge whether Jeremiah is a true or false prophet.

We are fortunate in that our passage reports the outcome of the trial. The princes—and now also 'all the people', who earlier were in league with the prosecution—speak for Jeremiah's acquittal on the strength of his testimony that Yahweh sent him with the message just given (v. 16b). For them, Jeremiah had evidently passed the test of the true prophet in Deut. 13.1-5. Some elders in attendance also aid the verdict of acquittal by recalling that Micah earlier predicted Jerusalem's destruction, and King Hezekiah did not put him to death (vv. 17-19).

What our passage does not say, but what we might reasonably infer now that we have looked more closely at the rhetoric of Jeremiah's defence, is that the prophet survived his trial in large measure because he managed to win over the bulk of his audience with a witness that combined assertion and non-assertion, authority and non-authority. This new type of rhetoric— a new *stance* really—so engaged his audience that they agreed to join him in his quest for truth. The ensuing engagement, no doubt, was just as important as Jeremiah's claim, 'Yahweh sent me', in bringing about a successful outcome to the trial. The engagement is also what likely evoked the timely testimony of the elders. This conclusion should not in any way be vitiated by the fact that Jeremiah needed the special protection of Ahikam son of Shaphan after the trial was over (26.24).

Chapter 28 is another familiar account that tells of Jeremiah meeting Hananiah the prophet during the time Jeremiah was preaching subservience to the king of Babylon. Jeremiah's message had been given earlier both verbally and symbolically to foreign envoys, to King Zedekiah, and after them to priests and a larger public (chap. 27). We expect the same basic message when Jeremiah faces off with the prophets. But not so. No authority-based preaching is delivered to the prophets' lead man, Hananiah son of Azzur, from Gibeon. The two meet in the Temple, and Hannaiah is first to speak

---

25. For a similar inclusio, see Huldah's oracle in 2 Kgs 22.15-20; cf. Lundbom, 'Poetic Structure and Prophetic Rhetoric in Hosea', p. 302.

in the usual assertive fashion. His word—ostensibly coming from Yahweh, since Hananiah is a Yahweh prophet—is that Babylon's power will be broken in two years, and Jeconiah (Jehoiachin), together with all the exiles, will return home. Jeremiah's response is as follows:

> **28** ⁶Amen! May Yahweh do so; may Yahweh make the words which you have prophesied come true, and bring back to this place from Babylon the vessels of the house of Yahweh, and all the exiles. ⁷Yet hear now this word that I speak in your hearing, and in the hearing of all the people. ⁸The prophets who preceded you and me from ancient times prophesied war, famine, and pestilence against many countries and great kingdoms. ⁹As for the prophet who prophesies peace, when the word of that prophet comes to pass, then it will be known that Yahweh has truly sent the prophet.

This response is similar to the one in chap. 26. Jeremiah's 'word' (דְּבַר) to Hananiah is a witness, basically, not preaching per se. He is again giving his views on true and false prophets. The speech breaks into two parts, each containing rhetorical moves the function of which are to probe the truth. Jeremiah begins by feigning agreement with his opponent: 'Amen! May Yahweh do so…' (v. 6), or, to put it another way, by granting his opponent permission to speak the word he has spoken. Either way what we have is another use, though a slightly different one, of *epitrope* or *permissio*.²⁶ The figure here contains irony in that Jeremiah neither agrees with Hananiah nor is he really granting what Hananiah has said. Another use of *epitrope* very similar to this is found in Micaiah's words to the king of Israel in 1 Kgs 22.15: 'Go up and triumph; Yahweh will give it [i.e., the enemy] into the hand of the king'.

What follows is a brief history lesson distinguishing prophets of doom from prophets of peace (vv. 7-9), the latter of whom Jeremiah then subjects to the other important test for true and false prophets in Deut. 18.22. This test was required when two prophets, both of whom were speaking in Yahweh's name, gave contrary messages. That is precisely the situation here, for Hananiah, as we have said, is a Yahweh prophet just like Jeremiah. According to Deut. 18.21-22 the false prophet is known by his word not coming to pass. The law of Deuteronomy makes no clear distinction between prophets of weal and prophets of woe, although since it says finally that people need not be afraid if the prophecy fails to come true, reference is no doubt to prophets preaching woe. Jeremiah, however, does make a clear distinction, and it is a different one. In it one sees another rhetorical move that classical rhetoricians called the *distributio*.²⁷ The *distributio* sets up distinctions for the purpose of argument. Here Jeremiah is arguing an important difference

---

26. See also 7.21 and 44.25b, which feign approval of evil behavior: also *epitropes*.
27. *ad Herennium* IV xxxv.

20. *Jeremiah and the Break-away from Authority Preaching* 253

between Hananiah and himself, Hananiah being a prophet of peace, and he being a prophet of doom. By subjecting prophets of peace to the test of Deut. 18.22, and then saying nothing more, Jeremiah leaves it to his audience to decide whether Hananiah has been truly sent by Yahweh, whether Hananiah has indeed spoken the truth, and whether Hananiah is in fact the true Yahweh prophet he claims to be.

After Hananiah has broken the yoke off Jeremiah's neck, Jeremiah turns and walks away. That Jeremiah later returns to judge Hananiah in most uncompromising fashion, and that our narrator pronounces for us a clear verdict on this prophet from Gibeon (v. 17), should in no way affect our estimate of what took place on this occasion when the two prophets met. Jeremiah could have preached to Hananiah the same authority-based message he had preached to the foreign envoys, the king, the priests, and the people, or indeed the same authority-based message that Hananiah had preached to him, but he did not.

Micaiah's speech in 1 Kings 22, as we mentioned, is similar to the one here, but Micaiah's rhetorical moves are supplemented by a clear word about the lying spirit in the mouths of prophets who predict victory for the king, and a sure word about the king's defeat (vv. 17-23). Jeremiah makes no comparable assertions.

With the other prophets dialogues are wanting. Amos in his spirited exchange with Amaziah simply delivers more authority preaching after the resident priest of Bethel rebukes him and tells him to go home (Amos 7.16-17).

Let us now turn to Jer. 3.1-5, the first of two Jeremianic speeches that show very clearly a break-away from authority preaching. The text reads as follows:

> 3 ¹'Look, a man sends away his wife
>   and she goes from him
> and becomes wife to another man
>   will he return to her?
> Would it not become greatly polluted
>   such a land?
> But you have whored with many lovers
>   and would you return to me?
>   —oracle of Yahweh.
>
> ²Lift up your eyes to the bare heights and see
>   where have you not had sex?
> Along the roads you sat for them
>   like an Arab in the wilderness
> You have polluted the land
>   with your whorings and your wickedness
> ³Therefore the showers have been withheld
>   and the latter rains have not come.

Indeed the brow of a whore woman has come upon you
>you refuse to be ashamed
⁴Have you not just now called to me 'My father
>trusted friend you are of my youth
⁵Will he bear a grudge forever
>will he be indignant to the end?'
Look now, you have spoken
>but are doing wrong
>>and are still capable!

The limits of this speech are fairly well-established.[28] Hebrew הֵן (v. 1) and הִנֵּה (v. 5) form an inclusio supporting these limits. The opening הֵן is best rendered 'Look!' or perhaps 'Listen now!' The speech is beginning with a call for dialogue. Deut. 24.1-4 is then summarized, a law that regulates remarriage. Yahweh is the speaker, and the law provides a good analogy to the covenant relationship he has with Israel. More precisely, Yahweh is putting forth an argument *a minori ad maius* (Heb. *qal vechomer*), which we can see from the mention of 'many lovers'. Then comes the question on which the entire speech turns, 'and would you return to me?'

The remainder of the speech is a spirited indictment against Israel the whore, complete with word plays, rhetorical questions, and hyperbole. Israel is stubborn and unashamed; for this reason, natural calamities have come upon her. Still she seeks—perhaps by recitation of a Temple liturgy (vv. 4b-5a)—a restored relationship with Yahweh.

The speech concludes by juxtaposing the people's pious words with their evil behavior, which continues unabated: 'Look now, you have spoken, but are doing wrong, and are still capable!' The speech contains no resolution. And no judgment. The question waiting to be answered is still the one posed at the beginning: 'and would you return to me?' The final הִנֵּה hearkens back to the opening הֵן, which helps bring the audience back. What will the audience answer?

The argument appears to set up an answer of 'no!' The nation cannot return to Yahweh. Yet when the speech is read in a larger context including 4.1-4, as some say it is supposed to be read,[29] a 'no' answer is less certain, for 4.1 begins, 'If you return, O Israel—oracle of Yahweh—to me you should return'. Looking again at the speech's key phrase, we note that it lacks the interrogative particle, which means the translation could just as well be 'yet return to me'. So rendered, the phrase is a hopeful plea for Israel's return. Reuven Yaron has in fact translated it this way, pointing out that

28. Lundbom, *Jeremiah: A Study in Ancient Hebrew Rhetoric*, pp. 37-39 (1997 edn, pp. 52-56).
29. So James Muilenburg, 'A Study of Hebrew Rhetoric: Repetition and Style', in *Congress Volume Copenhagen* (VTSup, 1; Leiden: E.J. Brill, 1953), p. 105; and John Bright, *Jeremiah* (AB, 21: Garden City, NY: Doubleday, 1965), p. 25, who follow the interpretation of Paul Volz, *Der Prophet Jeremia* (KAT; Leipzig: Deichert, 1928).

in the Talmud the rabbis used this statement to show how Yahweh's mercy was not subject to law.[30]

The very fact that the key phrase in the speech is open to diametrically opposed interpretations only underscores the point I wish to make. Jeremiah has abandoned authority preaching; the audience is left to conclude this speech as it wishes. What we are saying here is that different answers may have been given when the speech was first delivered, even if Jeremiah anticipated an unambiguous 'no!' And once the speech was followed by 4.1 in the composition that led finally to a book of Jeremiah, a conclusion to the question was supplied, one not necessarily the same as when 3.1-5 stood by itself. And different audiences through the ages have interpreted the speech's key line differently, as we have just seen.

This open-ended conclusion reminds us of Jesus' parable of the Lost (Prodigal) Son in Lk. 15.11-32. There we are left not knowing whether the older brother *returns* to the father, and goes in finally to join the party. We know the brother was invited, but not if he went in. The audience listening to the parable has to decide that, as it must decide simultaneously whether it too will respond to the father's kind invitation of salvation.

Jeremiah's speech in 3.1-5 contains all three classical argumentive appeals. There is an appeal to *logos* in the argument *a minori ad maius*. An appeal to *pathos* is made in vv. 4-5, where Jeremiah depicts the people's moving plea for divine favor. And the citation of Deut. 24.1-4 serves as an *ethos* appeal if the prophet intends not to be cast as someone bent on undermining covenant law.

In 5.1-8 we have a dialogue speech, which weighs in the balance Jerusalem and those inhabiting Judah's capital city. It has unmistakable echoes of the dialogue between Abraham and Yahweh over Sodom and Gomorrah (Gen. 18.23-32). In my earlier study, I delimited this speech to vv. 1-8. It consists of five stanzas, which can be demarcated by keywords and a change of speaker and/or audience. The whole is an expanded chiasmus (a b c b' a').[31] The speech goes as follows:

Yahweh to Jeremiah:

5   ¹Run back and forth in the streets of Jerusalem
        look please, and take note
     Search in her squares (to see)
        if you can find a *man*
(a)   If there is one who does justice
        and searches for truth
           that *I may pardon her*
     ²For if they say 'As Yahweh lives'
        surely in vain *they swear*.

---

30. Reuven Yaron, 'The Restoration of Marriage', *JJS* 17 (1966), p. 3.
31. Lundbom, *Jeremiah: A Study in Ancient Hebrew Rhetoric*, pp. 75-78 [1997, pp. 100-104].

Jeremiah to Yahweh:

(b)
³O Yahweh, your eyes
    do they not look for truth?
You struck them down, but they writhed not
    you annihilated them, but they refused correction
They have made their faces harder than rock
    they have refused to repent.

Jeremiah to Self:

(c)
⁴Then I said, but these are the *poor*
    they have no sense
For they know not Yahweh's way
    the justice of their God
⁵I will go to the *great*
    and I will speak with them
For they know Yahweh's way
    the justice of their God.

Jeremiah to Yahweh:

(b′)
But both alike had broken the yoke
    they had snapped the bonds
⁶Therefore a lion from the forest *will strike them*
    and a wolf from the desert will devour them
A leopard will prowl around their cities
    anyone going out from them will be torn apart
For their rebellions are many
    their regressions are great.

Yahweh to Jerusalem:

(a′)
⁷Why should *I pardon you*?
    Your children have forsaken me
        and have *sworn* by 'no-gods'
When I fed them to the full they committed adultery
    and to whore-houses they trooped
⁸They were well-fed lusty stallions
    each *man* neighing for his neighbor's wife.

The speech begins with Yahweh instructing Jeremiah and others who make up a search party (the imperative verbs are plural) that they should try to find *one* righteous man in Jerusalem. Yahweh expresses his overriding concern in the optative mode: 'that I may pardon her', namely, Jerusalem.

Jeremiah is next to speak (b), and he questions Yahweh about his passion for truth. This is a move simply to get audience attention, for Jeremiah knows that Yahweh has such a passion. Jeremiah continues in affirming his oneness with Yahweh by expressing outrage at precisely what outrages

Yahweh: the ineffectiveness of punishment in bringing about a change in people's behavior (cf. Amos 4.6-11).

In the center (c) the audience becomes privy to a dialogue Jeremiah had with himself while he was out on the mission. It occurred to Jeremiah that perhaps poor folk clung to wrongdoing because they did not know Yahweh's *torah;* if he went among society's upper class he would find such knowledge, and a people therefore who practiced justice and sought the truth. If Yahweh has a hope, so does Jeremiah.

In the next verse (b') Jeremiah shifts into the assertive mode, but since Yahweh is the addressee (the people are referred to in the third person), the discourse does not translate into authority preaching. Jeremiah first gives a sad report of the mission. Then, with vivid metaphors, he anticipates the consequences for Jerusalem. Here we see the big difference from Isaiah's 'song of the vineyard', where the audience was directly confronted with coming destruction. That was judgment preaching. Jeremiah, however, does not preach judgment except in the most indirect fashion. He may even be trying to forestall judgment, which is what Abraham was doing in the Sodom and Gomorrah dialogue. By expressing fears to Yahweh about what will happen to the people of Jerusalem, Jeremiah's impact on his audience is totally different from what it would be if he preached to the audience uncompromising judgment. Now, instead of them being angry and defensive, they will be fearful along with him. Jeremiah has made himself one with the people. Indeed, it is his oneness with *both* Yahweh and the people that makes Jeremiah a true divine mediator, the likes of Moses and Samuel (cf. 15.1). Identification with the people also makes Jeremiah a true rhetor, something he could not have been without making the break from authority preaching.

In the final section (a') Yahweh resumes the discourse. He now speaks directly to the people of Jerusalem, asking them the question on which this particular dialogue turns: 'How can I pardon you?' It is a question they will have to answer. The speech ends with more indictment, though a lesser amount than in 3.1-5. The point is, however, that there is no judgment and no answer to the pardon question. The speech ends in heavy silence.

The stereotyped v. 9 is a later addition, added also in 5.29 and 9.8 [9]; it reads:

> Shall I not punish them for these things?
> —oracle of Yahweh
> and shall I not avenge myself on a nation such as this?

With the speech having left open the matter of divine pardon, this double question—which is rhetorical—assists later audiences in formulating their answer. The speech is thus brought one step closer to authority preaching or discourse in the assertive mode. Even yet, the audience for whom the speech is now intended will still have the obligation—albeit a reduced one—to become sufficiently engaged with the prophet's message so it can choose for itself between divine punishment and divine pardon.[32]

---

32. This essay is dedicated with appreciation to the Rev. Douglas G. Cedarleaf, Evangelical Covenant Church pastor, of Minneapolis, MN. As a Fulbright Lecture it was given in May, 1989 at the Universities of Sheffield and Leeds in England, and at Uppsala University in Sweden.

Chapter 21

RHETORICAL STRUCTURES IN JEREMIAH 1*

Chapter 1 of the book of Jeremiah contains what is generally regarded to be the call and commission[1] of Jeremiah to be Yahweh's prophet. Its material, while important simply because it seeks to credential Jeremiah for the difficult ministry he must undertake, has added importance for those wishing to reconstruct the prophet's early career in that v. 2 of the superscription gives a precise date for anchoring the call in the 13th year of Josiah, that is, 627 BCE.[2]

* First published in *ZAW* 103 (1991), pp. 193-210.
1. The term 'commission' used here in chapter 1 is not without problems. Yahweh designates Jeremiah for the prophetic office in vv. 9-10, then again in vv. 17-19 the mandate is given to get on with the business of prophetic ministry. I use 'commission' in this article to refer to the mandate of vv. 17-19.
2. Cited in the article are the following commentaries and other works discusssing Jeremiah 1: Jerome, *S. Hieronymi Presbyteri Opera, in Hieremiam VI* (Turnhout: Brepols, 1960); J. Calvin, *Commentaries on the Book of the Prophet Jeremiah and the Lamentations* I (trans. John Owen; Grand Rapids, MI: Baker, 1979); J.G. Eichhorn, *Einleitung ins Alte Testament* III (Reutlingen: Johannes Grözinger, 1790); F. Hitzig, *Der Prophet Jeremia* (Leipzig: S. Hirzel, 2nd edn, 1866); E. Henderson, *The Book of the Prophet Jeremiah and That of the Lamentations* (London: Hamilton, Adams, 1851); K.H. Graf, *Der Prophet Jeremia* (Leipzig: T.O. Weigel, 1862); F. Giesebrecht, *Das Buch Jeremia* (HKAT; Göttingen: Vandenhoeck & Ruprecht, 1894); E. Sellin, 'Jeremia von Anatot', *NKZ* 10 (1899), pp. 257-86; B. Duhm, *Das Buch Jeremia* (KHC; Tübingen und Leipzig: J.C.B. Mohr [Paul Siebeck], 1901); B. Stade, 'Streiflichter auf die Entstehung der jetzigen Gestalt der alttestamentlichen Prophetenschriften', *ZAW* 23 (1903), pp. 153-71; C.H. Cornill, *Das Buch Jeremia* (Leipzig: Chron. Herm. Tauchnitz, 1905); A.S. Peake, *Jeremiah* I (CB; New York: H. Frowde and Edinburgh, 1910); S. Mowinckel, *Zur Komposition des Buches Jeremia* (Oslo: Jacob Dybwad, 1914); A. Condamin, *Le Livre de Jérémie* (Paris: Victor Lecoffre, 1920); K. Budde, 'Über das erste Kapitel des Buches Jeremia', *JBL* 40 (1921), pp. 23-37; F. Horst, 'Die Anfänge des Propheten Jeremia', *ZAW* 41 (1923), pp. 94-153; J. Skinner, *Prophecy and Religion* (Cambridge: Cambridge University Press, 1926); A.C. Welch, *Jeremiah: His Time and His Work* (Oxford: Oxford University Press, 1928); P. Volz, *Der Prophet Jeremia* (KAT, 10; Leipzig: A. Deichertsche Verlagsbuchhandlung, D. Werner Scholl, 2nd edn, 1928); G.A. Smith, *Jeremiah* (New York and London: Harper & Bros., 4th edn, 1929); F. Nötscher, *Das Buch Jeremias* (Bonn: Peter Hanstein, 1934); H. Birkeland,

Yet the chapter has its share of problems, many of the same in fact that crop up elsewhere in the book. For this reason divergent views are held on basic issues, among which can be listed the following: (1) the date and authorship of the composition, including the question of how the chapter has grown into its present form; (2) the correlation, if there is any, between the composition *qua* literary work and Jeremiah's actual prophetic experience; and (3) the composition's structure, that is, what basic parts are to be delineated and how these are seen to hang together. This last issue is a particularly pressing one and must admit to some kind of resolution if the chapter is taken to be a compilation of separate sources.

This essay will touch on all these issues, but will be concerned chiefly with what is last-mentioned. Briefly, it will be argued that if Jeremiah 1 is to be understood properly, and the larger chronological and historical issues associated with Jeremiah's call and the beginning of his career are to find satisfactory resolution, the macrostructures in chapter 1 must be recognized as being rhetorical in nature. Like other parts of the book of Jeremiah—indeed other parts of the OT—this chapter was written with the aim of being read aloud to a gathered congregation of people.[3] Simple but nevertheless effec-

---

'Grunddrag i profeten Jeremias förkunnelse', *SEÅ* 1 (1936), pp. 31-46; J.P. Hyatt, 'The Peril from the North in Jeremiah', *JBL* 59 (1940), pp. 499-513; J.P. Hyatt, 'Jeremiah', in *IB* 5 (ed. George A. Buttrick; New York: Abingdon Press, 1956), pp. 777-1142; J.A. Bewer, *The Book of Jeremiah* I (New York: Harper & Bros., 1951); A. Weiser, *Das Buch Jeremia 1-25,14* (ATD, 20; Göttingen: Vandenhoeck & Ruprecht, 8th edn, 1981; originally 1952); F. Augustin, 'Baruch und das Buch Jeremia', *ZAW* 67 (1955), pp. 50-56; H. Michaud, 'La vocation du "prophète des nations"', in *Maqqēl Shāqedh: La Branche d'Amandier* (Montpellier: Causse Graille Castelnau, 1960), pp. 157-64; H.H. Rowley, 'The Early Prophecies of Jeremiah in Their Setting', *BJRL* 45 (1962–63), pp. 198-234 (repr. in *A Prophet to the Nations: Essays in Jeremiah Studies* [ed. L.G. Perdue and B.W. Kovacs; Winona Lake, IN: Eisenbrauns, 1984], pp. 33-61); W.L. Holladay, 'The Background of Jeremiah's Self-Understanding: Moses, Samuel and Psalm 22', *JBL* 83 (1964), pp. 153-64; W.L. Holladay, *Jeremiah* I (Hermeneia; Philadelphia, PA: Fortress Press, 1986); J. Bright, *Jeremiah* (AB, 21; Garden City, NY: Doubleday, 1965); W. Rudolph, *Jeremia* (HAT; Tübingen: J.C.B. Mohr [Paul Siebeck], 3rd edn, 1968); J. Berridge, *Prophet, People, and the Word of Yahweh* (Zürich: EVZ, 1970); W. Thiel, *Die deuteronomistische Redaktion von Jeremia 1–25* (WMANT, 41; Neukirchen–Vluyn: Neukirchener Verlag, 1973); W. Thiel, *Die deuteronomistische Redaktion von Jeremia 26–45* (WMANT, 52; Neukirchen–Vluyn: Neukirchener Verlag, 1981); J.R. Lundbom, *Jeremiah: A Study in Ancient Hebrew Rhetoric* (SBLDS, 18; Missoula, MT: Society of Biblical Literature and Scholars Press, 1975 [repr. Winona Lake, IN: Eisenbrauns, 1997]); S. Niditch, *The Symbolic Vision in Biblical Tradition* (HSM, 30; Chico, CA: Scholars Press, 1983); W. McKane, *Jeremiah* I (ICC; Edinburgh: T. & T. Clark, 1986); R.P. Carroll, *The Book of Jeremiah* (OTL; Philadelphia, PA: Westminster Press, 1986); S. Herrmann, *Jeremia* (BK 12.1; Neukirchen–Vluyn: Neukirchener Verlag, 1986).

3. According to chap. 36, the first scroll of Jeremiah's prophecies was read aloud

tive techniques of Hebrew rhetoric lie embedded in the text, their function being to enhance the reception of the text before its ancient audience. Modern commentators, because they have paid insufficient attention to these rhetorical techniques, have failed to hear the text properly. As a result they have also failed to interpret it properly. Our first task as biblical critics and biblical exegetes is to hear the composition, insofar as it is humanly possible, in the way it was meant to be heard in its ancient setting.

The Superscription (1.1-3)

A few words at the outset about the superscription, which, in its present form introduces not chapter 1 but a larger Jeremiah book.[4] Here our concern is only with v. 2. Because v. 2 gives a specific date in the 13th year of Josiah, it is widely believed that originally the verse introduced only the call.[5] This introduction is repeated in v. 4, which is the first of four short superscriptions beginning the book, going more or less as follows: 'And the word of Yahweh came to me saying' (vv. 4, 11, 13, and 2.1). The repetition restores focus after v. 3, which is an added word about Jeremiah being active during the reigns of Jehoiakim and Zedekiah.

Jeremiah's Call and Commission: An Overview (1.4-19)

A Unified Composition

In the traditional view vv. 4-19 present in straightforward manner the call and commission of Jeremiah. These verses are assumed to form a unified composition, by which is meant not only that they combine to make up a literary unity, which they do, but that what they report is a single experience in the life of the prophet. The call proper appears in vv. 4-10,[6] and the words of commission, in which Jeremiah is told to get on with the business of prophetic ministry, are at the end in vv. 17-19. Midpoint in the chapter are two visions that are part of the call and commission. The whole is controlled by the date in v. 2. In the 13th year of Josiah, that is 627/6 BCE, Jeremiah is issued his call after which he immediately begins his prophetic career. This view was held or presupposed by virtually all scholars through the end of the 19th century, e.g. Jerome, Calvin, Eichhorn, Hitzig, Graf, and Sellin; also by scholars in more recent times, e.g. Welch, Rowley, and Berridge.

---

to a congregation in the Temple (v. 10) before it was read to a select audience in the Temple library and before it was read to the king.
 4. Chaps. 1–39, according to Graf, *Der Prophet Jeremia*, and Rudolph, *Jeremia*.
 5. So Stade, 'Streiflichter' (pp. 153-54), and Michaud, 'La vocation' (p. 158 n. 1).
 6. Already in Hitzig, *Jeremia*, p. 3, though his delimitation was actually vv. 5-10.

The Question of Jeremiah's Age

Early indications of strain on the traditional view, although not being perceived as such, came when Calvin questioned—actually ridiculed—the view of Jerome that Jeremiah began his ministry when he was very young.[7] Jerome had simply taken נַעַר in vv. 6-7 as 'young male' or 'boy', which was its usual meaning (in both his commentary and in the Vulgate he used *puer*). Since Calvin's time one meets up only occasionally with a scholar who believes that Jeremiah began his ministry when he was still young.[8] The majority of scholars push up Jeremiah's age as far as possible in order that he be at a reasonable level of maturity for the commencement of a public career. Some put his age between 23 and 25;[9] others at 18.[10] In support of a higher age it is pointed out that נַעַר, in some biblical passages, reaches up into a higher range of chronological age. The term can, for example, mean 'young man of marriageable age', 'soldier', or 'slave',[11] which leads some to suggest that the term may have more to do with societal status than with age.[12] Solomon refers to himself as a נַעַר after he has become king and is married (1 Kgs 3.7). We do not know his precise age. Yet King Josiah is a נַעַר at 16 but apparently not at 20 (2 Chron. 34.3). The Bible translations consistently opt for or else imply a young age for Jeremiah when translating v. 6:

Vulgate:	*quia puer ego sum*
Luther:	den ich bin zu jung
Swedish:	ty jag är för ung
NAB:	I am too young
King James:	for I am a child
NEB:	I am only a child
RSV:	for I am only a youth

---

7. Calvin, *Jeremiah and Lamentations* I, p. 31.

8. Eichhorn, *Einleiting* (p. 103) took this position, so also Birkeland, 'Grunddrag' (p. 32: 'i sin tidigaste ungdom') and Rowley, *Early Prophecies* (p. 222 [repr. p. 51], n. 127: 'his call came when he was very young').

9. Duhm, Cornill, G.A. Smith, Peake, Condamin, Volz, Nötscher, Weiser and Rudolph.

10. Skinner, *Prophecy*, p. 24, Bewer, *Jeremiah*; and Bright, *Jeremiah*, p. xxix. Among older commentators one occasionally meets up with a different chronology, e.g. Henderson, who dates Jeremiah's call in 629 (*Jeremiah and Lamentations*, p. vi) when the prophet is said to be 20 years old (p. 2).

11. BDB, p. 655.

12. J. MacDonald, 'The Status and Role of the *Na'ar* in Israelite Society', *JNES* 35 (1976), pp. 147-70, argues that נַעַר means 'young male of high birth'; H.P. Stähli, *Knabe-Jüngling-Knecht: Untersuchungen zum Begriff* נַעַר *im Alten Testament* (BET, 7; Frankfurt: Peter Lang, 1978), pp. 122-23, in discussing Jer. 1.6, says נַעַר here means underage ('young' or 'too young') in the sense of not yet having achieved the societal status of a man (אִישׁ).

It is interesting to note that the RSV uses 'youth', but in passages where Samuel is referred to it translates נַעַר as 'boy' (1 Sam. 2.11, 18, 21, 26; 3.1, 8). So age may still be a problem for the traditional view.

The Visions and Their Provenance
The onset of modern literary criticism brought with it more serious challenges to the traditional view. At issue now was the chapter's unity, also the hitherto accepted correlation between the picture given in the literature (i.e. vv. 4-19) and Jeremiah's actual life experiences. The two scholars most influential in pressing new source-critical points of view were Bernhard Duhm and Sigmund Mowinckel.

Source critics for the most part took chapter 1, or at least the bulk of chapter 1, to be 'source A', i.e. from Jeremiah himself—because of the 'I' form used throughout.[13] Yet increasingly it was believed that the chapter in its present form could not have come from the *hand* of Jeremiah, as was formerly thought, but must owe its compilation rather to some editor—if not Baruch, then another from a later period. Duhm sought originally to 'save' the chapter for Jeremiah by taking vv. 15, 16, and 18b as later additions, but he gave that up, concluding finally that the chapter was a 'mosaic' of separate fragments put together by a late editor (Ergänzer).[14]

New critical work served to lessen strains placed on the unified view, including some which had come to light only recently. Not infrequently it eliminated them altogether. With the chapter being viewed now as a compilation of fragments, the concern, in short, was to preserve the integrity of individual parts rather than the integrity of the whole. Duhm, for example, simply conceded that transitions in the chapter were not always well-fitting nor could one know, in every case, precisely how the individual parts fit together.[15]

Duhm and Mowinkel shared not all the same assumptions, nor did they arrive, to be sure, at the same conclusions. But they did agree on one thing, namely, that a major break was necessary between vv. 10 and 11. The superscription in v. 11, 'And the word of Yahweh came to me saying', signaled a new beginning. Duhm said:

> Die beiden Visionen, v. 11 – 16, sollen wohl ungefähr in dieselbe
> Zeit fallen wie die Berufungsvision v. 4 ff., doch stellt die Einführung
> 11: *Und Jahwes Wort kam zu mir* sie als selbständige Erlebnisse hin.[16]

Mowinckel was even more emphatic about the break. Speaking about the call, he said:

---

13. Giesebrecht (*Jeremia*, p. xx), Sellin (*Jeremia*, p. 261), Cornill (*Jeremia*, p. xxxix), and Mowinckel (*Komposition*, p. 20).
14. Duhm, *Jeremia*, p. 10.
15. Duhm, *Jeremia*, pp. 10, 13.
16. Duhm, *Jeremia*, pp. 10-11.

Diese ist mit V. 10 deutlich abgeschlossen. Mit der Formel 'das Wort
Jhwh's kam zu mir' wird immer etwas Neues eingleitet. Diese neue
Vision hat nichts mit 1,4-10 zu tin; sie steht hier im Anfang des Buches,
da sie gewissermaßen als Motto der ganzen Wirksamkeit des Jir. zu
betrachten ist, eine Anordnung, die wohl auf die 'Urrolle' und somit
auf Jir. selbst zurückgeht.[17]

For them the call was now reduced to just vv. 4-10. Hitzig, to be sure, had earlier delimited the call to vv. 4-10, but Duhm and Mowinckel see a more complete break. For Duhm the two visions—which in his view comprise vv. 11-16—are separate experiences from the experience of the call, although Duhm does concede they should probably derive from the same time as the call. Mowinckel, in speaking about the first vision, says it has nothing to do with the call.

Scholars have more or less followed the lead of Duhm and Mowinckel in limiting the call to vv. 4-10 and bracketing out the visions in vv. 11-16.[18] But not all are willing to sacrifice the unity of the chapter or the view that Jeremiah's commissioning and career beginning follow immediately after the call. Many for this reason take vv. 17-19 as a continuation of vv. 4-10.[19] This keeps the call and commission together, and for those concerned about preserving a correlation between literary presentation and Jeremiah's real life experiences, it keeps in tact the view that Jeremiah began his career immediately after the call. Duhm, however, takes another line. He says vv. 17-19 go better with what precedes than with vv. 4-10. Mowinckel, for his part, says vv. 17-19 derive not from Jeremiah but are a late addition which picks up on 1.8 and 15.20-21 (so too more recently Holladay).[20]

The disengagement of the two visions, particularly the second about the tilted pot signaling the approach of the foe from the north, takes the greatest amount of strain off the traditional view. First of all, it eliminates the problem created by שֵׁנִית ('a second time') in v. 13. The term appears in the superscription, 'And the word of Yahweh came to me a second time (שֵׁנִית)'. Now when it is recalled that this superscription is the third—not the second—in a series, and Yahweh's word is said to have come to Jeremiah two times prior (vv. 4, 11), we naturally want to know why it does not say here in v. 13 that Yahweh's word came to Jeremiah a 'third' time. This problem shows up in a continuous reading of the narrative, and has been noted already by Bright[21] and Berridge.[22]

---

17. Mowinkel, *Komposition*, p. 20.
18. Budde ('Kapital des Buches Jeremia', p. 30) and Thiel (*Jeremia 1–25*, p. 72).
19. Stade, Cornill, Volz, Rudolph, Bright, and Herrmann.
20. Holladay, *Jeremiah* I, pp. 24-25.
21. Bright, *Jeremiah*, pp. 7-8.
22. Berridge, *Prophet, People, and the Word of Yahweh*, p. 67.

But if the two visions are disengaged from the call, and said to have been transmitted independently as a pair before assuming their place in chapter 1—which is the way the argument usually runs—it makes sense, at least for an earlier time, for the second superscription to state that Yahweh's word came to Jeremiah 'a second time'. Kimchi notes that שֵׁנִית links the two visions, and he is cited in support of the view that originally the two visions had no connection with the call in vv. 4-10.[23] So here we have a case where the integrity of the parts can be affirmed when it is not possible to claim integrity for the whole. But again, the editor of the final composition has left us surely with an 'ill-fitting transition'.

A second reason for wanting to bracket out the second vision is that an early date for this vision creates historical and chronological problems. There is the identification of the foe from the north on the one hand, and the dating of the vision of the foe—also oracles about the foe in 4.5ff.—on the other. In the pre-critical period no such problems were recognized. It was assumed (e.g. by Calvin) that the foe was Babylon, and that Jeremiah early in his career—indeed at the very beginning—foresaw Judah's destruction at the hands of the Babylonians. But with the rise of critical scholarship came a change in the thinking about prophets and prophecy. Prophets were now said to be 'forthtellers', not 'foretellers', which is to say their words had to be placed over against events currently taking place, or, at the very least, against events about to take place shortly. A de-emphasis on predictive prophecy is seen in Wellhausen and all who came under his influence. Now if the vision of the foe comes to Jeremiah in 627, and he preaches about the foe in the years between 627 and 622 (which was a widely held view), Babylon at the time is not an imminent foe; rather it is a distant foe some 15-20 years away. Those holding the traditional view therefore had to find another foe, which they did by naming a people known as the Scythians. The Scythians were Indo-Aryan hordes that roamed Asia during the Late Assyrian Age.[24] By adopting the 'Scythian hypothesis', which many did,[25] the threat of the foe could remain in Jeremiah's earliest years, although doubts were expressed whether this foe ever did attack Judah. Many in fact who adopted the hypothesis concluded that nothing happened, leaving Jeremiah discredited and silent for a time.[26] The Scythian hypothesis has also had its share of detractors following the challenge of Wilke,[27] and not everyone holding the traditional

23. McKane, *Jeremiah* I, pp. 16-17.
24. So Herodotus, *History* I, 104-106.
25. See Rowley, 'Early Prophecies', pp. 199-200 n. 8 for bibliography.
26. Peake, *Jeremiah* I, p. 11; Rowley, 'Early Prophecies', pp. 200, 218.
27. F. Wilke, 'Das Skythenproblem im Jeremiabuch', in *Alttestamentliche Studien* (Festschrift Rudolph Kittel; BWAT, 13; Leipzig: J.C. Hinrichs'sche Buchhandlung, 1913), pp. 222-54.

view accepted it. Today the hypothesis is largely discredited, and scholars are back to identifying the foe as Babylon.[28]

So there continues to be a need to bring the vision of the foe nearer the Babylonian threat, which becomes real only after Nineveh falls in 612 BCE. Bracketing out the vision accomplishes this goal, for it allows one to date the vision later. Rietzschel, for example, dates both visions to the reign of Jehoiakim;[29] Bright too says both visions are later, but does not specify dates.[30] And we have said nothing thus far about scholars who deal with the same problem by challenging or otherwise reinterpreting the chronological notice in 1.2. These propose a lower chronology for Jeremiah, which puts the beginning of his ministry in the reign of Jehoiakim.[31] This issue is complicated and by no means settled. Suffice it is to say that when the two visions—particularly the second—are bracketed out and dated to a later time, a *bona fide* problem is eliminated.

We may conclude this overview by saying that no consensus has been reached on how to interpret Jeremiah 1. The traditional view that the chapter is a simple, straightforward, unified composition describing one experience in the life of Jeremiah is in need of modification. The view that the chapter is a compilation of fragments, for example, one incorporating two visions comprising vv. 11-16 and perhaps also a later commissioning report, also has problems. The difficulties with both views appear in my opinion to be structure-related. We need therefore to examine the text afresh with an eye for structure. And since this material originated in a religious community and was destined for use in a religious community, the structures contained will in all likelihood be rhetorical structures. Identifying these must be a first priority. Once this has been done we can go on to say something about fragments within the chapter and their possible provenance.

Rhetorical Structures in Jeremiah 1

In a previous study[32] I argued that the controlling structure of vv. 4-19 was a chiasmus in which the two visions occupied the center position. I argued further that the call expanded upon the vision of the almond rod and the commission expanded upon the vision of the tilted pot:

---

28. Weiser, *Jeremia 1-25,14*, pp. 43-44; Rudolph, *Jeremia*, pp. 48-49; Berridge, *Prophet, People, and the Word of Yahweh*, pp. 76-88.

29. C. Rietzschel, *Das Problem der Urrolle* (Gütersloh: Gütersloher, Gerd Mohn, 1966), p. 135.

30. Bright, *Jeremiah*, p. 7.

31. Horst, Hyatt, Holladay and McKane.

32. Lundbom, *Jeremiah: A Study in Ancient Hebrew Rhetoric*, pp. 96-99 (1997 edn, pp. 127-30).

A   Articulation of the Call (4-10)
     B   Vision of the Call (11-12)
     B'   Vision of the Commission (13-14)
  A'   Articulation of the Commission (15-19)

The view of Duhm and Mowinckel that vv. 11-16 are to be bracketed out is mistaken, I believe, on two counts: (1) the break at v. 11 is no 'new beginning'; and (2) after v. 16 there is no break at all. First let us look at v. 11. The superscription in this verse, 'And the word of Yahweh came to me saying', *repeats* the superscription of v. 4, which contains the same words. A look at other passages in the book where superscriptions appear in sequence will show the same sort of rhetoric. A good passage for comparison is 3.6-11, which reads:

> *And Yahweh said to me in the days of King Josiah*, 'Have you seen what she did, that faithless one, Israel, how she went up on every high hill and under every green tree, and there played the harlot? And I thought, After she has done all this she will return to me; but she did not return, and her false sister Judah saw it. She saw that for all the adulteries of that faithless one, Israel, I had sent her away with a decree of divorce; yet her false sister Judah did not fear, but she too went and played the harlot. Because harlotry was so light to her, she polluted the land, committing adultery with stone and tree. Yet for all this her false sister Judah did not return to me with her whole heart, but in pretence, says Yahweh. *And Yahweh said to me*, 'Faithless Israel has shown herself less guilty than false Judah.'

This passage content-wise is not the same as 1.4-12. The long section at the beginning is an allegory on Israel and Judah, two sisters of ill-repute. The short word at the end set off by the second superscription summarizes the point of the allegory. The superscriptions are also not worded exactly the same, but the rhetoric, that is, one superscription largely repeating another, is precisely what we have in 1.4 and 11. The second superscription, 'And Yahweh said to me', signals no break; at most it occasions a pause in what is a continuous narrative, one whose function is to restore focus or prepare the audience for the emphatic words to come. The new beginning is at v. 12.

In the covenant passage of 11.6 and 9 are two superscriptions, 'And Yahweh said to me', with intervening narrative. This may be another example of the same sort of repetitive rhetoric, but because problems of interpretation here are complex, we had better withhold judgement about this passage for the time being. It should simply be noted that the RSV has pre-empted an objective reading of v. 9 by adding the word 'again' ('Again the LORD said to me').

In the parable of the linen waistcloth in 13.1-9 are four superscriptions in a series: vv. 1, 3, 6, and 8. The passage reads:

> *Thus Yahweh said to me*, 'Go and buy a linen waistcloth, and put it on your loins, and do not dip it in water'. So I bought a waistcloth according to the word of Yahweh, and put it on my loins. *And the word of Yahweh came to me a second time*: 'Take the waistcloth which you have bought, which is upon your loins, and arise, go to Parat,[33] and hide it there in a cleft of the rock'. So I went, and hid it at Parat, as Yahweh commanded me. *And after many days Yahweh said to me,* 'Arise, go to Parat, and take from there the waistcloth which I commanded you to hide there'. Then I went to Parat, and dug, and I took the waistcloth from the place where I had hidden it. And behold, the waistcloth was spoiled, it was good for nothing. *And the word of Yahweh came to me*: 'Thus says Yahweh: Even so will I spoil the pride of Judah and the great pride of Jerusalem'.

Here the second superscription (v. 3) contains שֵׁנִית ('a second time') and the third (v. 6) מִקֵּץ יָמִים רַבִּים ('after many days'). Both very clearly signal time-lags. But not the fourth superscription in v. 8, which, like 3.11, prepares the audience for the climactic teaching. One normally assumes that this teaching came to Jeremiah immediately after he dug up the spoiled cloth. This final superscription also gives no indication of bridging literary fragments that at one time existed separately.

Chapter 24 makes a particularly worthwhile comparison to chapter 1 because it also contains a vision report—the only other one, in fact, which is found in the book of Jeremiah. Verse 1 begins, 'And Yahweh showed me' (הִרְאַנִי יהוה), and v. 4 continues with 'And the word of Yahweh came to me', the exact words of 1.4 and 11. This superscription again signals no major break, but like 3.11 and 13.8 is simply an introduction with emphasis on the interpretation that follows.

One additional passage of prose, somewhat larger, provides us with a final example of superscriptions used in sequence; it too contains שֵׁנִית. The passage is in chapters 32–33. Jeremiah 32.1-5 introduces the account of Jeremiah buying a field in Anathoth while he remained under house arrest in the court of the guard. Like the superscription beginning the book in 1.1-3, it is written in the third person. Verse 1 begins:

> *The word which came to Jeremiah from Yahweh* in the tenth year of Zedekiah king of Judah, which was the eighteenth year of Nebuchadrezzar.

Verses 2-5 give more background, after which there appears another superscription in v. 6 introducing the preferred subject, which is the report of Jeremiah buying the field. It says:

> *And Jeremiah said, The word of Yahweh came to me saying:*

---

33. I.e., to Parah, a town four miles from Anathoth. In the construct, פְּרָת, the town name, forms a play on words and is a deliberate association with the river Parat, viz. the Euphrates (cf. LXX).

In v. 26 is a third superscription introducing Yahweh's answer to a prayer Jeremiah has just addressed to him:

And the word of Yahweh came to Jeremiah saying:

Then in 33.1 a fourth superscription continues in the third person prefacing a word about hope and restoration for Jerusalem. This one contains שֵׁנִית:

And the word of Yahweh came to Jeremiah a second time (שֵׁנִית) *while he was still shut up in the court of the guard.*

The progression here, while not precisely the same as in chapter 1, is nevertheless similar. The beginning superscription (32.1) is a general introduction like 1.2. The second superscription (32.6) restores focus after intervening narrative. That was the function basically of 1.4. In both cases the audience is being alerted to the preferred subject that follows immediately, and is being told to pay heed. The third superscription (32.26) may appear at first glance to introduce a new revelation, but it does not. The prayer and answer form a dialogue, similar to what we had in the call. The fourth superscription (33.1), which contains שֵׁנִית, bridges a time-gap and signals a new revelation. The time-gap is not long, however, perhaps only days or weeks because Jeremiah is still under house arrest in the court of the guard. But there is a time-gap, also the onset of a new revelation. Evidence of both may perhaps be indicated by the chapter division at 33.

Returning to chapter 1, which in its present form is set forth as being a continuous narrative, it seems reasonable enough to take the superscription in v. 11 as a repetition of the superscriptions in vv. 2 and 4, and the superscription in v. 13—with שֵׁנִית—as a new beginning. And by 'new beginning' is meant a time-lag between the first and second visions. When Yahweh comes with his word 'a second time' he comes with a new revelation. In the other passages where שֵׁנִית occurs a time-lag between revelations is assumed.

Does שֵׁנִית bridge two originally separate narrative fragments? In 33.1 it is said to do so,[34] but not in 13.3. Jeremiah 13.1-9 is too short to be divided up into fragments. So we must conclude that שֵׁנִית does not necessarily imply a bridging of sources. It can, but it also cannot.

It remains to examine the break said to exist after v. 16. Many scholars make it; at the same time debate has been ongoing from the time of Duhm up to the present regarding divisions within vv. 13-19 and where they are to be made. Two arguments, actually, have been going on. One is of a minor sort, the other more major. The minor argument has to do with where the second vision ends. Duhm, as we mentioned, ended this vision at v. 16; so also did Mowinckel. Hitzig earlier in his outline delimited vv. 11-16; nevertheless,

---

34. See Rudolph, Bright, Thiel and Carroll.

when speaking of the second vision he referred to vv. 13-14. Today the tendency is to limit the second vision to vv. 13-14;[35] vv. 15-16 are explained in various ways, usually as some sort of expansion. Carroll[36] says that in both 11-12 and 13-14 'the brief exchanges (i.e., between Yahweh and Jeremiah) constitute the genre', and Amos 7.7-8; 8.1-2 are cited for support.[37] Reducing the second vision to vv. 13-14 makes it about the same length as the first vision. Duhm earlier noted the imbalance between the two visions when the second was extended to v. 16.

The major argument associated with the break after v. 16 concerns what to do with vv. 17-19. We noted earlier that Mowinckel was emphatic in bracketing out these verses as a later addition. Duhm was more tentative. He said:

> Wie der Schluß der Einleitung, v. 17-19, an das Vorhergehende anzuschließen ist, wird nicht recht deutlich gemacht. Er ist jetzt die Fortsetzung der Rede Jahwes in der zweiten Vision, die dadurch viel länger wird als die erste; natürlicher würde er sich eigentlich als Fortsetzung von v. 4-10 ausnehmen, aber das וְאַתָּה 17 ist doch wohl Gegensatz zu dem Ich v. 12 und 15.[38]

In my view, the contrast which he points out between וְאַתָּה ('but you') in v. 17 and הִנְנִי ('look I') in v. 15 is rhetorically significant; in fact it argues for keeping vv. 15-19 together. To get the full thrust of what is being said in these verses we must add another rhetorically significant term, וַאֲנִי הִנֵּה ('and I, look'), in v. 18. The overall thought of Yahweh's speech, which begins in v. 15 and concludes either at v. 18 or v. 19, proceeds as follows:

> [15]*Look, I* am calling all the tribes of the north ...
> (to) Jerusalem ...
> against all its *walls* round about
> and against all the *cities* of Judah ...
>
> [17]*But you* (Jeremiah), get dressed, go out and speak
> to (Jerusalem) ...
>
> [18]*And I, look* I have made you today
> into a fortified *city* ...
> and into *walls* of bronze against all the land ...

---

35. Skinner, *Prophecy and Religion*, p. 30; Augustin, 'Baruch und das Buch Jeremia', p. 53; Lundbom, *Jeremiah: A Study in Ancient Hebrew Rhetoric*, p. 97 (1997 edn, p. 128); Niditch, *The Symbolic Vision in Biblical Tradition*, pp. 45, 48-50; McKane, *Jeremiah* I, p. 20; Carroll, *Jeremiah*, p. 106; and Herrmann, *Jeremia*, p. 43.
36. Carroll, *Jeremiah*, p. 106.
37. So also Niditch, *The Symbolic Vision in Biblical Tradition*, p. 70.
38. Duhm, *Jeremia*, p. 13.

Not only do we have the contrast between 'I' and 'you', but also a repetition of הִנֵּה (cf. 1.6, 9) and another repetition (in reverse order) of 'walls' and 'city/cities'. Judah's fate is being contrasted with that of Jeremiah. Jerusalem's walls and Judah's cities will fall to the foe from the north; Jeremiah, however, with protection from Yahweh will like a fortified city and walls of bronze have his salvation assured.[39]

There is no break then after v. 16. The only break in vv. 13-19 is after v. 14 where the second vision ends, and that appears—like 11a—to be minor, since the vision has uncontested links to the beginning of Yahweh's speech in v. 15.[40]

Having concluded that the superscription in v. 11 is a repetition of the superscriptions in vv. 2 and 4, and that there is no break in the text after v. 16, the most compelling reasons for bracketing out the two visions are eliminated. The whole of vv. 4-19 makes perfectly good sense 'as is'.

The word comes to Jeremiah in his call, which includes the vision of the almond rod. It then comes a second time in the commission, which includes the vision of the tilted pot. There are two visions, two divine words, two experiences in the life of the prophet. This being so, we must now discuss briefly what the scope of each experience might have consisted of at different stages of development. And we must enquire also into larger questions of meaning and interpretation.

The Call and Commission Revisited

The Call (1.4-12)

The call as it now stands includes a vision. But was this always the case? Ever since the rise of critical scholarship it has been considered possible that the call may have undergone expansion. If so, we wish to know, if possible, what the call consisted of in its earliest articulation.

By reducing the call to vv. 4-10 scholars have pointed to the fact that 'audition' predominates over 'vision', although it is usually recognized that there is a hint of vision in v. 9 where Yahweh stretches forth his hand to touch Jeremiah's mouth.[41] Thiel suggests that the original call be limited to vv. 4-8 (less 7bβ); this would make it a pure audition report.[42] Such a view finds added support in that vv. 4-8 are delimited by an opening superscription and a closing formula of נְאֻם־יְהוָה. I suggested earlier that v. 5—which is poetry—stood at the beginning of an early edition of the book of Jeremiah

---

39. Lundbom, *Jeremiah: A Study in Ancient Hebrew Rhetoric*, p. 97 (1997 edn, p. 128).
40. Lundbom, *Jeremiah: A Study in Ancient Hebrew Rhetoric*, pp. 97-98 (1997 edn, pp. 128-29); Niditch, *The Symbolic Vision in Biblical Tradition*, p. 48.
41. Berridge, *Prophet, People, and the Word of Yahweh*, p. 31.
42. Thiel, *Jeremia 1–25*, p. 71.

where it formed an inclusio with 20.18.⁴³ Perhaps then v. 5 is the original kernel of Jeremiah's call. If so, a second stage of development could be the report of vv. 4-8 (although I see no reason to delete 7bβ). We must, in any case, allow for the possibility that the call narrative underwent expansion. But that does not force upon us a date for the final version in the middle- or post-exilic period. Growth could have taken place during Jeremiah and Baruch's own lifetime (36.32).

Even if the call was originally a 'pure audition report', we must be careful not to make too sharp a distinction between 'audition' and 'vision', assuming, for example, that each was a separate experience and the two were mutually exclusive, or that because Jeremiah disparaged visions (better: dreams) in 23.23-40 it would not have been possible for a vision to have been a genuine component of his own experience of call. According to 23.18 the true messenger is expected to both 'see' and 'hear' Yahweh's word in the divine council. Also that Jeremiah did in fact experience visions as other prophets did is plainly attested in chapter 24 and 38.21. In chapter 24 the form of the vision is no different from the form of the visions in chapter 1.⁴⁴

A more important question is what the call means in the text now before us. Virtually everyone notes its similarity to the call of Moses in Exodus 3–4, particularly at the point where Jeremiah puts up resistance. But those who hold the traditional view, as well as others who combine the fragments in some meaningful way, assume that Jeremiah's demur was short-lived. Perhaps this is because Yahweh appears to overpower him in the response of vv. 7-10. In any case, Jeremiah is believed to have accepted his call soon after it was issued. Reducing the call to vv. 4-8 does not materially affect this way of interpreting the outcome of the dialogue.

Yet it needs to be recognized that nowhere in the call—however it be delimited—is there any indication of acceptance on Jeremiah's part, nothing certainly approaching Isaiah's 'Here I am, send me' (Isa. 6.8). We know of course that Yahweh will have his way with Jeremiah, and that in the end he does have his way with Jeremiah; nevertheless, Jeremiah's silence here may still be an indication that some time needs to pass before the call can be accepted and his career as a prophet can be launched.

Reading on into vv. 11-12 with the thought that these verses continue the dialogue and form a part of the same basic experience, we find that the otherwise problematic remark which Yahweh makes in v. 12, 'I am watching over my word to do it', now yields perfectly good sense. Yahweh is promising to watch over and *fulfill* the word he has just spoken, which is everything affirmed in vv. 5-10 and what v. 4 designates as his 'word'. Yahweh is

---

43. Lundbom, *Jeremiah: A Study in Ancient Hebrew Rhetoric*, pp. 28-30 (1997 edn, pp. 42-44).

44. Niditch, *The Symbolic Vision in Biblical Tradition*, p. 70.

thinking along the same lines as Jeremiah. He knows his word requires fulfillment, and that a period of time will have to elapse before this fulfillment comes. The LXX of v. 12 reads 'my words' plural (τοὺς λόγους μου), which changes the meaning only slightly. The antecedent in this case appears to be 'my words' (τοὺς λόγους μου) in v. 9. According to this interpretation, Yahweh will watch over and fulfill the 'words' promised for Jeremiah's mouth. In my earlier study I opted for this reading,[45] but now, for reasons that will become clear in a moment, I prefer the MT reading 'word'.

If there is a time-lag of years instead of hours or days between the call and Jeremiah's acceptance of the call, it becomes possible to assign a younger age to Jeremiah when the call comes, which is to say, נַעַר in 1.6-7 can be simply translated 'boy' (so Bright; now NRSV). Jeremiah is then the approximate age of Samuel when he receives his call in the Shiloh sanctuary (1 Samuel 3). He is not the age of Moses, who, when called, was already a grown man (Exod. 2.11: וַיִּגְדַּל מֹשֶׁה). Jerome notes a difference in age between Moses and Jeremiah and says it explains the contrasting responses of Yahweh to their respective demurs. Because Moses was a grown man his resistance was met with a rebuke. Jeremiah, however, was treated with leniency because at a young age fear and timidity are considered admirable traits.[46]

I would suggest then that Jeremiah was a boy perhaps 12 or 13 when he heard the call to be Yahweh's prophet. The year was 627 BCE, the place Anathoth—not in the sanctuary but out in the open country. Jeremiah resisted saying he was only a boy, but Yahweh passed over his objection and proceeded to designate him for the prophetic office. Jeremiah need have no fear of those who would oppose him, for Yahweh would ensure his deliverance. Yahweh promised also to put his words in Jeremiah's mouth, which amounted to designating him the 'prophet like Moses' spoken about in Deut. 18.18. The dialogue closes with a sign (cf. Exod. 3.12). Yahweh directs Jeremiah's attention to a nearby almond blossom, and with a play on words (שָׁקֵד/שֹׁקֵד) he gives Jeremiah this assurance: 'I am watching over my word to do it'.

The Commission (1.13-19)

Jeremiah's commission sends him forth to do the work of prophetic ministry, and it is given in the context of the vision announcing the foe from the north. In light of our rhetorical analysis little can be said about expansion

---

45. Lundbom, *Jeremiah: A Study in Ancient Hebrew Rhetoric*, p. 98 (1997 edn, p. 129).

46. Jerome (*In Hieremiam VI*, 5) says, 'Detestatur officium quod pro aetate non potest sustinere, eadem uerecundia, qua et Moses tenuis et gracilis uocis esse se dicit. Sed ille quasi magnae robustaeque aetatis corripitur, huic pueritae datur uenia, quae uerecundia et pudore decoratur'.

within these verses, and even less about the possibility of fragments having had some prior existence. Verses 15-18 are a unit, and the likelihood that vv. 13-14 at one time had a separate existence appears remote. It is sometimes argued that vv. 15-16 are a late insertion because of the stereotyped—so-called 'Deuteronomic'—language in v. 16. Admittedly this verse has such language, but that by itself does not betray middle- or postexilic provenance. This is the rhetorical prose of Jeremiah's age,[47] and both content-wise and vocabulary-wise it is practically the same as a verse from the oracle of Huldah in 2 Kgs 22.17.[48]

It may be that v. 19 is an addition, the purpose of which is to create continuity with 1.8 and 15.20-21. If so, the passage could then be said to have experienced slight growth. But again, there is no reason to assign a late date to v. 19; it only need follow 15.15-21, which is normally dated not later than the reign of Jehoiakim.[49] One could, however, just as easily conclude that all of vv. 13-19 is one piece.[50]

The possibility would seem to be greater that vv. 4-12 and vv. 13-19 were originally separate accounts, particularly with the major break coming between vv. 12 and 13 and the call and commission now seen as separate experiences between which a span of years intervenes. Nothing conclusive, however, can be drawn from שֵׁנִית in v. 13. In the other two passages where the term occurs, שֵׁנִית in one case bridges sources (33.1), but in the other case does not (13.3). Yet neither passage assumes the time-lag we are proposing here. So the possibility should be left open that the call account, at one time, had a separate existence from the commission account.

I have argued that Jeremiah's acceptance of the call came later than the issuance of the call. How much later we cannot say, at least based on what information is available in chapter 1. To accept the call Jeremiah needs simply to be a young man able to reconcile himself to a great undertaking, someone who is also mature enough to begin preaching the words Yahweh puts into his mouth. A period of about four or five years, if Jeremiah is about 12 or 13 at the time of the call, would seem to be a minimum. This would put him at about 18. But as we have said, the data here in chapter 1 does not help us answer this question.

---

47. So J. Bright, 'The Date of the Prose Sermons of Jeremiah', *JBL* 70 (1951), p. 27, who cites the earlier judgments of W.O.E. Oesterley and T.H. Robinson, *An Introduction to the Books of the Old Testament* (London: SPCK, 1958), p. 304; also W.F. Albright in *BASOR* 70 (1938), p. 17, who said the Hebrew of the Lachish Letters was of the same basic style as the Deuteronomist and the Jeremiah prose.

48. J. Lundbom, 'The Lawbook of the Josianic Reform', *CBQ* 38 (1976), p. 298.

49. So Rudolph, Bright and Holladay.

50. Rietzschel, *Das Problem der Urrolle*, p. 135.

By the time the vision of the tilted pot comes, acceptance has already taken place. This vision and the message accompanying it bid Jeremiah to begin preaching immediately. Rashi and Kimchi note that the phrase in v. 17, חֲאֹזר מָתְנֶיךָ (lit. 'gird up your loins'), means to get ready for 'speedy and decisive action'.[51] This commission report must not be confused with Jeremiah's acceptance; it presupposes acceptance, but is not the acceptance itself. Yahweh dominates the discourse from beginning to end.

The commission report does, however, offer itself as a fulfillment of Yahweh's promise in v. 12. That seems to be what the superscription in v. 13 is trying to tell us when it says that the word of Yahweh came to Jeremiah a second time. The first time was the call, which concluded with a promise. Now the one writing the superscription tells us that this promise was fulfilled in Yahweh's second word of commissioning. Such an interpretation of course requires the MT reading 'word' in v. 12; the LXX reading 'words' has something else in mind, but that is another matter. All I am saying is that if one reads the MT v. 13 fulfills v. 12, the second vision fulfills the first, and the commission is a fulfillment of the call.

Taken together the four superscriptions in 1.4, 11, 13, and 2.1 advocate a 'theology of the divine word'. Yahweh's word has ongoing forward motion from promise to fulfillment:

    1.4   Yahweh's word comes to Jeremiah in the call
    1.11   Yahweh's word continues, promising fulfillment
    1.13   Yahweh's promised word is fulfilled
    2.1   Yahweh's word continues to be fulfilled as Jeremiah begins to preach

According to our revised picture of chapter 1, Jeremiah does not begin his career in 627 BCE. Only the call comes in that year. The beginning of his public ministry is later, how many years later we do not know. But judging simply from the dates that have been suggested, it could not have been before 622. If this be true, then the chronology of the traditional view must be revised. Jeremiah is no longer preaching in anticipation of Josiah's reform activities, that is, in the years 627-622, nor during this time is he announcing the arrival of some early foe from the north. This revision takes from the traditional view the greatest strains that have been placed upon it, and it does so without tampering with the chronological notices given in 1.2; 25.1-3; and 36.1-2.

A tentative reconstruction of the commission is as follows. Sometime after 622 Jeremiah receives the vision of the pot tilted on its side. It announces a foe that will wreak havoc over the whole land. The foe is not named, but it can be assumed to be Babylon. The focal point of the enemy will be Jerusalem and the cities of Judah. In the end Judah will be defeated. Yahweh is the primary actor who is doing all this, and it is because the

---

51. McKane, *Jeremiah* I, p. 22.

nation is guilty of gross covenant infidelity. But in his words of commission to Jeremiah, Yahweh promises the prophet what he will not promise Jerusalem: protection and deliverance. With this assurance Jeremiah is then able to begin preaching Yahweh's message to his people.

Chapter 22

RUDIMENTARY LOGIC IN JEREMIAH*

Logic among the Ancient Greeks
Aristotle and the Syllogism

Logic today and down through the ages owes a singular debt to the ancient Greeks, Aristotle (384–322) in particular, who developed syllogistic reasoning into a system in his *Prior Analytics* I.[1] Aristotle's name for logic was 'analytics'. At the heart of Aristotle's logic was the syllogism (συλλογισμός), which he defined as 'a form of words in which, when certain assumptions are made, something other than what has been assumed necessarily follows from the fact that the assumptions are such'.[2] An Aristotelian syllogism is a deductive argument, basically, an 'if…then' proposition: 'if α and β, then γ'. Typically it consists of three different categorical statements: two premises (one major and one minor), and a conclusion. The major premise is a generally accepted belief; the minor premise is a specific shared belief or observation; and the conclusion follows necessarily from the terms of the premises.[3]

Aristotle had precursors among the Greek mathematicians, rhetoricians, and philosophers of the 5th- and 4th-centuries. Mathematicians had to prove their theorems, while rhetoricians and philosophers had to develop ways of refuting the contentions of other rhetoricians and philosophers.[4] The latter individuals would tentatively accept the point of view of their adversary, then refute it by showing that it led to absurd consequences. One precursor

---

* First published in *Jeremiah Closer Up* (Sheffield: Sheffield Phoenix Press, 2010), pp. 10-22.

1. Aristotle, *Prior Analytics*, I-II (trans. Hugh Tredennick; LCL; Cambridge, MA: Harvard University Press, 1962); Ernst Kapp, *Greek Foundations of Traditional Logic* (New York: Columbia University Press, 1942), pp. vi, 60-74; Czeslaw Lejewski, 'Ancient Logic', *EncPhil* 4, pp. 513-16; G.B. Kereferd, 'Aristotle', *EncPhil* 1, pp. 151-62.

2. *Prior Analytics*, I, i 24b; cf. *Topics*, I (trans. E.S. Forster; LCL; Cambridge, MA: Harvard University Press, 1966), i 100a; *The 'Art' of Rhetoric*, I (trans. John Henry Freese; LCL; Cambridge, MA: Harvard University Press, 1967), ii 1356b.

3. Christopher Johnstone, 'Enthymeme', in Thomas O. Sloan (ed.), *Encyclopedia of Rhetoric* (Oxford: Oxford University Press, 2001), p. 248.

4. Lejewski, 'Ancient Logic', pp. 513-14.

was Zeno of Elea (c. 490), who Aristotle credited with being the founder of dialectic. Another precursor much admired by Aristotle was the most celebrated practitioner of argumentation in all of Greece, Socrates (470–399). Aristotle had precursors as well among the Sophists, for example Protagoras (490–421) and Prodicus (460–399), who were interested in the correct use of words. Not surprisingly, Aristotle learned a good deal also from Plato (428–347) after entering his Athenian Academy in 367, going on to make practical applications of Plato's philosophical theories.

Aristotle and the Enthymeme
Aristotle brought deductive logic into the study of rhetoric by recognizing a type of syllogism which he called the 'enthymeme'.[5] The term was employed by prior and contemporary writers, for example Isocrates (436–338) and Anaximenes of Lampaskos (c. 380–320).[6] Aristotle said, 'Rhetorical demonstration is an enthymeme, which, generally speaking, is the strongest of rhetorical proofs'.[7] He called it a 'rhetorical syllogism',[8] considering it a truncated syllogism in which one premise was omitted (or suppressed) because the audience could supply it.[9] An example of the enthymeme would be the inference of 'Socrates is mortal' from 'All men are mortal'. The missing premise, here the minor one, is 'Socrates is a man'.

Argumentation in Ancient Israel

We are unaccustomed to probe behind the great classical cultures of Greece and Rome in a search for earlier logical and rhetorical arguments, preferring to leave their origin and development to the Greek rhetoricians and philosophers, and the Roman rhetoricians, who came later. This is perhaps how it should be. After all, from where else in the ancient world do we derive the systematic treatment of logic and rhetoric given us by Aristotle, or the treatment of figures and modes of argumentation such as those coming down to us in the rhetorical handbooks of the *ad Herennium* and Quintilian's *Institutes*? Yet it seems fair to ask about the extent to which argument was understood by peoples of ancient Near East, who inhabited a world and shared a world view considerably older and different from that existing in the classical world of Greece and Rome.

If we peer into the Old Testament, which is the only real discourse that survives from ancient Israel, we find a select number of arguments being

5. Johnstone, 'Enthymeme', pp. 247-50; Thomas M. Conley, 'The Enthymeme in Perspective', *QJS* 70 (1984), pp. 168-87.
6. Conley, 'The Enthymeme in Perspective', pp. 172-74.
7. Aristotle, *Rhetoric*, I, i 1355a.
8. Aristotle, *Rhetoric*, I, ii 1356b.
9. Aristotle, *Rhetoric*, I, ii 1357a; II, xxii 1395b.

put to use. In Jeremiah, for example, one finds the *prostasis-apodosis* ('if... then') form, which is a deductive argument.[10] A couple of examples:

> *If* you return, Israel
> —oracle of Yahweh—
> to me return
> and *if* you remove your wretched things from me
> and do not waver about
> *then* you can swear 'By Yahweh's life'
> in truth, in justice, and in righteousness
> *then* nations shall bless themselves in him
> and in him shall they boast (Jer. 4.1-2).

> *If* these statutes depart
> from before me—oracle of Yahweh
> *then* the seed of Israel shall cease
> from being a nation before me—all the days (Jer. 31.36).

> *If* the heavens above can be measured
> and the foundations of the earth explored to the depths
> *then* I, I will reject all the seed of Israel
> because of all that they have done
> —oracle of Yahweh (Jer. 31.37).

This argument appears elsewhere in Jer. 12.16, 17; 33.20-21, 25-26; and in Deut. 28.1, 15.

In Jeremiah are also arguments *a fortiori* or *a minori ad maius* (Heb. *qal vechomer*), which is an argument from the lesser to the greater.[11] It is a 'how much more' argument:

> *If* with men on foot you have run and they have wearied you
> *how then* will you fare in a heat with horses?
> and (*if*) in a peaceful land you have fallen down
> *how then* will you do in the pride of the Jordan? (Jer. 12.5).

> Look, (*if*) those for whom there is no judgment to drink the
> cup must surely drink
> *then* are you one who will surely go free? (Jer. 49.12).

See also Jer. 3.1 and 25.29.[12]

Jeremiah made particularly good use of the rhetorical question in argumentation.[13] He uses the rhetorical question, sometimes a pair of them, as a

---

10. Jack R. Lundbom, *Jeremiah 1–20* (AB, 21A; New York: Doubleday, 1999; New Haven: Yale University Press, 2009), pp. 130, 325-26; Jack R. Lundbom, *Jeremiah 21–36* (AB, 21B; New York: Doubleday, 2004), pp. 486-87; Jack R. Lundbom, *Jeremiah 37–52* (AB, 21C; New York: Doubleday, 2004), pp. 587, 593.
11. Lundbom, *Jeremiah 1–20*, pp. 130, 646; *Jeremiah 37–52*, pp. 336, 586.
12. Lundbom, *Jeremiah 1–20*, p. 301.
13. Lundbom, *Jeremiah 1–20*, pp. 130-32.

foil for a more important statement he wishes to make. The rhetorical question is put to use in two types of argument. In one, a single or double question lifts up some paradigmatic behavior, a common happening, or something built into the natural order, which the prophet then follows by a (contrary) portrayal of human behavior that is scandalous. A couple of examples:

> Has a nation exchanged gods
>   even though they are no gods?
> But my people has exchanged its glory
>   for no profit! (Jer. 2.22).

> Can a maiden forget her ornaments
>   a bride her knotted cords?
> But my people has forgotten me
>   days without number (Jer. 2.32).

See also Jer. 5.22a, 23; 18.14-15; and somewhat differently, Jer. 13.23.

The other specialized usage in Jeremiah is the threefold question in the 'If...if...so why...?' (מַדּוּעַ...אִם...הֲ) form, which appears nine times in the book. Here two questions are a foil for the third, which expresses a troubling vexation. The vexation is often an incongruity the prophet has observed. A couple of examples:

> Have I become a wilderness to Israel?
>   or a land of thick darkness?
> So why do my people say, 'We are free to roam
>   we will no longer come to you?' (Jer. 2.31).

> If [people] fall down, do they not get up?
>   If one turns away, does he not return?
> So why has this people turned away
>   Jerusalem, the rebel perpetual? (Jer. 8.4-5a).

See elsewhere Jer. 2.14 (shortened); 8.19, 22; 14.19; 22.28; 30.6 (modified); and 49.1.

Jeremiah uses other arguments described in the classical rhetorical handbooks, for example *epitrope* (Jer. 26.14); *descriptio* (Jer. 26.15); and *distributio* (Jer. 28.8-9).[14]

The Enthymeme in Prophetic Preaching

It came as somewhat of a surprise to me to discover the enthymeme in preaching of the Hebrew prophets.[15] When the preaching of virtually all the 8th- to 6th-century prophets was set over against the homiletical rhetoric of

---

14. Lundbom, *Jeremiah 1–20*, p. 133; *Jeremiah 21–36*, pp. 292-93, 334-35.
15. Lundbom, 'Hebrew Rhetoric', *EncRhet*, p. 326.

Deuteronomy, it became immediately clear that what the prophets had done was simply to omit Deuteronomy's message that an Israel in violation of the covenant would be punished, and gone straight on to make their indictments (violation had occurred) and judgments (punishment will come). In order to reconstruct a complete syllogism for this preaching, if one is to be desired, the message of Deuteronomy has to be supplied:

[Deuteronomy: An Israel in violation of the covenant will be punished]
The prophets: Israel has violated the covenant
                Israel will therefore be punished

We can assume that the prophets' audience was fully capable of supplying the omitted premise, for which reason it did not have to be stated. Aristotle realized that speakers out to persuade crowds—even the most ignorant of speakers—were more successful in using the enthymeme, since crowds do not require all the steps of an argument, nor do they want all the added words.[16] The prophets, for the most part, were addressing crowds, so they too stood a better chance of persuading their audience by means of the enthymeme.

One may well ask at this point what date is then to be assigned Deuteronomy? The general consensus is that Deuteronomy is a 7th-century document, but many believe it embodies traditions out of North Israel, which would push the date of the traditions, at least, back into the 8th-century or earlier. In my view, the First Edition of Deuteronomy (chaps. 1–28) belongs to the reform of Hezekiah, which I date between 712 and 705. And I agree that this core document contains older material from North Israel, which could make preaching the conditional nature of the Sinai covenant contemporary with the 8th-century prophets, Amos and Hosea. It may be older. Yet the provenance of Deuteronomy is not crucial for maintaining the juxtaposition I am setting forth, since the idea that an Israel in violation of the covenant will be punished could have had currency at any time in Israel's history, long before the Deuteronomic Code and attendant homilies were written down on a scroll.

Rudimentary Logic in Oracle Clusters of Jeremiah

I now wish to present evidence that Jeremiah, or else the compiler of the Jeremiah oracles, expressed a rudimentary understanding of logic and argumentative strategy by arranging a select number of oracles into clusters of three, with the result that the prophet's preaching moved from a general principle to indictment to judgment. This could translate into a major premise, a minor premise, and a conclusion, in which case we would have an early form of syllogistic reasoning not unlike what Aristotle developed

---

16. Aristotle, *Rhetoric*, II, xxii 1395b.

later into a system. I am not suggesting that Jeremiah understood and employed syllogistic reasoning in his preaching, although that need not be precluded, only that when certain oracle clusters are carefully delimited and examined, we see in them a rudimentary form of Hebrew logic. This discovery owes a considerable debt to rhetorical criticism, which in the book of Jeremiah has made significant progress in delimiting prophetic oracles—in both poetry and prose—within their larger contexts.[17] And it is significantly aided by form criticism, for example in the isolation of messenger formulas ('Thus said Yahweh' and 'oracle of Yahweh'), and by paying close attention to content; also by noting section markings in the Hebrew text, the *setumah* and the *petuḥah*, which we now know to be very old, since they have turned up in the Dead Sea Scrolls.[18]

The Temple Oracles (Jer. 7.1-15)
Earlier scholars saw in Jer. 7.1-15 a 'Temple sermon' delivered by Jeremiah in 609, a summary of which appears together with narrative background in chap. 26. But they were troubled by a lack of coherence in the sermon, particularly between vv. 3-7 and vv. 12-14.[19] This sermon began with a call for covenant obedience, which differed only from the preaching of Deuteronomy in that people were being told to amend current behavior (vv. 3-7). The hope was expressed here that the nation could escape judgment and its people remain in the land. Then came a strident indictment of evils having been committed (vv. 8-11), and finally unmitigated judgment, which the prophet says would leave the Jerusalem Temple in ruins like what happened to Israel's first sanctuary at Shiloh (vv. 12-14). One is left to wonder, then, how people could be told in a single sermon to 'make good their ways and their doings' and thereby avert judgment, and then be hit with a harsh indictment and an even harsher judgment for having disobeyed the Sinai covenant.

The term 'sermon', however, is a misnomer, for not only is this preaching too brief to be much of a sermon, but more important, the verses are not a unified composition, but rather three self-contained oracles brought together into a cluster: Oracle I (vv. 3-7); Oracle II (vv. 8-11); and Oracle III (vv. 12-14). Each oracle possesses an integrity of its own, which if not eliminating the coherence problem entirely, at least significantly reduces it. Oracle I gives a general statement of principle, stating that a people amending their behavior by obeying the Sinai covenant will have ongoing existence

---

17. Lundbom, *Jeremiah 1–20*; *Jeremiah 21–36*; *Jeremiah 37–52*. On the delimitation of literary units as a first priority in rhetorical criticism, see James Muilenburg, 'Form Criticism and Beyond', *JBL* 88 (1969), pp. 8-10.

18. Lundbom, *Jeremiah 1–20*, pp. 63, 74; Jack R. Lundbom, 'Delimitation of Units in the Book of Jeremiah', in *The Impact of Unit Delimitation on Exegesis* (ed. Raymond de Hoop *et al.*; Leiden: E.J. Brill, 2009), pp. 146-74.

19. Lundbom, *Jeremiah 1–20*, pp. 458-59.

in the land. Oracle II is an indictment that covenant violation—on a grand scale—has occurred. And Oracle III announces unmitigated judgment. When the three oracles are brought together into a cluster, there is movement from general principle to indictment to judgment.

The three oracles are delimited by: (1) section markings; (2) messenger formulas (small caps); and (3) a use in each of the rhetorical device known as the inclusio (italics). The section markings cited are the three *setumah* breaks in the Leningrad Codex of the Hebrew Bible (M^L). The Aleppo Codex (M^A) and St Petersburg Codex of the Prophets (M^P) also have a *setumah* before v. 3, marking the beginning of the first oracle; the St Petersburg Codex has *a setumah* after v. 11, marking the end of the second oracle; and the Aleppo and St Petersburg Codices have a *petuḥah* after v. 15, marking the end of the larger unit. 4QJer[a] also has a section after v. 15. The text of Jer. 7.1-15 can then be delimited into three oracles as follows:

ס

I ³THUS SAID YAHWEH OF HOSTS, THE GOD OF ISRAEL:
Make good your ways and your doings and *I will let you dwell in this place*. ⁴Do not trust for yourselves in the deceptive words, 'The temple of Yahweh, the temple of Yahweh, the temple of Yahweh are these'. ⁵For if you really make good your ways and your doings, if you really act justly each man toward his fellow, ⁶the sojourner, the orphan, and the widow you do not oppress, and the blood of the innocent you do not shed in this place, and after other gods you do not go, to your own hurt, ⁷then *I will let you dwell in this place*, in the land that I gave to your fathers for all time.

II ⁸*Look*, you trust for yourselves in the deceptive words to no avail. ⁹Do you think you can steal, murder, and commit adultery, and swear to The Lie, and burn incense to Baal, and go after other gods that you have not known, ¹⁰and then come and stand in my presence, in this house upon which my name is called, and say, 'We are safe!' —only to keep doing all these abominations? ¹¹A robber's den is this house upon which my name is called in your eyes? As for me, *Look!* I have seen!—ORACLE OF YAHWEH.

ס

III ¹²Go indeed, would you, to *my place* that was *in Shiloh*, where I first made my name dwell, and see what I did to it because of the evil of my people Israel. ¹³Now then, because you have done all these doings—ORACLE OF YAHWEH—when I spoke to you—constantly I spoke—but you did not hear, and I called you but you did not answer, ¹⁴I will do then to the house upon which my name is called, in which you trust, yes to *the place* that I gave to you and to your fathers, as I did *to Shiloh*.

¹⁵So I will cast you away from my presence, as I cast away all your brothers, all the offspring of Ephraim.

ס

Each of the oracles contains a messenger formula. Oracle I is preceded by an embellished 'Thus said Yahweh of hosts, the God of Israel' (v. 3); Oracle II concludes with 'oracle of Yahweh' (v. 11); and Oracle III has 'oracle of Yahweh' in the middle (v. 13). The different locations of the formulas may be intentional, particularly if the oracles were originally delivered as a cluster.

Looking at rhetorical form, we see that all three oracles employ the inclusio, which is a verbal tie-in between beginning and end. The repeated words and/or phrases in the three oracles:

I	*I will let you dwell in this place...*		v. 3
	I will let you dwell in this place		v. 7
II	*Look*	הִנֵּה	v. 8
	Look!	הִנֵּה	v. 11
III	*my place ...in Shiloh...*		v. 12
	the place ...to Shiloh		v. 14

The inclusio in Oracle III supports bracketing out v. 15 as a later add-on, the purpose of which was to render a comparison between Judah and Ephraim (= Northern Israel).

So what we have in 7.1-15 is an introduction (vv. 1-2), three separate oracles (vv. 3-14), and an add-on (v. 15). Oracle I is preaching like Deuteronomy, although calling here for correction (v. 3: 'Make good [Amend] your ways and your doings'), suiting the tenor of the Josianic Reform. Oracle II is a strident indictment for covenant violation. Oracle III is riveting judgment.

Reducing these messages into a syllogistic argument would yield the following:

> Major premise: A people not violating the covenant can remain in the land
> Minor premise: This people, though feeling secure, has violated the covenant
> Conclusion: Yahweh will bring (this people and) this land to ruin.

It could be that this cluster of oracles is an editorial creation, and nothing more. But when all three oracles are compared with their summarization in 26.4-6, also with Jeremiah's defense in 26.13, the segments are seen to draw upon not just one oracle, but upon all three.[20] So Jeremiah may have spoken all three oracles in succession on one occasion, moving intentionally from general principle, to specific violation, to judgment. If so, we have a rudimentary logic in the preaching of Jeremiah.

---

20. Lundbom, *Jeremiah 1–20*, pp. 454, 459.

The Covenant Oracles (Jer. 11.1-13)

The same sequence of general principle, indictment, and judgment appears a second time in Jer. 11.1-13. Here is a prose segment containing three self-standing oracles on covenant obedience. In the larger unit is an introduction to Oracle I (vv. 1-3a); the text of Oracle I (vv. 3b-5a); Jeremiah's 'amen' to Oracle I (v. 5b); an introduction to Oracle II (v. 6); the text of oracle II (vv. 7-8); an introduction to Oracle III (vv. 9-10); and the text of Oracle III (vv. 11-13).[21] Two of the oracles have messenger formulas (small caps), and all get help in delimitation from the section markings in M^L. The three oracles go as follows:

פ

1-3a ...

I   ³ᵇY HUS SAID YAHWEH, THE GOD OF ISRAEL:
Cursed be the man who will not hear the words of this covenant ⁴that I commanded your fathers in the day I brought them out from the land of Egypt, out of the iron furnace: Hear my voice and do them, according to all that I commanded you, and you will be a people to me, and I, I will be God to you, ⁵that I may perform the oath that I swore to your fathers to give them a land flowing with milk and honey, as at this day.
...

ס

II   ⁷For I told your fathers emphatically in the day I brought them up from the land of Egypt—and unto this day—constantly told: Hear my voice. ⁸But they did not hear, and they did not bend their ear, but they went each in the stubbornness of their evil heart, so I brought upon them all the words of this covenant, which I commanded them to do, but they did not do.[22]

ס

...

ס

III   ¹¹THEREFORE THUS SAID YAHWEH:
Look I am bringing evil upon them, from which they will not be able to escape. And they will cry to me, but I will not hear them. ¹²The cities of Judah and the inhabitants of Jerusalem will go and they will cry to the gods to whom they burn incense, but they certainly cannot save them in the time of their evil. ¹³For the number of your cities equals your gods, Judah, and the number of the streets of Jerusalem is the altars you have set up to Shame—altars to burn incense to Baal.

ס

---

21. Lundbom, *Jeremiah 1–20*, pp. 614-20.
22. The oracle follows the reading in MT; the LXX has a shorter text (see Lundbom, *Jeremiah 1–20*, p. 618).

The other major medieval codices support delimitation with section markings. M^A and M^P have a *petuḥah* before v. 1, and M^A a *setumah* and M^P a *petuḥah* after v. 13, marking the beginning of the larger unit, and the end of Oracle III. M^A has a *petuḥah* and M^P a *setumah* before v. 6, marking the beginning of Oracle II. M^A has a *setumah* and M^P a *petuḥah* after v. 8, marking the end of Oracle II. M^A has *a setumah* and M^P a *petuḥah* before v. 11, marking the beginning of Oracle III.

Oracle I begins with a 'Thus said Yahweh, the God of Israel' messenger formula, and Oracle III with a 'Therefore thus said Yahweh' formula. Oracle II has no messenger formula.

These oracles do not contain inclusio structures like the oracles in 7.3-14, but they do have some nice word balances and smaller rhetorical structures.[23] They share the following vocabulary and phraseology in vv. 3-4, 7-8, and 10:

v. 3	who will not hear the words of this covenant	v. 8	they did not hear... the words of this covenant	v. 10	refused to hear my words... my covenant
v. 4	that I commanded your fathers in the day... from the land of Egypt Hear my voice and do	v. 7	that I commanded your fathers in the day... from the land of Egypt Hear my voice	v. 10	their fathers (2×)
		v. 8	but they did not do		

All three oracles focus on the covenant, which is the Sinai covenant undergoing renewal in the Josianic Reform (2 Kings 23). Oracle I (vv. 3b-5a) announces a curse on anyone not hearing the words of the covenant commanded to Judah's ancestors, after which comes an exhortation to hear Yahweh's voice and do the commands. Oracle II (vv. 7-8) indicts the ancestors for covenant disobedience, stating that punishment came as a result. Oracle III (vv. 11-13), preceded by a clarifying word to Jeremiah (vv. 9-10), promises judgment on the current generation, which the clarifying word says is engaged in a 'conspiracy' to return to the iniquity of the ancestors (vv. 9-10). The current generation has broken Yahweh's covenant made with the ancestors (v. 10b).

Reducing these oracles and editorial comment to a syllogism, we have a major premise, two minor premises, and a conclusion:

Major premise:	Cursed be anyone who does not hear and do the covenant
Minor premise:	The ancestors did not hear, and were cursed
Minor premise:	The current generation refuses to hear
Conclusion:	The current generation will be cursed.

---

23. Lundbom, *Jeremiah 1–20*, pp. 615-19.

The question of coherence has not arisen in these oracles largely because scholars have not assumed a single sermon, as in 7.1-15, but also because the supplementary prose of vv. 9-10 brings the indictment into the present and prepares for the judgment of Oracle III. The preaching moves clearly from a general curse on anyone who does not hear and do the covenant (Oracle I), to indictment of past and present generations for covenant violation (Oracle II and supplementary prose), to judgment on the current generation (Oracle III).

These three oracles could have been delivered in sequence on a single occasion, but if so, some editorial comment was required to get a syllogistic argument. Otherwise, we could take this argument as an enthymeme, where the audience was expected to supply the assumption that the current generation was no better than the former generation in refusing to hear (and do) Yahweh's covenant. In either case, the present oracle cluster becomes a full syllogistic argument only with the compiler's supplement, and the compiler is to be credited with the syllogistic argument. I suggested in my commentary that Oracles I and II fit well into the reform years of Josiah, and that Oracle III, because of its reference to a conspiracy, probably belongs to the early reign of Jehoiakim.[24] Either way, whether the argument was originally an enthymeme or a complete syllogism, whether it reflects the mind of Jeremiah or the mind of the compiler, or possibly both, there exists in the present text a clear movement from a general principle, to a specific violation of the principle, to judgment, another display of rudimentary logic in the preaching of Jeremiah.

Oracles to the Royal House (Jer. 21.11-14)

Our third example of an oracle cluster showing logical progression from a general principle to indictment to judgment is in Jer 21.11-14, which contains three oracles to Jerusalem's royal house. These oracles, unlike the others, are in poetry. The larger unit here consists of an introduction to the King Collection and Oracle I (vv. 11-12a); the text of Oracle I (v. 12b); the text of Oracle II (v. 13); and the text of Oracle III (v. 14).[25]

The three oracles are delimited by messenger formulas (small caps), and get partial support from section markings in M^L at the beginning and end of the larger unit. The M^A and M^P also have a *setumah* prior to v. 11, where a shift from prose to poetry occurs. One manuscript in the Cambridge Genizah Collection has a section after v. 12, separating Oracle I from Oracle II.[26] No medieval codex other than M^L has a section after v. 14, but the chap-

---

24. Lundbom, *Jeremiah 1–20*, p. 626.
25. Vv. 13-14 are not one oracle, as many commentators assume; cf. Lundbom, *Jeremiah 21–36*, p. 108.
26. Lundbom, *Jeremiah 21–36*, p. 109.

ter division is made before the return to prose in 22.1. The three oracles in 21.12b-14 state the following:

ס

¹¹⁻¹²ᵃ...

I   ¹²ᵇTHUS SAID YAHWEH:
Execute justice in the morning
        and rescue the robbed from the oppressor's hand!
Lest my wrath go forth like fire
        and burn so none can quench it
                on account of their evil doings.

II   ¹³Look I am against you, sitting one of the valley
        rock of the tableland—ORACLE OF YAHWEH
Those saying, 'Who can come down upon us
        and who can enter into our habitations?

III   ¹⁴But I will reckon upon you
        according to the fruit of your doings
            —ORACLE OF YAHWEH
And I will kindle a fire in her forest
        and it will consume everything around her.

ס

Oracle I is a general exhortation to the royal house to execute justice, lest Yahweh's wrath go forth like fire. Oracle II is an indictment for royal house pride about impregnability. Oracle III is judgment on the royal house for unspecified (evil) deeds, stating that the divine fire will indeed come. Reducing the messages to a syllogistic argument, which takes some reading between the lines, yields the following:

Major premise:	A royal house not executing justice will ignite the divine wrath
Minor premise:	The royal house sits confident (despite unjust deeds)
Conclusion:	(Unjust) deeds will bring divine wrath on the royal house.

One may prefer to label this an enthymeme, since the minor premise does not relate transparently to the major premise. The audience may be able to supply the unjust acts of the royal house, in which case it is unnecessary to state them in the argument. But we are probably not far from the truth if we imagine that the pride being censured in the indictment is going hand in hand with unjust deeds. 'The fruit of your doings' in Oracle III surely refers to unjust doings. There is, in any case, movement from a general principle to indictment to judgment, showing the same sort of logical progression seen in the other oracle clusters. In my commentary I suggested that these oracles were probably not spoken to the royal house directly, but to ordinary citizens in the Temple courtyard or some other public place,[27] which would support the argument being an enthymeme rather than a formal syllogism if the former is more suited to addressing the masses.

We must not think that the ancient Hebrew mind was incapable of thinking logically. The enthymeme was being used by the prophets 400 years before Aristotle, and a rudimentary form of syllogistic reasoning is evident in Jeremiah or a compiler of the Jeremiah oracles over 200 years before it was given classic definition by the great Athenian philosopher in his *Prior Analytics*, I.

---

27. Lundbom, *Jeremiah 21–36*, p. 110.

Chapter 23

THE DOUBLE CURSE IN JEREMIAH 20.14-18*

Jeremiah 20.14-18 is the last of the so-called confessions of Jeremiah found in chaps. 11–20 of the book of Jeremiah.[1] This confession, cast in poetry, concludes also the early edition of Jeremiah 1–20.[2] Its precise date and provenance are not known. In my view the passage emanates most likely from c. 605–604 BCE when hostilities peaked between King Jehoiakim and the prophet.[3]

* First published in *JBL* 104 (1985), pp. 589-600.
1. Cited in the article are the following commentaries and other works discussing Jer. 20.14-18: J. Calvin, *Commentaries on the Book of the Prophet Jeremiah and the Lamentations* III (Grand Rapids, MI: Eerdmans, 1950); F. Hitzig, *Der Prophet Jeremia* (Leipzig: Weidmannsche Buchhandlung, 1841); E. Henderson, *The Book of the Prophet Jeremiah and that of Lamentations* (London: Hamilton, Adams, 1851); C.F. Keil, *Jeremiah, Lamentations* (Grand Rapids, MI: Eerdmans, 1980); B. Duhm, *Das Buch Jeremia* (Tübingen: J.C.B. Mohr [Paul Siebeck], 1901); C.H. Cornill, *Das Buch Jeremia* (Leipzig: Chron. Herm. Tauchnitz, 1905); F. Giesebrecht, *Das Buch Jeremia* (HKAT; Göttingen: Vandenhoeck & Ruprecht, 1907); A.S. Peake, *Jeremiah* I (CB; New York: H. Frowde, 1910); A.W. Streane, *The Book of the Prophet Jeremiah Together with the Lamentations* (CBSC; Cambridge: Cambridge University Press, 1913); W. Baumgartner, *Jeremiah's Poems of Lament* (trans. David E. Orton; Sheffeld: Almond Press, 1988); P. Volz, *Studien zum Text des Jeremia* (Leipzig: J.C. Hinrichs, 1920); *Der Prophet Jeremia* (KAT; Leipzig: Deichert, 2nd edn, 1928); A. Condamin, *Le Livre de Jérémie* (Paris: Librairie Lecoffre, 1936); L. Prijs, 'Jeremia XX 14ff.: Versuch einer neuen Deutung', *VT* 14 (1964), pp. 104-108; J. Bright, *Jeremiah* (AB, 21; Garden City, NY: Doubleday, 1965); W. Rudolph, *Jeremia* (HAT; Tübingen: J.C.B. Mohr [Paul Siebeck], 3rd edn, 1968); G.P. Couturier, 'Jeremiah', in *The Jerome Biblical Commentary* (ed. R. Brown *et al.*; Englewood Cliffs, NJ: Prentice–Hall, 1968); J. Berridge, *Prophet, People, and the Word of Yahweh* (Zurich: EVZ-Verlag, 1970); J.R. Lundbom, *Jeremiah: A Study in Ancient Hebrew Rhetoric* (SBLDS, 18; Missoula, MT: Society of Biblical Literature and Scholars Press, 1975; 2nd edn; Winona Lake, IN: Eisenbrauns, 1997); W.L. Holladay, *The Architecture of Jeremiah 1–20* (Lewisburg, PA: Bucknell University, 1976); and N. Ittmann, *Die Konfessionen Jeremias* (Neukirchen–Vluyn: Neukirchener Verlag, 1981). For a list of the confessions see Bright, *Jeremiah*, p. xvi, or Berridge, *Prophet, People, and the Word of Yahweh*, p. 114 n. 1.
2. See my *Jeremiah: A Study in Ancient Hebrew Rhetoric*, pp. 28-30 (1997 edn, pp. 42-44).
3. *Jeremiah: A Study in Ancient Hebrew Rhetoric*, pp. 47-48 (1997 edn, pp. 66-67).

Without a doubt this is Jeremiah's most anguished cry. In it he invokes not one but two curses: the first on the day of his birth, the second on the man who brought his father the news. Poets ancient and modern have mused on why they were born,[4] but Jeremiah's words are unusually disquieting, because Yahweh, the one who commissioned him as a prophet from before he was born (1.5), is the preferred audience among all other audiences.[5]

Commentators through the years have judged the outcry extreme. Duhm calls it 'ein Ausbruch wütender Verzweiflung'; Sheldon Blank, 'a blast of unreasoned anger'.[6] Though Jeremiah's words have a striking parallel to Job chaps. 3 and 10, there is nothing in all the prophetic literature to which they may be compared. Zwingli[7] and Calvin both recognized that the outburst reflects a condition *in extremis*; nevertheless, they warn us not to emulate the prophet. Calvin comes right out and calls the statement blasphemy. Others perceive that Jeremiah borders on blasphemy (so also 12.1; 15.18; 20.7) even though he does not curse the divine name.

Because the emotional content is so high, difficulties inherent in the text are easily glossed over. Keil, for example, speaking of how the man who witnessed the birth and brought the news to Jeremiah's father could also be the one expected to kill Jeremiah in the womb, says, 'Jeremiah is as little thinking how this could happen as, in the next words, he is of the possibility of everlasting pregnancy'. A.S. Peake comments: 'And while the idea of the death at the hand of the messenger is extravagant, what but the extravagance could be expected in such an outburst as this?'

4. In Euripides' 'The Daughters of Troy' (*Euripides* I [Cambridge, MA: Harvard University Press, 1966], pp. 406-407), Andromache says:

> Mother, O mother, a fairer, truer word
> Hear, that I may with solace touch thine heart:—
> To have been unborn I count as one with death
> But better death than life in bitterness.

For early appearances of the 'wish never to have lived' in Greek and Hebrew sources, see the essay by David Daube entitled 'Black Hole', *RJ* 2 (1983), pp. 177-93. A song popular in America during the 1920s with the title 'I Wish I Had Died in My Cradle', written by Lew Brown and Max Friedman (New York: Shapiro, Bernstein, 1926), concluded with the words:

> I only wish someone had told me
> The love that you gave was untrue
> And I wish I had died in my cradle
> Before I grew up to love you.

5. For those who do not think Jeremiah addresses these words to Yahweh, see n. 8.

6. Sheldon Blank, *Jeremiah: Man and Prophet* (Cincinnati, OH: Hebrew Union College Press, 1961), p. 78.

7. Ulrich Zwingli, *Aus Zwinglis Predigten zu Jesaja und Jeremia* (Zurich: Berichthaus, 1957), p. 226.

We must recognize, too, before proceeding with any analysis of this poem, that subject matter alone requires *a priori* that Jeremiah be circumspect. Jeremiah cannot curse his mother or father (Exod. 21.17; Lev. 20.9). What he does is cite them indirectly, relating his mother to the fated day and his father to the fated messenger (vv. 14-15). Jeremiah also may not curse Yahweh (Exod. 22.27 [Eng. 28]; Lev. 24.10-16). Still he does manage to speak the Name, recalling who it was that overthrew Sodom and Gomorrah (v. 16). Jeremiah is also circumspect in that he does not explicitly address Yahweh as in the other confessions. Yet most agree that Yahweh is the addressee and that the question in v. 18 is directed at him.[8] Job, after broaching his birth question to an unspecified audience in Job 3.11, asks the same of Yahweh in 10.18.[9]

We begin our study by noting that there is no problem delimiting vv. 14-18 as a self-contained unit. Verses 13 and 18 contain early (i.e. pre-Masoretic) markings of closure, v. 13 the indicator ס, and v. 18 the indicator פ. Commentators too are in agreement that vv. 14-18 is a literary unit. The only puzzlement, which cannot be fully dealt with at the present time, is how vv. 14-18 relates to the verses preceding. This is an intriguing question to which various answers are given.[10] We may note simply that vv. 7-10 is another near-blasphemous confession and that vv. 11-12, to which an independent v. 13 has been added,[11] celebrates the prophet's deliverance from some danger that threatened him personally.

Rhetorical features of the poem have been described in my *Jeremiah: A Study in Ancient Hebrew Rhetoric*.[12] Briefly, the opening 'cursed be the day' (v. 14) balances 'cursed be the man' (v. 15). In classical rhetoric this repetition of אָרוּר ('cursed') would constitute an *anaphora*. Within v. 14 the beginning אָרוּר ('cursed') is contrasted by the final בָּרוּךְ ('blessed'). Within v. 15 the beginning אָרוּר ('cursed') contrasts the final שַׂמֵּחַ שִׂמֳּחָהוּ ('making him very glad'). These positive and negative terms set up a bitter irony

---

8. Baumgartner and Rudolph disagree, so also Blank, in 'The Confessions of Jeremiah and the Meaning of Prayer', *HUCA* 21 (1948), pp. 331, 351-53 n. 29. See further the discussion in Berridge *Prophet, People, and the Word of Yahweh*, pp. 38-39 n. 76.

9. Hitzig (*Jeremia*, p. 159) properly compares v. 18 with Job 10.18, a passage usually eclipsed by 3.11, yet one of great importance because here Job enters into open dialogue with Yahweh about why he was born.

10. Calvin discusses the relationship at some length. In his view, the controlling mood of chap. 20 is deliverance celebrated explicitly in v. 13. The expression in vv. 14-18 is what he felt *before* that deliverance took place. In my view vv. 7-18 is an editorial creation built in the same manner as the entire book of Lamentations. There words of faith and hope (3.19-39) are by design placed at the center. See further N. Gottwald, 'Lamentations', *Int* 9 (1955), pp. 330-35.

11. The end of v. 12 is marked as a closed (ס) section in the MT.

12. Lundbom, *Jeremiah: A Study in Ancient Hebrew Rhetoric*, pp. 46-48, 68 (1997 edn, pp. 65-67, 90).

about Jeremiah's birth. Something normally beautiful, something thought at an earlier time to be beautiful surely, is now loathsome and is rejected. The incongruity creates pathos in the audience. Keywords at the beginning and the end of successive double bicola make for literary closure, and for this reason I take v. 14 and v. 15 as verse units. The parallel structures of vv. 14 and 15, noted also by Ittmann,[13] give further indication of verbal and rhythmical sub-units in the poem. Verses 14, 15, and 16 all contain אֲשֶׁר in the same collocation, that is, beginning the second colon. Relative pronouns are, of course, always suspect in poetry;[14] consequently two of the three are deleted by Giesebrecht and Baumgartner. All, however, should remain. In this instance they are not prosaic overlay but an integral part of the poem. I do, incidentally, find evidence of prosaic overlay in v. 15 and will say more about that in a moment. But in poetry any word—even an אֲשֶׁר—should be retained as original when it appears the word is intentionally placed and when the poet seems also to have intended its repetition. There is another important אֲשֶׁר in v. 17—though it is the conjunction—and about that I will also say more in a moment. Finally, 'the day' (הַיּוֹם) in v. 14 makes an inclusio with 'my days' (יָמָי) in v. 18.

Turning now to content we see that vv. 14 and 15 announce the respective curses but do not fill them out. The 'filling out'—and then of only one of the curses—comes in v. 16. The same style of articulation is found in 17.5-6. In v. 16 we see that the curse is a simile type, known also from the ancient Near Eastern treaties.[15] A disagreement prevails, however, as to which curse is being brought to completion. Is it the curse on the man as the text states, or the curse on the day as Duhm and his followers argue? Duhm deleted 'this man' in v. 16 as a gloss and took v. 16 to be a continuation of v. 14. The subject of וְהָיָה (v. 16) was 'the day' (v. 14): 'Let (the day) be like the cities...' Verse 15 was merely 'ein Anhängsel' to v. 14, which contained the main point. Duhm simply wanted a closer parallel to Job 3.3-10, where the curse is on the day. In either case—whether Duhm is to be followed or the received text is to be read—only *one* of the two curses is fully articulated. Verse 17 is commonly labeled the 'reason' or 'motivation' for the curse of v. 16 (Ittmann).

One further observation on content. It has been argued, on the basis of vocabulary primarily, that v. 18 is a lament.[16] Form-critically then, the

---

13. Ittmann, *Die Konfessionen Jeremias*, p. 26.
14. G.A. Smith, *The Early Poetry of Israel and Its Physical and Social Origins* (London: British Academy and Oxford University Press, 1912), p. 11.
15. Delbert Hillers, *Treaty-Curses and the Old Testament Prophets* (Rome: Pontifical Biblical Institute, 1964), pp. 18-26, 74-76.
16. So Baumgartner, *Jeremiah's Poems of Lament*, p. 77, and Berridge, *Prophet, People, and the Word of Yahweh*, p. 39 n. 76.

structure of the confession contains roughly four parts: (a) the announcement of the double curse (vv. 14-15); (b) the completion of one of the curses (v. 16); (c) the reason for the completed curse (v. 17); (d) the final lament (v. 18).

The poem, as was mentioned earlier, has versification. Here I follow Volz, who makes a division into five parts (strophes). These coincide with the units delimited by our present verse numbers.[17] I prefer, however, with *BHK* and *BHS*, to scan vv. 14, 15, and 16 as double bicola, not tricola. Also in v. 15ab I take אֶת and along with Baumgartner לֵאמֹר as prosaic overlay and suggest we delete. With these minor adjustments the syllable counts for vv. 14 and 15 are as follows:

v. 14   4 : 6 = 10
                        24
         9 : 5 = 14

v. 15   4 : 6 = 10
                        24
         7 : 7 = 14

Verse 16 is longer. Reading the MT without alteration we have a syllable count for this verse as follows:

v. 16   10 : 10 = 20
                          38
         9 : 9 = 18

Verse 17 as it stands is three cola. The first colon is 10 syllables, the second 8, and the third 7. Verse 18 is also three cola, the first colon 9, the second 7, and the third 8. Totals are 25 (v. 17) and 24 (v. 18). We could proceed further to discuss a possible metrical structure for the entire poem and propose certain minor textual adjustments that would sharpen up the correspondences, but that we will forgo until after we have dealt with v. 17 and the problem of the messenger.

Most commentators perceive problems in vv. 16-17. Attention has focused mainly on the messenger who brings the news of Jeremiah's birth to his father. Duhm objects that the poem should occupy itself so long with the messenger—so much so that the messenger becomes the focal person. Duhm also does not think the messenger should be reproached for failing to kill the young babe. Both points are well taken. Even Keil and Peake sense some difficulty here, when they argue that a highly emotional cry need not be rational or coherent. Less compelling is Duhm's objection to the comparison between a man and a pair of cities, namely, Sodom

---

17. Volz, *Studien zum Text des Jeremia*, p. 174.

and Gomorrah.¹⁸ Duhm, nevertheless, has gained an impressive following with his emendation of v. 16,¹⁹ in part, no doubt, because of the parallel drawn to Job 3.3-10, but also because he relieves a hapless messenger of an admittedly heavy burden.²⁰

Two problems have been noted in v. 17. The first is how to read MT מֵרָחֶם. Though the preposition *min* normally means 'from', virtually everyone agrees that we must follow the LXX (ἐν μήτρᾳ μητρὸς) and the Syriac and translate 'in the womb'. Proposals for arriving at this reading vary.²¹ If we were to translate 'from the womb'—the idea being that death was expected to come at the moment of birth or shortly thereafter—an inconsistency would be created with the remainder of the verse, for there it states that the womb is to be for the dead babe a grave.

The other problem concerns the subject for לֹא־מוֹתְתַנִי ('he did not kill me'). If v. 17 expands the curse of v. 16 and provides for it a reason, the subject would naturally be the man (the messenger). But that is just our problem, for the man is an unsuitable candidate and it is a recognition of this fact that has sent commentators in search of alternate explanations. Duhm thinks custom would have dictated that it be a doctor. Prijs prefers to leave the subject indefinite, saying simply that it is whoever had the right to bring about the death.²² It could have been an angel of death or even God. These latter possibilities are supported by certain medieval Jewish commentators. Rashi (1040–1105 CE) supplied מלאך המות after מוֹתְתַנִי; Isaiah di Trani (d. c. CE 1280) supplied המלאך המותת. David Kimchi (1160–1235 CE?) thought the subject was God, who in Job's case did not shut the doors of his mother's womb (Job 3.10). In the nineteenth-century Henderson identified Yahweh as the subject, pointing out that he is named explicitly in the preceding verse. But no other commentator, so far as I know, has

---

18. Hillers rightly points out that Duhm does not really eliminate this problem, for the analogy he substitutes is every bit as opaque as the one he gets rid of; see Hillers, *Treaty-Curses and the Old Testament Prophets*, p. 75 n. 85.

19. Baumgartner adopted Duhm's proposal as is; a larger number (Volz, Rudolph, Couturier and others) accepted it as modified by Cornill. Cornill added 'that day' to give the improved reading, 'Let that day be like the cities.' Giesebrecht preferred the substitution of 'curse' for 'that man'.

20. This latter point is picked up by Rudolph (*Jeremia*, p. 132) and Couturier.

21. Hitzig, Henderson, and Keil interpret מֵרָחֶם to mean 'from the time still in the womb'. More recent scholars (Duhm, Cornill, Giesebrecht, Peake, Streane, Baumgartner, Condamin and Rudolph) emend to בְּרֶחֶם. Dahood repointed to מְרֻחָם and translated 'enwombed' ('Denominative riḥḥam, "to conceive, enwomb"', *Biblica* 44 [1963], pp. 204-205). Bright accepted this solution. Marvin Pope has suggested to me that since *bᵉ* and *min* are interchangeable in Ugaritic, *min* here could mean 'in'. See Pope's remarks in *Song of Songs* (AB, 7c; Garden City, NY: Doubleday, 1977), p. 518; cf. M. Dahood, *Psalms III* (AB, 17a; Garden City, NY: Doubleday, 1970), pp. 397-98.

22. Prijs, 'Jeremia XX 14ff.', pp. 104-108.

picked up on the idea that God might have been expected to kill Jeremiah in the womb.[23]

In my view, the problem lies with v. 17. No change is required in v. 16. That verse is a straightforward curse on the man, which follows and expands upon v. 15. My proposal is that v. 17 is the 'missing' curse on the day and that a colon has either dropped out or been dropped out at the beginning of the verse, which would have gone something like:

וְהָיָה הַיּוֹם הַהוּא כְּ_____

And let that day be like_____

Some famous day—a day of battle perhaps—was originally recalled by Jeremiah in order that he might compare it with his day of birth. The following considerations are put forth in support of this proposal: (1) The announcement of a double curse would seem to require the full articulation of a double curse. (2) If v. 17 is a filling out of the curse on the day instead of a reason for the curse on the man, continuity is broken between v. 16 and v. 17, which is precisely what we need if the problem of the messenger is to be eliminated. Stated positively, other subjects are now available for לֹא־מוֹתְתַנִי. (3) Verse 17 as it now stands begins with אֲשֶׁר, which is awkward. But with a prior colon in the verse this colon with the אֲשֶׁר is moved to the second position and the אֲשֶׁר is then in the same collocation as in vv. 14, 15, and 16. From a rhetorical point of view, this means an improvement of v. 17 as well as an improvement of the poem as a whole. (4) If v. 17 fills out the curse on the day, we have a chiasmus in vv. 14-17: day/man/man/day. Rhetorically this is another improvement for the whole poem. (5) With an additional colon in v. 17 the syllable count of this verse is more closely matched with v. 16, the verse to which it is parallel form-critically according to the revised scheme.

The first point is really the most important. The confession announces a double curse, but the poem as it now stands articulates only one curse in full: the curse on the man. The need for a full articulation of the curse on the day is required; Duhm sensed this and so did others who accepted his reinterpretation.

The colon proposed for v. 17a is modeled quite deliberately on וְהָיָה הָאִישׁ הַהוּא כֶּעָרִים in v. 16a. Verses 14 and 15, as already noted, are parallel and finely balanced. The prophets are known elsewhere to have spoken of significant 'days'. Isaiah remembered the 'Day of Midian' (Isa. 9.3 [Eng. 4]; cf. Judges 6–7); Hosea talked about the 'Day of Jezreel' (Hos. 1.11), and Ezekiel the 'Day of Egypt' (Ezek. 30.9). The 'Day of Jerusalem' is mentioned in Ps. 137.7.[24] An intriguing possibility here for Jeremiah would be

---

23. Rudolph explicitly rejects the idea, as does Keil earlier.
24. For Israel's memory of decisive days, see J. Muilenburg, 'The Biblical View of Time', *HTR* 54 (1961), p. 238.

an *earlier* 'Day of Midian' described in Num. 31.1-20. Israel on this day defeated the Midianites under Moses. It was the battle in which Balaam, the son of Beor, was killed. The victory however was tainted because soldiers were commanded to kill Midianite women and children and did not do it. As a result Moses judged them with severity. Included among this number would certainly have been some women who were pregnant. Had Jeremiah, say, recalled this particular day, the curse in v. 17 would have gone:

> And let that day be like Midian
> because he did not kill me in the womb
> So my mother would have been my grave
> and her womb forever great.

Suggestive as this is, particularly when it has Jeremiah building on a tradition about Moses, I make it only for purposes of concretizing my proposal. The proposal does not rest ultimately on the thesis that Midian stood originally in the text. I do think a colon now lost filled out the curse on the day, and I consider it possible that a curse formula similar to the one in v. 16a made mention in v. 17a of *some* particular day.

We must now address the question of who was to have killed Jeremiah in the womb. It is not the messenger of vv. 15-16. Was Jeremiah thinking perhaps of a soldier who in the heat of battle refrained from violating his pregnant mother when he could have violated her (cf. Amos 1.13)? This is possible. The subject of לֹא־מוֹתְתַנִי would then be indefinite and a comparison between some recent battle and one of the type described in Num. 31.1-20 would have to be assumed. Unspecified antecedents are known to exist in biblical Hebrew,[25] and because the subject here is delicate we should not be surprised to find the person going unnamed. Duhm's suggestion that a doctor would be the one to intervene is unlikely. We know of course from the Ebers Papyrus (c. 1550 BCE) that abortifacients were prescribed by doctors of ancient Egypt,[26] also that abortions were common during the Golden Age of Greece,[27] but whether medical abortions of any sort were performed in Israel during the seventh- and sixth-centuries BCE—or at any other time during the ancient Israelite period for that matter—is highly questionable. There is no evidence from the OT that Israel had indigenous doctors;[28] in

---

25. E.g. וַיֹּאמֶר לְיוֹסֵף in Gen. 48.1, and the classic וַיִּקְבֹּר אֹתוֹ in Deut. 34.6, about which later rabbis taught that Yahweh buried Moses.

26. C.P. Bryan (trans.), *The Papyrus Ebers* (trans. C.P. Bryan; New York: D. Appleton, 1931), p. 83.

27. Plato, *Republic* 5.461; Aristotle, *Politics* 7.14. The Hippocratic Oath (c. 400 BCE) forswears the use of any abortifacients; see further J.T. Noonan, 'An Almost Absolute Value in History', in *The Morality of Abortion* (ed. J.T. Noonan; Cambridge, MA: Harvard University Press, 1970), pp. 3-5.

28. Ancient Hebrew does not even have a noun for 'doctor'; it uses simply the

fact, it appears rather than Yahweh is the only real doctor for his people (Exod. 15.26; 2 Kgs 20.5; Ps. 103.3; cf. Deut. 32.39).[29] Not until we come to Sirach in the second century BCE do we find in Israel a passage extolling the virtues of the human doctor (Sir. 38.1-15).

The restructuring of v. 17 requires, I think, that we consider with new seriousness the idea that Jeremiah wanted Yahweh to kill him in the womb. With the colon 'because he did not kill me in the womb' in the second position in the verse instead of the first, that is, in v. 17ab, an association is natural with v. 16ab, 'which Yahweh overthrew without pity'. Henderson, I believe, has correctly located the subject for 'he did not kill me' in this prior colon: it is Yahweh. The thought goes as follows: Yahweh did overthrow the cities of Sodom and Gomorrah, but Jeremiah he did not overthrow. A variation of this very same theme appears in the promise of 1.13-19. There Yahweh says he will overthrow Jerusalem and its neighboring cities (v. 15), but Jeremiah he will not overthrow (v. 19). Jeremiah, it seems, is struggling in this confession with his earlier promise from Yahweh. In one dark moment he says he would just as soon forget it.

A word now about textual omissions. Critical scholarship of an earlier generation was preoccupied with textual *expansion*. The assumption was that the text contained what was originally spoken or written and something more, or, where ancient texts varied, the shorter version was the earlier or the more original. This *tendenz* impacted Jeremiah in a significant way, for there the LXX is one-eighth shorter than the Hebrew MT. It therefore must be the more original text.[30] Yet we have learned that the biblical text suffers

---

participial forms רֹפֵא and רֹפְאִים ('healer/healers'). When these terms denote human healers they are always foreigners (Gen. 50.2; Jer. 8.22; 2 Chron. 16.12; Job 13.4), and except for Gen. 50.2 such individuals are spoken of disparagingly.

29. The priest is a one-man health department when it comes to controlling the spread of diseases such as leprosy; otherwise he does not function in the role of doctor; see C. Weiss, 'Medicine in the Bible', *Scientific Monthly* 50 (1940), pp. 266-71. Yet it is entirely possible that the 'ordeal of jealousy' (Num. 5), over which the priest presides, could bring about an abortion. Abortion is suggested by the euphemistic expression of the 'thigh falling away'; see Freedman, Lundbom, 'beṭen', in *TDOT* 2 (Grand Rapids: Eerdmans, 1975), p. 98; G.B. Gray, *Numbers* (ICC; Edinburgh: T. & T. Clark, 1903), p. 48, who cites the view of H.W. Robinson; G.R. Driver, 'Two Problems in the Old Testament Examined in the Light of Assyriology', *Syria* 33 (1956), pp. 73-77; W. McKane, 'Poison, Trial by Ordeal and the Cup of Wrath', *VT* 30 (1980), pp. 474-78. According to Weiss, only the prophets practiced the art of healing, and even then they did so only on occasion. E. Neufeld, however, thinks that ancient Israel's medical practitioners were apothecaries who were organized into guilds (see Neh. 3.8) ('Hygiene Conditions in Ancient Israel [Iron Age]', *Journal of the History of Medicine and Allied Sciences* 25 [1970], pp. 428-29).

30. So F.M. Cross, 'The History of the Biblical Text in the Light of Discoveries in the Judean Desert', *HTR* 57 (1964), pp. 289-99; J.G. Janzen, *Studies in the Text of Jeremiah* (Cambridge, MA: Harvard University Press, 1973), p. 135.

just as much from omissions. Twenty-five years ago W.F. Albright, discussing Deut. 32.43, which in the Qumran text exceeds the MT by two cola and in the LXX exceeds it by four cola, had this to say about textual omissions:

> The seventh colon seems to have vanished from all our recensions, leaving the eighth colon a torso which may be variously interpreted. Of course, I should not insist on the correctness of my point of view, but it does accord with the increasing evidence from the Qumran Scrolls that our Hebrew originals, once edited in antiquity, suffered far more from omissions by copyists than from additions.[31]

Albright is directing his comments to the subject of textual transmission and is probably referring to omissions of an involuntary sort, for example, haplography, copying from incomplete manuscripts, etc. Nevertheless it is notoriously difficult, as any text critic knows, to decide to what extent scribal activity bears marks of intentionality. Now and then we make judgments on intentionality, for example, that someone intentionally omitted the substance of an argument between Cain and Abel in Gen. 4.8.

Here in Jer. 20.17 it is not hard to imagine why a colon such as the one we propose was deliberately omitted. It is infelicitous, to say the least, for Jeremiah to curse his birthday because Yahweh did not kill him in the womb. We said earlier that the line between blasphemy and nonblasphemy was a fine one with Jeremiah—that 'Prometheus' of ancient Israel.[32] For other ears, however, particularly those in a theological community, that line is more easily crossed, and when this happens the offense must somehow be removed. The chosen solution, I think, was to drop the colon beginning the curse on the day. This left a truncated v. 17 to continue the curse of v. 16, and the messenger was now made to carry an added burden for an added offense. I suppose also that by excising the curse from the text there would be the added effect of 'breaking' it, no small consideration surely for a tradition that must preserve Jeremiah from gross sin. Yet, as we noted, certain medieval Jewish commentators retained the original idea of divine intervention in the womb.

The addition of a colon at the beginning of v. 17 alters the poem's poetical, rhetorical, and formal structures. Though it is certainly possible for a poetic line to begin with אֲשֶׁר (see 5.22b; 8.17b; 13.25b; Job 9.15, 17), it is unlikely here because 17a begins a verse. I know of nowhere else in Jeremiah where this happens. Duhm proposed we read instead יַעַן אֲשֶׁר. But when the first colon of the verse is shifted to the second position, the entire poem benefits by another repetition of אֲשֶׁר:

---

31. W.F. Albright, 'Some Remarks on the Song of Moses in Deuteronomy XXXII', *VT* 9 (1959), p. 341.

32. S.H. Blank, 'Men against God—The Promethean Element in Biblical Prayer', *JBL* 72 (1953), pp. 1-13.

¹⁴Cursed be the day
   on which (אֲשֶׁר)...
¹⁵Cursed be the man
   who (אֲשֶׁר)...
¹⁶Let that man be like the cities
   which (אֲשֶׁר)...
¹⁷Let that day be like (Midian)
   because (אֲשֶׁר)...

The poem also contains a nice chiasmus: day/man/man/day.[33] The curse on the man follows a normal (or should we say expected) sequence. Its announcement is completed in the next verse. Both verses speak about delivered messages: v. 15 a birth report, v. 16 a war alert. The first curse, however, has to wait for completion until after the second curse is spoken in full. Verse 17 then completes the curse on the day, and in it Jeremiah comments once again on his mother. This hiatus—also the inversion of completions—is what makes the poem rhetorically noteworthy. Chiastic arrangements are now well known in Hebrew rhetoric[34] and are amply documented in other speeches of Jeremiah.[35]

An additional colon in v. 17 also changes its syllable count:

   v. 17   10 : 10 = 20
                               35
                8 : 7 = 15

The verse is now brought into line with v. 16, to which it is parallel in content. This represents another improvement structurally speaking. In my earlier study of this confession I suggested that v. 18 might also be minus a colon, in this case a second one beginning with אֲשֶׁר.[36] The entire poem would then consist of bicolic lines with each second colon of the verse beginning with אֲשֶׁר. I was impressed at the time with similarities between this poem and the one in 14.2-6.[37] I am now, however, open to the possibility that v. 18 may deliberately be shorter since it is a lament. On a smaller scale there is the well-known Qina rhythm of the bicolon, which measures 3.2 according to the stress system of Hebrew metrification. Here a tricolon following four double bicola serves in a similar way as a retardant. Only in this case it is for the poem as a whole.

---

33. Holladay finds a slightly different chiasmus in vv. 14-18 (*The Architecture of Jeremiah 1–20*, p. 133).

34. See most recently J.W. Welch (ed.), *Chiasmus in Antiquity* (Hildesheim: Gerstenberg, 1981).

35. Lundbom, *Jeremiah: A Study in Ancient Hebrew Rhetoric*, chap. 3.

36. Lundbom, *Jeremiah: A Study in Ancient Hebrew Rhetoric*, p. 47 (1997 edn, p. 65).

37. Lundbom, *Jeremiah: A Study in Ancient Hebrew Rhetoric*, pp. 67-68 (1997 edn, pp. 90-91).

23. The Double Curse in Jeremiah 20.14-18

It remains only to revise our form-critical structure from one having four parts to one with only three—though one may argue that the first two parts are really only one genre, namely, the curse. At any rate, the 'reason' is eliminated and we are left with the following content: (a) the announcement of the double curse (vv. 14-15); (b) the completion of the double curse (vv. 16-17); (c) the final lament (v. 18).

The whole poem I read as follows:

> ¹⁴Cursed be the day
>   on which I was born
> The day when my mother bore me
>   let it not be blessed.
>
> ¹⁵Cursed be the man
>   who brought the news to my father
> 'A son is born to you'
>   making him very glad.
>
> ¹⁶Let that man be like the cities
>   which Yahweh overthrew without pity.
> Let him hear a cry in the morning
>   and an alarm at noon.
>
> ¹⁷*Let that day be like (Midian)*
>   because he did not kill me in the womb
> So my mother would have been my grave
>   and her womb forever great.
>
> ¹⁸Why did I come forth from the womb
>   to see toil and sorrow
>   and end in shame my days?

If this proposal has merit, the confession is even more extreme than we had thought, for Jeremiah—in spite of language that is still nondirect—blames Yahweh for not killing him in the womb. Tradition, however, must temper bold (not to say reckless) statements made by its outstanding individuals. In this case, the modulation came early. Another modulation of this desperate cry appears extant in the text where it serves a function in composition. I refer to the way 1.5 is made to answer 20.18 in the first edition of the book of Jeremiah.[38] This bit of editorial handiwork takes the affirming words of Jeremiah's call and has them answer—or not answer, as the

---

38. I proposed in *Jeremiah: A Study in Ancient Hebrew Rhetoric*, pp. 29-30 (1997 edn, pp. 43-44) that chaps. 1–20 might be the *Urrolle*. That view has more support now in light of the recent study by L. Hicks, 'DELET and MᶜGILLĀH: A Fresh Approach to Jeremiah xxxvi', *VT* 33 (1983), pp. 46-66. Judging from the way scrolls were made in antiquity, Hicks estimates that the original scroll of Jer. 36 was between 18 and 24 MT chapters of Jeremiah (p. 66).

case may be—Jeremiah's deep existential question.[39] Jeremiah was born, the scribe-turned-theologian tells us, because Yahweh called him before he was born. The controlling theology of this early book of Jeremiah is then more or less on a par with the controlling theology of the early book of Job (3.1–42.6), from which we learn also that the ways of the Almighty are ultimately unknowable and inscrutable.

---

39. See my discussion of divine-human discourse in 'God's Use of the *Idem per Idem* to Terminate Debate', *HTR* 71 (1978), pp. 193-201.

Chapter 24

NEW COVENANT IN JEREMIAH AND LATER JUDAISM*

The term 'new covenant' occurs in Jer. 31.31, and only there in the Old Testament, denoting the basis on which a future relationship between God and his people will rest following the collapse of the Sinai (Mosaic) covenant and Israel's loss of nationhood in 587/6 BCE. This new relationship, which God himself will create, is anticipated in other terms by Jeremiah (24.7; 32.38-40; 50.5) and also by Ezekiel (Ezek. 16.60; 34.25; 36.27-28; 37.26), Second Isaiah (Isa. 42.6; 49.8; 54.10; 55.1-5; 59.21; 61.8), and Malachi (Mal. 3.1; cf. 2.1-9). The new covenant forms the centerpiece of a larger eschatological hope that includes a new act of salvation, a new Zion, and a new Davidic king. The belief in a new covenant existed among the Essenes of Qumran, but it was the Christian Church that laid real claim to Jeremiah's promise, establishing the new covenant finally as its charter of faith. In the New Testament the phrase 'new covenant' appears in Luke (22.20), in Paul's Corinthian correspondence (1 Cor. 11.25; 2 Cor. 3.6), and in the Letter to the Hebrews (Heb. 8.8, 13; 9.15; 'fresh covenant' in 12.24).

The New Covenant in Jeremiah

The new covenant prophecy in Jer. 31.31-34 is one of four brief eschatological sayings concluding an earlier edition of Jeremiah's Book of Restoration (chaps. 30–31). A rhetorical structure calls attention to the eschatological nature of these utterances ('Look days are coming' in 31.27, 31, 38; cf. 30.3), and indicates that the promised future will contain both continuity and discontinuity with the past (עוֹד, 'again' in 31.23, 39; and לֹא...עוֹד, 'not…again' in 31.29, 34a, 34b, 40).[1] Discontinuity gets the accent in the new covenant passage. Whereas the *torah* will remain in the new covenant and the obligation to comply with its demands will still exist, conditions

---

* First published in *ABD* 4 (New York: Doubleday, 1992), pp. 1088-90; repr. in *Jeremiah 21–36* (AB 21B; New York: Doubleday, 2004), pp. 465-74.

1. Jack R. Lundbom, *Jeremiah: A Study in Ancient Hebrew Rhetoric* (SBLDS, 18; Missoula, MT: Society of Biblical Literature and Scholars Press, 1975), pp. 32-36 (1997 edn, pp. 47-52).

for compliance will be vastly improved, because God promises to write his *torah* on the human heart.

Scholars have considered two related questions when discussing the concept of a 'new' covenant: (1) whether this covenant really is 'new'; and (2) whether the Sinai covenant, over against which the new covenant stands, continues to be viable. Zimmerli believes that Jeremiah announces the end of the Sinai covenant.[2] Von Rad agrees that the old covenant really was broken and that there is no attempt here, as in Deuteronomy, to re-establish it on the old bases; nevertheless, the revelation it contained is not nullified in whole or in part.[3] So far as content goes, the new covenant neither alters nor expands the old. What may certainly be said is that for Jeremiah the gulf between the new covenant and the Sinai covenant is greater than for any who preceded him. In my view, the new covenant cannot be reduced to a renewed Sinai covenant, such as took place on the plains of Moab (Deut. 5.2-3; 28.69 [29.1]), at Shechem (Joshua 24), or in Jerusalem at the climax of the Josianic Reform (2 Kings 23). Although this new covenant will have admitted continuity with the Sinai covenant, it will still be a genuinely new covenant, one that marks a new beginning in the divine-human relationship because (1) it is given without conditions, and is therefore eternal (cf. Jer. 32.40); (2) it will be written in the hearts of people in a way the Sinai covenant was not; and (3) it will be grounded in a wholly new act of divine grace, which is the forgiveness of sins (Jer. 31.34; cf. Ezek. 36.25-28).

The forgiveness of sins is not what undergirded the Sinai covenant; in fact, it played no part at all in that covenant's earliest formulation, or in the formulation of Deuteronomy. The act of divine grace undergirding the Sinai covenant was the deliverance from Egypt (Exod. 20.2; Deut. 5.6). In Deuteronomy, the nation is promised life if it obeys the covenant; if it does not obey, Yahweh will rain down a multitude of curses, the most serious of which will be the loss of the land. The essential Deuteronomy (chaps. 1–28) makes no provision for a restored divine-human relationship once the covenant is broken and the curses have fallen (Deut. 4.29-31 bases Yahweh's mercy on a remembrance of the covenant with the fathers—i.e., the Abrahamic covenant). Disobedience, says von Rad, is not the problem for Deuteronomy that it later became for Jeremiah and Ezekiel.[4] Deuteronomic theology is best summed up in Joshua's words to the people at Shechem: If you disobey the covenant, Yahweh will *not* forgive your sins; instead he will punish you (Josh. 24.19-20). This theology is carried over into the Holiness Code (Lev. 26.14-20), although there, provisions are made for the

---

2. W. Zimmerli, *The Law and the Prophets* (Oxford: Blackwell, 1965), p. 80.
3. G. von Rad, *Old Testament Theology* II (Edinburgh: Oliver & Boyd, 1965), pp. 212-13.
4. Von Rad, *Old Testament Theology* II, p. 270.

forgiveness of sins, after which Yahweh will begin again with Israel on the basis of his covenant with Abraham (Isaac and Jacob), and his remembrance of the land (Lev. 26.40-45).

The new covenant is new because Yahweh's *torah* will be written on the human heart.[5] The Sinai covenant was written on tablets of stone (Exod. 24.12; 31.18 *et passim*). In the homiletical rhetoric of Deuteronomy, however, the *torah* was supposed to find its way into the human heart (Deut. 6.6; 11.18; 30.11-14). But Deuteronomy knows—as does Jeremiah—that the heart is deceitful and layered with evil (Deut. 10.16; 11.16; Jer. 4.4). Jeremiah is the more negative in assessing the human condition. He says the heart is evil, stubborn, and rebellious (5.23), that sin is 'engraved' on the tablet of the heart (17.1), and that the heart is 'deceitful above all things' (17.9). In addition, he believes that the people have not the ability within themselves to make their relationship with God right again (2.25; 13.23).[6] Nevertheless, prior 'heart talk' in Deuteronomy and Jeremiah is background for and determines the articulation of the new covenant promise. If the law did not penetrate the human heart before, and this might still be debated (Ps. 119.11), it will with the new covenant in place, because Yahweh promises to make it happen (cf. Isa. 51.7). Jeremiah, on another occasion, says that Yahweh will give Israel a (new) heart to know him (24.7; cf. Deut. 30.6). Ezekiel expects for Israel a new heart and a new spirit (Ezek. 11.19; 18.31; 36.26), although in 18.31 people are told to make both for themselves—a demand, needless to say, incapable of fulfillment. Ezekiel alone imagines that human beings will have such a capacity.[7] The new heart and new spirit are otherwise understood to be gifts of divine grace.

According to ancient Hebrew thought, the 'will' took up residence within the heart,[8] so if the *torah* is to be written on the human heart, people will have the will to obey it. Moreover, they will no longer have to admonish one another to 'Know Yahweh!', for everyone will know him (Jer. 31.34). 'Knowing Yahweh' here as elsewhere requires the expanded meaning of 'knowing and doing the *torah*' (Hos. 4.1-2; Jer. 5.4-5). In Deuteronomy, people must continually be told, 'Be careful to do (the commands)' (5.1, 32; 6.3, 25; etc.), 'Take heed...lest you forget the covenant/Yahweh' (4.23; 6.12; 8.11; etc.). The liturgical injunctions in 6.6-9 and 11.18-20 admonish

5. Von Rad, *Old Testament Theology* II, pp. 213-14; M. Weinfeld, 'Jeremiah and the Spiritual Metamorphosis of Israel', *ZAW* 88 (1976), p. 28; H.W. Wolff, *Confrontation with Prophets* (Philadelphia, PA: Fortress Press, 1983), p. 54.
6. Von Rad, *Old Testament Theology* II, pp. 216-17; Bernard P. Robinson, 'Jeremiah's New Covenant: Jer 31, 31-34', *SJOT* 15 (2001), pp. 181-204.
7. M. Greenberg, *Ezekiel 1–20* (AB, 22; Garden City, NY: Doubleday, 1983), p. 341.
8. A.R. Johnson, *The Vitality of the Individual in the Thought of Ancient Israel* (Cardiff: University of Wales, 1964), pp. 77-79.

them also to keep Yahweh's words in their hearts as well as in other more conspicuous places. But in the end, admonitions such as these and more from the prophets were made to no avail. Disobedience exceeded all limits, and the Sinai covenant was undone.

In Jer. 32.37-41, which is a parallel passage to 31.31-34,[9] the covenant of the future is described as an 'eternal covenant' (בְּרִית עוֹלָם). The term 'eternal covenant' appears also in Jer. 50.2. Prior to this, only the unconditional covenants given to Noah, Abraham, Phinehas, and David were taken to be eternal.[10] Unconditional covenants were at home in southern theology, that is, in P traditions (Gen. 9.16; 17.7, 13, 19; Exod. 31.16; Lev. 24.8; Num. 18.19; 25.13) and psalms from the Jerusalem temple (Pss. 89.20-38 [Eng. 19-37]; 111.5, 9; cf. 2 Sam. 23.5). At some point before the Exile, possibly as a result of preaching by Isaiah, the covenants to Abraham and David were expanded so as to cover Jerusalem and the Temple (Isa. 37.33-35 = 2 Kgs 19.32-34; Pss. 105.8-11 = 1 Chron. 16.15-18; 132.11-18; cf. Isa. 31.4-5; Jer. 7.1-15). Ezekiel and Second Isaiah look forward to an eternal covenant between Yahweh and the nation (Ezek. 16.60; Isa. 55.3; 61.8), which they describe elsewhere as a 'covenant of peace' (Ezek. 34.25; 37.26; Isa. 54.10), or one in which Yahweh's Spirit will indwell the people (Ezek. 36.27-28; Isa. 59.21). These varied descriptions of the future covenant were part of the larger messianic hope taking shape at the time. The servant figure of Second Isaiah will personally embody the new covenant (Isa. 42.6; 49.8), and through this servant other nations will be brought into covenant relationship (Isa. 55.1-5).[11] One finds a universalism in Second Isaiah not present in Ezekiel. Finally, Malachi's 'messenger of the covenant' is cast as a priestly figure (Mal. 3.1; cf. 2.1-9).

The New Covenant in Later Judaism

In postexilic Judaism the covenant idea contains all the ambiguities characterizing the larger eschatological hope generally. National life has been reconstructed along the old lines, which is to say the Sinai covenant is again central, and the Law (*torah*) occupies a position of supremacy. In Nehemiah 9-10 a 'faith covenant' (אֲמָנָה in 10.1 [9.38]) is made to walk according to Yahweh's *torah* given through Moses. Ezra prays that the people will thereby return to the 'faithful heart' of Abraham (Ezra 9.7-8). At the same

---

9. Von Rad, *Old Testament Theology* II, p. 214.
10. D.N. Freedman, 'Divine Commitment and Human Obligation', *Int* 18 (1964), pp. 419-31 (repr. in *Divine Commitment and Human Obligation* I [ed. John R. Huddlestun; Grand Rapids, MI: Eerdmans, 1997], pp. 168-78).
11. J. Muilenburg, 'Isaiah', *IB* 5 (ed. George A. Buttrick; New York: Abingdon Press, 1956), p. 405.

time a new covenant is looked for in the future, at which time the Messianic Age will dawn. Bar. 2.35 speaks of an eternal covenant that will secure Israel's tenure in the land. In *Jubilees*, where the Law has eternal validity and the Messianic Age is thought to have already begun, an eternal covenant is described in which the people on their part will confess sin, and God on his part will create a holy spirit in the people and will cleanse them (*Jub.* 1.22-24).

Among the Essenes at Qumran, the new covenant finds fulfillment in a separated community (*yḥd*) that believes it is living in the 'last days'. This community has important similarities to the early Church. Members of the Qumran community swore an oath to uphold a covenant variously described as a 'covenant of God', an 'eternal covenant', a 'covenant of repentance', a 'covenant of steadfast love' (*ḥsd*), and a 'new covenant'. Essene covenant theology is contained in two sectarian documents found among the Dead Sea Scrolls: the *Rule of the Community* (1QS), known earlier as the *Manual of Discipline*, and the *Damascus Document* (CD), earlier called the *Zadokite Document*. The latter was known before the Dead Sea discoveries, two fragmentary medieval codices having been found in the genizah of the Cairo Synagogue in 1896, which were published in 1910.[12] The *Damascus Document* contains three references to a 'new covenant' that people have entered into 'in the land of Damascus', a cryptonym for their place of exile in the Qumran desert (cf. Amos 5.26-27).[13] Seven manuscripts of the *Damascus Document* were found in Cave 4, some tiny fragments also in Caves 5 and 6.[14] Also, in the *Pesher on Habakkuk* found at Qumran (1QpHab), there may originally have been a reference to the 'new covenant' in 2.3; however, the manuscript has a lacuna where scholars think 'covenant' once stood, leaving the reading uncertain and opinions about it divided.

The Essene Jews who separated themselves from the rest of Judaism and relocated in the Qumran desert did so in order to be reborn as the New Israel. According to Frank Cross, the word 'community' (*yḥd*) as used in the *Rule of the Community* is eschatological, that is, it means 'Israel of the New Covenant'.[15] People entering this new covenant were required to return to a serious study of the Mosaic Law. Required also of each member was strict obedience to the Law's demands as understood in light of interpretations

---

12. R.H. Charles, *The Apocrypha and Pseudepigrapha of the Old Testament* II (Oxford: Clarendon Press, 1913), pp. 785-834; C. Rabin, *The Zadokite Document* (Oxford: Clarendon Press, 1958).

13. These 'new covenant' references are CD 6.19; 8.21 = 19.33/34; and 20.12 in Rabin, *The Zadokite Document* and 8.15; 9.28, 37 in Charles, *APOT* II.

14. F.M. Cross, *The Ancient Library of Qumran* (Sheffield: Sheffield Academic Press, 1995), p. 72; *IDBSup*, p. 210.

15. Cross, *The Ancient Library of Qumran*, p. 71.

given by the priestly hierarchy. At the top of this hierarchy was the Teacher of Righteousness, the original leader of the sect and the author, perhaps, of the *Rule of the Community*. The *Damascus Document* is from a later period, after the Teacher's death.[16] The community bore an unmistakable stamp of legalism; nevertheless, that legalism was informed by the prophets, whose great legacy at Qumran was the conviction that sin lay deep within the human soul and only through repentance and purification was a restored relationship with God possible. The *Damascus Document* in 19.16 called the Qumran covenant a 'covenant of repentance' (*bryt hšwbh*). Repentance had to precede purification, which was accomplished in the initiatory baptismal rite.[17]

This new covenant was to be eternal. Whatever else this signified, it at least meant that anyone entering the covenant was expected to remain within it for life (1QS 3.11-12). The covenant was renewed annually, at which time all members underwent evaluation. This covenant had its obligations, and like the Sinai covenant, these obligations were fortified with blessings and curses (1QS 2.1-18). The *Rule of the Community* reads much like Deuteronomy. The main difference between the two is that in the former the older corporate sense is gone; the blessings and curses, for example, fall now upon individuals. The *Rule of the Community* does not forsee any abrogation of the covenant as a whole, nor does it imagine that noncompliance might lead to the community being destroyed. The same can be said of the Church. On the other hand, the individual responsibility presupposed in the *Rule of the Community* appears not to result from any inner motivation, at least not of the sort Jeremiah envisioned in his new covenant prophecy. God is said to have placed a holy spirit in the people of Qumran (1QS 3.7), but they still need admonitions to obey, as both the *Rule of the Community* and the *Damascus Document* make clear.

The new covenant idea undergoes no further development in Judaism. The Midrashim contain merely a few citations of Jer. 31.33 for purposes of focusing on the old problem of remembering the *torah*. Midrash Song of Songs 8.14 (*Cant. R.* 8.14) interprets the phrase about God writing the *torah* on the people's hearts to mean that God recalls for the people what they themselves have forgotten, and what has led them into error. More often in the midrashic literature the Jeremiah verse is given a meaning closer to the one it had originally: that forgetting the *torah* can be expected in the Present World, and only in the World to Come, when the *torah* is (truly) written on the heart, will people no longer forget it (*Qoh. R.* 2.1; *Cant. R.* 1.2; *Pes. R.* 107a; *Yal.* on Jer. 31.33; cf. St.-B.3, pp. 89-90, 704). Medieval

---

16. Cross, *The Ancient Library of Qumran*, p. 96.
17. M. Black, *The Scrolls and Christian Origins* (New York: Charles Scribners Sons, 1961), p. 94.

Jewish writers cited the Jer. 31.31-34 passage largely to refute Christological interpretations, for example, arguing that the Mosaic *torah* was not abrogated by Jesus and the Christian Gospel, but that in the Messianic Age it will be renewed and internalized in a new covenant lasting forever.[18] In the modern *Encyclopaedia Judaica* (1971–1973), there are no articles on 'new covenant' or 'eternal covenant', and in the article on 'covenant',[19] neither of these covenants is mentioned.

---

18. R.S. Sarason, 'The Interpretation of Jeremiah 31.31-34 in Judaism', in *When Jews and Christians Meet* (ed. Jakob J. Petuchowski; Albany, NY: State University of New York, 1988), pp. 103-109.

19. M. Weinfeld, 'Covenant', *EncJud* 5 (1971), pp. 1012-22.

The Gospels

Chapter 25

NEW COVENANT IN THE EARLY CHURCH
AND IN MATTHEW*

The Christian Church, from earliest times, claimed the promise of Jer. 31.31-34 and understood itself to be the people of the new covenant. It thought of itself as a new people (1 Pet. 2.1-10): Israel reborn, but a more inclusive Israel to which Gentiles now belong. It comes as a surprise, then, to find so little said in the New Testament about a new covenant.

New Covenant in the Gospel Tradition

The words 'new covenant' are placed on the lips of Jesus only in the longer text of Lk. 22.20, where, at the Last Supper, Jesus passes the wine and says, 'This cup...is the new covenant in my blood'. Scholarly opinion is divided over the originality of this reading, although the longer text does enjoy wide support. Among the modern English translations, the RSV, NEB, and REB omit the words, putting manuscript readings that contain the words in a footnote. The JB, NAB, NIV, GNB, and NRSV retain the words in the text. The longer Lucan text is thought by some to depend upon 1 Cor. 11.25, where Paul cites a Last Supper tradition antedating him, reflecting perhaps usage in the Antioch Church[1]: 'This cup is the new covenant in my blood'. Mark 14.24 records Jesus' words as, 'This is my blood of the covenant', a modification in the direction of Exod. 24.8.[2] Matthew 26.28 adds 'for the forgiveness of sins', which is new covenant language from Jer. 31.34.[3]

In some ancient manuscripts Mark and Matthew have the word 'new' added. Some form critics conclude that neither 'new' nor 'covenant' was

---

* Lecture given at Mount Miguel Covenant Village, Spring Valley, CA., on October 13, 2005. Portions were published previously in my 'New Covenant' article in *ABD* 4 (New York: Doubleday, 1992), pp. 1090-93, also in my *Jeremiah 21–36* (AB, 21B; New York: Doubleday, 2004), pp. 474-79.

1. J. Jeremias, *The Eucharistic Words of Jesus* (New York: Macmillan, 1955), pp. 127-31.

2. *TDNT* 2, p. 133; A. Richardson, *An Introduction to the Theology of the New Testament* (New York: Harper & Row, 1958), p. 230; cf. Heb. 9.20.

3. C.H. Dodd, *According to the Scriptures* (London: Nisbet, 1952), p. 45.

spoken by Jesus,[4] which is to say that the Last Supper liturgy was originally briefer and in the Synoptic passages has undergone expansion. Even if 'new covenant' was heard on the lips of Jesus just one time, he clearly did not focus on the concept in his preaching. But for the early Church, the Last Supper liturgy conveys the idea that Jesus' death, or his shedding of blood, seals the new covenant now made by God with humankind. Sacrificial terminology from Exod. 24.3-8, almost entirely absent in the prophets (but see Zech. 9.11), has come to dominate the covenant idea, where it takes on fresh new meaning.

New Covenant in Paul

Paul refers to himself and the Corinthian laity as 'ministers of a new covenant' (2 Cor. 3.6), where Jer. 31.31-34 appears to be in the back of his mind. This covenant has found expression in the *hearts* of the Corinthians, wherein the 'Spirit of the living God' resides (vv. 2-3). The new covenant therefore contrasts with the 'old covenant' of Moses (vv. 14-15), which was written on stone (v. 3).

Paul might have said more about the new covenant were it not for his concern to establish a more ancient base than Jer. 31.31-34 for the new faith in Christ. The important promise for Paul is the one given to Abraham, that through him all the families of the earth would be blessed. Paul grounds the blessings through Christ in the Abrahamic covenant so they may apply equally to Jews and Gentiles (Gal. 3.14). Paul must short-circuit the Sinai covenant if he is to realize his goal of evangelizing the Gentiles, for the Sinai covenant was made only with Israel (cf. Rom. 9.4; Eph. 2.11-13). Moreover, the Sinai covenant contains the law, which is now a burden to everybody—Jew and Gentile. In Paul's view, the law only brings people under its curses. But Christ, by dying on the cross, becomes himself a curse redeeming those under the law who have faith in him (Gal. 3.10-14). The new covenant, therefore, contains only blessings, making it just like the Abrahamic covenant. The Sinai covenant serves Paul only for the purpose of making a contrast with the Abrahamic covenant. In his allegory of Gal. 4.21-31, Paul sees the Abrahamic covenant (fulfilled through Sarah) leading to freedom, sonship, and the Jerusalem above; the covenant made at Sinai (called Hagar) leads to the present Jerusalem, that is, Jews and Judaizers, and thus slavery.

As a Christian, Paul has a major problem knowing what to do with the law (Torah). The law is supposed to belong to the new covenant, but the coming of Christ has eclipsed the law. Paul resolves this problem to some extent by seeing a development in the covenants. Among the former covenants,

---

4. R. Bultmann, *Theology of the New Testament* I (trans. Kendrick Grobel; New York: Charles Scribners Sons, 1951), p. 146; J. Jeremias, *The Eucharistic Words of Jesus*, pp. 110-15.

the Abrahamic covenant is primary, and is not annulled by the Sinai covenant coming later (Gal. 3.17). Paul exploits the dual meaning of διαθήκη as 'covenant' and 'will' (or 'testament') in Gal. 3.15-18 in order to make this point. The Sinai covenant when originally given was accompanied with great splendor, though it was a splendour that faded (cf. Exod. 34.29-35); now there is no splendour at all associated with this covenant because of the surpassing splendour of Christ, whose new covenant is eternal (2 Cor. 3.7-11). Paul also sees a development in the covenants when he views the Mosaic law as a schoolmaster that must discipline a people not yet mature (Gal. 3.23-24). With the coming of Christ, those having faith are no longer subject to their former schoolmaster (vv. 25-26). In Romans, Paul says that Christians are discharged from the law (Rom. 7.6), that Christ is the end of the law (10.4). Yet Paul does not want to dispense with the law; in fact, he calls it holy (7.12) and claims to uphold it (3.31). His other statements, however, distance him irrevocably from Judaism, for whom the law is central and eternally binding. For Paul, Christ is central, and the new covenant written by his life-giving Spirit surpasses all other covenants and is eternal.

Paul's law and grace dichotomy (Rom. 6.14) stems from the lack of a typology in his thinking between the new covenant in Christ and the Sinai covenant. Were such a typology made, Paul would have to concede that the Sinai covenant/law had its own accompanying act of divine grace, which was the Exodus from Egypt.

Paul's views on sin and reconciliation in Romans lack covenant language per se; nevertheless, they rest almost certainly on broad-based assumptions about the new covenant existing in the early Church. According to Paul's gospel, both Jew and Gentile are under the power of sin, both stand in need of forgiveness, and both are reconciled to God by Jesus' death on the cross. In Ephesians, too (whether or not it is Pauline), the blood of Christ is said to bring Gentiles near to God, even though formerly they were strangers to the covenants of promise (Eph. 2.12-13).

In Rom. 2.14-15, Paul seeks parity between Jew and Gentile by stating that upright Gentiles not possessing the Jewish law show, nevertheless, 'that what the law requires is written on their hearts'. Such people also possess a 'conscience' (συνείδησις). The first remark about a law-equivalent 'written on the heart' appears to be a borrowing from Jer. 31.33 (cf. St.-B. 3, pp. 89-90); the following remark about a 'conscience that bears witness' derives most likely from Stoic or Jewish-Hellenistic philosophy. Paul's precise understanding of how the new covenant manifests itself among the Gentiles is by no means transparent in these verses, but one should note that his thinking nevertheless runs parallel to Jeremiah's new covenant passage, where the promise of a law written on the heart is followed by the promise of a new inner motivation to know and do the law (Jer. 31.34).

In Rom. 11.25-32 the new covenant prophecy is given a most extraordinary interpretation, unlike any other in the NT, and certainly unlike any made subsequently by the Church Fathers. Elsewhere the referent for the new covenant is the Church, which is the New Israel; here the referent is the Israel that remains hardened to the Gospel.[5] Paul says that at some future time, when the full number of Gentiles has come in, and the Parousia of Jesus occurs, *all* Israel will be saved. Isaiah 59.20 is quoted in support of the Parousia, after which comes the new covenant prophecy:

> The Deliverer will come from Zion
>   he will banish ungodliness from Jacob
> and this will be my covenant with them
>   when I take away their sins (Rom. 11.26-27).

The new covenant prophecy here quoted cannot be identified with certainty. The first part, 'and this will be my covenant with them', is thought to be a continuation of the previous quotation of Isa. 59.20 into v. 21a. The second part, however, 'when I take away their sins', has to be from somewhere else. Some suggest that this phrase comes from Isa. 27.9b, which in the LXX compares nicely, except for the singular 'his sin'. The plural 'their sins' concludes the new covenant passage of Jeremiah (LXX 38.34), where also in v. 33 the beginning words are 'For this is the covenant'. Paul could then be giving a freely rendered abridgment of Jer. 31.31-34.[6] An abridgment of this same passage occurs in Heb. 10.16-17. Regardless of what passages make up this florilegium, Paul gives the new covenant promise its most inclusive meaning: he believes this covenant really is for everyone. He concludes by saying, 'For the gifts and the call of God are irrevocable' (Rom. 11.29), by which he means not just the covenant promise to Abraham, but also the new covenant promise. Both covenants are unconditional, eternal, and given for the salvation of all.

New Covenant in Hebrews

In the letter to the Hebrews the new covenant is given its most prominent place in the NT. Jeremiah's new covenant prophecy is quoted twice, once in its entirety (Heb. 8.8-12), and once in abridged form (10.16-17). For this NT writer, Christ is the great high priest of the heavenly sanctuary (7.26), one who 'has obtained a ministry which is as much more excellent than the old as the covenant he mediates is better, since it is enacted on better promises' (8.6). The Sinai covenant, here called the 'first covenant', was shown to be faulty because people under it turned up faulty (8.7-8a). Reference is

---

5. C.H. Dodd, *The Epistle of Paul to the Romans* (MNTC; London: Hodder and Stoughton, 1932), p. 182.
6. Dodd, *The Epistle of Paul to the Romans*, p. 182.

25. New Covenant in the Early Church and in Matthew

presumably being made to the first covenant's provisions for noncompliance, namely, the curses of Deuteronomy 28. The new covenant prophesied by Jeremiah has better promises: it contains an unconditional commitment by God to forgive sins; it is eternal (9.15; 13.20); and Jesus is the covenant's surety (7.22). According to Hebrews, Jeremiah in announcing this new covenant treats the Sinai covenant as obsolete. That obsolescence is just now being seen as the first covenant is ready to vanish away (8.13).

Jesus is the 'mediator of the new covenant' (9.15; 'better covenant' in 8.6; 'fresh covenant' in 12.24; cf. 1 Tim. 2.5-6; Isa. 42.6; 49.8). In Judaism the covenant mediator was Moses (cf. Gal. 3.19), and after his death the high priest.[7] Jesus becomes mediator of the new covenant by virtue of his death on the cross, which the author of Hebrews explains in priestly and sacrificial categories understood within Judaism (9.1-14). Special appropriation is made of the Day of Atonement ritual (Leviticus 16). As the high priest who enters once and once only the Holy Place with his own sacrificial blood, Jesus secures for God's elect their eternal redemption (9.11-12, 24-28; cf. 7.27). This death purifies human consciences (9.14; 10.22; cf. Rom. 2.15), something not possible with the earlier sacrifices (9.9).

The Holy Place—or Heavenly Sanctuary (9.24)—is for the elect also the Promised Land of rest and inheritance (4.9-11; 9.15). In raising the subject of inheritance, the author of Hebrews uses both meanings of διαθήκη: 'covenant' and 'will' (9.15-22; cf. Gal. 3.15-18). A will does not take effect until the death of the one who makes it, that is, the testator. Jesus is therefore the testator of the new covenant. At his death the elect receive their inheritance, which is redemption from transgressions under the first covenant. The blood performs the same function of ratification in the new covenant as it did in the old (9.18-21; cf. Exod. 24.6-8). The author echoes a common rabbinic theme when he says that without the shedding of blood there is no forgiveness of sins, or no atonement with God (9.22; cf. Lev. 17.11).

In the abridged quotation from Jeremiah in Heb. 10.16-17, the accent is on the concluding words of the new covenant promise, which is, that God will no longer remember the peoples' sins. Earlier in chap. 10 the author maintained that yearly sacrifices on the Day of Atonement—as well as daily sin offerings—were ineffectual because they had to be repeated. Jewish teachers would find such an argument unconvincing; indeed it is flatly contradicted in *Jub.* 5.17-18. Nevertheless, for the writer of Hebrews, Jesus makes the single offering of his body, which for all time perfects the sanctified elect (10.10, 14). Once the forgiveness of sins is granted, there is no longer any sin offering that can be made (10.18, 26).

The 'once for all' view of Jesus' sacrifice is matched in Hebrews with a 'once for all' view of repentance, enlightenment (baptism), and sanctification

---

7. Richardson, *An Introduction to the Theology of the New Testament*, p. 229.

of the believer. If one deliberately sins after coming to a knowledge of the truth, that person profanes the blood of the new covenant and has only God's vengeance to look forward to (10.26-31). This somewhat exaggerated view of Christian sanctification has the effect of recasting the new covenant in terms of the old; it also qualifies the 'blessings only' promise made to the Church. Although curses are not explicitly placed on individuals who lapse under the new covenant, they are implied (6.1-8; 10.26-31; cf. Gen. 17.13-14). The idea that deliberate sin makes a sin offering inefficacious is found in Num. 15.30-31 (*Yom.* 8.9 applies the same principle to the Day of Atonement ritual). But in a closing benediction the author of Hebrews prays that the Lord Jesus, 'by the blood of the eternal covenant', will equip the elect to do God's will (13.20-21).

New Covenant in Matthew's Gospel

The lack of a new covenant emphasis in the preaching of Jesus and in the Gospels generally is compensated for by Matthew in the writing of his Gospel. Matthew is more 'teaching' (*didache*) than proclamation of the gospel (*kerygma*),[8] probably being used didactically for those desiring to join the church, or for the newly joined once they had been baptized.

According to W.D. Davies, Matthew intends in his Gospel to depict Jesus as the 'new Moses' leading a 'new Exodus', the Sermon on the Mount being Jesus' 'new Torah (Law)'. Although this new Torah is considerably less burdensome than the old (Mt. 11.28-30), no antithesis is intended: the new comes to complete the old (5.17).[9] Benjamin Bacon saw things along similar lines, arguing that Matthew's Gospel is divided into five books modeled on the five books of the Torah: Genesis to Deuteronomy.[10] This makes it into a 'new Torah', or 'new Law'. Each little book within the larger book contained a narrative section, a sermonic section, and a closing formula stating that Jesus had finished his teaching. Bacon's outline went as follows:

Book I	3–4	Narrative
	5.1–7.27	Sermon: The Sermon on the Mount
	7.28-29	'And when Jesus finished these sayings…'
Book II	8.1–9.35	Narrative
	9.36–10.42	Sermon: The Missionary Discourse
	11.1	'And when Jesus had finished instructing his 12 disciples…'

8. J. Jeremias, *The Sermon on the Mount* (trans. Norman Perrin; London: University of London, 1961), pp. 19-23.
9. W.D. Davies, *The Sermon on the Mount* (Cambridge: Cambridge University Press, 1969), pp. 10-32.
10. Benjamin W. Bacon, *Studies in Matthew* (New York: Henry Holt and Co., 1930), pp. 80-90.

Book III	11.2–12.50	Narrative
	13.1-52	Sermon: Parables on the Kingdom
	13.53	'And when Jesus had finished these parables…'
Book IV	13.54–17.21	Narrative
	17.22–18.35	Sermon: Church Administration
	19.1	'Now when Jesus had finished these sayings…'
Book V	19.2–22.46	Narrative
	23–25	Sermon: End Times/Farewell Address
	26.1	'When Jesus finished *all* these sayings…'

The addition of 'all' in the final formula shows that a climax had been reached. Bacon's view was widely accepted with only a few reservations and modifications. The main problem with his structure, however, was that it left out material at the beginning and end of the Gospel. Davies said, 'The birth narratives are outside the main scheme of the work and, what is more important, the Passion of Jesus and his Resurrection are reduced to mere addenda'.[11]

An improved outline was proposed by Charles Lohr, who argued that the entire Gospel was arranged in a chiasmus.[12] The chiasmus is a rhetorical figure well known from classical literature, found to exist in large panels in the biblical discourse by Nils W. Lund. Lund showed how words and ideas often move up to a center point, which frequently is the climax, and then repeat in reverse order to the end.[13] Lohr's structure for Matthew, which also alternates narrative and sermon, is the following:

1–4	a					Narrative: Birth and Beginnings
5–7		b				Sermon: *Blessings*, Entering the Kingdom
8–9			c			Narrative: Authority and Invitation
10				d		Sermon: Mission Discourse
11–12					e	Narrative: Rejection by Present Generation
13						f Sermon: Parables of the Kingdom
14–17					e'	Narrative: Acknowledgement by Disciples
18				d'		Sermon: Community Discourse
19–22			c'			Narrative: Authority and Invitation
23–25		b'				Sermon: *Woes*, Coming of the Kingdom
26–28	a'					Narrative: Death and Resurrection

---

11. W.D. Davies, *Invitation to the New Testament* (Garden City, NY: Doubleday, 1966), p. 214.
12. Charles Lohr, 'Oral Techniques in the Gospel of Matthew', *CBQ* 23 (1961), pp. 403-435.
13. Nils W. Lund, *Chiasmus in the New Testament* (Chapel Hill, NC: University of North Carolina Press, 1942 [repr. Peabody, MA: Hendrickson, 1992]).

Here all the Gospel material is accounted for, and while Lohr's categories may not reproduce exactly what was in the Gospel writer's mind, the categories are convincing in the main. One sees here how the Parables of the Kingdom in chap. 13 become the center and climax of the Gospel, also how the 'woes' of chap. 23 intend to balance the 'blessings' of chap. 5. Jesus pronounces 'blessings' on the new people of the Kingdom (5.3-11), but on the old he pronounces 'woes' (23.13-36). This, I believe, makes Matthew's Gospel into a 'new covenant' document.

What Matthew has done is to adapt a form from international treaties of the ancient Near East, found also in Deuteronomy (Deut. 11.26-32; 28). In these treaties, and in Deuteronomy, the terms of the treaty/covenant are fortified by blessings and curses. Blessings and woes occur also in Luke's 'Sermon on the Plain' (Lk. 6.20-26), where there are four of each. Luke has adapted the same covenant form, only there the antithesis is obvious because the woes immediately follow the blessings. In Matthew, however, the antithesis is embodied in a rhetorical structure, which makes the contrast less obvious unless one reads the Gospel in its entirety, which is doubtless how it was read originally in the early church. Today, with only a portion of the Gospel being read at one time in public worship, or possibly the Sermon on the Mount being read as a whole, the contrast is lost because of too much intervening material between chaps. 5 and 23. If we read (aloud) the Gospel in its entirety, we will discern the rhetorical structure given it by Matthew, and will discern also that Matthew intends his Gospel to be a new covenant document: blessings are conferred on the new people of the Kingdom, and woes are heaped upon the scribes and Pharisees. The passages juxtaposed are the following:

> *Blessed* are the poor in spirit, for theirs is the kingdom of heaven
> *Blessed* are those who mourn, for they shall be comforted
> *Blessed* are the meek, for they will inherit the earth
> *Blessed* are those who hunger and thirst for righteousness, for they will be filled
> *Blessed* are the merciful, for they will receive mercy
> *Blessed* are the pure in heart, for they will see God
> *Blessed* are the peacemakers, for they will be called children of God
> *Blessed* are those who are persecuted for righteousness' sake, for theirs is the kingdom of heaven
> *Blessed* are you when people revile you and persecute you and utter all kinds of evil against you falsely on my account. Rejoice and be glad, for your reward is great in heaven, for in the same way they persecuted the prophets who were before you. (Mt. 5.3-12 NRSV)
>
> But *woe* to you, scribes and Pharisees, hypocrites! For you lock people out of the kingdom of heaven. For you do not go in yourselves, and when others are going in, you stop them.
> *Woe* to you, scribes and Pharisees, hypocrites! For you cross sea and land to make a single convert, and you make the new convert twice as much a child of hell as yourselves.

Woe to you, blind guides, who say, 'Whoever swears by the sanctuary is bound by nothing, but whoever swears by the gold of the sanctuary is bound by the oath'. You blind fools! For which is greater, the gold or the sanctuary that has made the gold sacred?...

Woe to you, scribes and Pharisees, hypocrites! For you tithe mint, dill and cummin, and have neglected the weightier matters of the law: justice and mercy and faith. It is these you ought to have practiced without neglecting others. You blind guides! You strain out a gnat but swallow a camel!

Woe to you, scribes and Pharisees, hypocrites! For you clean the outside of the cup and of the plate, but inside they are full of greed and self-indulgence. You blind Pharisee! First clean the inside of the cup, so that the outside also may become clean.

Woe to you, scribes and Pharisees, hypocrites! For you are like whitewashed tombs, which on the outside look beautiful, but inside they are full of the bones of the dead and of all kinds of filth...

Woe to you, scribes and Pharisees, hypocrites! For you build the tombs of the prophets and decorate the graves of the righteous, and you say, 'If we had lived in the days of our ancestors, we would not have taken part with them in shedding the blood of the prophets...' (Mt. 23.13-36 NRSV)

The blessings and the woes contain some striking comparisons and contrasts, which are italicized in the following chart:[14]

Woes	Blessings
'you lock people out of the *kingdom of heaven*' (23.13)	'poor in spirit/those persecuted... theirs is *the kingdom of heaven*' (5.3, 10)
'you make the convert... a *child of hell*' (23.15)	'peacemakers.. will be called *children of God*' (5.9)
'*blind* guides... *blind* fools... *blind*...' (23.16-19)	'the pure in heart... will *see* God' (5.8)
'you have neglected... *mercy*' (23.23)	'the *merciful*... will receive *mercy*' (5.7)
'you clean the outside of the *cup* and of the *plate*...' (23.25)	'those who *hunger and thirst* after righteousness ... will be filled' (5.6)
'you are like white-washed *tombs*... full of *the bones of dead men*' (23.27)	'those who *mourn*... will be comforted' (5.4)
'you build the *tombs*... and decorate the *graves*...' (23.29)	
'that upon you may come all the righteous blood shed on *earth*' (23.35)	'the meek... will inherit the *earth*' (5.5)

In closing should also be noted some important differences between Matthew's new covenant document and the covenant document of Deuteronomy:

1. Matthew tones down the language. The Greek μακάριοι (blessed) and οὐαι (woe) translate the Hebrew אַשְׁרֵי and הוֹי, both milder terms than the

---

14. Adapted with minor changes from J.C. Fenton, *The Gospel of St. Matthew* (Pelican NT Commentaries; Baltimore, MD: Penguin Books, 1963), p. 368.

בָּרוּךְ (blessed) and אָרוּר (cursed) of Deuteronomy. Jesus does not go so far as to curse the scribes and Pharisees. Luke, too, tones down the language of Jesus.

2. The blessings and woes in Matthew are simply announced; neither are conditional, as in the international treaties or in Deuteronomy, which is to say, they do not depend upon obedience or disobedience to any legal demands of the new covenant. The blessings are simply conferred on the new people of the Kingdom, who receive them without price. Similarly, the woes are simply laid upon the scribes and Pharisees as a current indictment. Jesus is speaking here as a prophet, not as a lawgiver of Deuteronomy.

3. The blessings of Matthew's new covenant come first, not last, as in Deuteronomy and the international treaties. It is as if Jesus wants to get them out ahead of everything else, and not make his audience wait for a warning or judgment expected at the end.

4. With the blessings and woes spoken to different audiences—the blessings on the new people of the Kingdom (5.3-11), and the woes on the old (23.13-36)—the new people receive neither woes nor curses, only blessings. This is important, reflecting precisely the new covenant as announced by Jeremiah in Jer. 31.31-34, which is unconditional and eternal. Matthew believes there can be no abrogation of the new covenant, and no destruction of the Church (cf. Mt. 16.18).

Chapter 26

CLOSURE IN MARK'S GOSPEL*

The thesis here is one I presented many years ago to students in a Christian Origins class I was teaching at the University of California, Berkeley. It offers an interpretation of the abrupt, yes, shocking conclusion to the Gospel of Mark in 16.8. Since this amazing verse continues to arouse wonderment in all who read it, the time has perhaps come for me to share my idea with a broader audience.

Ideas should have some 'sitting time' before going into print, although perhaps not as long as this idea has waited. Samuel Johnson said admiringly of Alexander Pope (1688–1744) that Pope's publications were never hasty, never sent to the press until they had lain two years under his inspection. And the celebrated Roman rhetorician, Quintilian (c. 35–95 CE), cited with approval advice of Horace, who, in his *Art of Poetry*, urged that publications not be hurried but 'kept in store till the ninth year comes around'.[1] So better late than too early.

There is another reason why I want just now to share this study on a Gospel text with an audience of seminary colleagues, students, pastors, and church laity. Very often I hear the complaint, particularly from pastors and lay folk, that modern biblical scholarship produces a small yield, where I take 'yield' to mean theological insight and usefulness in the life of the church. The complaint is not always well-founded, but much of the time it is, and those of us in the profession need to do more than we are doing to make critical study of the Bible relevant to life in the church and in the world. This modest contribution, which is an exercise in rhetorical criticism, will show, I hope, how modern critical study of the Bible can produce tangible results with regard to Christian witness and evangelism, for the strange ending of Mark's Gospel speaks a positive and powerful word about both.

The Abrupt Ending in Mark

With the rise of critical scholarship the original ending of Mark's Gospel is now put at 16.8. The verse reads:

---

* First published in *Seminary Ridge Review* 9/1 (2006), pp. 33-41.
1. *Quintilian I: The Orator's Education: Books 1–2* (trans. Donald A. Russell; LCL; Cambridge, MA: Harvard University Press, 2001), p. 51.

> So they [the women] went out and fled from the tomb, for terror and amazement had seized them, and they said nothing to anyone, for they were afraid (NRSV).

At least three supplements have been identified in the manuscript tradition. The largest and most common supplement of vv. 9-20 is absent in Codex Sinaiticus, Codex Vaticanus, and other important ancient witnesses, and appears in neither the Tischendorf (1869–72) nor Wescott and Hort (1881) editions of the Greek New Testament. Eusebius and Jerome say the verses are wanting in almost all Greek manuscripts known to them.[2] Having vocabulary, style, and content that is definitely non-Markan, these verses seem clearly to have been quarried from other Gospels and Acts, and added later, perhaps in the second century.[3] Two shorter supplements are also attested, and no wonder, with v. 8 concluding: ἐφοβοῦντο γάρ, 'for they were afraid'. In Greek this conclusion is even more jarring, with the final word being the conjunction γάρ.[4]

Not only does Gospel tradition remedy this seeming infelicity with supplements of a more positive nature, but both Matthew and Luke, assuming that they are later than Mark, contain correctives of their own. Matthew says: 'So they [i.e., the women] departed quickly from the tomb with fear and great joy, and ran to tell his disciples' (Mt. 28.8). Luke says: '...and returning from the tomb they [i.e., the women] told all this to the eleven and to all the rest' (Lk. 24.9).

Interpretations of Mark's abrupt ending, which Wellhausen, Meyer, Lightfoot, and others took to be original, vary. Some see it as a climactic expression of Mark's 'messianic secret' idea (cf. 1.34). Others propose solutions that would bring Mark in line with Matthew and Luke, giving the ancient audience—and us too—a more desirous ending. We know, do we not, that eventually the women did as commanded (v. 7). They told the disciples, Peter, and others that Jesus had risen from the dead. Many have imagined, therefore, that an original ending, once present, is now lost.[5]

The solution to this puzzlement about Mark's abrupt ending at 16.8 is to be sought, in my view, in a correct understanding of Hebrew rhetoric and composition, which has been carried over into all three New Testament Gospels by writers familiar with the Hebrew Scriptures, our Old Testament, and familiar also, quite possibly, with literary works

---

2. Vincent Taylor, *The Gospel According to St. Mark* (London: Macmillan & Co., 1952), p. 610.
3. F.C. Grant, 'The Gospel According to St. Mark', *IB* 8 (New York: Abingdon Press, 1951), p. 915.
4. Taylor, *The Gospel According to St. Mark*, pp. 603-609; C.S. Mann, *Mark* (AB, 27; New York: Doubleday, 1986), pp. 81-82, 659.
5. Taylor, *The Gospel According to St. Mark*, p. 609.

employing similar techniques throughout the classical world. I am concerned here with a single device that ties the end of a composition in with its beginning, what biblical scholars now call the *inclusio*.[6] Classical scholars refer to the same as 'ring composition' in works of Greek and Roman authors.

The Inclusio in Hebrew Composition

It is now well documented that ancient Hebrew composition made extensive use of the inclusio. It was employed in all types of Hebrew discourse—narrative, genealogical lists, prophetic oracles, psalms, and other genres appearing in our Old Testament. It was also employed on a larger scale to tie entire compositions together, what today we call 'essays' and 'books'. The inclusio is doubtless a thought pattern, but its identification in the biblical text is most convincingly argued when words and phrases at the beginning of a composition are seen to repeat at the end. The repetition sends a signal to the audience that the discourse has come to an end. Repeated words and phrases also drive home points the speaker wishes to emphasize, compare, or contrast. On some occasions the same establish subtle continuities and convey weighty theological truths. The modern reader must then be alerted to this structure in biblical discourse, for in structure is meaning and in some cases also a message.

The inclusio is the primary controlling structure in Deuteronomy 1–28, where it functions to close individual sermons as well as an early edition of the book.[7] The inclusio tying together the First Edition of Deuteronomy is the following:

Deut. 1.1-5
These are the words which Moses spoke   אלה הדברים אשר...משה
to all Israel beyond the Jordan...beyond   אל־כל־ישראל...
the Jordan, *in the land of Moab*, Moses   בארץ מואב...
undertook to explain *this law*:...   את־התורה הזאת

---

6. The term was used by Ed König in his *Stilistik, Rhetorik, Poetik in Bezug auf die biblische Literatur* (Leipzig: Dieterich'sche Verlagsbuchhandlung, 1900), p. 350, and became widely employed after the appearance of Dahood's *Psalms I–III* (AB, 16, 17, 17A; Garden City, NY: Doubleday, 1966, 1968, 1970). Muilenburg also made use of the term in his 'Form Criticism and Beyond', *JBL* 88 (1969), pp. 9-10. On classical scholars' use of the term 'ring composition', see my essay, 'Rhetorical Criticism: History, Method and Use in the Book of Jeremiah', in *Jeremiah: A Study in Ancient Hebrew Rhetoric* (Winona Lake, IN: Eisenbrauns, 2nd edn, 1997), pp. xix-xliii; Lundbom, *Jeremiah 1–20* (AB, 21A; New York: Doubleday, 1999), pp. 76-79.

7. See Lundbom, 'The Inclusio and Other Framing Devices in Deuteronomy I–XXVIII', *VT* 46 (1996), pp. 296-315.

Deut. 28.69 [29.1]
>   *These are the words of the covenant which*
>   Yahweh commanded *Moses* to make *with*
>   *the people of Israel in the land of Moab*,
>   beside the covenant which he made with
>   them at Horeb

אלה דברי הברית אשר...
את־משה...
את־בני ישראל בארץ מואב

The inclusio performs an important compositional function in the book of Jeremiah, where it brings closure to successive editions of the book.[8] The nearly-final book of Jeremiah, before chap. 52 was added, is given closure by a briefly-worded inclusio similar to the one in Deuteronomy 1–28: the opening phrase repeats at the close, informing the audience that the book reporting Jeremiah's words and deeds is now concluded. This inclusio occurs only in the Hebrew Masoretic text, where it is an add-on in the expanded colophon of Seraiah ben Neriah (51.59-64):

Jer. 1.1
>   *the legacy of Jeremiah...*

דברי ירמיהו...

Jer. 51.64
>   *...the legacy of Jeremiah*

...דברי ירמיהו

Keywords come here at the beginning of 1.1 and at the end of 51.64.

An inclusio ties together an earlier Jeremiah composition comprised of chapters 1–20, what I have called the First Edition of the book of Jeremiah:[9]

Jer. 1.5
>   Before I formed you in the belly I knew you
>   and before *you came forth from the womb* I declared you holy   תצא מרחם
>   a prophet to the nations I made you

Jer. 20.18
>   Why this: *from the womb came I forth*   מרחם יצאתי
>   to see hard times and sorrow
>   and my days end in shame?

Here the keywords are inverted: 'you came forth/from the womb' // 'from the womb/came I forth'. Of greater importance, however, is a theological statement created by the collocation, namely, that Yahweh's words of call now serve to answer Jeremiah's wrenching question: 'Why came I forth from the womb?' Jeremiah came forth from his mother's womb because Yahweh called him before he came forth, long before. Von Rad, commenting

---

   8. Lundbom, *Jeremiah: A Study in Ancient Hebrew Rhetoric* (Missoula, MT: Society of Biblical Literature and Scholars Press, 1975), pp. 23-60 (1997 edn, pp. 36-81).
   9. Lundbom, *Jeremiah: A Study in Ancient Hebrew Rhetoric*, pp. 28-30 (1997, pp. 42-44); Lundbom, *Jeremiah 1–20*, pp. 93-95, 229.

on the confession in 20.14-18, says: 'the God whom the prophet addresses no longer answers him'.[10] True, in chapter 20 Jeremiah's question does not receive an answer. But when the First Edition of the book of Jeremiah is heard in its entirety, an answer is given to the suffering prophet. This answer is embodied in the book's structure, and an audience alerted to structure will get the message our ancient scribe meant to convey.

The Inclusio in Matthew and Luke

The New Testament, despite its use of Greek and an indebtedness here and there to Greek thought and Greek modes of argumentation, contains a goodly amount of Hebrew idioms, thought forms, and argumentative strategies. It also preserves a rich legacy of Hebrew rhetorical devices and modes of composition, known to us primarily from the Old Testament. One of these rhetorical devices is the inclusio, which occurs often in the discourse and written composition of the NT. In both it effects closure in much the same way that it does in the OT.[11]

In his little *Matthew* commentary in the Pelican series, J.C. Fenton notes that the end of the First Gospel returns to the beginning.[12] The inclusio there is created in a final redaction, where the great biblical affirmation, 'I will be with you',[13] is brought in to show that God, in Christ and in the Holy Spirit, has come to dwell and will continue to dwell with his people to the close of the age:

Mt. 1.23
    ...and his name shall be called Emmanuel,
    which means *'God with us'*   μεθ' ἡμῶν ὁ θεός

Mt. 28.20
    ...and lo, *I am with you* always, to the   ἐγὼ μεθ' ὑμῶν εἰμι
    close of the age

The final verses of 28.19-20 are generally agreed to be a later addition, referring as they do to Christian baptism in the name of the triune God.

---

10. Gerhard von Rad, *Old Testament Theology* II (Edinburgh: Oliver & Boyd), p. 204.

11. See J.C. Fenton, 'Inclusio and Chiasmus in Matthew', in *Texte und Untersuchungen zur Geschichte der altchristlichen Literatur 73: Studia evangelica* (ed. Kurt Aland; Berlin: Akademie-Verlag, 1959), pp. 174-79; also Nils Lund's *Chiasmus in the New Testament* (Chapel Hill, NC: University of North Carolina, 1942 [repr. Peabody, MA: Hendrickson, 1992]), which develops the same basic thesis with regard to large chiastic panels in the NT.

12. J.C. Fenton, *The Gospel of Saint Matthew* (Pelican New Testament Commentaries; Baltimore, MD: Penguin, 1963), p. 43.

13. This bedrock OT promise occurs in Gen. 28.15; Exod. 3.12; Jer. 1.8, 19; 15.20; Isa. 41.40; 43.5, and elsewhere.

With an Emmanuel (= God with us) prophecy existing already in 1.23, we cannot speak here of a strictly supplemental theology to Matthew's Gospel; nevertheless, the add-on verses give the 'God with us' theme an emphasis it might not otherwise have, and are in keeping with Matthew's tendency throughout to stress the continuity of the Gospel message with earlier OT revelation. I would conclude, then, that the 'God with us' theme in Matthew's Gospel achieves the prominence it now has due to a later writer who added 28.19-20 to the Gospel proper. In creating an inclusio between 1.23 and 28.20, this ancient scribe established continuity between the earthly Jesus, the 'God with us', and the risen Jesus, God's 'I am with you' to the close of the age.

Luke's Gospel, in a similar yet different way, also ends where it began: in the Jerusalem Temple. After Jesus' departure at Bethany the disciples return to the Temple in Jerusalem, which hearkens back to Zechariah's presence in the Temple when he received the divine visitation.[14] An inclusio for this Gospel is made from the following verses:

Luke 1.64-68
...and immediately [Zechariah's] mouth was
opened and his tongue loosed, and he spoke,
blessing God...and he prophesied saying,   εὐλογῶν τὸν θεόν...
'Blessed be the Lord God of Israel'   Εὐλογητὸς κύριος ὁ θεὸς τοῦ Ἰσραήλ

Luke 24.50-53
...and he [i.e., Jesus] *blessed them*   εὐλόγησεν αὐτούς...
and *while he blessed them* he parted   ἐν τῷ εὐλογεῖν αὐτὸν αὐτοὺς
from them, and they returned to
Jerusalem with great joy, and were
continually in the Temple *blessing God*   εὐλογοῦντες τὸν θεόν

The verbal repetition puts the accent on 'blessing God', which occurs in the Temple at both the beginning and end of Luke's Gospel. At the beginning, the aged Zechariah is blessing God in the Temple after his tongue had been loosed (1.64-68), and at the close, the disciples are blessing God in the Temple after their return from Bethany (24.50-53). This blessing theme is given added weight in Luke's Gospel by Elizabeth's words to Mary in chapter 1: '*Blessed are you* (Εὐλογημένη σὺ) among women, and *blessed* (εὐλογημένος) is the fruit of your womb' (1.42). So the inclusio in this case lifts up a theme well-integrated into the Gospel as a whole, one that carries over also into Acts, where it says that the disciples must remain in

---

14. G.W.H. Lampe, 'Luke', in *Peake's Commentary on the Bible* (ed. Matthew Black and H.H. Rowley; London: Thomas Nelson and Sons, 1962), p. 843; Joseph A. Fitzmyer, *The Gospel According to Luke (X–XXIV)* (AB, 28A; Garden City, NY: Doubleday, 1985), p. 1591.

Jerusalem after Jesus' departure until the Holy Spirit is poured out upon them (Acts 1.4-5).

The Inclusio in Mark

Here in the Gospel of Mark we have the abrupt ending of the women leaving the tomb on Easter morning and not saying anything to anyone. They had just been told by the divine messenger that Jesus was risen, and that they should tell the disciples and Peter that they would see him in Galilee. A solution to this unsatisfying conclusion, which seems not to have been considered, but which is eminently plausable, is that here, as in the other Synoptics, closure is created by an inclusio tying together the end of the Gospel with its beginning. The actions of the women at the tomb, along with the prior command of the divine messenger, are being contrasted by this Gospel writer with Jesus' command to a leper healed at the beginning of his ministry, and actions of that leper occurring subsequently (1.40-45). The relevant verses:

Mk 1.44-45
    And [Jesus] said to him, 'See that
    you say nothing to anyone;   μηδενὶ μηδὲν εἴπῃς
    but *go,* show yourself to the priest...   ...ὕπαγε
    But he went out and began to proclaim   ὁ δὲ ἐξελθὼν ἤρξατο κηρύσσειν
    loudly, and to spread the word   πολλὰ καὶ διαφημίζειν τὸν λόγον

Mk 16.7-8
    But *go, tell* his disciples and Peter   ...ὑπάγετε εἴπατε
    that he is going before you to Galilee...
    and they went out... and said nothing to   καὶ ἐξελθοῦσαι...
    anyone for they were afraid.   καὶ οὐδενὶ οὐδὲν εἶπαν

The contrast is unmistakable: the healed leper is commanded to show himself to the priest, and not to say anything to anyone, yet he goes and tells everyone. The women, for their part, are commanded to tell the disciples of Jesus' resurrection and forthcoming appearance in Galilee, but they depart the tomb in fear, saying nothing to anyone. One act of disobedience gets the good news of Jesus out, another act of disobedience translates into silence about news infinitely better.

Geography, too, is a key component in Mark's inclusio. Whereas for Luke the Gospel story begins and ends in Jerusalem, and in Jerusalem God's promise of the Holy Spirit will be realized (Acts 1.4-5), for Mark the Gospel story begins and ends in Galilee, and in Galilee a future promise will be realized. The point has frequently been made that Mark's leper story in 1.40-45 is loosely connected to its context, whereas in both

Matthew (8.1) and Luke (5.12) attempts are made to give the story a context.[15] Nevertheless, Mark's miracle story does take place in Galilee, which is where Jesus' ministry began.

Mark's audience, upon hearing his Gospel read aloud from start to finish, can be expected to make the connection between the women's actions on Easter morning and that of the healed leper reported at the Gospel's beginning. In both cases an explicit command was disobeyed, but any final reckoning will probably count the women's disobedience less serious than that of the healed leper. Mary Magdalene, Mary the mother of James, and Salome were among the faithful, devoted women of Gospel tradition, members of Jesus' 'inner circle', like the Twelve. In Mark we know that the disciples consistently get a 'bad press' for their lack of faith and understanding. Now the women receive a bit of the same for their Easter morning behavior. Actually, both acts of disobedience, that of the leper and that of the women, will doubtless fade into insignificance when all is said and done, because the good news of Jesus ends up being preached despite all human efforts—intentional or otherwise—to keep it quiet.

The message for the Markan church should be clear. Within the church, surely, are members of an 'in group' who are failing to get out the good news of Jesus' resurrection, while at the same time rank 'outsiders', who have been impacted by God's saving work, cannot in their exuberance and unspeakable joy be kept quiet, and must tell everyone they meet about it. These individuals may have come into the church from nowhere, or may still be outside the church. In any case, no one told them to be about the work of evangelism, in fact, some within the church may have told them to refrain, but they are doing it anyway, advancing the gospel cause more than those inside the church. There is a shame element at work here, which is occasionally necessary to get people who should be doing the work of witnessing, but are not, out doing it. The abrupt ending of this Gospel is then a 'wake-up call' to the Markan church, giving them a model from the glorious day of Easter that they would do well not to emulate. It remains for them to decide for themselves what it is they should be doing.

In the present-day, within the church and without, are people witnessing to the good news of Jesus' healing grace and his resurrection from the dead, who are perceived by others as not having the warrant to do so. Some doubtless are without a warrant. I am not concerned to identify who these people might be, except to note that such are around. What needs to be learned from Mark's Gospel is that people who should be out telling the good news of Jesus are simply not doing it, and they should be. Does this mean that every follower of Jesus must be an evangelist? Yes and no. Not everyone must be primarily engaged as an evangelist, for the church is a

---

15. Taylor, *The Gospel According to St. Mark*, p. 185.

body consisting of many members, and each member has its own primary function (1 Corinthians 12). But having said this, all who bear the name of Christ must be willing, ready, and about the business of testifying to Jesus' healing grace in their lives, and Jesus' glorious resurrection from the dead, when the opportunity presents itself. Too many Christians today are saying nothing to anyone, and for such people the abrupt ending in Mark's Gospel is intended.

> We confess to you, Lord, the unrest of the world,
>   to which we contribute and in which we share.
> Forgive us that so many of us are indifferent to the needs of our fellows.
> Forgive our reliance on weapons of terror,
>   our discrimination against people of different race,
>   and our preoccupation with material standards.
> And forgive us Christians for being so unsure of our good news
>   and so unready to tell it. Amen.[16]

---

16. Adapted from Caryl Micklem (ed.), *Contemporary Prayers for Public Worship* (ed. Caryl Micklem; Grand Rapids, MI: Eerdmans, 1967), p. 35.

Indexes

Index of Biblical References

Old Testament

Genesis		18.8	76	38	85, 231
1	242	18.10	75	39	85
1.6	227	18.13-15	75	42–43	91
1.7	227	18.14	75	43.14	90
2–11	65, 66, 67	18.16–19.28	75	48.1	297
3	67, 79	18.17-21	76	49	85
3.6	101	18.17-19	75	49.18	85
4.8	299	18.20-21	75	50.2	298
4.24	139	18.22	75, 76		
9.16	306	18.22b	75	*Exodus*	
11–12	70	18.23-32	74, 75, 77,	2.11	273
11.1-9	67, 84		255	3–4	272
11.3-4	68	18.23	77	3	91, 93, 94,
11.4	68, 69, 84	18.25b	77		95, 96, 97
11.7	69	18.26	77	3.4	93
11.9	68	18.33	76, 79	3.8	93
11.10-32	84	19	79	3.10-15	93
11.10-27	68	19.1	75	3.12-15	4, 8
12–50	66, 67	19.13-14	76	3.12	4, 93, 94,
12.1–25.18	65	19.13	76		273, 327
12.1-3	67, 68, 70,	19.14	78, 221	3.14	4, 89, 93,
	84	19.15	75		94, 95, 96
12.2	68, 69, 84	19.16	76, 79	3.14a	95
12.3	68	19.17-38	79	3.14b	93, 95, 96
13.8	217	19.24	76	3.15	4, 93, 96
14	77	19.25	76	4	94, 242
15	67	19.27-28	77	4.10-13	94
17.7	306	19.27	76	4.12	94
17.13-14	318	19.29	79	4.13	90
17.13	306	19.30-38	79	4.15	94
17.19	306	22	73, 74, 75	15	3, 131,
18–19	74, 75, 79,	25.19–50.26	65		136, 143,
	80, 155	28.15	327		166
18	vii, 73-80	31.21	154	15.3	38, 134
18.1-15	75	32.22-32	174	15.6	38
18.1	76	37–50	85	15.11	38
18.2	75	38–39	85	15.16b	38

Index of Biblical References

15.16cd	136	*Leviticus*		1.2-4	107
15.26	298	16	317	1.5	107, 108,
16.23	90	17.11	317		130, 233
17.1-7	218	20.9	292	1.6–3.29	23, 104,
20–23	102	24.8	306		110
20.2	304	24.10-17	99, 101	1.6-36	104
20.13-15	100	24.10-16	292	1.6	105
20.17	101	26.14-20	304	1.28	193
21	114	26.40-45	305	2–3	110
21.17	292			3.29	105
22.3b-4	227	*Numbers*		4	118
22.27 [28]	292	5	298	4.1-43	119
23	114	15.30-31	318	4.1-40	110
23.14-17	111	15.32-36	99, 101	4.23	205
23.14	111	16	217	4.25	126
23.17	111	18.19	306	4.28	4
23.31	154	20.1-13		4.29-31	304
24.3-8	314	23–24	131	4.44–30.20	117
24.6-8	317	23.18	13	4.44-49	108, 109,
24.8	313	24.5	12		110, 118,
24.12	305	24.7	12		119
31.16	306	25.13	306	4.44	105, 107,
31.18	305	27.14	217		110, 130
32.7-8	99, 101	31.1-20	297	4.49	110
32.10	214			5–28	110, 242
32.11	214	*Deuteronomy*		5–26	121, 123
32.19	214	1–28	viii, 4, 8,	5–11	108, 110-
32.22	214		102-120,		11, 118,
32.34	94		106, 117-		119, 122,
33	91, 93, 94,		18, 119,		127
	96, 97		120, 122,	5ff	108
33.1a	95		123, 230,	5	107, 110
33.2	94		173, 233,	5.1-33	110
33.12-23	95		281, 304,	5.1	105, 108,
33.12-17	94, 95		317, 325,		110, 305
33.14	94		326	5.2-3	304
33.17	95	1–4	107, 108-	5.6	304
33.18-23	8		10, 118,	5.17-19	100
33.19-20	95		119, 121,	5.21	101
33.19	89, 95, 97		242	5.27–6.3	105
33.19a	95	1-4.40	108	5.32	305
33.19b	95	1-3/4	107, 119	6.1–11.25	110
33.20	95	1–3	110, 115	6.1	105
33.20a	95	1.1-5	105, 106-	6.3	105, 111,
33.21-22	95		108, 109,		305
34.1	95		110, 117,	6.5	104
34.6	95		118, 119,	6.6-9	110, 111,
34.7	48		122, 325		305
34.29-35	315	1.1	105, 107,	6.6	305
			233	6.12	305

Deuteronomy (cont.)		13.6 [5]	116	27.11-14	148		
6.25	305	13.7-12 [6-11]	113, 115	28	71, 121, 123, 320		
7.6-8	97	13.7 [6]	113				
8.1-20	105	13.13-18		28.1	279		
8.7-10	105	[12-17]	113, 115	28.15	279		
8.11	305	13.14 [13]	113	28.20	126		
9.18	126	13.19 [18]	112, 113	28.69–32.47	105		
9.25	90	14.1-21	112, 113-14, 233	28.69 [29.1]	105, 117, 118, 119, 122, 304, 326		
10.16	305						
11	110	14.1-2	113				
11.16	305	14.2	5, 105, 233				
11.18-20	110, 111, 305	14.3-8	113	29–34	117, 118, 119, 120, 123, 130		
		14.9-10	113				
11.18	305	14.11-20	113				
11.22	111	14.21	5, 105, 113, 114, 233	29–30	120, 128, 242		
11.26-32	320						
11.26-31	110			29	118		
11.32	105, 110, 111	14.22–15.23	112, 114	29.1-14 [13]	118		
		15.12-18	87	29.1 [28.69]	118		
12–28	108	16.1-17	111	29.8 [9]	118		
12–26	108, 110, 111, 122, 123	16.16-17	111	29.11 [12]	118		
		16.18–17.13	114, 115	29.13 [14]	118		
		16.21-22	114	29.20 [21]	128		
12–18	111, 114, 118	17.1	114	29.24-26 [25-27]	127		
		17.9	114				
12	111-12, 113	17.8-13	217	29.24	126		
		17.12	114, 219, 229	30.6	305		
12.1	5, 105, 110, 112, 113, 233			30.11-14	305		
		17.14-20	114, 115	30.15-20	120		
		18	120	31–34	106, 107, 108, 118, 120		
12.2-3	112	18.1-8	114				
12.3	13	18.9-22	114				
12.4-14	112	18.15-22	115	31–32	127, 129		
12.15-28	112	18.18	115, 130, 273	31.1-13	107		
12.29-31	112			31.9	128, 129		
12.32	5	18.20-22	115, 116, 117	31.16	126, 129		
13–26	112			31.20	129		
13–18	114-17, 115	18.20	116	31.24-30	106, 127		
		18.21-22	252	31.24	108, 127		
13	112-13, 114, 115, 116, 120	18.22	116, 117, 252, 253	31.25-26	129		
				31.26	106, 127, 128		
		19-26/28	118				
13.1-5	251	19.16-19	217	31.28	106		
13.1 [12.32]	112, 113, 118, 233	21.5	217	31.29	126		
		21.18-21	99, 101	32	3, 108, 118, 120, 123, 124, 128, 130, 132, 134, 299		
13.2-7 [1-6]	113, 115, 116, 117	24.1-4	254, 255				
		26.16	105, 110				
13.2-4 [1-3]	115, 116	27	117, 119, 122				
13.3 [2]	113						
13.4 [3]	113	27.1-8	117				

Index of Biblical References

32.1-43	xii, 131-49, 146-48, 149	32.18	133, 139, 141, 145	32.38	133, 146		
				32.38b	135, 142		
		32.19-22	132, 137, 138	32.39-42	132, 135		
32.1-28	viii			32.39-40	136		
32.1-3	131, 132, 137, 145, 146	32.19	132, 135, 145	32.39	131, 132, 133, 146, 298		
		32.20	145				
32.1	131	32.21	131, 138, 145	32.39a	138		
32.2	133			32.40	138, 146		
32.3	38, 133, 134.137	32.22	133, 137, 145	32.41	131, 146		
				32.42	133, 134, 137, 146		
32.4-9	132, 137, 140	32.23-27	132				
		32.23	131, 132, 145	32.42b	38, 134		
32.4	132, 133, 145			32.43	131, 132, 134, 139, 145, 146. 299		
		32.24-25	131				
32.5	145	32.24	145				
32.6	133, 141, 145	32.25	145				
		32.26	145	32.43b	38, 134		
32.6a	135	32.27	133, 135, 139, 140, 145	32.44-47	106, 127		
32.7	132, 133, 145			32.46	106, 127		
				33	131, 143, 144, 166		
32.8	140, 145	32.27b	38, 135				
32.8b	144	32.28-33	132, 140	33.1	105		
32.9	38, 133, 134, 135, 137, 139, 140, 145	32.28	132, 138, 145	33.2-8	131		
				33.8	218		
		32.29	131, 145	33.10	217		
		32.30-32	131	33.29b	144		
		32.30	135, 141, 145	34	107		
32.10-14	132, 142			34.6	297		
32.10	132, 145	32.30b	138	34.10	129		
32.11	131, 133, 145	32.31	133, 138, 145				
32.12	133, 135, 145	32.32	145	*Joshua*			
				1	107		
32.14	131, 133, 134, 142, 145	32.32a	138	7.20-26	99, 101		
		32.32b	140	15.55	154		
		32.33	133, 140, 145	19.26	154		
32.14b	38, 134			24	242, 304		
32.15-22	124, 125, 126	32.34-38	132, 138, 142	24.2	154		
				24.3	154		
32.15-18	132, 140, 142	32.34	131, 132, 141, 146	24.14	154		
				24.15	154		
32.15	132, 145	32.35	133, 146	24.19-20	304		
32.15a	140, 142, 144	32.35b	138				
		32.36	131, 133, 135, 138, 146	*Judges*			
				5	3, 131, 166		
32.15b	140, 141			5.3	38		
32.16	131, 141, 145	32.37-38	135	5.8	38		
		32.37-38a	141	5.10	38		
32.17	141, 145	32.37	135, 144, 146	5.12	38		
32.17b-18	142			5.19	38		

Judges (cont.)		3.7	262	22.51	152
5.23	38	4.3	83	22.54 [53]	126
5.27	38	5ff	67		
6–7	296	8	69	*2 Kings*	
13	155	9.9	126	1–2	xii, 151,
19	79	11.8	126		152, 155,
20	79	11.33	126		160, 202
20.34-48	99, 101	12.26-31	103	1	152, 153,
		12.33	126		154, 155,
1 Samuel		13.1	126		156, 157,
1.24	90	13.2	126		158, 160,
2	221	14.9	126		161
2.10	218	14.15	126	1.1	151
2.11	263	15.30	126	1.2–3.8	203
2.18	264	16.2	126	1.2-16	151, 155,
2.21	263	16.7	126		202
2.26	263	16.13	126	1.2	152, 153,
3	273	16.26	126		202
3.1	263	16.33	126	1.3	203
3.8	263	17–19	152	1.4	158
12	242	17.1	186	1.6	158, 194
15.22	187	17.7	126	1.9	153, 154,
15.33	158	17.35	126		156, 203
23.13	90	17.37	126	1.10a	156
25	154	17.38	126	1.10b	156
25.21	221	18	116, 154,	1.11	156
			160	1.12a	156
2 Samuel		18.13	116	1.12b	156
7	66, 67, 69,	18.18	126	1.13-15	203
	70, 84	18.19	116, 224	1.13-14	156
7.1	71	18.27	196	1.15	153, 203
7.5-11	192	18.40	116, 158	1.15a	156
7.9	70	19.2	161	1.15b	156
7.13	69	19.7	155	1.16	158
7.29	70	19.10	126	1.17-18	151, 152,
9–20	66	19.14	126		202
11	99, 101	20.39	182	1.17	152
11.1	71	21	99, 101,	2	150, 152,
12	246		152		155, 156,
12.1-4	182	21.22	126		157, 158,
12.7	182	22	116, 160,		161
15–18	71		253	2.1-18	151, 155,
15.20	90	22.6	116, 224		159, 202
22.14	204	22.15	194, 252	2.1	153, 154,
23.5	306	22.17-23	253		158
23.11	127	22.17	126	2.2-3	153
		22.28	117	2.2a	156
1 Kings		22.42	152	2.2bα	156
1–2	66, 67	22.44 [43]	126	2.2bβ	156
3.3	126	22.51-53	152, 202	2.3a	156

2.3bα	156	22.3-20	129	16.12	298	
2.4-5	153	22.3-11	129	17.7-9	103	
2.4a	157	22.3	129	19.8-11	217	
2.4bα	157	22.8–23.25	118	26.17	158	
2.4bβ	157	22.8-14	83	34.3-7	123, 128	
2.5a	157	22.8-10	5, 167	34.3b-7	123	
2.5bα	157	22.8	121, 127, 128	34.3	122-23, 262	
2.5bβ	157					
2.6-8	153	22.11	128	34.13	5, 119, 167	
2.6a	157	22.12-20	129	34.24	127	
2.6bα	157	22.13	127	35.1-19	123	
2.6bβ	157	22.14-15	124			
2.7	157, 158, 203	22.15-20	251	*Ezra*		
		22.15	194	9.7-8	306	
2.9-13	202	22.16-20	6, 124, 173			
2.9-12	152, 153	22.16-17	124, 125	*Nehemiah*		
2.11	158	22.16	124, 127, 234	3.8	298	
2.12	159			8	119	
2.13-14	153	22.16a	124	8.1	119	
2.15-22	153	22.17	126, 127, 274	8.9	119	
2.16	158			9–10	306	
2.17	158	22.18-20	124	10.1 [9.38]	306	
2.19-22	151	22.20	234			
2.23-24	151, 153	22.20b	124	*Esther*		
2.25	152, 153, 155, 202	22.51-53	151	4.16	90, 91	
		23	286, 304			
3.1	152	23.1-3	129	*Job*		
3.14	161	23.2	128	3	291	
6.17	161	23.3	128	3.1–42.6	302	
8.1	90	23.4-20	121, 123, 128	3.3-10	293, 295	
12.4 [3]	126			3.10	295	
13.14	159, 160	23.5	126	3.11	292	
14.4	126	23.8	126	9.15	299	
15.4	126	23.19	126	9.17	299	
15.35	126	23.21-23	123, 129	10	291	
16.4	126	23.21	128	10.18	292	
16.13	126	23.22-23	129	13.4	298	
16.15	126	23.24-25	129	37.4	204	
17.11	126	23.24	128			
17.16	126	23.25	128, 129	*Psalms*		
17.17	126	23.26	126	1	42	
18.18	82	23.30	108	1.1	15	
19.32-34	306			1.6	137	
20.5	298	*1 Chronicles*		2.1	141	
21.6	126	2.4-15	85	6	53	
21.15	126	16.15-18	306	10.1	141	
21.22	126			13	53	
22–23	121, 122, 128, 129	*2 Chronicles*		15.1	141	
		11.13-17	103	18.14 [13]	204	
		13.9-2	103			

Psalms (cont.)		Proverbs		10.19	193
22	53, 130, 260	7.19	12	11.1	176
		10.13	235	19.6	214
25	143	11.12	235	27.9b	316
25.1-3	136	14.1	14	28.10	195
28	53	14.11	14	28.13	195
30	53	15.8	14	29.9-10	195
31	53	15.21	235	30.1-7	234
31.13	53	25.1	82	30.7	183
33.7	11	26.1-12	83	30.30	204
33.12	13	26.4-5	84	31.1-5	234
34	143			31.4-5	306
35	53	Song of Songs		34.2a	137
35.17	141	8.14	308	34.5a	137
37.30	12			34.6c	137
42.6 [5]	38	Isaiah		34.8a	137
42.12 [11]	38	1–39	86	36.3	82
43.5	38	1–5	86	37.33-35	306
49.6 [5]	141	1	85	38.13	212
51.7	14, 15	1.3	185	40–66	167
52.3 [1]	141	1.4	86	40.1-11	143
52.9 [7]	15	1.18	12, 231	41.8-10	97
57.10	13	5–6	85-87	41.40	327
58.2 [1]	141	5	86, 87	42.6	303, 306, 317
60.3	214	5.1-7	182, 247, 248		
73.1	221			42.14	181
74.1	214	5.3	247	43.4	97
82	43	5.4	247	43.5	327
89.20-38		5.5-6	247	44.23	134
[19-37]	306	5.7	175, 247	44.23c	38, 134
94.9	14	5.8-30	247	44.24–45.13	136
102.29	12, 13	5.8-25	170	47.1-4	134
103.1	13	5.8-22	86	47.4	38, 134
103.3	298	5.16	86	48–51	38
105.8-11	306	5.19	86	48.2	38, 134
111.5	306	5.24	86	49.8	303, 306, 317
111.9	306	6	85, 86, 87		
113	143	6.1–9.6	86	51.7	305
119.11	305	6.1-11	86	51.15-16	38, 134
119.68	14	6.1	86	53.3	12
119.168	15	6.3	4, 86, 168	54.5	38, 134
123.4	13	6.5	86, 87	54.9-10	97
128.3	14	6.8	272	54.10	303, 306
129.3	12	6.9-10	195	54.15	38, 134
129.7	13	7–8	86	55.1-5	303, 306
130.5	15	9.3 [4]	296	55.1	136
132.11-18	306	9.6	86	55.3-5	97
137	143	10.1	86	55.3	306
137.7	296	10.5	86	55.10-11	91
		10.15	188	59.20	316

59.21	303, 306	1.6-7	262, 273	2.1–4.4	33
59.21a	316	1.6	262, 271	2.1	261, 275
61.8	303, 306	1.7-10	272	2.2-3	44
66.13	185	1.7bβ	271, 272	2.2	33
		1.8	264, 274, 327	2.2b-3	33, 47
Jeremiah				2.4	33, 47
1–51	107	1.9-10	259	2.5-9	6, 30, 34,
1–39	261	1.9	271, 273		44, 47-48,
1–24	44	1.10	6, 32, 177,		100, 138,
1–20	24, 28, 29,		263, 264		140, 175
	33, 34, 35,	1.11-16	263, 264,	2.5a	141
	46, 55,		266, 267,	2.6	248
	107, 290,		269	2.7	50
	301, 326	1.11-12	192, 267,	2.8	219, 248
1	viii, 31, 33,		270, 272	2.9	39, 47,
	40, 249,	1.11	261, 263,		139, 142
	259-76,		264, 267,	2.11	30, 188
	259, 260,		268, 269,	2.12	32, 192,
	261, 263,		271, 275		198
	265, 266,	1.11a	271	2.13	47, 139,
	268, 269,	1.12	267, 270,		180
	272, 274,		272, 273,	2.14-19	31
	275		274, 275	2.14	30, 52,
1.1-3	34, 46,	1.13-19	33, 269,		189, 280
	261, 268		271, 273,	2.18-19	234
1.1	326		274, 298	2.18	30, 39
1.2	259, 261,	1.13-14	267, 270,	2.19	176
	266, 269,		274	2.20-28	41
	271, 275	1.13	261, 264,	2.20	32, 180,
1.3	261		269, 274,		192, 193,
1.4-19	263, 266,		275		248
	271	1.14-19	261	2.20b	41
1.4-12	267, 271,	1.14	271	2.22	280
	274	1.15-19	267, 270	2.23-24	180
1.4-10	40, 261,	1.15-18	274	2.23	248
	264, 265,	1.15-16	270, 274	2.23a	41
	267, 270,	1.15	263, 270,	2.25	248, 305
	271		271, 298	2.25b	41
1.4-8	271, 272	1.16	126, 263,	2.26	184
1.4ff	263		267, 269,	2.27	32, 196,
1.4	261, 264,		270, 271,		248
	267, 268,		274	2.27b-28a	175
	269, 271,	1.17-19	259, 261,	2.27c	41
	272, 275		264, 270	2.28	32, 47, 193
1.5-10	261, 272	1.17	270, 275	2.29	39, 141
1.5	32, 33, 34,	1.18	177, 270	2.31	30, 52,
	42, 46, 55,	1.18b	263		189, 248,
	56, 193,	1.19	270, 274,		280
	271, 272,		298, 327	2.32	30, 188,
	301, 326	2	43		280

Jeremiah (cont.)

2.33-37	47, 48-50	4.15	39, 193	5.23	30, 280, 305		
2.33	32, 195	4.17	181	5.24	248		
2.35	248	4.19-22	249	5.25	61		
2.36-37	234	4.19	168, 170, 197, 249	5.27	184		
2.36	176	4.19c	39	5.29	31, 41, 51, 257		
2.37	48	4.20	184	5.30-31	196		
3.1-5	6, 30, 35, 39, 174, 198, 249, 253-54, 255, 257	4.21	141	5.31	32, 219		
		4.22	32, 173	5.31b	142		
		4.22c	139	6.1-7	44, 48, 249		
		4.23-26	6, 170, 201	6.1	193		
		4.26b	137	6.4-5	30, 197		
3.1	30, 186-87, 198, 254, 279	4.29	39, 183	6.7	185		
		4.31	181, 248	6.8-12	30, 44, 48, 249		
		4.31a	39				
3.2	193	5.1-9	47, 50-51	6.8	140		
3.3	180	5.1-8	6, 30, 34, 35, 48, 50, 79, 80, 100, 138, 140, 175, 198, 249, 255-56	6.9	44		
3.4-5	255			6.10	32, 182		
3.4b-5a	254			6.13-15	41		
3.5	254			6.14	168, 248		
3.6-11	57, 183, 267			6.15	39		
3.11	268			6.16-17	248		
3.12	33	5.1	6, 32, 50, 177	6.20	39, 189		
3.15-18	40			6.22-24	41		
3.19-20	5, 199	5.2	39	6.24	181		
3.20	184	5.3	194	7	71		
3.21	39	5.4-5	197, 249, 305	7.1-15	47, 56-57, 71, 282-84, 287, 306, 383		
3.22b-25	42						
3.23	183	5.5b	137				
3.24-25	40	5.6	39, 51				
4.1-4	254	5.6c	39, 137	7.1-2	57, 284		
4.1-2	30, 186, 279	5.7	198	7.1	57		
		5.7a	141	7.2	57		
4.1	254, 255	5.8	32, 180, 181	7.2b-8.3	40		
4.2	248			7.3-14	56, 284, 286		
4.3-4	33	5.9	31, 41, 50, 51, 257				
4.3	33			7.3-7	6, 57, 173, 282		
4.4	32, 127, 181, 305	5.10b-11	140				
		5.12	248	7.3	57, 284, 383		
4.5ff	265	5.13	192				
4.5	6, 32, 177, 248	5.15-17	168-69, 170	7.4	168		
				7.5-7	30		
4.6b	39, 137	5.17	31, 198	7.5-6	6		
4.7	176, 180	5.18-19	40	7.6	126		
4.8b	39, 137	5.19	126, 248	7.7	57, 284		
4.9-12	40	5.21	173	7.8-11	6, 57, 173, 282		
4.9	176	5.22a	30, 280				
4.13	181, 193	5.22b	299	7.8	57, 284		
4.14	32						

7.9	6, 32, 99, 126, 177	8.22	15, 30, 52, 189, 280, 298	11.19	248		
7.11	57, 126, 283, 284			11.20	54		
				11.21-23	40		
		8.23 [9.1[	52	12.1-6	42		
7.12-15	44, 57	9.2-5 [3-6]	31, 53	12.1	291		
7.12-14	6, 57, 173, 282	9.2 [3]	53	12.3	5		
		9.4	175, 193	12.5	30, 187, 279		
7.12	57, 126, 284	9.8 [9]	31, 41, 51, 257				
				12.7	6, 177		
7.13	57, 126, 284	9.11-15 [12-16]	40	12.13	33		
		9.12 [13]	126	12.13b	142		
7.14	57, 284	9.18 [19]	39	12.14-17	40		
7.15	57, 283, 284	9.18b [19b]	137	12.16	279		
		9.21 [22]	140	12.17	279		
7.17-20	127	9.22-25 [23-26]	40	13.1-9	267, 268, 269		
7.17	126, 177	9.22	181				
7.18	126	10.1-10	31	13.1	267		
7.19	126	10.6-7	31, 174	13.3	267, 268, 269, 274		
7.20	127	10.10	31				
7.21	196, 252	10.11	47	13.6	267, 268		
7.22-23	191	10.12-16	41	13.8	267, 268		
7.28	181	10.16	39, 134	13.9-14	40		
7.29	40	10.18	198	13.18	224		
7.33-34	6	10.19-21	42	13.22	182		
7.33	177	10.19	249	13.23	280, 305		
7.34	177	10.22	39	13.25b	299		
8.4-5	30, 32, 52, 189	10.23-25	42	13.26	182		
		11–20	249, 290	14.1–15.4	42		
8.4-5a	280	11.1-13	285-87	14.2-6	300		
8.6	5, 181	11.1-3a	285	14.7-9	42		
8.6b	47	11.1	286	14.8-9	39		
8.7	140, 185	11.3-4	286	14.10	196		
8.8	81, 82	11.3b-5a	285, 286	14.11-16	40		
8.10	39	11.5b	285	14.12	177, 184		
8.10b-12	41	11.6	177, 267, 285, 286	14.18	39		
8.11	168, 248			14.19-22	42		
8.12	39	11.7-8	285, 286	14.19	52, 280		
8.13-17	30, 34, 48, 175, 249	11.8	286	15.1	257		
		11.9-17	40	15.2	196		
		11.9-10	285, 286, 287	15.1-2a	40		
8.13	140			15.3-4	40		
8.14	194	11.9	267	15.10-14	40		
8.16	32	11.10	286	15.10	198		
8.17b	299	11.10b	286	15.13-14	41		
8.18-21	30, 42, 47, 51-52, 197, 225, 249	11.11-13	285, 286	15.15-21	42, 249, 274		
		11.11	286				
		11.13	286	15.16	130		
8.19	30, 52, 280	11.17	126	15.16b-17	130		
8.22–9.1 [2]	32, 47, 52-53, 170-71	11.18-23	42	15.18	39, 291		
		11.18	6, 176	15.19	176		

Jeremiah (cont.)		20.9	249	21.8-9	185
15.20-21	264, 274	20.10	35, 53, 248	21.9	177
15.20	327	20.11-13	43, 53	21.11-14	287-89
16.1-18	40	20.11-12	292	21.11-12a	287
16.4	177	20.12	54, 292	21.11	287
16.9	177	20.13	54, 292	21.12	127, 287
16.11-13	30	20.14-18	viii, 31,	21.12b-14	288
16.11	126		42, 46, 47,	21.12b	287
16.21	40		55-56, 144,	21.13-14	287
17.1-4	40		174, 199-	21.13	287
17.1	140, 305		200, 290-	21.14	127, 287
17.3-4	41		302, 292,	22–23	24, 248
17.5-8	30, 42, 185		300, 301,	22.1-6	40
17.5-6	293		327	22.1	288
17.9	305	20.14-17	296, 300	22.8-9	40
17.12-13a	171	20.14-15	292, 294,	22.9	126
17.13-16a	30, 42, 52,		301	22.10	191
	249	20.14ff	290, 295	22.11-12	40
17.13	183	20.14	292, 293,	22.14-19	42
17.14	176		294, 296	22.20	196
17.15	248	20.15-16	297	22.22	192
17.16b-18	42	20.15	292, 293,	22.24-27	40
17.27	127		294, 296,	22.26	224
18–45	24		300	22.28	52, 280
18.6-12	40	20.15ab	294	22.29	32, 168,
18.6	185	20.16-17	294, 301		198
18.7	32	20.16	293, 294,	22.30	32, 198
18.14-15	30, 188,		295, 296,	23.1-8	40
	280		299, 300	23.5-6	40, 41
18.18	32, 181	20.16a	296	23.12	39
18.19-23	42	20.16ab	298	23.16-17	40
18.20	5	20.17	293, 294,	23.18	48, 272
18.23	194		295, 296,	23.19-20	41
19.1–20.6	249		297, 298,	23.21-22	48
19.4	126		299, 300	23.23-40	40, 272
19.7	177	20.17a	296, 297,	23.23-24	190-191
19.8	177		299	23.29	248
19.13	126	20.17ab	298	24–36	xii, 44
20	55, 292,	20.18	33, 34, 39,	24	33, 44,
	327		46, 56,		268, 272
20.1-6	219		272, 292,	24.1	268
20.3	35		293, 294,	24.4	268
20.6	176		300, 301,	24.7	303, 305
20.7-18	292		326	24.9	177
20.7-13	47, 53-54,	21–45	87	24.10	177
	249	21–23	28, 34, 46	25	44
20.7-10	6, 42, 53,	21	34, 46, 55	25.1-3	275
	174, 292	21.1-10	249	25.6	126
20.7	54, 176,	21.1	34, 46	25.7	126
	291	21.8-10	120	25.9	177, 185

Index of Biblical References

25.10	177	30.3	59, 303	32.12	83		
25.13a	44	30.5–31.22	57	32.24	184		
25.14	126	30.5	39	32.26	269		
25.27	6	30.6	280	32.29	126		
25.29	30, 187, 279	30.8-9	40	32.30	126		
		30.10-11	41	32.32	126		
25.30	212	30.17	183	32.37-41	306		
25.33	40	30.23-24		32.38-40	303		
25.38	212	31.4-5	6, 32,136, 169, 177	32.40	304		
25.38b	137			33	269		
26–29	249	31.7	6	33.1	269, 274		
26–28	117	31.15-20	5	33.4	184		
26	44, 56, 71, 249, 252, 282	31.15	39, 200	33.10	177		
		31.16-17	198, 200	33.11	177		
		31.18-19	200	33.14-16	41		
26.1-19	24	31.20	189, 200-201	33.20-21	279		
26.2	183			33.25-26	279		
26.4-6	284	31.23-40	47, 57-59	34–35	87-88, 249		
26.12-15	6, 173, 250	31.23-34	40, 58	34	31, 87		
26.12	6	31.23	58, 303	34.20	177		
26.13	284	31.27	303	35	31, 44, 87		
26.14-15	190	31.28	323	36/37-45	44		
26.14	30, 280	31.29	303	36	44, 83, 260, 301		
26.15	6, 190, 280	31.31-34	303, 305, 306, 309, 313, 314, 316, 322				
26.16b	251			36.1-8	45, 81		
26.17-19	251			36.1-2	275		
26.24	251			36.4	83		
26.35/36		31.31	303	36.10-11	83		
27–29	44	31.33	308, 315, 316	36.10	261		
27–28	225			36.26	82		
27	251	31.34	58, 304, 305, 313, 315	36.32	82, 272		
27.2-11	225			37–44	28		
27.8	177			37.10	194		
27.12-15	225	31.34a	303	38.21	272		
27.16-22	225	31.34b	303	38.34 [LXX]	316		
28	251	31.35-40	58	44.3-6	127		
28.1-16	225	31.36-37	186	44.3	126		
28.2-4	6	31.36	30, 279	44.5	126		
28.6-9	194-95, 252	31.37	30, 279	44.6	177		
		31.38	303	44.8	126		
28.6	252	31.39	303	44.12	177		
28.7-9	252	31.38-40	40	44.15	126		
28.8-9	30, 190, 280	31.40	58, 59, 303	44.17	126, 177		
		32–33	268	44.18	126		
28.17	253	32	249	44.19	126		
29	24	32.1-5	268	44.21	126, 177		
29.18	177	32.1	268, 269	44.23	126		
30–33	28	32.2-5	268	44.25	126, 196		
30–31	24, 40, 53, 57, 303	32.4	184	44.25b	252		
		32.6	268, 269	45	45		

Jeremiah (cont.)		51.35	248	4.1-2	305
45.1-5	45, 107	51.38	176	4.1	216, 221,
46–51	24, 28, 40,	51.44	32, 181,		227, 247
	44		192	4.1b	227
46.3-4	178	51.54	39	4.2	100, 227,
46.5	198	51.59-64	45, 83,		230
46.7-8	189		107, 326	4.4-10	221, 222,
46.17	183	51.59	83		223
46.18	154	51.64	326	4.4-8	218
46.20	168	52	326	4.4-6	220, 223,
46.23	140				225, 231
46.25-26	40	*Lamentations*		4.4	222, 223,
46.27-28	41	1–2	6, 34, 45,		235
47.3	39		100	4.4a	220, 221,
47.6	32, 198	3.19-39	292		222, 226,
48.2	193	3.64	126		227, 231
48.3	39			4.4b-9a	226, 227,
48.15	171	*Ezekiel*			228, 229,
48.46	142	11.19	305		230, 231
49.1	52, 280	12.25	90, 91	4.4b-5	224
49.7	189	16.60	303, 306	4.4b	216, 217,
49.8	178	18.31	305		219, 220,
49.12	30, 187,	21.27	168		221, 222,
	279	23	183		224, 225,
49.15	171	24	242		226, 227,
49.19	212	30.9	296		228, 229
49.26	39	34.25	303, 306	4.5-8	221
49.30	178, 192	36.25-28	304	4.5-6	217, 219,
50.2	306	36.26	305		222
50.5	303	36.27-28	303, 306	4.5ff	222
50.6	184	37.26	303, 306	4.5	219, 220,
50.7	183	44.23-24	217		222, 223,
50.20	194				224, 228,
50.22	39	*Hosea*			230
50.35-38	6, 31, 35,	1–3	216	4.5a	228
	169, 198	1.11	296	4.6	221, 222,
50.41-43	41	2	179		223, 224,
51.11-14	174	2.4 [2]	221		229, 230
51.15-19	41	4	216, 225,	4.6a	217
51.19	39, 134		235, 247	4.7-8	230
51.20-23	32, 169,	4.1–5.7	216	4.7	221, 224,
	177, 198,	4.1-10	viii, 216-		229
	234, 248		31, 216,	4.8	221, 229
51.20b	234		219, 220,	4.8a	217
51.22	184		227, 230,	4.9a	216, 217,
51.23c	234		231, 247		225, 226,
51.31-35 [LXX]	107	4.1-4a	227, 230,		227, 229,
51.34-45	6, 34, 44,		231		230
	48, 138,	4.1-3	221, 222,	4.9b-10	227, 230
	175		226, 227		

4.10	227, 230, 235	8.13	232	1.2–2.16	208	
		8.13a	237, 238	1.2	181, 203, 204, 211, 212	
4.11-14	172, 226, 227, 229, 234, 235, 236, 237, 238	8.13b	238			
		8.14	236			
		9.3	232	1.2b	204	
		9.16	179	1.3–2.16	204	
		10.1	179	1.3–2.3	35, 205	
4.11-12	234	10.3	224	1.3-5	204	
4.11	235	10.5	219, 224	1.5	205	
4.12	235	10.7	224	1.8	205	
4.12a	235	10.10	224	1.10	205	
4.13	238	10.11	179	1.12	205	
4.13b	237	10.13	181	1.13	297	
4.14	231, 235, 236	10.14	224	1.15	205	
		10.15	224	2.2-16	208	
4.14ab	238	11.1-4	5, 199	2.3	205	
4.14c	235	11.1	179	2.5	205	
4.15	236	11.3	179	2.6-16	208	
4.16	180	11.5	232	2.6-8	206	
4.16b	247	11.8-9	5, 199	2.9–3.8	203	
4.17	196	11.10	212	2.9-16	209	
4.19	223	11.11	232	2.9-12	208	
5.1	224	12.1	181	2.9	171, 208	
5.3-4	172	12.2	232	2.10-12	207, 208	
5.10	218	12.4-5a	174	2.10	208	
5.13-14	234	12.6 [5]	38, 134	2.11-12	174	
5.14	180, 212	12.7	180	2.11	208	
6.4	180	12.10	182	2.11b	246	
6.9	219	13.7-8	212	2.12	208	
7.4	53	13.12-13	180	2.13-16	205, 209	
7.7	181	13.14	175	2.13/14-16	208	
7.8	179			2.13	208, 209	
7.11-12	234	*Joel*		2.14-16	174, 206, 209	
7.11	180, 232	1.4	7, 178			
7.16	180	1.19-20	174	2.14	209	
8	236	2.19	177	2.15	209	
8.1	213	2.28-29	175	2.16	203, 205, 208, 209	
8.3	213, 214	3.14	168			
8.5	viii, 213-15	3.16	181	3.1-8	209	
		4.16 [3.16]	212	3.1	203, 204, 209, 210	
8.7	181					
8.9-13	172, 226, 227, 229, 232, 234, 235, 236-37, 238	*Amos*		3.2	203, 204, 209, 210	
		1–2	35, 196, 206, 225, 245	3.3-8	187-88, 206, 209, 210, 211	
		1.1	211			
8.9	179, 232, 236	1.2–3.8	viii, xii, 202-212, 204, 209, 211	3.3-6	210, 246	
				3.4	211	
8.10	238			3.6	203, 210	
8.11	237			3.7-8	210	

Amos (cont.)		7.10-11	225	Haggai	
3.7	210	7.11	225	1.4	187
3.8	179, 203,	7.14-15	171, 248	1.13	155
	204, 210,	7.14	191		
	211, 246,	7.16-17	225, 253	Zechariah	
	248	7.17	225	9.5	176
3.8a	211, 212	8.1-3	245	9.11	314
3.8b	211	8.1-2	192, 270	10.8	90
4.1-3	246	8.5-8	206	11.4-14	183
4.1	179, 203,	8.9-10	171		
	224	9.6	38, 134	Malachi	
4.4-5	196, 206			2.1-9	303, 306
4.6-12	206	Micah		3.1	303, 306
4.6-11	257	1.10	192	4.5-6	150
4.13	38, 134	2.11	196		
5.1	203	3	247	APOCRYPHA	
5.2	171	3.2-3	175	Wisdom of Solomon	
5.4-6a	174	5.4 [5]	205	6.17-19	6, 178
5.5	193			19.17	80
5.8-9	206	Nahum			
5.8	38, 134	1.9-11	173	Sirach	
5.10-12	171			3.16	14
5.19	208	Habakkuk		38.1-15	298
5.21-24	206	2.16-17	170		
5.26-27	307			Baruch	
6.4-6	206	Zephaniah		2.35	307
7	225	1.2-6	170		
7.1-9	245	1.2-3	170	PSEUDEPIGRAPHA	
7.7-8	270	1.5-6	170	Jubilees	
7.8	225	1.15	170	1.22-24	307
7.9	225	2.2	170	5.17-18	317
7.10-17	245	2.4	193		
7.10-13	207				

NEW TESTAMENT

Matthew		5.7	321	10.25	151
1–4	319	5.8	321	11–12	319
1.23	327, 328	5.9	321	11.1	318
3–4	318	5.10	321	11.2–12.50	319
5–7	319	5.17	318	11.14	150
5	320	7.1-5	87, 231	11.28-30	318
5.1–7.27	318	7.28-29	318	12.24	151
5.3-12	320	8–9	319	12.27	151
5.3-11	320, 322	8.1–9.35	318	13	319, 320
5.3	321	8.1	330	13.1-52	319
5.4	321	9.9	81	13.52	81
5.5	321	9.36–10.42	318	13.53	319
5.6	321	10	319	13.54–17.21	319

Index of Biblical References

Matthew (cont.)		6.20-26	320	3.6	303, 314
14–17	319	15.11-32	255	3.7-11	315
16.7-8	329	22.20	303, 313	3.14-15	314
16.14	150	24.9	324	8–9	21
16.18	322	24.50-53	328		
17.10-13	150			Galatians	
17.22–18.35	319	John		3.10-14	314
18	319	4.21-24	72	3.14	314
19.1	319	8.2-11	231	3.15-18	315, 317
19.2–22.46	319	8.13	150	3.17	315
19.18	100	8.48	150	3.19	317
19.22	319	8.51-53	150	3.23-24	315
20.1-5	98	8.52-53	150	3.25-26	315
23–25	319	19	92	4.21-31	314
23	320	19.22	90		
23.1-39	81			Ephesians	
23.13-36	320-21, 322	Acts		2.11-13	314
		1.4-5	329	2.12-13	315
23.13	321	2.14-36	241		
23.15	321	2.17-18	176	1 Timothy	
23.16-19	321	23.1-5	218	2.5-6	317
23.23	321				
23.25	321	Romans		Hebrews	
23.27	321	2.14-15	315	4.9-11	317
23.29	321	2.15	317	6.1-8	318
23.35	321	3.31	315	7.22	317
26–28	319	5.3-5	6, 178	7.26	316
26.1	319	6.14	315	7.27	317
26.28	313	7.6	315	8.6	316, 317
28.8	324	7.12	315	8.7-8a	316
28.19-20	327, 328	8.29-30	7, 178	8.8-12	316
28.20	327, 328	9.4	314	8.8	303
		9.18	97	8.13	303, 317
Mark		10.4	315	9.1-14	317
1.34	324	10.14-15	7	9.9	317
1.40-45	329	11.25-32	316	9.11-12	317
1.44-45	329	11.26-27	316	9.14	317
10.19	100	11.29	316	9.15-22	317
13.1-2	72	16.22	81	9.15	303, 317
14.24	313			9.18-21	317
16.7	324	1 Corinthians		9.20	313
16.8	323, 324	11.25	303, 313	9.22	317
16.9-20	324	12	331	9.24-28	317
		15	92	9.24	317
Luke		15.5-9	92	10	317
1	328	15.10	91	10.10	317
1.42	328			10.14	317
1.47	12	2 Corinthians		10.16-17	316, 317
1.64-68	328	3.2-3	314	10.18	317
5.12	330	3.3	314		

Hebrews (cont.)		*1 Peter*		*Jude*	
10.22	317	2.1-10	313	1.3	240
10.26-31	318	2.4-10	72		
10.26	317			*Revelation*	
11.5	150	*2 Peter*		5.5	212
12.24	303, 317	2.6-8	80	10.3	204
13.20-21	318			21.22	72
13.20	317				

INDEX OF AUTHORS

Abarbanel 10
Abba, Raymond 94, 96
Ackroyd, Peter R. 66, 90, 95
Adams, John Quincy 17
Adams, Robert M. 81, 82
Adler, Joshua 106
Adler, Mortimer J. 19
Akiba, Rabbi 83
Albrektson, Bertil 90
Albright, William F. 93, 94, 103, 143, 274, 299
Allcock, Philip J. 155
Alonso Schökel, Luis 22, 104
Alt, Albrecht 90
Alter, Robert 139
Alexander, T.D. 79
Anaximenes 278
Andersen, F.I. 205, 208, 210, 211, 212, 216, 217, 220, 222, 223, 226, 229, 231
Anderson, Bernhard W. 71, 132, 155
Anderson, Robert T. 82
Apollonius 21
Aquila 213
Aristotle 3, 4, 5, 19, 26, 31, 97, 165, 166, 277, 278, 281, 289, 297
Arnold, Carroll C. 16
Arnold, William R. 27, 89, 90, 93, 95
Asbjørnsen, Peter Christian 82
Athanasius 121
Auerbach, Erich 73, 74, 80
Augustin, F. 260, 270
Avigad, N. 83

Bacon, Benjamin 318, 319
Baker, Aelred 9
Baldwin, Charles Sears 16, 17
Barnes, William 154
Bauer, Marvin G. 16
Baumgartner, Walter 42, 52, 90, 210, 290, 292, 293, 294, 295
Bea, A. 23, 104

Beethoven, Ludwig 21
Begrich, Joachim 42
Ben Asher 61
Benware, Wilbur A. 68
Bergfalk, Bradley J. 31, 81
Bernhardt, K.-H. 89, 94
Berridge, J. 260, 261, 264, 266, 271, 290, 292, 293
Bertholet, Alfred 89
Bertman, Stephen 21
Best, Thomas 8
Betz, Hans Dieter 20
Bewer, J.A. 260, 262
Bird, O. 19
Birkeland, H. 259, 262
Bitzer, Lloyd 19
Black, C. Clifton 23, 27, 33
Black, Edwin 19, 26
Black, J.S. 66
Black, Matthew 308, 328
Blank, Sheldon H. 291, 292, 299
Blayney, Benjamin 40
Bock, Alfred 156
Bonamartini, Ugo 9
Booth, Wayne C. 16
Bos, Lambert 11
Boys, Thomas 23
Brandt, William J. 91, 178
Braulik, Georg 106
Bream, Howard N. 143
Breit, Herbert 102
Bridston, Keith R. 241
Briggs, Charles 10
Bright, John 35, 122, 254, 260, 262, 264, 266, 269, 273, 274, 290, 295
Brown, Lew 291
Brown, Raymond 290
Brown, S.L. 219, 221
Bryan, C.P. 297
Bryant, Donald C. 17, 18, 19, 30, 31

Brueggemann, Walter 67
Buber, Martin 32, 93
Budde, Karl 221, 222, 259, 264
Bühlmann, Walter 90
Bultmann, Rudolph 313
Bussby, Frederick 9
Buttrey, T.V. 21
Buttrick, George A. 22, 38, 103, 134, 152, 233, 260, 306

Calvin, John 216, 217, 218, 220, 221, 222, 223, 259, 261, 265, 290, 291, 292
Cao, Jing xiii
Carney, T.F. 21
Carpenter, J. Estlin 65, 75, 93, 126
Carroll, R.P. 260, 269, 270
Carrubba, R.W. 21
Carruth, W.H. 41, 77
Cassuto, U. 69
Cedarleaf, Douglas 258
Charles, R.H. 307
Cheyne, T.K. 235
Child, James Francis 17
Childs, Brevard 90, 94, 96
Christensen, Duane L. 106, 115, 118
Chrysostom, John 121
Cicero 3, 17, 165, 166
Clayton, Hugh 43
Clines, David J.A. xii, 73, 77
Cohen, A. 218, 221
Cohen, H. 217
Coleman, S. 218, 219
Collins, J.R. 80
Condamin, A. 23, 34, 45, 100, 104, 203, 259, 262, 290, 295
Conley, Thomas M. 278
Connors, Robert J. 16, 17, 20, 32
Conrad, Edgar W. 143
Corbett, Edward P.J. 17, 18, 19, 20, 26, 243
Cornill, C.H. 259, 262, 263, 264, 290, 295
Corré, Alan D. 7
Couturier, G.P. 290, 295
Crafer, T.W. 221
Crenshaw, James 33, 82
Cripps, R.S. 203, 204, 210
Cross, Frank M. 94, 123, 152, 298, 307, 308
Culver, Dwight W. 241
Cyprian 227

Dahood, M. 15, 38, 49, 214, 228, 232, 233, 295, 325
Daube, David 7, 159, 161, 291
Davies, G. Henton 82
Davies, Philip R. 73, 77
Davies, W.D. 318, 319
Dawn, Marva J. 160
DeRoche, M. 219, 221, 222, 223
Dodd, C.H. 313, 316
Douglas, Stephen A. 25
Driver, G.R. 298
Driver, S.R. 70, 75, 89, 90, 91, 94, 102, 108, 110, 122, 126, 131, 132
Drummond, Alexander M. 18
Duckworth, George E. 21
Duhm, Bernhard 41, 86, 225, 232, 235, 259, 262, 263, 264, 267, 269, 270. 290, 291, 293, 294, 295, 296, 297, 299
Dundes, Alan 156
Durham, John I. 82, 90

Eichhorn, J.G. 259, 261, 262
Eissfeldt, Otto 66, 67, 121, 122, 127
Elliger, Kurt 235
Ellis, P.F. 66
Euripides 21, 291
Eusebius 324
Evans, Ray 92
Ewald, H. 94

Feigin, S. 225, 229
Fenton, J.C. 321, 327
Fischel, Henry A. 7, 178
Fisher, Walter R. 19, 26
Fitzmyer, Joseph A. 328
Fohrer, Georg 67, 77, 121, 122
Follis, Elaine R. 143
Forster, E.S. 277
Fox, Michael V. 23
Freedman, David Noel 8, 35, 65, 66, 67, 69, 71, 76, 86, 94, 95, 97, 98, 99, 100, 101, 121, 123, 143, 144, 148, 203, 205, 208, 210, 211, 212, 216, 217, 220, 222, 223, 226, 229, 231, 232, 234, 235, 298, 306
Freese, John Henry 277
Friedman, Max 291
Fuller, Reginald C. 23

Index of Authors

Gadd, C.J. 81
Galbiati, H. 23, 104
Gamaliel, Simeon ben 193
Gaster, T.H. 159
Gevaryahu, Haim M.I. 106
Gevirtz, S. 232
Giesebrecht, F. 259, 263, 290, 293, 295
Gildersleeve, Basil 21
Ginsberg, H.L. 83, 143
Glasser, Arthur F. 241
Goedicke, H. 143
Good, Edwin M. 35, 85, 235, 236
Gordis, Robert 83, 206, 217, 221
Gottwald, Norman 66, 129, 292
Goulder, M.D. 152
Graf, K.H. 259, 261
Grant, F.C. 324
Graves, Richard L. 32
Gray, George Buchanan 15, 232, 298
Gray, John 152, 156, 158, 161
Green, David E. 67, 77
Greenberg, Moshe 305
Greenwood, David 151
Gregory, G. 7, 15, 22, 39
Griffin-Collart, E. 19
Grimm, Jacob 82
Grimm, Wilhelm 82
Grobel, Kendrick 313
Gunkel, Hermann xi, 23, 41, 42, 43, 53, 69, 77, 79, 159, 244

Hallevy, Jehuda 94
Hanson, Paul D. 71
Haran, Menahem 35, 83, 143
Harford-Battersby, G. 68, 75, 93, 126
Harper, William R. 203, 204, 209, 210, 211, 219, 221, 222, 235
Harrelson, Walter 132, 155
Harvey, Julian 43
Haupt, Paul 94
Hayakawa, S.I. 89
Heathcote, Arthur W. 155
Henderson, E. 259, 262, 290, 295, 298
Herder, J.G. von 7, 69
Hermann, Th. 222
Herodotus 21, 265
Herrmann, S. 260, 264, 270
Hertzberg, H.W. 70
Heschel, Abraham J. 193
Hicks, L. 301

Hillel 7, 186
Hillers, Delbert 293, 295
Hitzig, F. 259, 261, 264, 269, 290, 292, 295
Holladay, William L. 33, 123, 130, 225, 260, 264, 266, 274, 290, 300
Holmer, Paul 241
Holmgren, Frederick C. 31, 81
Homer 21, 73
Hoop, Raymond de 37, 282
Horace 21, 323
Horne, Thomas 11
Horner, Thomas M. 42
Horst, F. 259, 266
Hort, J.A. 324
Howes, Raymond F. 18
Huddlestun, John R. 67, 98, 205, 306
Hudson, Hoyt 16, 18
Huesman, John E. 214
Huffmon, Herbert 43
Humenik, Julia xiii
Hunger, Hermann 45
Hunt, Everett Lee 16, 17, 18, 26
Hutchins, Robert M. 19
Hyatt, J.P. 260, 266

Ibn Ezra 217, 219
Immerwahr, Henry 21
Isocrates 278
Ittmann, N. 290, 293

Jacob, E. 155
Jakobson, Roman 9
Janzen, J.G. 298
Janzen, Waldemar 203
Jebb, John 9, 23
Jeremias, J. 313, 318
Jerome 121, 229, 259, 261, 262, 273, 324
Johnson, A.R. 305
Johnstone, Christopher 277, 278
Josephus 131, 150
Junker, H. 220

Kamphausen, Adolf 131
Kaplan, Mordecai 86
Kapp, Ernst 277
Keil, C.F. 290, 291, 294, 295, 296
Kennedy, George 20, 27, 241, 242, 243, 245
Kennedy, John F. 25

Kereferd, G.B. 277
Khomeini, Ayatollah 240
Kimchi, David 217, 218, 219, 221, 231, 265, 275, 295
King, Martin Luther, Jr 25
Kittel, Rudolph 41
Kleinert, P. 105
Klostermann, A. 102
Klyn, Mark S. 18, 27
Köhler, Ludwig 44
König, E. 22, 325
Koptak, Paul E. 31, 81
Kovacs, B.W. 260
Kraeling, Carl H. 81, 82
Kramer, Samuel N. 7, 87, 166
Krebs, Johann T. 11

Labuschagne, Casper 115
Lagarde, Paul de 90
Lambert, W.G. 83
Lampe, G.W.H. 328
Landsberger, Benno 81
Lausberg, H. 233
Lejewski, Czeslaw 277
Lemke, Werner E. 122
Lenchak, Timothy A. 102
Lesko, Leonard 90
Ley, Julius 41
Liebreich, Leon 86
Lightfoot, John 324
Limburg, J. 155, 206, 211
Lincoln, Abraham 25
Lindars, Barnabas 90, 95
Lipinski, E. 82, 83
Livingston, Jay 92
Loader, J.A. 76, 80
Lohfink, Norbert 23, 104, 105, 108, 110, 112, 113, 117, 118, 119, 127, 128, 129, 220, 222, 225, 231
Lohr, Charles 319, 320
Lowth, Robert 3, 4, 7, 9, 10, 11, 15, 22, 39, 40
Lugt, Pieter van der 26
Lund, Nils W. 8, 23, 34, 45, 48, 104, 106, 138, 140, 153, 174, 207, 237, 319, 327
Lundbom, Jack R. 8, 29, 31, 33, 34, 35, 39, 41, 42, 43, 44, 45, 46, 47, 49, 50, 51, 52, 53, 55, 56, 57, 69, 83, 84, 87, 95, 100, 106, 107, 108, 118, 129, 136, 137, 138, 139, 140, 142, 144, 202, 208, 226, 228, 229, 230, 234, 238, 247, 251, 254, 255, 260, 266, 270, 271, 272, 273, 274, 279, 280, 282, 284, 285, 286, 287, 289, 290, 292, 298, 300, 303, 325, 326
Luria, B.Z. 106
Luther, Martin 95

Maarsen, I. 217
MacDonald, B. 80
MacDonald, J. 202
Malena, Sarah 202
Mann, C.S. 324
Margalit, B. 226
Marks, John H. 68, 75
Marsh, James 7, 68
Mayes, A.D.H. 118
Mays, J.L. 203, 204, 205, 209, 210, 213, 221, 222, 235, 236
Mazzocchi, Alessio Simmaco 9
McCarthy, Dennis J. 103, 221
McConville, J.G. 112
McEvenue, S. 23, 104
McGavern, Donald A. 241
McKane, William 260, 265, 266, 270, 275, 298
McNeil, Krista xiii
Meek, Theophile J. 10, 35
Mendenhall, George 66, 103
Menzies, A. 66
Meyer, Heinrich 324
Meyers, Carol L. 65, 84
Miano, David 202
Michaud, H. 260, 261
Michaud, J.F. 10
Micklem, Caryl 331
Millard, Alan R. 82
Moe, Jørgen 82
Mohrmann, G.P. 18
Montague, Gene 25, 27, 31, 32, 35
Montgomery, J. 151, 152, 153, 156, 158, 159
Moran, William L. 23, 104, 105, 108
Morgenstern, J. 79
Morrow, Amanda R. xii
Moulton, R.G. 22, 29, 37
Mowinckel, Sigmund 35, 45, 82, 119, 167, 205, 259, 263, 264, 267, 269, 270
Mozart, Wolfgang 21

Muilenburg, James xi, 8, 15, 22, 23, 24, 25, 26, 27, 28, 29, 30, 31, 32, 33, 37, 38, 39, 41, 43, 45, 82, 83, 94, 95, 97, 103, 104, 132, 133, 134, 135, 136, 137, 139, 141, 143, 151, 153, 155, 167, 177, 233, 254, 282, 296, 306, 325
Myers, Jacob M. 143
Mylonas, George E. 7
Myres, J.L. 21

Nestle, E. 121
Nethercut, William R. 21
Neufeld, E. 298
Newing, Edward G. 143
Nicholson, E.W. 103, 108, 117, 122
Niditch, S. 260, 270, 271, 272
Nielsen, Eduard 82
Nilsen, Thomas R. 18
Nötscher, F. 259, 262
Nogalski, James D. 42
Noonan, J.T. 297
Norwood, Gilbert 21
Noth, Martin 71, 82, 107, 108, 117, 119, 121, 167
Notopoulos, James A. 29, 37, 233

O'Connell, Robert H. 26
O'Connor, M. 65, 84
Oesterley, W.O.E. 274
Olbrechts-Tyteca, L. 19, 74, 89, 240, 245
Oliver, Robert T. 16
Olrik, Axel 156
O'Neill, James 16, 18
Orton, David 42, 232, 290
Owen, John 259

Pasor, Georg 11
Paton, Lewis B. 122
Paul, Shalom M. 35, 203, 205, 209, 210, 211
Peake, A.S. 259, 262, 265, 290, 291, 294, 295
Pearl, Chaim 68
Perdue, L.G. 260
Perelman, Chaim 19, 74, 89, 91, 240, 245
Perrin, Norman 318
Pettinato, Giovanni 94
Petuchowski, Jakob J. 309
Pfeiffer, Robert 102, 122

Pindar 21
Plato 278, 297
Plutarch 21
Politis, Konstantinos D. 80
Pope, Alexander 323
Pope, Marvin 295
Porter, J.R. 82, 90
Prijs, L. 290, 295
Prodicus 278
Propertius 21
Protagoras 278

Quintilian 3, 4, 17, 31, 97, 165, 166, 243, 278, 323

Rabin, C. 40, 307
Rad, Gerhard von 55, 65, 66, 68, 69, 70, 71, 75, 77, 79, 85, 93, 102, 103, 104, 105, 106, 117, 119, 142, 159, 304, 305, 306, 327
Rainey, Anson F. 82, 83
Rashi 68, 217, 275, 295
Reinesius, Thomas 10
Rendsburg, Gary 143
Rendtorff, Rolf 75
Richardson, A. 313, 317
Richardson, H. Neil 154
Ricoeur, Paul 96, 240, 244
Rietzschel, Claus 35, 266, 274
Roberts, J.J.M. 143
Robinson, Bernard P. 305
Robinson, David Moore 7
Robinson, H. Wheeler 298
Robinson, T.H. 274
Rofé, Alexander 33, 151
Rose, Mark 21, 202
Ross, James F. 155
Rossi, Azariah de 4, 9, 10
Rost, L. 66
Rowley, H.H. 121, 167, 260, 261, 262, 265, 328
Ruben, P. 235
Rudolph, W. 35, 213, 260, 262, 264, 266, 269, 274, 290, 292, 295, 296
Russell, Donald A. 323
Rushdie, Salman 240

Sandberg, Carl 6
Sarason, R.S. 309

Scaliger, Julius 11
Scherer, Karl 90
Schoettgen, Christian 4, 8, 9, 10, 11, 13, 14, 15
Scott, Fred Newton 16, 17
Scott, R.B.Y. 86
Seitz, Gottfried 106
Sellin, E. 259, 261, 263
Sinor, Denis 81
Skehan, Patrick W. 131
Skinner, John 75, 79, 86, 148, 153, 159, 259, 262, 270
Skutsch, O. 21
Sloan, Thomas O. 3, 277
Smith, Barbara Herrnstein 29, 233
Smith, George Adam 38, 108, 131, 132, 133, 134, 153, 219, 259, 262, 293
Smith, P.A. 26
Smith, W. Robertson 89, 94, 221
Snaith, Norman H. 152, 158
Socrates 97, 278
Soggin, J.A. 204, 209
Speiser, E.A. 69, 75, 84, 85, 227
Spohn, Gottlieb L. 11
Stade, B. 259, 261, 264
Stähli, H.P. 262
Stalker, D.M.G. 67, 77
Steele, R.B. 21
Steinmann, Martin, Jr 16
Stewart, Charles J. 18, 27
Stewart, Donald C. 16, 26
Streane, A.W. 290, 295
Szikszai, S. 152

Taylor, Vincent 324, 330
Theodoret 121
Theodotion 213
Thiel, W. 260, 264, 269, 271
Thiele, Edwin R. 152
Thomas, D. Winton 82, 119, 167
Thomson, George 21, 32
Tischendorf, Constantin von 324
Tournier, Paul 92
Trani, Isaiah di 295
Trask, W.R. 73
Tredennick, Hugh 277
Trible, Phyllis 26
Trueman-Dicken, E.W. 65
Turner, L. 77, 79

Ulrich, Eugene 139, 143, 144

Van Rooy, H.F. 118
Van Seters, John 75, 76, 77, 79
Van Unnik, W.C. 136
Van der Woude 136
Vaux, Roland de 79, 90, 95
Vergil 21
Volz, Paul 254, 259, 262, 264, 290, 294, 295
Vriezen, T.C. 89, 136

Walter, C.T. 11
Weaver, Purcell 19, 74, 240
Weber, R. 227
Weinberg, Bernard 30
Weinfeld, Moshe 103, 104, 106, 108, 117, 119, 305, 309
Weiser, Artur 122, 260, 262, 266
Weiss, C. 298
Weiss, M. 206
Welch, Adam C. 103, 259, 261
Welch, John W. 34, 300
Wellhausen, Julius 41, 65, 66, 75, 108, 119, 121, 122, 153, 213, 220, 222, 265, 324
Wescott, B.F. 324
Westermann, Claus 43, 68, 97
Wette, W.M.L. de 121
Wharton, James 68
Whitman, Cedric H. 21, 29, 37
Whybray, N. 75
Wichelns, Herbert 16, 17, 18, 19, 23
Widengren, Geo 143
Wilke, F. 265
Williams, Ronald J. 82
Winans, James Albert 16, 18, 26
Wilkinson, John 19, 74, 240
Wolff, Hans Walter 65, 68, 103, 203, 204, 205, 207, 208, 209, 210, 211, 213, 220, 221, 222, 223, 231, 235, 236, 237, 305
Woolbert, Charles H. 26
Wright, G. Ernest 103, 108, 117, 119, 132

Yaron, Reuven 255

Zeno 278
Zimmerli, Walther 68, 304
Zwingli, Ulrich 291

www.ingramcontent.com/pod-product-compliance
Lightning Source LLC
Chambersburg PA
CBHW070933230426
43666CB00011B/2427